CAMBRIDGE LATIN AMERICAN STUDIES

EDITORS

MALCOLM DEAS

CLIFFORD T. SMITH   JOHN STREET

20

STUDIES IN THE COLONIAL HISTORY
OF SPANISH AMERICA

THE SERIES

STUDIES IN THE COLONIAL HISTORY OF SPANISH AMERICA

MARIO GÓNGORA

Professor of History, University of Chile, Santiago

TRANSLATED BY

RICHARD SOUTHERN

CAMBRIDGE UNIVERSITY PRESS

CAMBRIDGE

LONDON · NEW YORK · MELBOURNE

Published by the Syndics of the Cambridge University Press
The Pitt Building, Trumpington Street, Cambridge CB2 1RP
Bentley House, 200 Euston Road, London NW1 2DB
32 East 57th Street, New York, N.Y. 10022, USA
296 Beaconsfield Parade, Middle Park, Melbourne 3206, Australia

Library of Congress Catalogue Card Number: 74-19524

ISBN: 0 521 20686 3

First published 1975

Printed in Great Britain
at the
University Printing House, Cambridge
(Euan Phillips, University Printer)

CONTENTS

Contents

PREFACE

This book is intended to make certain aspects of the colonial history of Spanish America more accessible at university level; some of these aspects are new; others have already been studied, but all of them, I must confess, have a particular appeal to me. An attempt has been made, on the basis of research carried out so far and with specific reference to its findings, to present a picture of some of the more important topics of that history, the understanding of which I consider to be indispensable to a full knowledge of that period. No attempt has been made, however, to cover the entire field, because, obviously, certain topics lie outside the range of my capabilities or interests. The better general histories that have appeared in the last few decades contain chapters devoted to specific topics, some of which are omitted from this study; this study, on the other hand, contains considerations of other topics not previously discussed. Rather than write a general history or summary of the period, I have preferred to concentrate my attention on certain problems or series of problems which throw light on the course of history as a whole, and on which I believe that I can make original observations, based on my own previous research, or express reflections and opinions suggested by the researches of others. This book, therefore, occupies an intermediate place between the general history and the monograph, although it occasionally takes on the characteristics of both types of study. The studies are interpretative, in the sense that they represent an attempt not only to provide information but also to demonstrate the historical trends and tendencies underlying the events, institutions and ideas described, in the hope of achieving a fuller understanding of those trends. The treatment of specific topics within each chapter has been arranged with this end in view.

In accordance with the character of the book, notes have been dispensed with almost entirely, except for a small number which are to be found at the end of the book; most of the references have simply been incorporated into the text. In the Bibliography, an attempt has been made to include all the books and articles which I have found to be of value in writing the present work until *ca.* 1970/72. This list does not include the printed sources –

chronicles, letters, legal compilations, doctrinal texts, accounts of travellers and so on – which comprise the basic and best-known documentary sources. These have been omitted, both to save space and also because such sources are easy to find through references in the secondary works quoted in this study.

I must express my thanks to Dr Richard M. Morse of Yale University, who first suggested that I should write such a book; to Malcolm Deas of the Centre of Latin American Studies of the University of Oxford, for his friendly advice and assistance; and, as always, to my wife, for her unfailing help in the task of revising the text.   M.G.

GLOSSARY

Adalid. Military leader, commander of a *cabalgada* or warrior-band.

Adelantado. In the Indies, title of the actual or future discoverer and conqueror of a particular territory.

Ají. Chili pepper (*Capsicum longum*).

Alcabala. Sales tax, levied on all commodities except foodstuffs.

Alcalde mayor. In the Antilles and Central America, the judge, appointed by the Crown, of a Spanish city or an Indian *pueblo.* He exercised both executive and judicial functions.

Alcaldes ordinarios. The head elected magistrates of the City Council.

Alcaldes provinciales de la Santa Hermandad. Officials responsible for the apprehension and prosecution of criminals within the jurisdictional area around a city.

Alférez mayor. Honorary municipal official, who carried the Royal Standard in religious processions and military parades. His office was the *Alferazgo mayor.*

Algara. Cavalry foray into enemy territory, with the object of capturing booty.

Alguaciles. Subordinate judicial officials, constables. However, the *Alguacil Mayor de Corte,* the *Alguacil Mayor de Audiencia* and the *Alguacil Mayor de Cabildo* were officials of high prestige. The office was the *Alguacilazgo.*

Almojarifazgo. Customs duty.

Audiencia. The supreme judicial and administrative authority in each territory.

Ayuntamiento. Municipal corporation. The term is virtually synonymous with *Cabildo* (*q.v.*).

Baquiano. Experienced guide, scout.

Benemérito de Indias. Direct descendant of the conquistadors and earliest settlers.

Cabalgada. See *Algara.*

Cabildo (*secular*). City Council; municipal corporation of a Spanish city or an Indian *pueblo.*

Cabildo eclesiástico. Cathedral chapter.

Caja Real. Royal Treasury.

Caja de comunidad. Community chest, into which were paid the revenues of an Indian *pueblo.*

Camote. Sweet potato (*Ipomoea batatas*).

Capitulaciones. Agreements signed between the Crown and a discoverer or future conquistador, stipulating the conditions of the proposed undertaking and the profits due to the various participants.

Cédula, Real Cédula. Royal decree, of a general or specific nature.

Censos. A mortgage contract, frequently perpetual and frequently with the church.

Glossary

Chácaras. Suburban smallholdings.

Compaña. Community formed by a conquest band.

Comunidades. In the Indies in the sixteenth century, the word was used in the sense of insurrections headed by municipal corporations (by analogy with the revolt of the *Comuneros* in Castile in 1520). It was still used in this sense in Paraguay in 1725–35 and in Socorro (New Granada) in 1781.

Concertaje. The *mita* (*q.v.*) in the rural areas of New Granada and Quito, which gave rise to a class of Indians (*indios conciertos*) established on the Spanish-owned *haciendas*.

Contadores. Comptrollers, auditors.

Corregidores. Chief judicial and administrative officials of a Spanish city or Indian *pueblo*, appointed by the Crown or its local representative.

Costa y minción, a su. At his own expense and risk.

Cuatequil. Aztec system of forced labour, the forerunner of *repartimiento* (*q.v.*).

Dehesa. Communal grazing lands around Spanish cities.

Doctrinero. Parish priest of an Indian community.

Ejido. Communal grazing land for domestic animals, belonging to a Spanish city or Indian *pueblo*.

Encomienda. In the Indies, the grant of the personal service or tribute of a group of Indians to a Spaniard (the *encomendero*).

Entretenimiento. Pension, annuity.

Escribano. Notary.

Estancia. Land granted for cattle-raising.

Fieles ejecutores. Municipal inspectors of weights and measures.

Fiscal. Judicial official of the *Audiencia*, attorney, public prosecutor; in Indian *pueblos*, a native catechist and churchwarden, working under the supervision of the parish priest.

Gañán. Free rural journeyman-labourer.

Hacienda Real. Royal Exchequer.

Hidalgo, hidalguía. Gentleman (by birth or designation); the quality of one so described.

Ingenio. Sugar-mill.

Letrado. Lawyer, jurist.

Macehuales. (Mexico) ordinary Indians, subject to tribute.

Mandón. Native acting as foreman or overseer of a group of Indians.

Mercedes. Grants (of *encomiendas*, lands, mines, etc.).

Mita. In South America (originally only in Peru), a group of natives assigned to forced labour on a shift basis in the Spanish-owned mines, farms, textile workshops and building projects.

Mitayo. Native assigned to the *mita* (*q.v.*).

Moradores. Inhabitants of a city, other than the *vecinos* (*q.v.*).

Naborias. Household Indians, of a quasi-servile status.

Obraje. Textile workshop.

Oficiales reales. The Treasurer, the Comptroller, the Factor and (occasionally) the *Veedor* (*q.v.*) of each *Caja Real* (*q.v.*).

Oidor. Judge of the *Audiencia.*

Pardos. Mulatto soldiers serving in the militia.

Partida. The appropriate section of the *Siete Partidas,* the legal code compiled by King Alfonso X, the Wise, of Castile and León (1252–84).

Patronato. Right of patronage (Crown control of appointments to benefices) in the Church in Spain and in America.

Pecho. In Spain, personal tribute. The persons subject to this were called *pecheros*; by extension, this term was used of all members of the plebeian class, as opposed to the *hidalgos* (*q.v.*) and nobility, who were exempt from tribute.

Peón. In Spain, a *vecino* (*q.v.*), other than the nobility and gentry. In America, a worker.

Peonaje. The system of employment (frequently debt-servitude) of the *peón* (*q.v.*).

Procurador. A legal representative; more specifically, in the colonial *cabildo* the representative of the citizens within the *cabildo.*

Propios. Lands or income belonging to the municipality.

Quinto real. The fifth part, appropriated by the Crown, of booty taken in war and of mined gold and silver.

Quipu. Mnemonic device, consisting of a cluster of coloured and knotted threads, used for keeping statistical records in the Inca Empire and in early Colonial Peru.

Rancheadores. Robbers, raiders.

Realengo. Royal domains and properties.

Receptor de penas de cámara. The official responsible for the fines and other pecuniary sanctions imposed by the *Audiencia.*

Recopilación de Indias. Legal compilation of 1680, which codified the general legislation for the Indies.

Regidor. City councillor.

Repartimiento. Synonym of *encomienda* (*q.v.*); system of labour regulation, similar to the Peruvian *mita* (*q.v.*); a proportion of distributable commodities, trade in which was monopolised by the *Corregidor de indios* in his town.

Rescate. Barter; random.

Residencia (Juicio de). Legal inquiry held at the end of the term of office of senior officials, who might be accused of crimes of commission or omission committed during their tenure.

Tapias. See *naborias.*

Terrazguero. Tenant in a contract of *terrazgo* (the renting of a small plot of arable land).

Trapiche. Sugar-mill; grinder (for ore).

Vecino. 'First-class citizen' of a Spanish city, both in the Peninsula and in the New World, possessing full municipal and civic rights and privileges.

Veedor. Inspector.

Visita. Special administrative inquiry into alleged malfeasance on the part of any public body or official.

Yanacona. (Peru, Chile and the River Plate region). Indian taken from his district of origin and working for Spanish masters as a household servant, or on the *chácaras* (*q.v.*) and *haciendas.*

CHAPTER I

THE CONQUISTADORS AND THE REWARDS OF CONQUEST

Bands of warriors in the Reconquest of Spain

The men who undertook the discovery, conquest and settlement of the Indies followed methods and were impelled by collective motivations which both had their origins in the remote past. In order to understand these methods and motivations fully, it is necessary to situate them in their European historical context, even though one must still take into account certain radical modifications brought about by the geographical distance constituted by the Atlantic Ocean, and by action in lands and among races that were quite unknown.

The expansion of Europe from the eleventh century onwards was not the work of peoples, nor even of empires and kingdoms, but rather of spontaneously organised movements and groups of very varying orders of magnitude and importance: bands of Norman warriors in southern Italy; the great collective impulses of the Crusades; the orders of chivalry operating in the Levant, the Baltic and the Iberian Peninsula; companies of Catalans in the Byzantine Empire; and, finally, in Spain, the great process of Reconquest, reflected in the activities of military leaders, orders and even groups of French crusaders, working in loose collaboration with the Christian kingdoms of the peninsula. In all these cases, the recognition or explicit approval by the Church or by the States officially sanctioned, rather than created, enthusiasm for the Holy War, the eschatological motivations of which sustained the Crusades – in short, the spirit of adventure and its realisation. Moreover, similar phenomena appeared outside the boundaries of Christendom: one only has to remember the Muslim warriors of the Holy War (ahl al-ribat).

In the Iberian Reconquest, to a greater extent than in other cases, one is conscious of the presence of the State in the shape of Castile-León, Aragon and Portugal; however, even those kingdoms entrusted part of the task of the regaining of the national territory to small autonomous military forces which, however, consented to be part of a larger mission. At that time, Spain was conceived as a land to be won, with southern frontiers which were always of a provisional character, and still unpacified frontier areas – the

'Extremaduras' – which were in a state of continual warfare (Maravall, 1954). It was, therefore, quite reasonable for the kings to make grants of lands not yet in their possession, and to grant far-reaching rights and privileges to the potential settlers, who were, on the other hand, entrusted with the task of conquering and defending the territory concerned – an undertaking which the grants were designed to encourage. Promises, on the one hand, and free enterprise, on the other, were to be the distinguishing characteristics of Spain's expansion.

In 1089 the Cid persuaded King Alfonso VI of Castile and León to grant him all the castles and lands that he might reconquer from the Muslims, with the right to bequeath them to his successors. This leader had told the King that 'all that he did and won, he did and won for the King's sake, and that those knights and that company which he had in the lands of the Moors he maintained without any expense to the King...for he expected his recompense from the Moors and from their lands' (*Primera crónica general*, 561, quoted by the Muslim chronicler Ben Alcama). Another document which throws light on the Holy War in the peninsula was the privilege granted by the Emperor Alfonso VII to the Aragonese military confraternity of Belchite in 1136 (Rassow, 'La Cofradía de Belchite', *Anuario de historia del derecho español*, III, 1926): the confraternity pledged itself 'never to make peace with the pagans, but to harass and wage war against them constantly'; in return, the King granted them all the lands, castles and towns that they might capture from the Moors, and exempted them from payment of the *Quinto real* (Royal fifth), which was usually payable on all booty captured. The conquest to be carried out by the king's vassals was subject, then and for all time, to the deduction of a percentage of the resulting profits, usually the *Quinto real*, which was due to the king in token of his overlordship.

The Iberian Orders of Santiago, Calatrava, Alcántara and Montesa, and the international ones such as the Templars and the Knights Hospitallers, carried out on a greater scale this task of prosecuting a war that was both a Holy War and a drive for territorial expansion. These great monastic-cum-military organisations on the frontier subjected this warfare, which was prosecuted on a small scale by autonomous bands, to strict rules and discipline, and they also carried out a policy of internal colonisation (Bishko, 1965); but, after the phase of conquest was over, towards the end of the thirteenth century, they simply settled down to the enjoyment of their baronial possessions and privileges.

The cities and towns of the Extremaduras and the frontiers continually carried out, in Moorish lands, hit-and-run raids of the *cabalgada* or *algara* type, in the course of which the participants captured horses, livestock and slaves, all of which could be used in barter-trade; the spoils were distributed in accordance with strict rules laid down in the *fueros* (customary privileges). The association of this type of warrior life with the migratory sheep-grazing of New Castile, La Mancha and Extremadura constituted a peculiarly apt geographical framework for the warrior-bands of the Reconquest, and was to have an important genetic influence on the future society of Spanish America (Bishko, 1952, 1965; Carande, 1952).

The Reconquest led to the formulation of a system of political justice which placed great emphasis on concepts derived from the royal duty of rewarding and granting favours to men who had distinguished themselves in war. Liberality on the part of kings and lords, an essential virtue according to the ethic of nobility, was one of the qualities most extolled in the chronicles and in the manuals written for the education of princes. The king should be 'open-handed', according to the Second *Partida*; he should 'honour' everyone according to his deserts, according to the same *Partida* (X, 3), a principle which in the sixteenth century Gregorio López was to formulate more explicitly by stating that this meant making grants according to a person's merits. Prizes and rewards are regulated in detail in an entire section of the Second *Partida*. Chronicles, biographical sketches and full-length biographies written in fifteenth-century Castile indulge in interminable eulogies of the splendid generosity displayed in the granting of favours to their vassals by kings and lords.

Castilian expeditions in Africa and the Canaries

When the Reconquest of Spain's territory – except for the frontier with the small kingdom of Granada – had been completed in the second half of the thirteenth century, the great overseas expansion began. The kings of Aragon carried out military operations in Algiers and Tunis, and conquered Sicily and Sardinia. Of greater interest, however, from the point of view of this study, were the overseas conquests, in the Byzantine Empire in general and particularly in Greece, of the famous Company (*universitas*) of Catalan knights and *almogávares* (invaders). Chiefly recruited among those who had taken part in the fighting on the frontier in Spain, these experts in the capture of booty suddenly came to the forefront, from 1300 onwards, in the history of the Byzantine Empire, and their leader became a 'Caesar'. Subsequently they ruled for eighty years in Athens and Thebes, living as a Company apart from the Greek population employing both feudal and municipal forms of government; these Catalan adventurers provided,

3

as it were, a rehearsal of what was to take place in the conquest of the Indies.

Castile, on the other hand, expanded by 'passing the sea and going into the Realm of Africa', as Alonso de Cartagena put it in 1435: Barbary, the Atlantic coast of Africa as far as Guinea, and the Canaries. This process of expansion required financial capital to build ships, provision them and pay the men (though the sailors were attracted less by the promise of a daily wage than by that of the fruits of slave-raiding and piracy).

The commercial enterprise of Catalans, Majorcans, Basques, Asturians, Portuguese, Andalusians and Genoese secured the financial base, through the acquisition of loans and the establishment of commercial companies for each expedition, and, later on, for the colonisation of the Canaries (Wölfel, Verlinden, Sancho de Sopranís, Magalhaes Godinho). It is, however, necessary to emphasise, as does Ramos (1965), that commerce was a secondary activity and that the essential element in these enterprises was the sheer adventure inherent in them, the coastal raiding. Furthermore, enterprises of overseas conquest had been regulated in detail in the *Partidas*.

The nucleus of conquerors – the *caudillo*, or military leader, and his *compaña*, or followers – remained unchanged in this new sphere, both on the high seas and overseas. The forms of organisation and the underlying assumptions of the warrior-bands of the Reconquest are clearly recognisable: recruitment on a voluntary basis, but authorised by the State; the granting of future feudal rights over the lands to be discovered and conquered (for example, the grants made in the Canaries to Luis de la Cerda by Pope Clement VI and to Juan de Bethencourt by Henry III of Castile); the distribution of booty according to strict rules; the *Quinto real* levied on all booty captured; *Adelantados* appointed by the Crown but who nevertheless were obliged to finance the conquests, in return for a high percentage of the profits. Above all, there was no modification of the traditional notion that the participants in an enterprise of conquest had a right to be rewarded for their personal efforts and the expenses that they had incurred. In the proclamation that was circulated throughout Andalusia to recruit men for the expedition of the *Adelantado* Juan Rejón to the Canaries in 1480 – which was to be a royal, rather than a baronial, army – the 'venturers' who enlisted were promised that 'they will be given *repartimientos* there in accordance with their quality and services' (Zavala, 1935, 69); and in the *capitulación* signed with Pedro de Vera and his partners for the conquest of Great Canary Island, also in 1480, the King granted the remission of all the *Quintos* on captured slaves, hides, tallow and fish, for the term of five years, in view of 'the toil, venture and risk

4

incurred for their persons and property, and the ships and men which they are to supply for the said conquest', and they were also granted remission of the *Quintos* on booty that they might capture in other islands inhabited by infidels (Navarrete, I, 541). The concept of a Holy War against Islam was broadened to include the new peoples encountered on the coast of Africa and the off-shore islands; but the enterprise also had a missionary element, which had been absent in the case of Spain and which constituted an innovation. The concepts of Holy War and of Mission occasionally conflicted in the course of the fifteenth century in the Canaries, and some bishops and the Papacy attempted to restrain overt slave-raiding expeditions (Wölfel, 1930; Zavala, 1935).

The legal instruments which constituted the 'técnica de la esperanza' – 'technique of hope', as it is expressed in Ramos (1965, 100) – were the *capitulaciones* which the Crown signed on so many occasions during the fifteenth century with the conquerors. The term *capitulaciones*, that had been used so often to denote the privileges granted to Muslim and Jewish minority groups living under Christian rule, was now used to signify the privileges granted to those who enlisted for an enterprise and committed themselves to it. The captains used to form trading firms and acquire financial loans in order to fulfil their obligations; but the basis of the human relationships was still the old Castilian *compaña*, consisting of the military chieftain and his warrior followers, who had to be rewarded with their shares of the booty.

The expeditions to the Indies

Although the initial objective of the Catholic sovereigns had been to establish in the Indies entrepôts for the trade in gold, on the Portuguese model and as a Crown monopoly, keeping overseas only a small garrison of soldiers and the indispensable minimum of settlers, the basis of the enterprises was still, originally, the personal initiative of the discoverer in possession of a duly signed *capitulación*. The legal formulae and the techniques employed in the enterprises of Africa and the Canaries were transferred to the Indies, at first without any significant modifications, until fresh geographical discoveries and previously unforeseen developments caused an immense increase in the magnitude of those enterprises.

The *capitulación* authorising the discoveries of Columbus provided that, in the event of new islands and continents actually being discovered and conquered, he would receive a percentage of the royal profits derived from commerce, trade and barter, and the same document conferred several jurisdictional and governmental privileges. That is to say, the enterprise of discovery was broadened to include all the other possible objectives of the 'conquest', a word which was still employed in the strict etymological sense of the 'search' for something worth acquiring. Very soon, the commercial forces based in Andalusia – chiefly of Spanish or Genoese origin – were bringing pressure to bear to ensure for themselves the monopoly of the supply of goods to the entrepôt in Hispaniola, and also to obtain licences for barter-trade and discovery in lands not discovered by the High Admiral, particularly on the mainland. These efforts resulted in the voyages of Ojeda, Yáñez Pinzón, Juan de la Cosa, Americo Vespucio, Niño, Guerra, Lepe and Bastidas, between 1499 and 1504. The second voyage of Ojeda in 1502, as Governor of Coquibacoa, is of particular interest because of the personal participation in the expedition of the two merchants who had advanced the money for it, and, more especially, because Ojeda, rather than confining himself to barter-trade on the coast, wanted to penetrate into the interior and find the sources of the gold; as a base, he built some forts, which constituted the first Spanish attempt at settlement on the South American continent (Ramos, 1961). Although the expedition was a complete failure, it was, nevertheless, a symptom of a new trend towards permanent territorial dominion, based on criteria more far-reaching than purely commercial considerations.

However, the real base for the conquests, in the strict sense of the word, was to be Hispaniola, the principal nucleus of Spanish settlement – the most probable figure for the total population, that given by Las Casas for 1509, was 300 *vecinos* (*Historia general*, II, 374) – and the chief administrative headquarters. In a gradual process which took place between 1493 and 1505, the Genoese-Portuguese conception of a fortified entrepôt and a royal monopoly of the barter-trade in gold gave way to the concept of a permanently populated colony, where the Spanish *vecinos* could be maintained by Indian labour. This process has been described in detail in recently published research (Zavala, 1935; Meza Villalobos, 1971; Pérez de Tudela, 1956). There gradually developed a policy of encouraging mining operations, and lands and tax concessions were granted to the *vecinos*. Bobadilla proclaimed that kings 'were not farmers or merchants, nor did they require those lands for their own profit, but for the succour and relief of their vassals' (Hernando Colón, quoted in Pérez de Tudela, 1956, 177). Gold was obtained from the Indians not only by barter but also by means of the tribute paid by the chiefs to the king. The Spanish settlers lived grouped together in the city of Santo Domingo and in smaller towns; the instructions given to Ovando in 1501 and 1503 and the *capitulaciones* signed

6

with Luis de Arriaga in 1501 provided a legal definition for the urban base of the population. The hired colonists of earlier years disappeared, giving place to the *vecinos*, who owned town and country houses and cattle ranches, and were authorised to trade in all commodities (with certain exceptions, small in number but extremely valuable – for example, precious metals, slaves, salt and horses), and to elect the *Ayuntamientos* and *Cabildos*. The *vecinos* mined gold, and devoted themselves to agriculture and cattle-raising, thanks to Indian labour which was organised by law on a basis of personal service according to the *encomienda* system, by the *Real Cédula* of 20 December 1503, the purpose of which was to establish a convenient method for evangelisation of the natives and to encourage the settlement and systematic planting of crops on the island. In other words, the Crown was renouncing the concept of a monopolistic entrepôt on the Portuguese model, and legal definition was given even at this early stage to a specifically Castilian type of settlement, based on property-owning colonists, who paid to the Crown only its fifth share of precious metals, the customs (the *almojarifazgo*), and tithes for the maintenance of the Church.

Hispaniola was to be the starting-point for the bands of conquistadors during the boom years of the island's economy (1505–10), and it was to be men left without *encomiendas* who were to form the mass of those groups based on voluntary association which were to conquer Puerto Rico, Cuba, New Spain, Central America and Venezuela. Moreover, the men of Darien and Panama were to reach the Inca Empire and conquer every province of it. Other groups of conquistadors were to found the New Kingdom of Granada and La Asunción, at the other end of the continent.[1] These events took place in accordance with a compact time-schedule, from 1508 (Puerto Rico) to 1540–53 (Chile); the conquests of the River Plate region and the areas north of the Aztec Empire were, however, postponed as being of only peripheral importance. The process of conquest, according to Chaunu (1959), was still expanding, between 1525 and 1535, in absolute and, above all, in relative terms; between 1535 and 1540 the process of advance reached a 'plateau' as far as Spanish dominion over the native population was concerned. Subsequently, the conquest of the less densely populated parts of the continental land mass took place at a very much reduced rate (VIII, 147).

The origin of the conquistadors reflected the entire gamut of the social spectrum of Castile, with the sole exception (save for a few insignificant cases) of the families of the grandees. Of the ninety-one conquistadors who received *encomiendas* in Panama in 1519 and 1522, one finds three *hidalgos* (to which, however, one must add ten Basques and men from the hill region of

Santander, regions where everyone, regardless of origin, was considered an *hidalgo*); five squires; twelve retainers of nobles; ten men with professional qualifications or drawn from the urban middle class; twenty craftsmen; eleven farmers; three pilots and ships' masters; eleven seamen; seven described themselves as being without occupation and, moreover, declined to declare that of their fathers (this group included Diego de Almagro and Sebastián de Benalcázar); and nine gave no information on this point. To summarise the findings of this inquiry, we might say that, of those ninety-one men, forty-one small farmers, craftsmen and members of the middle class had come from a completely non-military background in Spain, but in the Indies they had become transformed into conquistadors. The remaining fifty, because they were *hidalgos*, were retainers of nobles or, because they belonged to the category of adventurers without known occupation, had already been military men in the peninsula. Not only did the *encomenderos* of Panama come from very varied social origins, but also their regional origins were just as varied. Of the eighty-eight who declared their origins, Andalusians (34.7 per cent) predominated by a wide margin, followed by Extremadurans (21.4 per cent) – the totals being twenty-nine and eighteen men respectively. Less important numerically were the men from Santander and the Basque provinces (ten), New Castile (eight men), Old Castile (seven) and León (five). Asturias and the kingdom of Aragon had only one or two representatives. Finally, there were three Italians and two Levantines, apart from four men whom it was not possible to classify (Góngora, 1962, III). A predominant place was, therefore, held in the case of Panama (the earliest settlement so far discovered of a city founded by conquistadors) by the men of Andalusia and Extremadura, and, with regard to social rank and occupation, civilians were only barely outnumbered by military men.

These figures give an idea of the trends observable if a large sample is considered. However, although men of lowly social origin from Andalusia were numerically preponderant, for the obvious reason of their proximity to the port of embarkation, Extremadura and the two Castiles had a marked qualitative advantage; particularly Extremadura, the most poor and rural province, which was largely owned by the Military Orders of Santiago and Alcántara. The encouragement of individual initiative provided by poor agricultural land, and the pattern of chivalrous conduct exemplified by the Orders (even though by 1500 this was not much more than a memory) undoubtedly contributed to this process of qualitative selection.

Around 1512 the decline in the Indian population of Santo Domingo constituted the most urgent problem in the settlement of the Indies. From that time, therefore, bands of *rancheadores* sent by the *vecinos* began to move to the 'useless islands', or even as far as Venezuela, to capture natives for use as slaves in the principal island. In groups of fifty or sixty, *baquianos*, expert guides and trackers employed by the *vecinos* of Puerto Plata, were commanded by their *adalides*, as happened in the case of the raids on the Barbary Coast carried out at the same time.

An enterprise on a larger scale, with the participation of conquistadors acting on their own account, has been described by Bernal Díaz del Castillo in the first chapter of his famous work: a group among those who had reached the mainland and found themselves out of employment through lack of opportunities asked Pedrarias Dávila for authorisation to go to Cuba, which from 1515 onwards was beginning to acquire importance economically, 'because there was nothing left to conquer', since Balboa had already completed his task. In Cuba, Velázquez, the *Adelantado*, promised to assign Indians to them, but time passed and he never fulfilled this promise; thereupon they decided 'to join forces, one hundred and ten of us comrades who had come from the mainland and others who were in Cuba but who had no Indians, and we enlisted under a *hidalgo* called Francisco Hernández de Córdoba, who was a rich man and had a village of Indians in that island, who was to be our captain; to set out on our own account to search for and discover new lands, thus to find employment for ourselves'. They had refused, according to Bernal Díaz, to become mere slave-raiders in the employ of Velázquez; they bought three ships (one of them acquired with a loan furnished by the *Adelantado* himself), ships' stores, glass beads to trade with the Indians, enlisted a chaplain and a *Veedor* (the official responsible for collecting the *Quinto real*) and finally set sail from San Cristóbal, Cuba. This is a classic description of a voyage of discovery carried out at the *costa y minción* of the participants. The collective motivation was obvious enough to Bernal Díaz: the surplus of men, in relation to the *encomiendas* available, was the impulse underlying this venture, this migration, from one land to another. It should be added that the same outlet was sought by *vecinos* indebted or ruined by the death of their Indians, like those who went with Velázquez himself from Hispaniola to Cuba in 1511 (Las Casas, *Historia general*, II, 506). The *encomienda* was, therefore, both the prize of conquest and the stimulus to further conquest; it was the mainspring of the collective movement: this was clearly recognised, even thirty or forty years later, in Peru, by La Gasca and Cañete, when they authorised fresh conquests to relieve the pressure imposed by the arrival of a new wave of Spaniards in that country. It was 'in order to rid these realms of people...who could not all find sustenance in this land', as La

Gasca put it when he reported to Spain in 1548, that he had sent an expeditionary force to Chile under Pedro de Valdivia. The Viceroy Cañete had special authorisation from Charles V to send out fresh expeditionary forces: there were at that time in Peru a thousand men with adequate means of support – according to the report of Cañete himself, made before leaving for Spain in 1555 (Levillier, *Gobernantes del Perú*, I, 252) – and there were a further seven thousand who were redundant, who 'say that they are as good as the others; there is nothing else for it but to rid the land of them and, because there are so many of them, this can only be done by means of making fresh discoveries'. This policy resulted in the steady expansion of the Empire from Peru towards Chile, Upper Peru and Tucumán, between 1548 and 1557.

In addition to this underlying tendency, however, there were actions resulting from the personal initiative of the *caudillos*. Even Bernal Díaz, anxious as always to emphasise the role of the common soldier in the conquering armies, still had to admit that Francisco Hernández de Córdoba had an *encomienda* and was a rich man before he took over command of the enterprise. The same is true of the three leaders in Panama who between 1524 and 1526 signed a contract for the discovery and conquest of Peru, and of Pedro de Valdivia, who had an *encomienda* in Porco before he left for Chile in 1540; Hernán Cortés, although he did not figure as a colonist of the first rank, either in Hispaniola or in Cuba, nevertheless had Indian servants and owned ranches, and had been Secretary to the Cabildo in Azua and an *alcalde ordinario* in Santiago, Cuba. All those men left behind their fortunes and incurred enormous debts to finance the new expeditions. The governors and *Adelantados* who did not participate directly in the expeditions sometimes contributed large sums from their personal fortunes to finance the new enterprises; and, although they sometimes had recourse to spending money which had already been collected in the Royal Exchequer during the previous governorship, their excuse for behaving thus was the same as that given by Cortés at the end of his Fourth Narrative Letter: he had indeed, up to 1524, taken 62,000 gold pesos, but before that he had spent all he had, and had incurred debts of 30,000 pesos, and the profits for the king had been over 1,000 per cent. Thus, whereas the common soldier in the conquering armies was spurred on chiefly by material need, the *caudillos* were moved to a greater extent by the urge to imperial expansion.

The enterprises of conquest, especially those overseas, required the support of considerable monetary capital. For this reason, they presuppose the previous economic development of Hispaniola and Cuba, which had enriched Spanish and foreign *encomenderos* and merchants. Recently published research has emphasised the contribution of merchants from Genoa, Florence, Nuremberg and Augsburg in the first decades of trade and finance in the Indies (Verlinden, Otte, Friede, Ruth Pike), independently or in association with Spaniards, acting both directly and through factors. The methods used in the sugar-cane industry in the islands – which replaced the mining wealth lost by the decline of the Indian population – owed much to the Genoese, who had perfected such methods in their plantations in the Levant, the Canaries and Madeira (Verlinden). The sugar-cane grown by Hernán Cortés on his estates was purchased by a Florentine firm (Melis). For expeditions of discovery and conquest, the Genoese lent money to or went into partnership with Rodrigo de Bastidas, the *Bachiller* Fernández de Enciso, Juan Ponce de León, Oviedo, Hernando de Soto and Sebastian Cabot; and they worked in close association with Diego Velázquez (Pike, 1966, V). The connection of the Welser firm with the conquest of Venezuela, from the city of Coro, between 1529 and 1546, is the most obvious example of the participation of High German finance capital in the government and trade of the Indies.

One must not, however, forget the participation of Spanish capitalists in the enterprises of conquest. The Licentiate Gaspar de Espinosa, the *alcalde mayor* of the government of Castilla de Oro under Pedrarias Dávila, led slave-raiding expeditions from Darién, which acquired enormous plunder; he had a prosperous *encomienda*, sugar plantations, and carried on trade in clothing with Nicaragua; later, from Panama, he gave decisive financial support to Pizarro's third expedition to Peru, and, carrying on an active correspondence with Spain, spread the news of the sensational victories and plunder of Cajamarca, while at the same time he engaged in trade with the new colony from the isthmus (Lohmann, 1968). The conquest of Nicaragua by Francisco Hernández de Córdoba, the founder of León and Granada, was organised by Pedrarias, who assumed responsibility for one-third of the expenditure incurred, signing an agreement with the Treasurer, the *Contador*, the Judicial Lieutenant-General of the Spanish Main and Francisco Hernández himself, the captain of the guard, who together put up the other two-thirds of the total cost of the enterprise (1523). This expedition sought to take advantage of the discovery already made by Gil González de Avila and, although the original intention stemmed from Pedrarias, the real entrepreneur, in the financial sense, was a certain Juan Téllez, partner and business agent of the senior Crown official in the government, and the holder of an *encomienda*. He was to be the man who would overcome the difficulties, persuade the Crown officials to invest capital, contribute money himself and impose the captain, Hernández, as leader of the expedition; he went personally to Nicaragua, immediately began to engage in trade in order to supply the conquistadors, bringing ships from Panama and Nata, and eventually found a place at the side of Pedrarias when the latter became Governor of Nicaragua (Góngora, 1962, 44–59).

However, this contribution of businessmen in the fitting out of ships, the acquisition of horses and slaves, the supply of arms and rations, and financial advances to the *caudillos* – a contribution that was particularly costly in the case of overseas conquests, which required more capital than in overland expeditions – did nothing to modify the basic and more ancient structure of the warrior-band, which was a legacy of the Spanish Middle Ages. Underlying the capitalistic system of association there still existed the traditional military and governmental relationships. The *caudillo*, in addition to being the military leader, usually possessed, in the form of a signed *capitulación*, the promise of the future governorship of the territory concerned, so that he possessed political powers and jurisdiction in addition to purely military ones. Pizarro, by the terms of the Toledo *Capitulación* of 1529, not only became the potential governor of New Castile but also the potential overlord of native vassals. The conquering force was a military association formed by the *caudillo* and his *compaña*, with legal and customary rules governing the distribution of booty, based on extremely popular and long-established concepts; yet it was something more than a spontaneously formed band, because it was authorised by the king or by his representatives in the Indies, and its leader usually held governmental appointments. A member of the band, once enlisted, could not leave it, under pain of death, in accordance with military law.

The distribution of the booty accruing from forays and expeditions shows, more clearly than anything else, the soldiers' assumptions concerning their rights to the rewards of conquest. The deeds of distribution provide clear documentary evidence of the constitution of the *compañas* and of the underlying military and economic notions. The distribution was carried out by comrades-in-arms elected from among the entire band. The first measure was to separate from the pile the *Quinto real* and any offerings promised to the Virgin or to monastic houses, and then the common debts were decided upon. This at times caused serious problems. In Cartagena in 1534, Pedro de Heredia had returned from the Sierra de Abreva. When his band proceeded to distribute the booty, they first subtracted from the total the shares won by the eight horses which had accompanied the expedition – the shares being collected by the horses' owners; then the cost of daggers, hardware, machetes and axes; the shipwrights' fees; the travel expenses of the attorney who was to go to Castile as the legal representative of the *compaña;* the horse which had been bought to carry the gold and so on. The remaining booty was then divided into 153 equal parts: the deed mentions only the total number of shares, without giving details as to who received what; the value of each share was just over 193 pesos (Góngora, 1952, 59–62). In a provisional deed of distribution of booty granted in 1524 to the followers of Francisco Hernández de Córdoba in Nicaragua, there was more differentiation in the amount of the shares. The Negro slaves and the Spanish servants in the employment of certain rich conquistadors, and the horses and mares, did not receive individual shares, but part of the shares granted to their masters. The standard share was of 250 gold pesos in value for each conquistador, or occasionally for a couple of them who had formed a business partnership for all financial purposes and had contributed Indian slaves or *naborias,* axes and equipment to such a partnership. Some of the conquistadors were indebted, and their shares were transferred to wealthier men who had supplied them with equipment or had paid off their previous debts in Panama. Pedrarias Dávila was given the jewel to which a governor had a customary right. The Crown Officers, Pedrarias (who, as a partner, had supplied ships, Negroes and horses) and Juan Téllez (the most important financial backer of the enterprise), all received shares of over 1,000 pesos in value (Góngora, 1962, 44–59). In contrast to the previous occasion, on this one the higher officials and the financial backer received shares markedly greater than those of the ordinary conquistadors; as it turned out, the gold sent on that occasion from Nicaragua turned out to be of very low quality, with a high copper content. In the famous distribution of the ransom of Atahualpa, according to the Report of Pedro Sancho de la Hoz, the conquistadors were classified as *caballeros* (that is, 'cavalrymen' or 'knights') and 'infantes' ('infantrymen' or *peones*), and accordingly received differing shares. Francisco Pizarro, by reason of his military rank, and the ships and the horse which he had contributed, received 57,220 gold pesos and 2,350 silver pesos; while his favourite brother, Hernando, received 31,080 gold pesos and 1,267 silver pesos. However, Juan and Gonzalo Pizarro, Hernando de Soto, Pedro de Candía and Sebastián de Benalcázar all received shares of a value amounting to between a third and a fifth of that received by their *caudillo.* The *caballeros* received between 8,000 and 9,000 gold pesos and 362 silver pesos, and the *peones* approximately half this amount. The *vecinos* of San Miguel de Piura, who had not been able to be present in Cajamarca when the Inca was captured, received more modest, but significant, shares, subtracted from the common stock. The enterprises of conquest, even though recruitment for them was on a voluntary basis, usually sought the support of all the *vecinos* of the city from which they set off; voluntary initiative was thus combined with official organisation. A city such as Santa Marta, which was situated in an extremely barren region and where the distribution of *encomiendas* took place at a later date, was still, in 1535, living off the booty brought back by the cavalry forays which went out 'to discover the secrets of the land', and always brought back a certain amount for the *vecinos* who stayed behind in the city (Góngora, 1962, 35–6).[2]

The system of equal shares of the old *compaña*, based on the right to a share of the plunder, was, at a certain point in history, replaced by an economic system based on private property; this change is, in general, marked by the distribution of *encomiendas*. Darién, between 1514 and 1520, derived its principal income from the gold, pearls and slaves brought back by the *cabalgadas*, which offset the imports of foodstuffs and clothing from the Caribbean islands; the quantity of mined gold was insignificant. When, however, the centre of gravity of the Spanish Main was displaced to Panama, slave-raiding expeditions became less frequent, *encomiendas* were distributed and put on an organised basis, gold was mined, using the pacified Indians as a labour force, although the *encomenderos* also processed gold, using their own Indians. The expeditions took place, no longer into the interior of the jurisdictional area of that governorship, but towards Nicaragua or Peru. The stage of slave-raiding and mere conquest gave way to one of peaceable domination, based principally on the *encomienda* system. The *encomenderos*, moved by their own self-interest, took measures to suppress raiding (Góngora, 1962, 16–26).

One example of exceptionally long duration of the period of military expeditions and *cabalgadas*, each one of which was liable to last for months or even years, took place in Coro under the government of the house of Welser, the big bankers of Augsburg who in 1530 had displaced the other German capitalists who had been active two years before. The German governors or their agents became closely associated with the conquistadors in their search for 'the secrets of the land' and, indeed, for those of the South Seas or of El Dorado. The *Wanderlust* of the conquistadors led them, on one occasion, to the south of Lake Maracaibo, and they rejected the settlement offered them by Jorge de Spira: 'most of the Spaniards said that they did not want to be settlers at all, but to set forth and discover the Interior. There were hardly ten of them that wanted to settle' (quoted in Friede, 1961, 343). The higher-level agents of the Spanish government during that period took the same attitude: Dr Navarro, who had gone out on an expedition after some fugitives and had been defeated by them, simply joined them and went off with them to the pearl island of Cubagua; Pedro de Limpias and the Licentiate Francisco de Carvajal made raids into the interior in search of slaves and treasure, just as had been done by Alfinger, Spira, Federman and Hutten (Aguado, III, 183–4, 187, 190, etc.). The operative factors were the general tendencies of all the conquistadors, and the peculiar regional characteristics of Coro (the barrenness of the soil), rather than any premeditated intention on the part of the Germans (Friede, 1961). It is true that the latter sponsored the expeditions into the interior – this was stated openly by the factor of the Welsers in 1535 – because in this way almost all the Spaniards would be able to pay off the debts which they had incurred with the firm (Oviedo, III, 56): the latter supplied clothing, rations, horses and equipment, all, of course, at very high prices, in view of the *de facto* commercial monopoly which it enjoyed in that area. For each expedition, the *compaña*, through its deputy, sent gold ore of varying quality to be smelted, the product of forays against the Indians and of barter-trade with them. From 1535 onwards, the official account books show records of barter-trade carried on by individuals, a symptom of the transition implied in the dissolution of the old system of common owner-ship of the *compaña*. However, the latter was ceasing to be the normal organ of representation vis-à-vis the governors, for from 1533 onwards its place was taken by the *Cabildo* of Coro, which at that time was beginning to acquire a degree of autonomy, both in its composition and its general attitude (Ramos, 1961). With the arrival in 1546 of the Licentiate Pérez de Tolosa, there was an end to the period of major expeditions into the interior which were provoked, in Coro as elsewhere, by the sheer surplus of Spaniards – as had been recognised by Spira, who arrived in 1534 with a large-scale expedition (Aguado, III, 91) – but also by a more deep-rooted and less mechanical inducement: the hope of finding El Dorado. Further-more, Venezuela was not only a land of gold but also a source of slave labour that could be utilised in the economy of the Caribbean islands: the *vecinos* of Cubagua, after the decline of the pearl fisheries, made a living by this trade until the New Laws abolished slavery. Jerónimo de Ortal, arriving in 1534 to take up his appointment as Governor of Paria and finding the place without resources, took to slave-raiding, making use of the experience in this field of his captain, Agustín Delgado, who had taken part in the expeditions from the Canaries to Africa before joining similar enterprises in the Indies (Aguado, III, 438). This constitutes valuable evidence of the continuity (in certain respects) existing between the enterprises of the Canaries and those of the Caribbean and Venezuelan regions.

Nearly all the conquests, in the strict sense of the term, had their original starting-point in the Indies themselves, and were undertaken by *vecinos* who had arrived there independently or in the fleets that were brought from Spain by Ovando, Diego Colón, Pedrarias and so on. In 1501 unmarried men had been prohibited from setting off 'in the retinue of' certain people, in order to avoid the participation of elements dangerous to public order in the colonies. Most of those who sailed in the fleets were *vecinos* who were given a free passage and an allowance for the early stages of their residence. Paid soldiers generally comprised only a small proportion of the total passengers. The Instructions imparted to Pedrarias Dávila bear the marks of the Spanish conception of colonisation and permanent settlement, and war against the natives was authorised only if the latter refused allegiance to the Crown. The underlying supposition was that the *vecinos* would settle down without difficulty. Their transformation into 'conquistadors' was to happen when they reached the Caribbean or the Spanish Main; the tendency to associate in warrior-bands organised for conquest proved stronger than the concept of mere colonisation and settlement.

The expeditions to the River Plate region, which were entirely independent of those in the Caribbean (the original starting-point of the Indian conquests), were not very different in character. Some of them, such as that of Díaz de Solís, took place entirely at the King's expense. That led by Pedro de Mendoza, in 1535, which was over 2,000 strong – one of the biggest expeditions that ever set off for the Indies – was financed by considerable contributions on the part of the Governor and of many of his followers, and founded the nucleus of settlement of Asunción, which was to display the characteristics of the conquistadors to such a marked degree: Oviedo, who witnessed a military parade of those men from Seville, commented on their martial appearance (III, 364). The subsequent expeditions of 1570–81, whose methods of recruitment have been studied in detail by Konetzke (1952), showed characteristics which at first sight appear contradictory. The Instructions recommended that, in enlisting men for the expedition, preference should be given to married men accompanied by their wives, small farmers and craftsmen and others of peaceable disposition. Yet, at the same time, in some of the expeditions, the commanders-cum-entrepreneurs were authorised to hold recruiting parades, with drum and fife, in the cities of Andalusia, something that until then 'had not been seen for the Indies' and designed to attract, above all, men of an adventurous spirit.

Conquest and settlement

The Iberian 'conquests' on the Barbary Coast, in the Canaries and in the Americas were, strictly speaking, 'searches', attempts to win men, treasure and lands on the frontiers of Christendom with the infidels, the most ardently sought prize, according to the traditional Hispanic preference, being treasure rather than arable land (Pedro Corominas, 1917). As a result, in Spanish America, the urge to wander prevailed for some time over the tendency to permanent settlement, and slave-raiding was preferred to the organisation of the *encomienda* system. While that period lasted, although, of course, some cities were founded, they were principally conceived of as starting-points for enterprises of conquest. The only real exception was the city of Santo Domingo, for there the development of the city took place before the wave of 'conquests'. As for Mexico, it had been, in any case, a populated centre in Indian times.

The commanders of the conquistador bands sometimes became genuine founders of cities and of politically cohesive territories, thus setting themselves apart from the innate tendencies of the warrior-bands, in so far as their individual qualities and political abilities gave a new direction to the interests and objectives of the group as a whole. Hernán Cortés provides the classic example of a type of conquistador completely different from Hernando de Soto, of whom Gómara felt able to write: 'He did not people the land, and thus he died and he destroyed the men who followed him. They will never do real good, those Conquistadors who do not, above all things, people the land' (quoted in Durand, 1953, I, 40). Cortés, by throwing off his allegiance to Velázquez, who had ordered him only to make a voyage of maritime discovery and to engage in barter-trade in gold, found it imperative to found a city in Veracruz, with the support of his own faction, and had himself elected Governor by the new *Cabildo*. The fundamental legal concepts of the *Partidas*, the primacy of the interests of royal overlordship over all others, played an important part in the presentation of this *fait accompli* to the King, in the First Letter (Frankl, 1962; Konetzke, 1948, 1963). From Veracruz, Cortés marched into the interior towards Tenochtitlán, fighting all the way and playing off one Mexican city against another, making masterly use of all his prestige in his dealings both with the Indians and with his comrades-in-arms, manipulating Moctezuma for political ends, suppressing Indian worship and advancing incessantly, step by step, towards power. Yet he was something more than the strong-willed and realistic politician who has so often been compared to the princes and tyrants of the Renaissance. He was also a *founder*, in the sense that he immediately realised the magnitude of the civilisation that had been conquered, and wrote an eloquent exposition of the aptitudes, occupations and way of life of the Aztecs – even though it is true that he always envisaged it from the point of view of civilisation rather than from that of spiritual culture – and he was able to draw from that estimate a fundamental conclusion, which was capable of shaping a new Indian policy. He took stern measures to curb private forays on the part of his followers (for example, in the Instructions given to Francisco Cortés, 1524) and atrocities committed by his Indian allies. He fully recognised the conditions necessary for the founding of a city: in the case of Cholula he expressed admiration, in his Second Letter, for the fertility of the cultivated land, the irrigation works and the availability of open land for the raising of livestock; he concluded that, of all localities, it was the best one for settlement by Spaniards. He took into account the fact that it was impossible to establish there the same system of personal service that had been established in the islands and which had led to the annihilation of the Indians; but he also knew the human material with which he was dealing – the ordinary soldier of the conquistador armies ('...because all, or most of them, think only of doing with these lands what they did before with the islands that they peopled, that is to say, to plunder and destroy them utterly, and then abandon them'). He therefore concluded '...and because it seems to me that it would be very wrong on the part of those who have experience of the past, to take no steps to remedy the present and the future, taking due care to correct those things that led to disaster in the aforesaid islands, especially because this land, as I have said many times to Your Majesty, is such a great and noble one' (Fourth Dispatch). He was afraid that there would be a rebellion if the Indians were not shared out as personal vassals, and he reminded the Spanish authorities of the War of the *Comunidades*: in the Fourth Dispatch, he actually used this word ('it were a good thing, since there had been a *Comunidad* in Castile, that there should be one here', according to some discontented conquistadors).

The conclusion which Cortés drew from all this was his idea of the *encomienda* as an institution for settlement and military defence – perhaps the closest approximation in the Indies to a genuine feudal system. Despite the orders promulgated by the King in 1523, he assigned the natives to provisional *encomiendas*, insisting, in the face of the Crown's demands, on the inadequacy of the strictly regalist solution which consisted of giving the conquistadors state pensions or incomes, the financial source of these being the tribute which the King was supposed to receive from the natives. To follow such a policy would involve entrusting the military defence of the

country to a regular army, which would be both costly and ruinous to the
Indians as well as to the Spaniards, in view of the habits of the soldiery. If,
however, one were to establish *encomiendas* of a type where the *encomendero*
was responsible for providing horses and arms for the defence of the land
in proportion to the number of Indians entrusted to his care and jurisdiction, and in which the rapacious exploitation of Indian labour would be
attenuated precisely because the institution was an hereditary fief of the
encomendero's family, and he would therefore look after his Indians out of
self-interest – such an institution seemed to Cortés to solve the problem.
The rootlessness of the Indians would be halted if personal service were to
be instituted on a portion of land actually within the area of the Indian
pueblo, and if the unavoidable departures from that area to lend service in
the houses or on the farms of Spaniards were strictly controlled by legal
measures. The *encomendero* was to reside in the appropriate city, marry
there or bring a wife from Spain and plant wheat and vines in his Indian
pueblos (see Cortés' Fourth Letter, the Ordinances for the good government and good treatment of the Indians, the *Memoriales* [Official Reports] of
1528 and *ca* 1537 and the Report to the Licentiate Núñez).

In contrast to pure regalism, the ideas of Cortés may be regarded as those
appropriate to a people of rural and military stock, based on notions both
popular and aristocratic, with an organic concept of economic interests. The
Spaniards, he said in his Report of 1537, will not settle permanently 'if they
do not have the means to maintain themselves in such a way that their own
interest obliges them to settle and forget their former state, and this will
certainly not happen unless Your Majesty gives them a share, so that, in
defending their own particular share, they defend that of Your Majesty,
which is the entirety'. He conceived of the *encomienda* as a permanent system
of strict entail based on primogeniture. However, his popular brand of
conservatism was applied not only to the Spaniards but also to the Indians:
the newly conquered land should be governed according to its ancient laws
and customs, 'for if one bears in mind the magnitude of the population, one
must conclude that if they had not ordered their affairs aright they would
not have maintained their numbers for such a long time, nor diminished so
drastically as soon as their ancient customs were disrupted' (Report of 1528).
Moreover, his opposition to Regalist solutions during the 1530s was based
not only on his heart-felt convictions, but on the defence of his own
overlordship, which was threatened by the continual interference of the
Audiencia: the latter had appointed *Corregidores* in the Indian *pueblos* within
the Marquisate of Cortés, 'low-born and ill-bred people, who think of nought
but their own profit and self-interest' (Report to the Licentiate Núñez).

In a wider sphere, one can comprehend the mentality of Cortés as a founder and coloniser when one observes that, even in his Third Letter, he envisaged the establishment of two centres of settlement in the Pacific to serve as bases for discoveries in the Ocean, and initiated undertakings which he was to continue to support even after the end of his tenure of office as Governor; in the Fourth and Fifth Letters he was to outline projects for the exploration of the Spice Islands, and also for the discovery of the Northwest Passage by the Atlantic or the Pacific route.

Cortés represented *par excellence* the type of conquistador who was the founder of a permanent and compact centre of political government on the mainland; this process marks the passing of the phase of political control over the islands and the coast, the period of geographically limited occupation and of exclusive dedication to barter-trade in gold and to *cabalgadas*; this now gave way to a system of 'settlement'. The fundamental aspects of the new system were to be: cities defended by the *encomenderos* living in them, with powerful *Cabildos* under their control; the conservation of the Indian peoples and of the authority of their *caciques*; personal service within the same *pueblo*, the old tribute paid by the Indians to their overlords being replaced by labour performed for the new lords of the land; supervision by the local authorities of all the natives' movements; hereditary bequeathment of the *encomienda*. The system established by Cortés was so faithful a reflection of the real needs of the Conquest that subsequent legislation, albeit after a few hesitations, was to extend it throughout the Indies. However, in the other areas of considerable settlement it did not always have the same coherence, nor were governors always able to apply it consistently. In Chile, for example, where Pedro de Valdivia was undoubtedly a good 'founder', the *encomienda*, as a system, had a more destructive and disruptive effect on the native population than was the case in Aztec Mexico (Jara, 1961; Góngora, 1970). In Paraguay, which was inhabited by poor Indians of the Guarani culture, without a class of overlords, and where the women occupied themselves in agricultural labour, the Spaniards established a subsistence economy which dispensed with the use of money, based on large-scale miscegenation. The lack of precious metals encouraged the conquistadors to carry out *entradas* in various directions, and to capture Indian slaves, with the help of their Indian auxiliaries from Paraguay. Service was conceived by the Indians as based on blood-relationship and agricultural tasks were performed by the womenfolk. Very large numbers of Indian men and women were employed in domestic service. The Governor, Martínez de Irala, was eventually obliged to abandon the practice of slave-raiding forays, owing to the legal prohibitions, and he then established the system of *encomiendas* and the confinement of the Indians to their native *pueblos*. Basically, however, Paraguay remained outside the Cortés model of government based on overlordship, and came to support a *mestizo* society based on an agriculture of subsistence (Elman Service, 1951).

Hernán Cortés outgrew the purely American sphere of activity and became a prominent figure in the Renaissance nobility of Spain, a hero glorified by López de Gómara and Cervantes de Salazar (John H. Elliott, 1967); but at the same time he continued to be an overlord of Indians on his enormous 'states' in southern and central Mexico, and a *granjero* engaged in planting sugar-cane; nor did he ever abandon his plans for fresh discoveries in the Pacific. This dual aspect was not present in the case of the other great conquistador, Francisco Pizarro, whose sphere of activity was exclusively American (Porras Barrenechea, 1941); he maintained the unity of the Inca Empire and also founded capital cities, and was an implacable disciplinarian: 'Of those who went with the Marquis to the Conquest', Pedro Pizarro was to write long afterwards, 'not a man would touch an ear of maize without leave from their commander.' However, his inability to control the behaviour of the other conquistadors made Peru, both under his rule and for a further thirty years, until the government of Viceroy Cañete (or, to be more exact, that of Francisco de Toledo), a prime example of an anarchic Hispanic political milieu; it was like an epitome of the era of the conquistadors, excessively turbulent and violent, though not without its outstanding figures.

Rights to the rewards of conquest and the rebellions of the conquistadors

From the very heart of the Spanish Middle Ages there had been derived the profound conviction that the conquistador who had rendered signal service, the *benemérito*, especially the one who had served *a su costa y minción*, without placing any financial burden on the king, had a prescriptive right to a reward in the lands he had conquered. As it was grandiloquently expressed by that typical popular representative of the Conquest, Bernal Díaz, his children and grandchildren could truthfully say 'my father came here to discover and win these lands at his own expense, and he spent his own patrimony on the enterprise, and he was one of the first conquistadors'.

The *Capitulaciones* constitute the foundation of the argument put forward by the discoverers and conquistadors in their disputes with the Crown, which was always desirous of limiting or evading its commitments. The heirs of Columbus in their lawsuit with the Crown, and the Admiral himself in his will, reminded the sovereigns of that family's enterprise and the expenditure which it had incurred ('...when I served you by discovering the Indies; I say served you, but it appears that I gave them to you, as if they were my own property...'), and they insisted that the Crown was under a contractual obligation to fulfil its promises.[3] Even more emphatically, in a Report of 1540 on the maritime discoveries which he was sponsoring, Hernán Cortés stated that 'it was not possible to take from me nor to suspend the right or possession which I have acquired by virtue of the said contract and *capitulación* made by Your Majesty and under your Royal mandate, because it is a binding contract involving mutual obligations, and Your Majesty, according to the law, is obliged to fulfil what was contracted and provided for in your Royal name with me so many years ago.' Gonzalo Pizarro, writing to Charles V himself around 1544, stated that 'in some matters Your Majesty has forgotten your Royal word pledged to the Conquistadors in the *capitulaciones* which he signed with the Marquis my brother' (Pérez de Tudela, *Documentos*, I, 363–5). The *Capitulaciones*, like the *fueros* of the Middle Ages, enshrined the prescriptive rights of the conquistador.

Discipline among the bands of conquistadors and obedience to the governor depended, to a large degree, on the equitable distribution of the booty and, subsequently on the granting of *encomiendas* and *mercedes*; and, in addition to this distributive justice, on generosity in all matters affecting the soldiers' interests, and on their willingness to abandon what was already acquired for the sake of further conquests. Jerez takes care to point out that Pizarro, in San Miguel, when he had to send some ships to Panama, did not take possession of the gold belonging to the *compaña*, but took it as a loan, promising to return it to the common stock the next time gold refining was carried out. In the distribution of the Cajamarca treasure, according to Jerez and Zárate, Pizarro proceeded with both justice and generosity when he first rewarded his immediate companions, who had taken part in the capture of Atahualpa; after that, however, he took care to distribute smaller shares and profits to the companions of Almagro, the *vecinos* of San Miguel and even to merchants and seamen who had arrived after the victory. Such generosity certainly gave proof of the wealth of the newly-discovered land in the eyes of public opinion in Panama and the other 'older' lands. An equitable distribution of booty was very difficult to achieve, because, as Zárate observes, 'each one thought that, though he were given the Governorship itself, it still would not be sufficient reward'. The generosity of Almagro to his companions became legendary. All these occasions, show the political instinct of the leader of the warrior-band.

The overlordship of the *caudillos* was the effective form of government in the era of the Conquest, but they depended on the uncertain support of those voluntarily constituted groups of men. The *Cabildos*, in so far as they articulated the aspirations of the conquistadors, serving as intermediaries between the band and the *caudillo* and providing the scene for a continuous interaction of forces, were, therefore, of outstanding importance in those early times, because they gave legal form to real political situations. Oviedo gives a vivid account of the swift rise of Balboa in Darién. He had arrived there hidden in a wine-cask, fleeing from Santo Domingo to escape his creditors; in the new territory he encouraged the election of *alcaldes ordinarios* to take over the government from Ojeda and his lieutenant Enciso, until such time as the King could make a definitive appointment; and he, as a mere *alcalde*, was 'almost a lord'. When the *vecinos*, 'some of them insisting that there should be one leader appointed to rule over them' (Las Casas), sent envoys to Diego de Nicuesa requesting that he come and assume the governorship, Balboa and the *regidores* who supported him arranged for a popular vote against accepting his appointment, arrested Nicuesa and put him on board a brigantine, alleging that through his fault they had missed the opportunity of taking part in an *entrada* which would have made a profit of 50,000 pesos. In the case of Cortés in Veracruz, the *Cabildo* was the institution that decreed the rejection of the authority of Velázquez, because he had forbidden them to found a city, and thus was preventing the increase of the King's overlordship and the opportunities for the conquistadors to gain *mercedes* in the new land. Bernal Díaz describes the political background of the agreement, and the manœuvres of the friends of Cortés and the adherents of Velázquez; how Cortés 'made a great show of refusing', and how he established, as a condition, that he was to be awarded a one-fifth share of what was left after the *Quinto real* had been deducted. This act has been interpreted as the application of municipalist notions or of a form of political Thomism, according to which sovereignty was reassumed by the People in order for it to contend against a tyrannical authority (in this case, that of Velázquez); moreover, at this time the Castilian War of the Communities was at its height (Giménez Fernández, 1948). Some have noted the influence of the monarchical legal principles of the *Partidas*, as a juridical ideology manifested in the documents supporting the act (Frankl, 1962). The incident may, rather, be interpreted as the expression of notions typical of the conquistadors. The strongest motivation was the desire to be rewarded in the land that they had just discovered and which was proclaimed as being rich in gold. They looked on it as their just due, as a kind of reasonable natural law, even though it lacked any theoretical foundation. The *procurador* of the *Cabildo* of Santiago, Chile, in 1541, in presenting his submission in the same terms as the *vecinos* of Veracruz had done twenty-two years before, emphasised the fact that Pedro de Valdivia knew, better than any other leader who had come from Peru, who had conquered the new land and who could, in consequence, justifiably expect rewards.

In this atmosphere of turbulence and adventure, there was nothing surprising in the manœuvres of the *caudillos*, and of the internal factions within each *Cabildo*. One can see this from Oviedo's descriptions of the factions in Honduras during the 1520s, and from the disputes after Valdivia's death between the different cities of Chile, each of which proposed its own candidate as governor, as described in the chronicle of Mariño de Lobera. In the last resort, however, the convictions, feelings and expectations of all the participants were fundamentally the same, and this similarity favoured the rise to power of the *caudillo* best able to capitalise on this complex of sentiments.

In Asunción, the Crown authorised the election of governors by the people as a whole, during the interim period before the King sent out a new governor. This was an extraordinary grant of municipal democracy, accorded to what was the most isolated province in the Indies. Ruy Díaz de Guzmán has left us a vivid description of these elections. Despite them, however, in the early years, effective command was in the hands of Martínez de Irala, who was Governor three times, the second time after the imprisonment of the *Adelantado* Alvar Núñez Cabeza de Vaca in 1543. The deposition of the latter, according to the traveller Ulrich Schmidel, was the result of his harsh treatment of the conquistadors, particularly with regard to the distribution of booty. The *Commentaries* written by the notary Pedro Hernández declared emphatically that the settlers who rose in rebellion in the name of 'liberty' felt threatened by the Ordinances which forbade the removal of Indian men and women from their lands for impressment into domestic service. There is no doubt that Irala, the royal officers and the members of the *Cabildo* were striving to achieve their common liberty, in the sense in which the conquistadors understood the term: this 'liberty' was at the same time a juridical, a political and an economic motivation for their behaviour.

In the settlement of Hispaniola the system which had overwhelmingly prevailed had been the grant of positions of power in accordance with purely Regalist principles, and, on the basis of such principles, the interests of bureaucratic cliques in Spain itself; an example of this was the grant of *encomiendas* to persons absent in the peninsula (Giménez Fernández, 1953). The conquests put an abrupt end to such practices, and the Crown was obliged to recognise its obligation to reward the services of the '*indianos*' (namely, those who had distinguished themselves in the Conquest of the Indies). In 1525 instructions were given to Luis Ponce de León to make grants of land in New Spain to all those who had served, and subsequently, in 1528, the King announced this policy of 'recompensing the aforesaid services and labours' of the conquistadors and the earliest settlers, for the specific purpose of persuading them to settle on the lands concerned. The Instructions imparted to the Viceroy Mendoza in 1535 and the *Cédula* addressed to Pizarro in 1536 in effect proclaimed the same basic principle. Further detailed provisions reserved not only *encomiendas*, but judicial offices, the appointments of *corregidor, alguacil* and so on, to the conquistadors or their descendants. An exactly similar policy was followed with regard to ecclesiastical benefices.

This principle gave rise to the requirement of supplying legal proof of personal merit and of services rendered by those claiming a *merced*. Such judicial proofs – of which there were an enormous number in the first century of Spanish domination – must, of course, be regarded with some scepticism as historical records. Their real documentary value, however, is of a different nature: they contain the definition of the qualities which a 'good' conquistador or settler was expected to possess. In the first place, he was expected to have taken a direct part in military operations; he was to have come *a su costa y minción*, to have brought with him armed companions – Spaniards, Negroes and *yanaconas* – and horses; donations and loans to military expeditions were taken into account; and, finally, note was taken of the hospitality which he had displayed in giving board and lodging to poor soldiers. A 'good settler' was a man who had provided seeds and trained the Indians in his *encomienda* in the care of livestock; who had undertaken the construction of ox-carts, mills and shipyards in the new territory; who had treated his Indians well, and encouraged their conversion to Christianity; who had persuaded his relatives and friends to come from Spain and settle; who had been loyal to the Crown during rebellions; who had been a 'good public servant' when holding appointments in local councils; and, above all and most emphatically, who was an *hidalgo* and whose style of life was that of a 'man of honour'. These judicial proofs, to a greater extent than any other source, provide a picture of the system of values prevailing at the time.

The New Laws of 1542 represent the most determined attempt on the part of the Crown to impose its authority on the situations and notions which had resulted from the Conquest. This reform was not in any sense the direct outcome of the ideas of Las Casas; it stemmed, rather, from an undercurrent of criticism which emerged from the moral preconceptions and the emphasis on natural law which was generally accepted in cultured circles in Spain at the time; the majority of the Council of the Indies, around 1542, wanted to abolish the *encomienda* system of personal service and to put a stop to the process of conquest, in order to avoid the total annihilation of the Indians. The views expressed both in the Council and at the Valladolid *Junta* suggested, as an alternative to the existing *encomienda* system, the establishment of feudal tenures for jurisdictional and tributary purposes, or of simple State pensions (*entretenimientos*); Ramírez de Fuenleal, the former President of the second Mexican *Audiencia*, and subsequently Bishop of Cuenca and President of the Valladolid Chancery, was the speaker who suggested solutions most at variance with the process of conquest and the *encomienda* system, especially since he proposed the abolition of the heredi-tary character of the latter institution (Pérez de Tudela, 1958). The New Laws did, in fact, deal a series of mortal blows to the conquistadors: the *Audiencias* (constituted by *letrados*) were henceforth to be the only bodies empowered to authorise new discoveries, and the decision to establish new settlements was to lie with the Council of the Indies; trade and barter with unpacified Indians was to be carried on in a peaceable manner, in order to leave the way clear for missionary endeavours; Indian slavery was to be completely abolished; existing *encomiendas* were to be supervised, with a view to eliminating the use of human labour for transporting goods and other personal services deterimental to the health of those rendering them; excessively large *repartimientos* were to be curtailed, with a view to recom-pensing conquistadors who had been left destitute; *repartimientos* held by officials and ecclesiastics were to be abolished; finally, and this provision was of great importance, *encomiendas* were to lapse at the death of their present holders. There is no trace in the New Laws of strictly feudal solutions on the European model, as had been suggested by some members of the Council; the only measure taken the following year was that of granting *corregi-mientos* and State pensions to the *vecinos*; in other words, the Crown was adopting a more decidedly Regalist position.

In New Spain, the protests of the *vecinos* and ecclesiastics succeeded in persuading the Viceroy and the Crown's 'Visitor' that the abolition of the *encomienda* system was impossible and inopportune; all that was achieved in that territory, as was the case throughout the Indies, was the abolition of Indian slavery. The *encomienda* system, however, was stubbornly defended. The Dominican Friars of the Viceroyalty stated that the Indians were lacking in constancy and that settlement by Spaniards was essential, and that this should take the form of a stratified social system, because the richer were then able to maintain the poorer citizens; the *Corregidor* system was inferior to that of the *encomienda*, both from the point of view of ensuring just treatment of the Indians and from that of the Royal Treasury. Were it not for the trade in and circulation of goods carried on by the *encomenderos*, wrote Francisco de Terrazas, the King would be nothing more than the 'lord of maize-fields and cotton saddle cloths, and not of the treasure which at present Your Majesty collects every year'; and New Spain provided an outlet for the poor of Castile. Cristóbal de Benavente, the *Fiscal* of the *Audiencia*, wrote that the occupation of the most fertile lands by the Indians made Spanish agrarian colonisation impossible; furthermore, in one of the most strongly-worded passages of his report, he emphasised that the conquistadors considered that they had a 'natural right by reason of the services which they had rendered' and because of the royal promise implied in the law providing for the duration of the *encomienda* for two natural lives, which constituted a quasi-contractual obligation. 'The attempt to govern this land in accordance with the same laws that are in force in Spain will not be tolerated, and there is nothing reprehensible in altering and modifying statutes and laws to adapt them to different times and different places' (CoDoIn, first series, 7, 532; Paso y Troncoso, *Epistolario de Nueva España*, IV, 99–114).

Although, in New Spain, the ruling circles argued their case and obtained an easy victory over the Emperor himself (1545–6), in Peru the proclamation of the New Laws led to the Civil Wars of 1544–8, and this conflict was prolonged in the rebellion of Hernández Girón and Sebastián de Castilla in 1553–4. Few incidents in the colonial history of the Americas have been more vividly recorded, in all their drama and even their 'picturesque' aspects, by contemporary chroniclers and, later, by modern historical research. The only matter that interests us here is the opinions of the conquistadors with regard to the events. The documentary records are, of course, in agreement as to the imprudence and turpitude of the Viceroy, Blasco Núñez de Vela, which was in sharp contrast to the behaviour of Antonio de Mendoza in Mexico. Of the former official Cieza de León wrote: 'Since he had come from Spain, where the King's Majesty is obeyed to such a degree that any measure or command, however harsh it may appear and by whomsoever it be enforced, is executed and fulfilled without any hesitation...he did not know the devious habits of the people who had lived in this realm, and the licence that they had enjoyed in past times', so he publicly proclaimed the Laws (*Guerra de Quito*, XXXIII). The strict enforcement of these Laws in the Indies, the land where it had become traditional for laws to be suspended on the grounds that they were inappropriate to the *milieu*, was, in the eyes of his contemporaries, the cardinal error committed by Blasco Núñez: 'they were more scandalized by the language he employed and by his gruff behaviour than by the Ordinances themselves', according to Gómara. The result was the armed insurrection originating in Cuzco, with the appointment of Gonzalo Pizarro as *procurador* and Chief Justice. Apart from their central argument, which hinged on the breach of the royal promise to recompense services rendered – a breach implied in the New Laws – the *letrados* also frequently insisted that laws required the assent of the subjects, in this case of the *vecinos*, 'who were the entire citizenry of the realms of Peru' (Gómara, *Historia de las Indias*, 250). As in so many other insurrections in the Americas, recourse was had to medieval ideas and terminology. The key word was now 'liberty' – not only to Pizarro, but also, for example, to Alvaro de Oyón, who led a rebellion in Popayán in 1553, styling himself 'the captain-general of liberty' (Friede, 1954).

The conquistadors believed that they constituted 'the land', in contrast to the intrusive royal officials. Gonzalo Pizarro, in a letter to Manuel de Estacio, wrote that 'what those from Spain wanted, even though they pretended otherwise, was to enjoy the fruits of our sweat and toil and, with their well-washed hands, to possess what we won with our blood' (Pérez de Tudela, *Documentos*, I, 84). And to Charles V he wrote that 'by those who have come from there [Spain] we have been robbed, ill-treated and oppressed and your Royal Treasury has been laid waste, simply because they come here filled with greed and ill-versed in the ways of this land' (*Documentos*, I, 363). The followers of Pizarro refused to accept the view of La Gasca that the King was the real creator of the wealth of the Governor of Peru and of his brothers, on the grounds that he (the King) had made them a grant of land on the Spanish Main and authorised them to raise the military force with which they conquered Peru. La Gasca compared the King to a lord who had granted a barren tract of land to a poor man so that the latter and his dependants might enrich themselves by working it for the term of their natural lives. Such a strictly legalistic interpretation of the conquests was not at all convincing to the rebellious conquistadors.

'There are in each province many more people without *encomiendas* than there are with them.' This fact, which was only too obviously true, was asserted by two participants in the 1542 *Junta*; their intention was to emphasise that those adversely affected by the New Laws were only a minority (Pérez de Tudela, 1958). According to this historian, the *encomienda* system operated not only to the detriment of the Indians, but also to that of the poorer Spaniards, who had been excluded from the spoils by a powerful caste and by certain governors who systematically favoured that oligarchy or their own immediate retainers. He admits, however, that the poor soldiers in Peru were the most loyal supporters of Gonzalo Pizarro, and they were sometimes rewarded, on the orders of Gonzalo Pizarro, by being allowed to marry the widows of *encomenderos* (Pérez de Tudela, 1963, XLI–XLII). This soldiery, often dispersed throughout the land as a result of unsuccessful forays, maintaining itself at the expense of the Indian *pueblos*, and often living in fear (according to a Pizarro supporter from Collao) 'on account of things that they had done, some of them serious, and others of little account' (Pérez de Tudela, *Documentos*, I, 178), came to constitute the strongest support of Pizarro in that land filled with 'men at a loose end' desirous of preserving their 'soldierly liberties'. There were friars – these were another highly combative element among Pizarro's followers – who preached in the same terms as a certain Dominican in Trujillo: 'you know and understand that you must treat the soldiers well and share with them what you have' (Pérez de Tudela, *Documentos*, II, 133). The fact is that, at the critical moment when the conquistadors had thrown off their allegiance to the King, and were resolved to defend their interests and what they conceived to be their rights and legitimate expectations, the dividing line between the contending parties was not determined by the rank attained by individuals but by personal loyalty to the King or to Gonzalo Pizarro; underlying allegiance to the latter there was, less explicitly, the adherence to a general feeling of solidarity uniting all the conquistadors in the Americas against the Crown's bureaucracy. The great ability of La Gasca – and his conduct had the prior support of Charles V, who had already given way over the question of the abolition of the *encomiendas* – lay in his avoidance of the attitude adopted by Blasco Núñez. La Gasca himself, basing what he said on recollections of his experiences in Peru, wrote in 1554 concerning the insurrection of Hernández Girón that the poorer conquistadors, 'an excessively numerous crowd, with their pretensions and their cupidity', 'relatives or friends or retainers of the *vecinos*', were those who encouraged the latter to place further exactions upon the Indians (Pérez de Tudela, *Documentos*, II, 509–10), and for this reason they were the foremost champions of the *encomienda* system, contrary to what the *letrados* in Spain might imagine. Diego Fernández corroborates the opinion of La Gasca when he voices the view of one of the conspirators in Sebastián de Castilla's insurrection in Cuzco in 1553, namely that the *Audiencia* of Lima, by eliminating personal service from the obligations involved in the *encomienda* system, was causing economic hardship in the land. The *vecinos* could now no longer support their own families, let alone the poorer Spaniards, who were too many in number and who wandered about as if lost, some of them in Condesuyo, Collao and Potosí, or in uninhabited places because they had no clothes with which to dress 'in accordance with their station', and taking potatoes and *chuño* (the dried potato of the Altiplano) from the Indians in order to have something to eat – 'the land will come to such straits of poverty, that men will look for some one to serve and they will find no one' (Diego Fernández, II, II, 1).

While the poorer conquistadors might have expected more from the 'liberty' proclaimed by Gonzalo Pizarro than from the laws and justice dispensed by the State, the *encomenderos* were determined to maintain their position as overlords. Some members of the 1542 *Junta* were sufficiently perceptive to realise this: Francisco de los Cobos considered that granting them a pension, even if it meant a larger income than they were getting at the time, 'will not satisfy them, and it will appear to them that they are merely being paid a salary from the State's account, whereas if they receive the same amount as a result of a *repartimiento* it will seem to them that they possess a perpetual estate'. The Count of Osorno put it more explicitly: 'Since the Spaniards in the Indies are of the same rank and station as we who are here, and are accustomed to command men, I believe that they would prefer to have a smaller income, provided that they are left with a few Indians, than to have a larger one without them' (Pérez de Tudela, 1958, 507).

Between 1510 and 1550, therefore, there were formed in the Indies bands of conquistadors which formed the spearhead of Spanish settlement and colonisation. These associations were formed outside the framework of the official structure prevailing in the cities, and were usually organised by groups of settlers who had already enriched themselves by way of the *encomienda* system, and enjoyed the financial support of money-lenders and merchants; the lower-level participants were, on the other hand, poor settlers without *encomiendas*. Although these bands were motivated by a spirit of adventure, they were nonetheless subject to military sanctions and jurisdiction, and sometimes even included leaders provisionally appointed to head and staff new governorships. The entire enterprise was founded on promises of reward and the hope of adventure. The band enjoyed its own long-standing right to booty, derived from the Reconquest of Spain. As on the frontier between Christendom and Islam, in the Indies there arose a

30

new human type which was to dominate the history of the early decades of the sixteenth century, and fill the ranks of all the institutions established: governors, *Oidores*, royal officers, the secular clergy, the *letrados*, merchants, craftsmen, ordinary *vecinos*, Negro auxiliary labour, friendly Indians, were all, in their way, 'conquistadors'. There were no purely 'civil' cities or institutions. The first settlers on Hispaniola had to suppress the rebellion of Higüey, and later found themselves involved, in some way or other, in military expeditions to Puerto Rico and Cuba, or in the slave-raids carried out in the 'Useless Islands' or on the Main. Only Viceroys like Mendoza or Velasco, or a character like La Gasca, or such *Audiencia* members as Ramírez de Fuenleal or Vasco de Quiroga, or such bishops as Zumárraga or, above all, the mendicant friars, represented a contrasting style of spiritual outlook.

The conquests constituted in each province 'the land' (*la tierra*), in the political sense of that medieval term: the unified polity of possessions, settlement, institutions and power. Herein lay the strength of the resistance of the conquistadors to the New Laws and to the State with its legislation and its bureaucracy. The conviction of having won the new land as volunteers, not as paid servants (the soldiers received pay from the leading conquistadors, but the latter lived and fought at their own expense) was the mainspring of the resistance; it was felt that the State was violating commitments guaranteed by the *Capitulaciones* and the Laws.

Towards the end of Spanish domination, one catches an echo of this same conviction in the pamphlet written by the exiled Jesuit Juan Pablo Viscardo, encouraging the movement for independence. When their ancestors, according to his *Letter to the American-born Spaniards* (1798), went to the New World,

they set out, at their own cost, to gain themselves a new living, and faced immense weariness and very great dangers. (Herrera says that all the conquests were carried out at the expense of the conquistadors themselves, without the government spending anything.) The great success which crowned the efforts of the conquistadors of America gave them, it appeared, a right which, even though it were not entirely justified, was at least more solidly founded than that of the ancient Goths of Spain, to enjoy the fruits of their valour and their labours. Yet their natural affection for their native land led them to give to it, as a generous tribute, their immense acquisitions; they could not doubt that a service both gratuitous and important should fail to obtain for them proportionate recognition, according to the custom of that century, in the shape of rewards for those who had contributed to extending the domains of the nation...If we consult our annals for the past three centuries, we shall see there the ingratitude and injustice of the Court of Spain, its untrustworthiness in the fulfilment of its obligations, first towards the great Columbus, and then towards the other conquistadors, who had given it dominion over the New World, subject to explicitly expressed conditions. We shall see the later history of those generous men struck down by official contempt, and besmirched with the hatred of those who libelled, persecuted and ruined them.

Fray Servando Teresa de Mier, in Book XIV of his *History of the Revolution of New Spain* (1813) and in his *Description of the Constitution Granted to the Americas by the Kings of Spain Before the Invasion of the Old Despotism* (1820), took up and amplified the theme of the *Capitulaciones* granted to the conquistadors, to the extent of suggesting the existence of an American Magna Carta dating from the first half of the sixteenth century, and subsequently destroyed by bureaucratic despotism (Góngora, 1965).

It is not easy to find, in the entire history of Spanish America, more obvious evidence than that provided by these writers of historical continuity, as they accord a new relevance to a past episode of political consciousness.

THE SPANISH EMPIRE IN THE INDIES: FROM CHRISTENDOM TO THE SYSTEM OF NATION STATES

The Bulls of Alexander VI

The kings of Castile might have justified their possession of the islands where Columbus landed solely on the grounds that they were the first occupiers, a right already recognised in a provision of the *Partidas* originally inspired by Roman law (*Partida* II, 28, 29), or on the grounds that it was a conquest of infidel lands, as had been the case in the Canaries. In the opinion of some jurists, this alone would have sufficed, but the Catholic Sovereigns wanted, despite this, to obtain Papal legitimisation of their claim and thus achieve juridical continuity with the Bull *Aeterni Regis* of 1481, which had established the demarcation between the Portuguese and Castilian zones on the Atlantic coast of Africa, thus giving sanction to the earlier Treaty of Alcaçobas. It is possible that they were thinking along the same lines as King Duarte of Portugal in 1436, when he addressed the Pope as follows:

Even though some make efforts to wage war and occupy on their own authority places held by the infidels, nevertheless, since the Earth is the Lord's and the fullness thereof, and He left to Your Holiness power over the entire globe, those who possess parts of it by the express authority and permission of Your Holiness shall appear to possess them by special licence and permission of God [De Witte, 1953, quoted and discussed more fully in Lopetegui-Zubillaga, 1965, I 58].

And years later, in 1510, Ferdinand the Catholic wrote to his ambassador in Rome, during the campaigns in North Africa, suggesting that the Pope should authorise his conquest by Apostolic Bull, in view of the legal doubts that had arisen:

they say that in law it is not licit for Christian princes to wage war in all the lands of the infidels, except in the realm of Jerusalem, unless the said infidels wage war against the Christians, or war be declared against them by the Supreme Pontiff...[and] we would not wish to be lacking any additional grounds there may be for the justification of the conquest [Lopetegui-Zubillaga, *ibid.*]

The famous texts, which 'donate, concede and assign', and, in some other passages, even 'invest' the Sovereigns with the 'full, free and all-embracing authority and jurisdiction' over the islands and mainland discovered by Columbus, so long as they were not already in the possession of any other Christian prince, and which also established, in a most emphatic manner, the obligation of sending missionaries at the king's expense, were of decisive importance in the creation of the Spanish Empire in the Indies. The original title based on discovery and the taking of possession tended to become eclipsed, and the subsequent *Compilation of Laws* of 1680 had the effect of prolonging the concept of Papal donation – which was already obsolete in the sphere of international relations – until the very end of the Empire.

As Giménez Fernández has pointed out, the Bulls of 1493, in addition to their practical usefulness as legal instruments,

> were the reflection of a transcendental metaphysical system – the Christian one – which, even when considered in isolation from the topical and chronological characteristics of the time when the Bulls were formulated, constituted an inexhaustible source of ideological expression in the differing circumstances which supervened with the passing of time...For this reason, throughout the period of Spanish domination in the Indies, there was never any ideological movement directed towards the reform of the existing legal situation, nor any change of direction in the government of the State, whose adherents did not, on one pretext or another, refer to the historical fact of the Bulls of Pope Alexander relating to the Indies for theoretical support, interpreting them in the light of their own social, political and juridical concepts.[1]

The problems, at times intractable, involved in the Bulls, their chronology, exegesis and legal interpretation, pragmatic motivations and doctrinal bases, have constituted a perennial source of controversy, with practical repercussions from the sixteenth to the eighteenth centuries, and as the source of theoretical and historical problems from the nineteenth century onwards. The historians of international law in the last century, and the historians of legal Spanish theory in this, have considerably amplified the conception which contemporary writers had of the Bulls, but they have by no means resolved all the anomalies involved. We still do not know, for example, if the documents concerned, which were published between May and September 1493 can be regarded as being in a definite chronological succession; and, if that is the case, whether the last Bull (*Dudum Siquidem*) had the effect of repealing the second one (*Inter Coetera*, published 4 May): the latter established the famous line of partition, whereas the former donated to the Castilians any islands and continents that they might discover sailing by the westward route towards the East, and also by the southern route to India (Giménez Fernández, 1944, 290–4). It is, moreover, doubtful if the famous theory of Bodin, according to which the Bulls made the King of Spain a feudatory of the Holy See, can be legitimately deduced from the textual formulae employed in the document in which the Catholic Sovereigns placed the new lands in subjection or submission to the Pope, and the latter in his turn donated them to the Sovereigns, using in this context the word 'investiture' and other terms implying a transfer of dominion. Certain German historians, and also Giménez Fernández and Weckmann, incline to the view that a 'feudal' relationship was established, but García Gallo disagrees with this. Weckmann has suggested that the islands were placed in special subjection to the Pope in the medieval sense of the term, according to the provisions of the Donation of Constantine; but this view has been contested by García Gallo (1957–8, 660 ff.). Finally, Giménez Fernández has denied the existence of a missionary objective in the first voyage (1492–3); but in this matter he has, in the opinion of the author, been convincingly refuted by García Gallo (*ibid.* 634 ff.)

It would exceed the scope of this study to examine all these problems, since its purpose is the consideration of long-term implications, without examining in detail the Bulls themselves and the circumstances in which they were published. What is of greater interest, for present purposes, is the subsequent process of interpretation and theoretical elaboration of the basis of Spanish dominion in the Indies, which began in the early years of the sixteenth century and which looks back to the Bulls of 1493 and the theories of the Middle Ages in its desire to legitimise the new Empire.

The theocratic interpretation of Spanish dominion

Because the Bulls were official decrees, they only rarely alluded explicitly to their own theoretical foundations. However, overtly theocratic theories can be found in Papal documents of the fifteenth century. For example, *Dominator Dominus*, promulgated by Pope Eugene IV, stated that 'the Lord God Almighty, who rules Heaven and Earth, entrusts to us for this purpose the task of being His representative on Earth, and of exercising His illustrious kingship over peoples and realms' (De Witte, 1958, 465). The Bull *Ineffabilis et summi*, which entrusted the conquest of Africa to the King of Portugal, began by quoting the text of Jeremiah 1: 10 ('See, I have this day set thee over the nations and over the kingdoms, to root out, and to pull down, and to destroy, and to throw down, to build, and to plant'). Such cases are, however, undoubtedly exceptional, and the bases of the theory must be looked for in doctrinal works.[2]

After the promulgation of the Bulls of Alexander VI, the Spanish and Portuguese Kings had entered into direct negotiations to modify the line of partition, and mutually agreed not to request the Pope to modify these arrangements; they did, however, declare that they would request Pontifical confirmation of the Treaty of Tordesillas; this confirmation took place, at Portugal's request, in 1506. Portugal arranged for yet another Papal intervention in its favour, in 1514, but this was the last Papal *démarche* in this sphere.

The crisis of conscience provoked by the sermon preached by the Dominican Montesinos in Santo Domingo in 1511, when he attacked the *encomienda* system, provoked Ferdinand the Catholic to announce officially that he was the legitimate ruler by virtue of the Bulls; there was no mention of title based on discovery or on possession (see his letter of March 1512 to Diego Colón). On the occasion of the *Juntas* held at Burgos and Valladolid in 1512–13, which regulated the *encomienda* system, some of the participants submitted written opinions, and even full-length treatises, which contain the first theoretical formulation of the basis of Spain's dominion over the Indies.

By far the most important of such treatises and pronouncements, that entitled *De Insulis Oceanicis*, by the jurist Juan López de Palacios Rubio, whom Las Casas praised as being both a just man and an effective practical champion of the Indians, but condemned for his theoretical pronouncements, in glosses in the margin of the copy of the manuscript in his possession. In his treatise he was trying, according to the somewhat over-harsh judgment of Las Casas, 'to flatter the King and avoid vexing him'. Following the same argument that he applied to the defence of the deposition of the King of Navarre by Pope Julius II – whose support Ferdinand obtained in order to deprive the King of Navarre of his kingdom on the grounds that he was allied to a schismatic (namely, the King of France) – Palacios Rubio asserted the transmutation of the authority of the chieftains of the islands, who were now subject to the King of Castile, into the full political dominion of the Pope over the entire globe – a full dominion, though not a direct one. According to the oft-repeated medieval allegory, the Pope had two swords, but he ceded the temporal sword to the Emperor and the Kings.

The work of Palacios Rubio begins with the first-hand accounts that had arrived from the Indies, which still described them as an earthly paradise, and went on to quote the Biblical prophecies concerning the preaching of the Gospel throughout the world, which had created such a deep impression on Columbus. In the view of Palacios Rubio, Columbus had not reached India, because nothing which resembled that country had been discovered, but new lands, the last beyond Ultima Thule, of which Seneca had spoken; its inhabitants were not Christians, but lived in accordance with Natural Law and might be saved through 'baptism of desire' up to the actual moment when the Gospel was preached to them.

The outlook of Palacios Rubio was not specifically eschatological; it was, rather, an increased emphasis on the duty of missionary activity and the propagation of the Faith. To a greater degree than any direct eschatological interpretation, what is evident is the doctrine of the Pope's kingship in the spiritual and temporal spheres, 'for the spiritual cannot subsist for long without the temporal'. The emphasis on the dual power of the Pontiff is not, in the work of Palacios Rubio, a purely legalistic consideration, but is based on the Scriptural notion of Christ as King and High Priest, at Whose coming all the kingly authorities of the Earth will by law lapse – the Spanish jurist was thinking of the historical scheme based on the Five Monarchies outlined in the Book of Daniel. Even though Jesus Christ refrained from using his temporal kingship over earthly things, he sometimes used that power. The expulsion of the money-changers from the Temple was one example of this, as were the miracles and the driving out of devils. The Pope had received both powers as the Vicar of Christ the Priest-King, not only over the baptised, but also in law over the infidels, owing to the abrogation of earthly kingdoms at Christ's coming; even though the overlords of infidel peoples might still in fact be in power, this was, as it were, with the consent of the Church, for the latter, like Christ, did not desire to use her power except for just cause, to bring people to the Faith, rather than merely provoke wars and depredations. Palacios qualified this ecclesiastical absolutism with a considerable number of practical reservations: the infidels still had due possession of their property, they could not be punished for mere unavoidable infidelity, war could not be waged against them unless the truth was first declared to them, nor could they be enslaved unless there was a prior cause for a just war, nor could they be forced to accept the faith and baptism. Legally, however, the radical nature of this thesis was unaffected: the Church might choose the Catholic king as the most suitable and 'such a concession could be made by the Church as a matter of right, because she is the supreme ruler of all nations, independent of all laws and endowed with a power that cannot be questioned'; the Church could entrust the conquest of the infidels to a Christian king, admonishing them to receive preachers and submit to the Church, on pain of a just war being waged against them.

37

The treatise of Palacios Rubio produces an overall impression different from that of a merely pragmatic and flattering pronouncement, as Las Casas described it. There is a certain enthusiastic Biblical inspiration in his proclamation that now is the time to preach the Gospel to all the newly discovered nations, to form them into one flock under One Shepherd.

The authority on whom Palacios Rubio relies most consistently is that of Enrico de Suso, Cardinal-Bishop of Ostia, known as Ostiensis or Hostiensis, who wrote a commentary on the Decretals (1271) dissenting from the moderate dualism of the commentators on the Decree of Gratian and placing the maximum emphasis on the absolute unity of the Church's authority, even over infidels; his treatise was an important contribution to the debate about the Indies.

It would, however, be unjust to see in theocracy only a 'pseudo-conservative' legalism inspired by Roman law (Dempf, 1929). There is, underlying it, the mystique of Christendom, stemming from Gregory VII and, more especially, St Bernard (Ullmann, 1955, 427 ff.). The Pope is the Vicar of Christ (not only of St Peter), and he is the indispensable guarantee of the unity of the Body of Christ, a body which embraces all kingdoms, with their peoples and their clergy. Christ is the Priest-King, after the order of Melchisedek, and so is the Pope, to whom all this power has been transferred. Innocent III adopted the legacy of the formulae of St Bernard, together with the well-known simile of the two swords. Historical and symbolic speculation regarding the prophecy of Daniel saw in the Kingdom of Christ the Fifth World Monarchy, to which had been 'transferred' all dominion since the Incarnation. Innocent IV, in his struggle with Frederick II, no longer regarded the Donation of Constantine as a basis of Papal power, but merely as a restitution or recognition of the Kingdom of Christ to His Vicar.

These were – among many others – the theocratic themes which Ostiensis and the later Guelph canon lawyers were to formulate in their treatises: Egidius Romanus, Ptolemy of Lucca, Augustinus Triumphus, Alvarus Pelagius, the Abbot Panormitano, St Anthony of Florence and Silvester of Prierias (a contemporary who brings us to the time of Vitoria), not to mention the Castilian humanist Rodrigo Sánchez de Arévalo. The Bull *Unam Sanctam* published by Boniface VIII is the official formulation of this 'political Augustinianism', of this *reductio ad unum*. Looking at these treatises as a whole, one may say, as Wilks (1964, 254 ff.) emphasises, that there exists a 'temporal power' as distinct from the Papal power, but rather, merely that there is a temporal 'office' or 'ministry', a sword which the Pope does not wield, but which executes his will; the differentiation of functions is maintained as a general rule, but political power is reduced, fundamentally, to theocratic unity.

Palacios Rubio, when dealing with the law governing the State internally, employs the image of the king as 'Vicar of God' in temporal matters, a concept derived from the *Partidas*; and he adds, furthermore, the idea based on Roman law of a pact of submission, by the terms of which the people originally transferred its power to the emperor (or king), and he tries to reconcile this notion of a social pact with that of a Divine vicariate. Neither aspect is clearly compatible with the theocratic interpretation of the Bulls, nor does he, in this work, make any effort to integrate these concepts.

From such heterogeneous arguments there emerges a characteristic which seems peculiar to Spanish juridical thought. Whereas Gallicanism asserted the absolute superiority of the King of France in temporal matters, his 'divine right' which made him independent of the Pope, and, in addition, placed limits on the Pope's power in purely ecclesiastical matters by using the bishops as a counterweight, Spanish Regalism had a very different internal structure. The *Siete Partidas*, the fundamental source of late medieval and modern legal ideas, may be extremely monarchistic in political matters, but they are Ultramontane in their approach to canon law, because they were based on commentaries on the Decretals. There never was, in Spain, from the time of the *Partidas* until the late seventeenth century, Regalism of the Gallican or Anglican kind, still less philosophical Regalism of the kind expounded by Dante or Marsilius of Padua. This juridical tradition combined a monarchism based on Roman law with Papalist canon law: this was not, as some have thought, merely a pragmatic avoidance of the issue, but a peculiar juxtaposition of the two concepts, appropriate to a kingdom situated on the warring frontier of Christendom, militant in its orthodoxy and at the same time enjoying great political autonomy vis-à-vis the Papacy.

Apart from Palacios Rubio we have a record, among the opinions put forward by the members of the 1512 *Junta*, of those of Fray Bernardo de Mesa and the Licentiate Gregorio, the priest, through the testimony of Las Casas and, what is of greater importance, that of the Dominican Fray Matías de Paz. His *De dominio Regum Hispaniae super Indos* discusses both the theses of Innocent IV and Ostiensis and the Thomist solution to the problem of whether infidel princes can lose their pre-existing political dominion over subjects recently converted to Christianity, a situation which frequently occurred in the Indies. St Thomas decided, despite the principles of Natural Law which he maintained with regard to infidels, in favour of the view that the ecclesiastical power could depose them and transfer their dominion to Christians: superior beings should judge inferior ones, and not the other way about; but the use of that superiority was to be conditioned by the need to avoid scandal (*Summa Theologica*, II, II, q. 10, a. 10). Paz agreed with the opinion of the great theologican, reconciled it with that of Ostiensis and concluded that it was legitimate to occupy certain regions – at least, so that they could serve as a base for missionary activities. Although a just war may be waged against them by Christians, the ignorance of the infidels is not culpable and they can with justice defend themselves, and they should not be enslaved when taken prisoner. This state of *impasse* represented by a war in which both sides were fighting justly led Paz to recommend, with great emphasis, good treatment of the natives (Beltrán de Heredia; Zavala, 1954).

The military mission

The fusion of conquest and Christian missionary activity was practised in the Middle Ages above all on the frontiers of Germany. The wars of Charlemagne were followed by mass baptisms which were virtually compulsory. Among the Wends of the Middle and Lower Elbe, the Crusade of 1147 meant, simultaneously, conversion and submission to the Saxon nobles; the effectiveness of conversion was due, more than to any other factor, to German immigration into the area. From 1200 onwards there were successive crusades and conquests carried out by the Order of Sword-Bearers in Livonia, as a sort of military mission sponsored by Archbishop Adalbert of Bremen. Then the Teutonic Order was established in Prussia. In contrast to the Spanish military orders, which were established for territorial conquest, without any missionary objective, the territory of Prussia was granted in 1226 by the Emperor to the Teutonic Order, with the simultaneous objectives of conquest and missionary activity.

The Canaries witnessed, from the conquest of Juan de Bethencourt onwards, the same process of warfare combined with missionary activity, and this continued throughout the fifteenth century; and here too there was some contradiction between the two activities – as had occurred in Prussia previously – which provoked the intervention of certain bishops and of the Papacy to counter slave-raiding forays. The Portuguese enterprises, on the other hand, were more exclusively a crusade and a search for Prester John, without any genuine development of the missionary concept (De Witte).

In such conditions, and as a result of the previous experience in the Canaries, Castile found itself burdened with the missionary obligation imposed by the Bulls of Pope Alexander VI. Columbus, in his letter to

Santángel and Sánchez (February 1493), expressed his satisfaction and his hope that the Sovereigns would encourage the conversion of the newly discovered peoples; furthermore, he had carried letters to friendly princes in which Ferdinand and Isabella proclaimed that they were sending Columbus in the service of God and for the increase of the orthodox Faith, in addition to their own interest in the enterprise; so that there is authentic proof of the missionary objective even in Columbus's first voyage, before the Bulls (V. D. Sierra, 1953; García Gallo, 1957-8, 634-44). The oft-quoted will of Isabella the Catholic made the same assertion in 1504.

The new lands incorporated into the kingdoms of Castile were, therefore, a typical mission field. Little is known about the degree of fulfilment of the tasks inherent in this obligation in the first years of settlement in the Caribbean, beyond the establishment of the first dioceses, in 1504, and the granting of universal royal patronage in the Indies, in 1508. The group of Reformed Dominicans led by Fray Pedro de Córdoba was the first to provoke a confrontation between missionary activity and the interests of the Spaniards in the colonies. Out of the *Juntas* of 1512-13, convened to discuss these problems, there arose, in addition to general measures to regulate the *encomienda* system, the famous *Requerimiento* of 1513, which was first used in the great expedition of Pedrarias to Castilla del Oro in the following year.

This document gave legal form to the requirement formulated by Palacios Rubio and Matías de Paz – namely, that the natives should realise the legal bases of Spanish dominion and should offer their submission and declare their readiness to receive the Gospel, on the promise of not losing their liberties and property if they did so, giving them due time to consider the matter. They were promised that they would not be forced to become converted to Christianity. But they were also threatened, if they delayed in recognising the conquest, with being attacked and enslaved. The strictly doctrinal part of the announcement was extremely succinct: it merely affirmed the existence of one God, Who had created the world and man, and the dispersal of peoples, among them the American Indians themselves, the world-wide power of the successor of St Peter and his donation of power to the kings of Castile; these were, so to speak, the premises on which the subsequent preaching of the clergy was based. Las Casas submitted the *Requerimiento* to a devastating scrutiny; he admired the man who wrote it, Palacios Rubio, but he reproached him with sharing the opinion of Ostiensis; what he attacked, above all, in the document was the irrational nature of the demand that the Indians should abandon their liberty for the sake of a creed utterly unknown to them (*Historia*, III, LVIII). The point was that Las Casas based his outlook on the concept of a peaceful mission, which he had already described theoretically in *De unico vocationis modo*; but the *Requerimiento* was a legacy of the medieval 'military mission', which envisaged the conquest as a necessary and prior subjugation designed to clear the way for missionary activity. This was a notion characteristic of a warrior culture, motivated by the thirst for political and religious domination and for booty; and this notion had, moreover, been nourished from the eleventh century onwards by the crusaders' mentality, which was transferred to other lands, in a passionate desire to achieve conversion at all costs, before the fulfilment of the eschatological expectations – a bold application of the Gospel's injunction to *compelle eos intrare*. Since the missions to the Mongol and Tartar realms in the thirteenth century, Rome had adopted a new stance, characterised by the dispatch of envoys and peaceable invitations to accept Christianity (Leturia, 1930, 170 ff.). The Spanish 'military mission', which took definite shape from 1513 onwards, was based on ingenuously legalistic premises which ignored a whole series of ethnographic problems and proclaimed in attorney's language the duty of submission based on religious truths, though without directly compelling anyone to accept the Faith; if the invitation were refused, it would mean war, with all its consequences, in order to establish the missionary State. There is no doubt as to the serious view which Palacios Rubio and Paz – among others, of whom we have no knowledge – took of the *Requerimiento*; but the point of view of Oviedo – a perceptive and sardonic one – also displays a crudely realistic reaction in the face of legalistic naïvety (*Historia*, III, xxix).

After the Granada Regulations of 1526, the *Requerimiento* was conceived of as a process of persuasion which was not supposed to be instantaneous, thus avoiding a mere notarial formality, and its application was to be the responsibility of the ecclesiastics taking part in the enterprise of discovery or conquest, in order to prevent the outbreak of slave-raiding forays, to which the soldiery were prone. From 1542 onwards – according to Hanke (1941) – the *Requerimiento* is no longer stipulated in the *Capitulaciones*; the Instructions imparted in 1559 in New Granada forbade having recourse to war except in self-defence or to punish Indians who had hindered preaching, and promised ten years' exemption from tribute to those who submitted and became converted. The notion of a predominantly peaceful process of colonisation emerges from the Instructions given to Viceroy Cañete for Peru, in 1556, for Charcas in 1563 and so on, and finally, above all, in the great Ordinances for Discovery and Settlement published by Philip II in 1573, with the well-known substitution of the word 'conquest' by that of 'pacification'. It must, however, be pointed out that during the really active era of the conquests (1510–50) this concept of the 'military mission' predominated almost exclusively; its disappearance coincided with the overall ebb of the rhythm of the conquest, so that the legal modification of 1573 did not fundamentally affect the actual process. It is, however, of interest as a symptom of the effect of Spanish criticisms on the process of conquest. Some thinkers did envisage the possibility of discovering, settling and preaching peaceably. Furthermore, it is worth bearing in mind that Christendom had a different attitude towards the powers of the Far East than towards America. The letter written by Charles V to the Eastern princes in whose lands Zumárraga and Betanzos wanted to travel and preach, extending the missionary expansion from New Spain, is a very different document from the official *Requerimiento* (Diego de Encinas, *Cedulario Indiano*, IV, 221). The missionary objective appears in a more sophisticated and developed form than in the legal document; there is no invitation to submit, but only to listen to preaching and, perhaps, enter into trade relations. It was this difference in attitude which was later to inspire the Jesuit Father José de Acosta to classify the infidels according to differing levels of political and cultural achievement.

The Empire of Charles V in the Indies

As has been pointed out by Juan Manzano (1948, 1951–2), the process of incorporation of the Indies into the kingdoms of Castile passed through various distinct juridical phases between 1492/3 and 1516. Discovered as the result of an enterprise of the Sovereigns of Castile and Aragon in 1492, they already belonged to them by that prescriptive right recognised in the *Partidas*; the Bulls of 1493 granted those lands to the Sovereigns on a personal basis, but provided that the inheritance was to pass after their death to the rulers of Castile and León, not those of Aragon. With the death of Ferdinand the Catholic in 1516, the Indies became, for Joan the Mad and her son Charles V, an inherited estate, which belonged inalienably to the realms of Castile. The fact that the *procuradores* of American cities applied for and obtained the Provisions of 1519, 1520 and 1523, which confirmed that inalienability, only had the effect of corroborating and ennobling this status: for a Spanish city, to be 'free' meant to belong to the king – to be part of the royal estate, and not subject to any national or foreign overlord, was an honour and a guarantee of increased liberty. Furthermore, on Hispaniola, this measure put a stop to any attempt on the part of Diego Colón or his heirs to convert the island into their personal fief. As for the motive of Ferdinand and Isabella in requesting that at the deaths of the two spouses the Indies should be incorporated into the Crown of Castile and not that of Aragon, Manzano (1948) has suggested that this might be explained by the same reason alleged by Mariana in the similar case of Navarre in 1515: Ferdinand preferred that these newly acquired territories should not be governed by the Aragonese statutes, which provided for more feudal rights and privileges, but by the more Regalist ones of Castile. In the opinion of the author, the other motive adduced by Mariana in the case of the annexation of Navarre (*Historia de España*, 29, 24) was more likely to be dominant in the case of America: Castile had more men and more resources with which to defend the Indies than Aragon could provide.

From 1516 onwards, there appears in the list of royal titles (together with the names of the other realms of the peninsula) that of 'King of the Indies, islands and Mainland of the Ocean Sea'. Furthermore, the same committee of *procuradores* of the cities of Hispaniola which in 1518 requested the solemn declaration of inalienability also requested a seat in the Cortes of Castile; but this request was denied.

The King of Castile and of the other realms of the peninsula became 'Emperor of the Romans' as a result of the election that took place at Frankfurt at the end of June 1519, but he was not crowned by the Pope until 1530, in Bologna. The Spanish Crown now inherited, owing to the dynastic politics of the Habsburgs, the 'Roman' universalism which had been handed down through the Middle Ages. Spain had, indeed, been familiar with an 'imperial' system before, but it had been confined to the restricted sphere of the peninsula itself: it had its 'empire', based on its possession of the cities of León and Toledo, during the tenth to the twelfth centuries; and its notion of a 'monarchy of Spain' transcending the various Christian realms, of which there is documentary evidence in various fifteenth-century writers, such as Rodrigo Sánchez de Arévalo and Diego de Valera. The imperial election of 1257, when Alfonso X was elected – the election was disputed and the usual Papal coronation did not take place – had little effect on Spanish political conscience. As if to make up for this, there is an entire corpus of Messianic 'imperialist' literature during the reign of the Catholic Sovereigns (Maravall, 1954, 494ff.; Américo Castro, 1949).

This study is not the appropriate place to provide a full interpretation of the content of the Empire and of the imperial idea of Charles V. Studies of this notion have emphasised the Dantesque-Ghibelline contribution of the Chancellor Gattinara (Rassow, 1945; Brandi, 1941); or the notion of harmony among the Christian princes and of defence of the Church, without implying a total domination (Menéndez Pidal, 1937); or the Erasmian, Reforming and Conciliar concept, expressed by Alfonso de

Valdés and Gattinara after the sack of Rome in 1527 (Bataillon, 1959; Vicens Vives, 1959). The attitude of the Spaniards towards the Empire which had fallen to their lot was complex and changeable in the decades between 1520 and 1550. The notions of most of the citizens and clergy appear to have been, it is true, much more deeply rooted in the traditional context of the 'kingdom', a concept foreign to 'transcendant Burgundian illusionism' of Empire (Maravall, 1960, 78; Jover, 1958). The Dominican school of Salamanca, from Francisco de Vitoria onwards, was definitely anti-imperialistic in its outlook.

Nevertheless, Spain was universalist in the sense that Christendom and the struggle against Islam could always count on popular support, particularly at the critical moments of the conquests of Tunis and Algiers, which were to awake the crusading spirit afresh, after it had already been stirred by the campaigns of Cisneros in Africa. The presence of Hernán Cortés at the battle of Algiers may be regarded as symbolic of the continuity of meaning in the Spanish conquests in America and Africa.

If we confine our attention to the American theatre of operations, it may be asserted that there is not much documentary evidence of imperialist ideas. The letters of the conquistadors to Charles V are addressed, as a matter of etiquette, to 'His Sacred, Catholic Majesty', a title which had at first provoked such a scandal in Castile; the letters contain other allusions to his 'Caesarian' attributes. Such formalities must have represented an increase of the King's dignity in the eyes of the conquistadors.

Oviedo's *Compendium of the Natural History of the Indies*, printed in Toledo in 1527, gave popular currency in its dedication to the term 'your Western empire of the Indies, islands and mainland of the Ocean Sea', instead of the simple word 'realm' included in the King's official titles; at the end of the same dedication he repeats the words 'Western empire' and attributes its origin to Columbus. However, at the beginning of Book I of his *General and Natural History* (1535), he contented himself with asserting that those Indies were now part of the empire of the Royal Crown of Castile, so that we cannot conclude that the idea expressed in 1527 – that of a 'Western empire' – was very deeply rooted in Oviedo's thinking; but it can at least be said that its formulation in so popular a work as that of 1527 must have made some impression.

To Cortés, however, the notion of empire was much more strongly felt, as has been pointed out by Victor Frankl.[3] The first relevant text can be found in the Second Letter, where, filled with admiration for the characteristics of the new land, he writes that Charles 'can once more style yourself emperor, with just title, and with no less merit than that of Emperor of

Germany, which, by the Grace of God, Your Sacred Majesty possesses'. To judge from the context of this Letter, Cortés envisaged this empire as compatible with the continuance of the various realms of the Indian monarchs, particularly with that of Moctezuma, who swore full fealty to the Emperor, but continued to exercise sovereignty over Tenochtitlán. In the Fourth Letter, when describing the ships which he had ordered to be built at two points on the Pacific coast, he states that they will be the cause of Charles's winning many more realms and kingdoms than he possessed already and that 'nothing will be lacking for Your Excellency to become monarch of the world'. In addition to the Pacific, he was interested in making voyages of discovery between Pánuco and Florida (discovered by Ponce de León), continuing northwards along the Atlantic coast as far as the passage to the 'South Sea' recently navigated by Magellan, which would make it easier to reach the Spice Islands by a route shorter than that of the Straits of Magellan, and the ships would come and go between the realms and kingdoms of the Emperor; and even if the passage were not found, they would in any case discover new lands which would be of use. Furthermore, from the South Sea, too, ships were to set out in search of the long-desired North-west Passage. In the Fifth Letter, he again applies to the monarch titles which were unfamiliar in Castile, calling him not only 'Your Majesty' but also 'Your Excellency' and 'Your Greatness'.

It may, therefore, be said that Cortés' notion of empire was based both on the unity of New Spain, conceived of as a polity formed by a number of realms and cities, which he compared to the 'German' Empire but without in fact knowing the real structure of that Empire and its relationship to Rome. On the basis of this notion, the idea of a universal monarchy appeared to Cortés – and this was a more original concept – as an empire based on the dominion of the ocean and the sea routes, including America and the Spice Islands. This second concept, which found expression in the Fourth Letter, corresponded more closely to the new enterprises and experiences of the Spaniards, and he was careful not to apply strictly the term 'empire' to that total polity, thus associating it with the more sacred interpretation of the concept; he simply termed it a 'monarchy of the world' in the more strictly geographical sense.

The ambitious maritime plans of Cortés never came to fruition, and Spain never secured control of the North-west Passage. Nor was the German 'Holy Roman Empire' to remain indefinitely subject to the Spanish Crown, and it became increasingly restricted to Germany itself after Charles's abdication. As Charles came to give greater emphasis to Spain and make it the effective centre of his dominions – Castile, after all, was paying for his great wars – it was possible to consider uniting the Spanish Crown and the Empire. The ambitious plans of 1548–52 envisaged an imperial succession alternating between the two branches of the House of Austria. This arrangement would have preserved continuity with the medieval Empire and the new Monarchy of Spain and the Indies. But the German wars imposed a different outcome, and all that was left was the dynastic connection of the Habsburgs, and the (not always consistent) inclination towards a common policy. What was established instead was a 'Western' and Atlantic monarchy which nevertheless still retained control over the western Mediterranean; it was therefore master of both the ancient and medieval sea *par excellence*, and of the 'Modern' Ocean, since it included the Low Countries, Spain, North Africa, the Canaries and the Indies. Control of the western Mediterranean made possible dominion over the coast of Africa and Italy, and the continuance of that interminable European mission, the containment of the Turkish Empire. This Hispanic monarchy was, however, 'modern'; it lacked the intransferable mystique of the Holy Roman Empire.

The missionary empire, according to the theories of Las Casas

In the Indies under Charles V there was another theory of empire; this one was the result of authentic experiences in the New World, which were certainly very different from the discoveries and maritime plans of Cortés: these theories were embodied in the concept of Las Casas of the imperial sovereignty of the kings of Spain over the principalities, *cacicazgos* and Indian communities. The notion was, of course, part of the untiring efforts of Las Casas to save the Indians from conquest and its results – slavery, the *encomienda* system and so on.

The imperial ideology was to find more mature expression in Las Casas when he was an old man, and, on being accused of denying the legitimacy of the Spanish Empire, he wished to be seen, on the contrary, as its greatest and most authentic champion; he defended it, however according to the notions which he himself defined, which differed greatly from those of the settlers and officials.

Of course, the elements of this ideological system are to be found from a very early stage in his career as a reformer in the Indies. In the years when he was expounding his projects to the Flemish favourites of Charles V (1517–19), he defended the liberty of the natives, basing his arguments on the Bulls, the will of Isabella the Catholic and the opinions of jurists and theologians submitted to the Juntas of Burgos and Valladolid in 1512 and

1513. He drew from all these documents the conclusion that the natives were under no obligation to serve private individuals, and he asserted the ability of the natives to receive the Catholic faith and attain a reasonable standard of political organisation, in contrast to the theory that they were *servi a natura* which was supported by the Bishop of Darien. He put forward the idea of peaceful penetration by missionaries supported, from a distance, by a few fortified strong points with a mere handful of settlers. (Giménez Fernández, 1960, 11). It was not, however, until he entered the Dominican Order that his doctrine received its fullest elaboration. His letter of 1531 to the Council of the Indies contains the fundamental doctrinal assertion that the king derives all his rights from the Bulls of Alexander VI; these he understood to imply the obligation to carry out missionary activity in order to bring into the Church those who had been invited 'at the eleventh hour' – the Indians (*BAE*, 110, 43 ff.). At about the same time, when he began to write his *General History*, he based his thinking on a very free paraphrase of the Bulls of 1493, and first of all asserted the obligation to evangelise, 'disregarding all dangers and travails whatsoever, and even more so private temporal interests'. But in addition, so that the Catholic Sovereigns 'as though moved by a purpose in some way their own should labour with some hope of satisfying their temporal interests', he affirmed that they were 'supreme governors, as it were sovereign emperors, over all the kings and princes and realms of these Indies' (*General History*, I, LXXIX). This was the basis of the doctrinal argument of Las Casas against Ostiensis and his most recent supporter as regards the American question, Dr Palacios Rubio, because that theocratic line of argument did away with the precisely defined interconnection of ends and means on which Las Casas based the Pontifical title, replacing it by a pure and simple donation, even though accompanied by a missionary objective. The indignant marginal notes written by Las Casas in the manuscript of Palacios Rubio are evidence of that disagreement. He found it necessary to reduce the donation to a mere intermediary instrument.

The juridical exposition of his theory of a Missionary Empire appears as a consistent line of thought in his *Thirty Most Juridical Propositions*, his *Treatise in Proof of the sovereign empire and universal principality which the Kings of Castile and León have over the Indies*, and in the work which he wrote as a very old man, *The Treasures of Peru*. In other words, all these systematic expositions of his theory were written after the great debate at Valladolid, in 1551, 1553 and 1565; and what is noticeable in the last work (the *Treasures*) is a new emphasis on Natural Law which goes a long way to diminishing the force of his principal argument regarding the Bulls.

The *Thirty Propositions* and the *Treaty in Proof* are works of extremely compact and homogeneous construction (*BAE*, 110). The sovereign imperial authority of the King of Castile, Las Casas untiringly affirmed, was quite compatible with the local sovereignty of the Indian monarchs, which were in their turn based on Natural Law which is common to all peoples; for the communities require some authority for their 'governance and continuance'. Infidelity does not make void Natural Law, nor the *Jus Gentium* which is its most direct derivative, affirms Las Casas, reiterating in several different ways a thesis already propounded by St Thomas. The Spanish Emperor should preserve the just laws and good customs of the Indians and abolish the bad ones, 'which were not many in number', without depriving them of their temporal goods, as had happened in practice as a result of the conquests, which had been, as he put it, a mission after the Mohammedan style. The Indian lords were to lose their right to make war upon one another and to make general laws; 'their liberty is to some extent abolished or diminished', he states in the *Treatise in Proof*; but that loss was more than offset by the better policies and laws which Christianity would bring in its train. The plurality of stratified overlordships presents no real difficulty, he affirms in the same work; it is the normal situation in Europe, where kings enjoy an overriding sovereignty, dukes or counts sovereignty in a more restricted sphere, and even the small landowner and the tenant enjoy possession in accordance with both civil and natural law. There are differing grades and kinds of jurisdiction, and this involved no inherent contradiction. The political system of medieval Europe, therefore, with its graduated powers, appeared to Las Casas as a good model for the régime he desired for the Americas.

However, the theoretical problem which he cannot evade, and does not attempt to, is that of the source of legitimacy of the imperial power of Spain. He rejects all the fictions employed as a basis of title – for example, the greater geographical proximity of the Indies to Spain (this argument had been used with regard to the Canaries by Alonso de Cartagena) – and also idolatry, human sacrifices and unnatural vice among the Indian peoples. He rejects also the application of the *servi a natura* theory of Aristotle, according to which those less illumined by natural reason owed obedience to the wiser (the argument advanced by John Major, Palacios Rubio, Bishop Quevedo and Juan Ginés de Sepúlveda), the greater prudence of the Spaniards and so on. The only legitimate title was the Bulls of Alexander VI, interpreted as implying a missionary obligation: but the theoretical problem arose when the Papal donation was contrasted with Natural Law and the *Jus Gentium*, which favoured the Indians, since in this case one could not even speak of a just war of self-defence or for the recovery of territory, an argument which might be advanced in the case of the Muslims and, at that time, more specifically, the Turks. One sees here, in the works published during the 1550s, a major dialectical effort to reconcile these extreme points of view, rejecting on the one hand the theocratic theory in its purest formulation – that of a total and effective kingship of Christ and the Church, which implied the lapse, at least *de jure*, of the power of the infidels, and, on the other hand, the interpretation based exclusively on Natural Law and the absolute denial of the sovereignty of Spain and the Pope.

The theoretical basis of his argument was that of 'indirect' Papal power (a term which, according to Carro, 1944, 176, was first used in the thirteenth century by Vincent of Spain and later by the Thomist and Gallican thinker John of Paris, around 1300; but which Carro, 244, considers, with good reason, to be less accurate than the term employed by Juan de Torquemada in the fifteenth century – power *ex consequenti*). In these works Las Casas reveals himself as a medieval thinker, following a well-established tradition.[4] 'However great and powerful they [States and properties] may be, they are of less consequence, of less value and substance and importance, than men and the actions of men.' The accessory should be subordinate to the principal, and 'priority should be given to the Faith and to spiritual matters'. In this sense, the Pope

has power over all the world and over all the faithful and the infidels within it, and over all their temporal goods and property and secular States, and even more so when it shall appear to him that with just cause it is needful and fitting for him to guide and direct both the faithful and the infidels (though in different ways) along the path of eternal life, and with this end to remove obstacles and impediments in the way of its fulfilment, that is to say *in ordinem ad finem spiritualem*.

The Pope incontrovertibly possesses such power as the Vicar of Christ. It is not clear, in the writings of Las Casas mentioned above, whether he attributes to Christ only a sacerdotal, and not a temporal, sovereignty in this world; he confined himself to saying that Christ could have changed the kingdoms of this earth, but did not do so, and that He taught His apostles to behave with humility: the school of thinkers arguing for what might be called 'indirect power' throughout the Middle Ages had affirmed that Christ possessed only a spiritual kingdom in the course of the actual history of mankind (Leclerc, 1959, commenting on Buenaventura, Aquinas, John of Paris, Gerson and so on). Although on this point Las Casas does not appear to have very clearly defined views, he is quite unambiguous in emphasising the Papal obligation to evangelise the infidels, 'an obligation inherited from Jesus Christ'; the Pope owes a debt to the infidels, Jews, Greeks and Gentiles, he asserts, quoting St Bernard; if he intervenes to restrict the political rights of the infidels, this is not because he is exercising an absolute right according to Roman law but as part of his obligation to evangelise them. Both the Pope and the king of Spain have rights which are dependent on their prior obligation to evangelise. By virtue of that duty 'to guide and direct men towards the end of sanctity', he may limit the exercise of political rights, even of those based on Natural Law and the *Jus Gentium.* Unity is restored, in the medieval sense of the term, in this new hierarchical order of rights and duties, and by virtue of that eminently medieval notion of a right exercised subject to the fulfilment of a duty.

The Pope acts 'occasionally' (*casualiter*) in temporal matters, according to a well-known decretal of Innocent III dealing with this subject, 'and therefore not regularly, nor on every occasion and for every cause'. He can, therefore, entrust a Christian prince with the task of discovering and making detailed observations of new lands, and send missionaries, and even depose an infidel sovereign who hinders preaching, thereby applying the principle of the 'just' cause for war; in that case, however, it does not automatically follow that he may deprive the successor of that sovereign of his inheritance, nor the people of the right to choose new rulers.

The king of Spain is not, however, a mere deputy of the Pope; the latter may 'honour him, and exalt him by giving and granting to him an almost imperial crown'; the Catholic Sovereigns, according to the splendid words he uses in Proposition XV, are 'architectural apostles (*apóstoles arquitectónicos*) of the Indies', which is 'the highest dignity that kings ever had over this earth'. Wilks (1964, 57) points out that, in the view of Aquinas, justice in the prince is 'architectural' – that is, it is the attribute of the author of a grand design (*Summa Theologica*, III, II, 58, 6) – and that legislators are, in a sense, like architects; this idea is derived from Aristotle's *Ethics* (I, 1), according to which the *techne architectonike* is the establishment of proper control over ends and means. According to the *Dictionary* of Juan Corominas, the use, in Las Casas, of the term 'architect' is the earliest known literary example in Spain.

Las Casas, in his *Treatise in Proof*, expresses himself as a medieval Thomist. As in St Thomas, the natural and the supernatural order are on planes which are distinct – nature in the Aristotelian sense has been recovered as an idea, in contrast to pure Augustinianism – but not separated. The more elementary things are perfected and ascend towards the

highest things, towards which they have an 'obediential' capacity, which restores as a basis of all things Christian and theocratic unity, by other methods than those envisaged in St Augustine's theology or in canon law.[5] On the basis of this interpretation, Las Casas asserts that the jurisdiction of the Indians after baptism 'will be formed, that is to say perfected...Because all human power and jurisdiction is imperfect and without form, if it is not informed and perfected by spiritual jurisdiction...and thus no power or jurisdiction is perfect without faith; but this does not mean that it is null or illegitimate' (*BAE*, 110, 422). He also points out, in this connection, that the formula of consecration of kings expresses such an 'approval and perfectioning' of royal power by spiritual power.

In the *Treasures of Peru*, however, we find a different intellectual approach, this time more strictly based on Natural Law and rational argument. According to the earlier treatises, the Pope could depose the infidel sovereign who hindered or harmed the preaching of the Faith. In the *Treasures*, the effect of the Bulls and of Spanish dominion is more clearly subordinated to the consent of the natives to dominion, government and the payment of tribute, and for all these ends a long period of persuasion on the part of the missionaries is necessary. The Papal donation is not a dogma of the Faith and has been disputed by Catholic thinkers. Prior to consent, the kings have only a right 'to the thing' (*jus ad rem*), rather than 'over the thing' (*jus in re*).

Medieval Thomism and the sense of underlying unity are very much attenuated in this work; the entire theory of the 'indirect' power of the Pope over temporal things has given way to an interpretation more exclusively based on Natural Law of the nature of political assent, a notion derived from Aristotle and Roman law; this interpretation was more 'modern'. Might this be due, perhaps, to the influence of Vitoria and Soto? There is only one quotation from Soto. What were Las Casas' real views on this subject? These are problems involving the internal coherence of the concepts concerned, and the same problems arise whenever one examines the works of Las Casas in detail. The inherent complications and contradictions have often been pointed out (Bataillon, Pérez de Tudela) and emphasised (Menéndez Pidal, 1963).

The impressive moral and political struggle waged by Las Casas endowed his theory of a 'missionary empire' with a certain durability and force. It is not necessary to repeat at this stage the abundant evidence of the well-known confrontation between groups based on conflicting interests and ideologies, since this has already been fully described by Hanke (1949), Manzano (1948), Bataillon (1966), Giménez Fernández (1953–1960) and so on. In the Philippines, where Legazpi had been instructed to behave peaceably towards even the Muslims (1565), the Dominican Bishop Fray Domingo de Salazar maintained in a treatise (published by Hanke, 1943) that the Pope had not received temporal power (he based this assertion on that of St Paul that 'no one who fights for God may involve himself in secular matters'), and could not have authorised the levying of tribute from the natives until they had been baptised. The king has only a 'divine and supernatural governorship' according to the Bulls, and this in no way resembles that which he enjoys in his European possessions, for it is as superior to the latter 'as the spiritual exceeds the corporal'. After the Faith has been voluntarily received, then government may be consolidated. Towards the end of the century, in 1596, his successor in office, also a Dominican, Miguel de Benavides, reaffirmed the 'indirect' Papal power and the concept of the missionary empire, quoting in support of this contention thinkers ranging from St Thomas to Vitoria, Soto and Báñez, and even that recent classic exponent of indirect power, Robert Bellarmine. In the Philippine mission field, however, the *Oidor* of the *Audiencia*, the Licentiate Melchor de Avalos wrote, in 1585, two letters (also published by Hanke, 1943) defending the expeditions against the Muslims in Borneo and the other islands, whom the friars also classed as 'peaceful', and he quoted repeatedly from Ostiensis – whose writings, in his view, facilitate the interpretation of the Bulls of Alexander VI – and from writers of his own century such as Palacios Rubio, Alfonso de Castro, Gregorio López, Focher and Dr Navarro. Moreover, he did not intend to make any original contribution to the debate, but merely to justify the Spanish *cabalgadas* by an appeal to legal authorities. In addition, Avalos was familiar with Las Casas, who 'although he treated of some matters well, did so in too exaggerated and far-fetched terms'. Documents such as this make it possible for us to assess the extent to which the jurists writing at the end of the sixteenth century were maintaining theories identical to those advanced at the beginning of that century, as far as theocracy was concerned, even though controversy had, of course, made the arguments more sharply defined: direct power, full donation, indirect power, missionary empire had all become the tools of argument.

Although Las Casas had supporters among the Franciscans (for example, he received a letter from some friars of that Order in Chile in 1562, denouncing ill-treatment of the Indians), it is obvious that the famous letter of the Franciscan Motolinía in 1555 to Charles V represents a doctrinally distinct point of view, quite apart from obvious differences resulting from temperament and varying interpretations of the best way in which to defend the Indians. The Franciscans were unreservedly in favour of exclusively missionary activity. The king of Spain, according to Motolinía, is the 'leader and captain' responsible for seeing that the kingdom of Christ 'is established and spread and preached to these infidels'.'It is needful to hasten matters...and those who will not listen to the Holy Gospel of Jesus Christ of their own free will, must be forced to do so; for in this case one must bear in mind the proverb, it is better that good should come to pass by force than that evil should come to pass voluntarily.' He does not, therefore, accept the outright condemnation of the conquests, and in that very letter urges that the conquest of Florida be undertaken. In this letter, and in his *History of the Indians,* he pointed out with complete frankness the abuses, atrocities, slavery, ill-treatment of labour in the mines and so on; but now, he says, the *Audiencias* and the Viceroys have put an end to these abuses; the real reason for depopulation has been the epidemics. Despite all the plagues which have beset the Indians, like those that afflicted Egypt, many people have been saved from idolatry, human sacrifice and so on. From the Franciscan point of view, the conquests, despite their attendant evils, had opened the way for the Gospel, which must be preached throughout the world, as an ineluctable obligation, until the end of all things. Las Casas' mistake lay in the fact that he was trying to go back to the beginning, instead of trying to modify a process that was already taking place.[6]

The strugle to legitimise Spanish possession was a very long one. In Mexico, according to Motolinía's letter, at the time of the Viceroy Mendoza, the *caciques* renewed their fealty to the King, who thus acquired a fresh title. The controversy appears to have been more heated in Peru, where it took the form of a diatribe against the Inca system of government. Juan de Matienzo, in his *Government of Peru* (1957), considered it tyrannical because it tried to maintain the natives in a state of poverty and continuous labour, without allowing them to profit from it and employing them in monumental and costly public works, like the Pharaohs and the Greek tyrants; they sacrified youths, deported whole peoples from their homes and so on. Spain held Peru with just title derived from the imperial rank of Charles V, which made him monarch of the whole earth, from the tyranny of the previous Inca overlords and from the Papal Bulls.

The struggle to acquire just title acquired a drastic character under the Viceroy Toledo, who had been instructed in 1568 to restore to their *caciques* the vassals of which they had been deprived. It is not necessary to describe more fully this aspect of the Viceroyalty of Toledo, which has received adequte treatment (Levillier, 1935; Manzano, 1948). It should merely be pointed out that Peru could have been the ideal field for establishing an empire over free native subjects, for in Vilcabamba the descendants of Manco Inca survived, sometimes trading with the Spaniards, sometimes being solemnly received in Lima, but always maintaining a quasi-independence in their places of refuge and giving asylum there to runaway Spanish soldiers. The defeat and much-publicised execution of Tupac Amaru in 1572, which was strongly criticised as an excessively harsh measure, put an end to this possibility. Furthermore, the *Informaciones* describing the Incas and their tyranny, based on reports from some two hundred *caciques* and old men who could interpret the *quipus* in Jauja, Guamanga, Cuzco and Yucay, provided further fuel for the theoretical controversy. In spite of the assertion of Levillier (1935), and the authentic traditions of which we catch a glimpse in these *Informaciones*, there is still the possibility that our information is distorted, either through the intervention of the interpreters employed, or by reason of problems common to all inquiries of this nature. Sarmiento de Gamboa's *History of the Indians*, which is largely based on these reports, has been highly praised by Porras Barrenechea as an authentic 'rhapsody of the heroic age' of the Incas.

The Anonymous Document of Yucay (1571) attacked Las Casas on the grounds that he was badly informed about Peru, since he did not know that the Incas were tyrants and the *curacas* merely their officials, not true lords. According to this work, the tyranny of the Incas had nevertheless constituted, as had the Roman Empire, a 'preparation for the Gospel', because it left behind it a unified polity to be conquered for the Christian Faith; on the other hand, Las Casas, by maintaining intact (at least theoretically) the power of the *caciques*, who were lords just as they had been before, had made it possible for them to hinder the introduction of the Faith. But his entire theory collapses in Peru if one demonstrates – according to the Anonymous Document – the tyranny of the Incas and thus clears the way for the legitimacy of Spanish rule. The author of the letter, in order to emphasise the importance of the problem, maintained that there were Spaniards who wished to marry women of the Inca royal clan, and then raise the realm in rebellion under their leadership, as soon as they heard that the King was not the rightful lord.

The governors of Peru and the jurists who supported them advanced a theory which was in some respects the opposite of that of Cortés in Mexico. Whereas the latter came to admire the institutions and the civilisation of the conquered people – and his attitude was reflected by so many clergy and jurists in New Spain – in Peru, on the other hand, the official ideology adopted an increasingly condemnatory attitude towards the Inca system. Polo de Ondegardo was an exception to this rule.

Around 1570, the doctrinal controversy reached its ultimate development in Peru under Viceroy Toledo, and then ceased somewhat abruptly. The great compilation prepared by the Visitor and President of the Council of the Indies, Juan de Ovando, which enshrines the ultimate legislative ideal of the sixteenth century in the Americas, considered that right to rule over the 'State of the Indies' – an expression which recurs several times (Maurtúa, 1906) – had a sufficient basis in the Pontifical concession, and also by right of discovery, which was interpreted by Ovando as a 'Providential' revelation to the Catholic Sovereigns. Another eminent Spanish jurist, Gregorio López, in his Note 3 to Law 2, paragraph 23 of the Second *Partida*, after giving a good summary of the theories of direct power and their refutation by Vitoria, inclines to the latter's view. However, as a heart-felt supporter of positive law, he left the supreme dominion of Spain unchallenged, while arguing for missionary penetration based on fortified strong points and trade, making war only in cases of extreme necessity, to defend preachers or converts; offensive war was permissible only to prevent human sacrifice.

The historical significance of Vitoria and his school

The theories of Las Casas, on the one hand, and the official Spanish view of full sovereignty based on the Papal donation, on the other, are both clearly perceptible trends in the history of the Indies in the sixteenth century. Both theories asserted the obligation to evangelise the Indians, but Las Casas rejected the concept of the 'military mission'; both theories accepted Spain's rule, but the official interpretation conceived of it as an outright monarchy, whereas Las Casas wanted to transform it into a mere tutelary trust, vaguely 'imperialist' in conception, over Christian Indian realms, and over Spanish colonies exercising no sovereignty over the natives.

In contrasting these two schools of thought, it is not easy to discern the historical role played by Vitoria. Las Casas quotes him only rarely, albeit with approval, as he quotes his disciple Soto. Bataillon (1958) has demonstrated the fictitious nature of the traditional story that Las Casas recommended to Charles V the abandonment of the Indies, and the monarch was dissuaded by Vitoria. Similarly, he has also pointed out that the order of Charles V, dated 1539, prohibiting further debate to avoid the scandal caused by his titles being openly disputed in Salamanca, was probably drafted with Vitoria in mind. In other words, from the Emperor's point of view, the most 'dangerous' theory was that of Vitoria, not that of Las Casas. This might explain why the *Relectiones* were published so much later, in 1557, and in France. It should also be borne in mind that Sixtus V went so far as to put the works of Vitoria and Bellarmine on the Index, on the grounds that they impugned the direct temporal power of the Papacy. The theoretical 'danger' of Vitoria was not, therefore, unnoticed by the highest authorities.

The other problem, however, is to decide what influence this theory had in America. It is true that the 'military mission' as a notion acceptable to legislators (that is to say, to the conscience of the ruling circles in Spain) began to lose ground as early as the Provisions of Granada of 1526, which emphasised persuasion rather than war. In the 1530s the news from Peru and the execution of Atahualpa provoked indignation in clerics such as Vitoria and, almost certainly, in wider circles. The Dominicans, acting independently of the Crown, persuaded Paul III to issue the Bull *Sublimis Deus* in 1537; this asserted the ability to receive the Faith, and also the liberty and rights to property of the natives. The Cortes held at Valladolid in 1542 (petition 94, quoted by Manzano, 1948) protested at the depopulation of the Indies as a result of the atrocities committed by the Spaniards. It is, however, difficult to deduce from these diffuse expressions of criticism the extent of the direct influence of Vitoria (Pérez de Tudela, 1958). The quotations made at the end of the century are equivocal, almost decorative, and alien to the spirit of Vitoria: this is true both of the statements of an *Oidor* in the Philippines who defended the conquests and that of an Augustinian advocating the enslavement of the Araucanians (Hanke, 1943). In 1571, in a full-scale propaganda campaign waged in Peru to demonstrate the tyranny of the Incas, the butt of the attacks was Las Casas: he was assailed in the Anonymous Document of Yucay, which accused him of being the author of the idea that the Inca was rightful lord of Peru, and by Juan de Ovando, from his post in the Council of the Indies, who arranged for a royal order confiscating the manuscripts of Las Casas which lay in the monastery of San Gregorio in Valladolid. There were not, however, any attacks on Vitoria, nor, obviously, any further application of his ideas as direct measures; even though, quite evidently, the injunction of the Ordinances for Discoveries of 1573 to carry out a peaceful mission, based on persuasion, trade and amity, when new lands were discovered, instead of embarking on conquest, indicates that legislation was subject to the influence of the views of all the opponents of conquest and of the military mission. Both the school of Salamanca and Las Casas himself, and such jurists as Gregorio López, and the friars of the various Orders, must have created a set of attitudes which, through so important a jurist as Juan de Ovando, from his position at the head of the administration of the Indies, led to the abolition of the traditional *Requerimiento*, which in practice had degenerated into a mere formality.

Even though there is no such explicit influence of Vitoria in the Indies, as recent writers have sometimes suggested, it is impossible to deny his important role in the history of European thought, precisely because his views were more strictly theoretical than were those of Las Casas. What took place in the Spain of Charles V was the assertion of the rights of the nation state and the denial both of the universal power of the emperor and of direct Papal power over temporal things – in other words, the negation of the medieval concept of Christendom. Apparently, this had already happened as a result of other trends – for example, Gallicanism, with its basic presupposition that the king of France recognised no superior in temporal matters. Vitoria's innovation, however, was that in addition to this assertion of the prerogatives of nation states (which might have been influenced by the tendencies inherent in the national monarchies of Spain, on account of his birth, and of France, because of his studies at the Sorbonne), he proclaimed the subordination of the State (the *Res Publica*) to the *Jus Gentium*. The latter was no longer simply a notion embracing all men, it was 'inter-national'; it appertained to States in their relations with one another, which were governed by a system of coexistence based on Natural Law. The problem of America was thus subsumed into a vaster and more theoretical problem.

Attitudes of this nature endow the Thomism of Vitoria and of his successors Domingo de Soto, Covarrubias, Molina and Vázquez de Menchaca with 'modern' characteristics alien to both Papal and imperial universalism and, as a result, passing beyond the intellectual horizons of their great medieval master. Even though St Thomas maintained that the supernatural order did not annul nature but, on the contrary, ennobled it, and the entire political doctrine of the school of Salamanca was based on this presupposition, it appears evident, in the author's opinion, that St Thomas would never have thought of the overall unity of mankind as being assured, not by the conjuncture of universal powers, but by rational principles embodied in a purely human law on the Stoic model. In Vitoria we can see the interaction of purely Thomist ideas (the perfect 'republic', as described in *De Regimine principum*) and humanistic and Stoic influences which are 'modern' in cast. This modernity of outlook was to be even more evident in Vázquez de Menchaca (Reibstein, 1949).

In contrast to these circles imbued with Renaissance learning, the intellectual universe of Las Casas, which was the fruit of American experiences and themes, was much less homogeneous intellectually, but it nevertheless possessed an intrinsic meaning: it represents the overlapping of the Thomist concepts of Natural Law and the notion of the peaceful mission, the latter being the hallmark of Las Casas' entire thought; the important role which he attributes to the Bulls and to the concept of Empire as a missionary enterprise made his outlook more 'medieval', on the whole, than that of Vitoria.

The decline of the Bulls as a factor in international politics

The 1520s witnessed the offensives of the French Atlantic ports towards the Caribbean, in the form of expeditions by corsairs. Beginning with the expedition of Verrazano in 1523, the French were searching for the North-west Passage to the South Sea, and this search was to lead them eventually to undertake the colonisation of Canada. Thereafter, the basic presuppositions of French foreign policy were to be: the freedom of the seas and of coastal trade; the legal validity of effective possession as against mere discovery, and its conferment of a title of sovereignty to be respected by any Europeans arriving on the scene subsequently; and rejection of the multilateral applicability of the Bulls of Alexander VI and of the Treaty of Tordesillas. The first demand that '*mare sit commune*' was voiced in a dispatch of 1538 (G. A. Rein, 1925, 133). In 1541, Francis I made the famous observation that he would like to have seen Adam's will in order to know how the universe had been divided among his heirs. The interests connected with privateering, cod-fishing and the discovery of a new passage to the Spice Islands were reinforced, from the middle of the sixteenth century onwards, by a military and colonialistic impulse that inspired the Huguenots under the leadership of Coligny in their attempts at settlement in Florida and in 'Antarctic France'. The Spaniards, when negotiating with them, used to base their reasoning on the same arguments employed by the discoverers and conquistadors in their disputes with the king of Spain – namely, that 'it is not just that others should come and enjoy the fruits of the labours and expense incurred by those who discovered the said Indies' (1559, quoted in Rein, 1925, 133).

The truce of Vaucelles (1556) and the Treaty of Cateau-Cambrésis (1559) first gave expression, in clauses that remained purely verbal and were handed down as a tradition among diplomats, to the famous principle later to be adopted by the English – 'no peace beyond the line [of amity]'. Beyond the longitude of the Azores and the Tropic of Cancer, there was to be no peace, nor, legally, was there to be war, between the nations of Europe: 'the strongest in those parts are to be the masters'. This implies the complete rejection of the underlying premises of the pacts between Spain and Portugal and of the Papal Bulls, in the opinion of Rein (211); what was more, the principle was to be replaced by its exact converse: the agreement designed to avoid conflict between Christian princes in overseas territories gave way to the axiom that war was the normal state of affairs 'beyond the line'; this war, however, was not legitimate, and was of no fundamental importance to the European powers engaged in it. Nothing expressed the new European consensus regarding the Americas so eloquently as this axiom, which after Cateau-Cambrésis remained unchallenged for over a century. The notion of the universality of the Pope's power and of his jurisdiction over the seas and lands situated on the frontiers of Christendom gradually faded into oblivion from the mid-sixteenth century onwards. Such lands were now thought of as being left free for occupation by fleets or adventurers, who set out to seize booty or acquire territorial dominion at the expense of the earlier occupiers. The kings and States of Europe denied responsibility for these forces, but reaped the fruits of their initiative; their war against rival States was 'underhand', to use the word current in Elizabethan England.

This marked the beginning of the golden age of the corsairs, pirates and buccaneers of the Caribbean, and of settlement by the French, the Dutch and the English in Canada, Virginia, the Lesser Antilles, Jamaica, Guiana, Honduras and elsewhere. Spain was forced to make a *de facto* abandonment of the rights granted to it by the Bulls and the Treaty with Portugal, owing to its inability to colonise and defend the entire continent and the islands, particularly the Lesser Antilles, which became the principal nuclei of settlement for foreign planters and buccaneers and bases for smuggling and piracy. Of the larger islands, Jamaica and the western part of Hispaniola were lost to Spain in 1655 and 1679.

The *de jure* recognition of the new situation may be dated from the Anglo-Spanish Treaty of Madrid (1670), the seventh clause of which proclaimed that the King of Great Britain 'shall have, hold and possess for ever, with full rights of sovereignty, property and possession, all the lands, regions, islands, colonies and dominions situated in the West Indies or in any other part of America, which the said King of Great Britain and his subjects at present hold and possess'. The principle of permanent war overseas gradually gave way to the recognition of a right of dominion based on possession, a principle that was also recognised in Europe. On subsequent occasions (in 1678, 1697 and 1713) clauses relating to American territories and frontiers are included in the most important European treaties. The filibusters, a relic of the preceding era, vanished from the scene in the last decades of the seventeenth century.

Thus the law of Christendom was replaced by international law governing relations between States, after an interregnum of some one hundred and twenty years – an interregnum which, of course, in the history of America and particularly of the Caribbean, was to be prolonged throughout the eighteenth century.

In any case, the law of Christendom was gradually falling into desuetude from the mid-sixteenth century onwards, annulling the force of the Papal and Spanish-Portuguese lines of demarcation, and being replaced by the principles of effective occupation and the freedom of the seas. The religious unity of the New World was disrupted by Dutch and English colonisation: the image of modern Europe began to be reflected in the Americas, through a process which began at that time and is still continuing in the twentieth century. The peculiar characteristics of the Americas – the conception of them as a different and special place, a mission field or, alternatively, a region given over to illicit war, began to disappear, in law, from the end of the seventeenth century. International legal instruments tended towards the consolidation of a unified juridical structure, and to the homogeneity of the two worlds, by virtue of modern conceptions based on Natural Law, which found their first expression in Spain and were later developed by Dutch and German jurists.

The later Spanish juridical reassertion of the right to dominion

In the *Book of Spiritual Governance* (*Libro de la Gobernación Espiritual*), the first part of the legislative plan evolved by Juan de Ovando as Visitor and President of the Council of the Indies, in 1571, it was stated that God had thought fit to 'reveal miraculously' the West Indies in the time of the Catholic Sovereigns, and had decreed that the Pope 'should entrust and grant to them and to their successors as Kings of Castile and Leon the kingdom, government and rights of discovery of that new and unknown world and the conversion of the barbarous peoples and nations which might be found there'. This was still the official position of Spain and the basis of its legislation; it had undergone no internal modification, even though it had diminished greatly in international relevance. This text expressed, in an ornate style that already appeared baroque, the theocratic, rather than merely juridical, basis of authority, firmly grounded on a revelation of Divine Providence and involving a religious obligation.

It was around the middle of the sixteenth century that various clerics of the Mendicant Orders were developing a doctrinal theory according to which the King of Spain, in the Indies, was the Pope's Vicar by virtue of his missionary attributes, and were drawing from it important juridical conclusions which far surpassed the mere question of ecclesiastical patronage. We will consider this aspect in more detail at a later stage.

The most systematic juridical formulation of the problems of legitimisation of dominion in the seventeenth century was provided by Solórzano Pereira in his *Disputationes de Jure Indiarum* (1629) and his *Política Indiana* (1648), which enjoyed an unrivalled prestige in the official and legal circles in the Indies for a century and a half. Although it is quite true to say that it is rarely original on decisive points (Ayala, 1946, 100), this does not detract from the significance of the work as a whole as an expression of legal thought. At times he had to deal with a dialectical adversary of the stature of Hugo Grotius – it was around this time when the *Mare Liberum* (1608) was contested by Serafim de Freitas, who defended the rights of Portugal – and the struggle was, of course, very unequal.

The peculiar contribution of Solórzano in the field which we are considering here is an eclecticism which blurs certain differences of principle (for example, in the case of the school of Salamanca, which enjoyed too great a prestige for him to refute it, but with whose underlying premises he fundamentally disagrees). He resolves the doctrinal controversy, after paying due attention to contrary opinions, by adopting a position which, despite everything, makes it possible for him to reaffirm Spain's rights. Throughout Book II of *De Jure Indiarum* and chapters IX to XII of Book I of the *Política Indiana*, he again considers all the matters which had given rise to controversy in the previous century, and attempts to reach solutions which will not unduly disturb the prevailing preconceptions.[7] When considering the arguments of Sepúlveda in favour of 'natural' slavery, he incorporates the more recent assessment of Acosta of the differing levels of civilisation attained by the natives. When he considers the question of the 'imperial' title, he admits that to the school of Salamanca and Gregorio López, the imperial title had no validity or force within Spain itself. When speaking of the political rights of the infidels, he expresses his approval of Ostiensis (who, as he put it, was more widely supported and was more useful for the Catholic faith), and he corroborates his opinion with the resounding words of St Augustine 'all the actions of the infidels are sinful...because without faith in Christ it is impossible to live uprightly, and freewill without the grace of Christ is worthless except for committing sins', and with St Thomas's dictum (from the *Summa Theologica*, II, II, q. 10, a. 10, and quoted only partially) that the Church may deprive the infidels of political power over the faithful. The Bulls, interpreted literally, confer full and integral dominion: Bellarmine, who was at first inclined to the contrary opinion, had declared that at the time he had not yet seen the Bulls themselves, so that Solórzano finds it possible to cite him as a supporting authority. The granting of Ireland to Henry II of England by Pope Adrian IV and the Portuguese Bulls constituted unambiguous historical precedents of the plenary content of the Bulls of Alexander VI. After making this point, however, Solórzano did not insist that the Pontiff enjoyed direct power in temporal matters, but accepted the Thomist *via media* of 'indirect' power, which was quite sufficient to justify the transference of power in the case of the Indies. There is nothing very original in this line of thought; but what is really significant, in our opinion, of the 'Spanish seventeenth-century' attitude are the historical-cum-religious titles adduced to justify dominion, which Solórzano employs against the enemies of Spain.

Solórzano, at that very moment of fierce controversy with the mass of anti-Spanish polemical literature which had been published in Europe, quoted, as signs of the action of Divine Providence, passages from Scripture which might be interpreted in a figurative or allegorical manner as alluding to the role of Spain in the Indies, texts already employed in controversy by Oviedo, Acosta, Torquemada, and others, and subsequently compiled in the lengthy treatise of Fray Gregorio García on the origin of the American Indians. To these he added the Aztec prophecies described by the missionaries, the existence of the cross as a religious symbol among so many different tribes, the inspired projects of Columbus and the Catholic Sovereigns, the apparitions of St James and of the Virgin in the battles of Cuzco and Arauco, and all kinds of similar prodigies. However, he also cites the contrary opinion of Vitoria, who doubted the miracles, in view of the atrocities and abuses committed by the conquistadors; and that of Acosta, who considered, as a problem of the utmost relevance, in his *De procuranda indorum salute*, the scarcity of miracles in the early stages of the evangelisation of the Americas. To this Solórzano doggedly retorts that, in any case, there had in fact been miracles attested by reliable authorities – for example, the miraculous cures narrated by Alvar Núñez Cabeza de Vaca. The author makes his own convictions quite plain, but also gives consideration to adverse opinions, in the course of a learned polemic which takes into account more than the purely rational evidence available. What did, in Solórzano's view, provide certitude, a kind of *ultima ratio* of the history of human kingdoms, was St Augustine's concept of Divine Providence, manifested in the punishment of the impious and fluctuations in the fortunes of kingdoms. Augustinianism and the historical perspective, in these thinkers of the Baroque Age, present a marked contrast to Thomist thinking based on Natural Law and the total absence of historical sense in the school of Salamanca of the sixteenth century.

The intellectual development of Solórzano led him to employ in his arguments a wealth of historical material, which he pressed into the service of his Spanish nationalism and Regalism. From the reign of Philip II onwards, the 'Caesarist' imperialist notions characteristic of the era of Charles V had been increasingly abandoned in Spain. What was now needed, to carry on the titanic struggle with the northern powers, was for thinkers who supported the Spanish State and Church to demonstrate the greatness of the new monarchy that was southern and western, Mediterranean and oceanic, Spanish and American, a combination represented by all the allegorical figures on the title page of the *Política Indiana*. It had to be defended, for example, against Bodin, who belittled the Spanish Empire in the Indies by describing it as a mere Papal fief. It was necessary to counter the attacks based on the Black Legend (for example, in the *Politics*, I, xii), though not without asserting that there was no justification for past and future abuses, and not without piously imploring God to remit their richly deserved punishment. As part of the polemic itself, Solórzano makes his *apologia*. He lays great emphasis on the title 'Catholic Sovereigns', which dated from long before the capture of Granada, ever since the convert Reccared appeared at the Council of Toledo, or since Alfonso I was King in Oviedo (734). In order to exalt his sovereigns still further, he not only points out that they have always been orthodox and defenders of the Faith, but that they have also been anointed and endowed with the power to cure scrofula (the 'King's Evil'), like the kings of France and England, who were able to cure scrofula after their consecration. This last point reveals the extent to which the theoretical defenders of Spain, at this extremely critical juncture, were willing to concede the thaumaturgic prestige of the northern monarchs; as a learned argument, however, it was extremely difficult to support with documentary evidence, which never enjoyed the enormous power of French popular beliefs in the 'miracle royal', the importance of which as a national myth has been emphasised by Marc Bloch. Solórzano is on more solid ground when he speaks of the immense geographical extent of the 'Catholic monarchy' across lands and oceans, a circumstance which made it possible to defend the Catholic religion on a world-wide scale.[8] Solórzano cautiously employs the term 'monarchy' (not 'empire'). Fray José Laínez, however, referred to Philip IV in 1641 as 'Catholic King of the Spains and Emperor of America' (Jover, 1949, 212). One official, Pedro Mejía de Ovando, in his *Practical Book or Report* (*Libro o Memorial Práctico*) of

1639 (MS., National Library, Madrid) stated that Alexander VI, disposing of temporal things by virtue of his power over spiritual things, as the Popes had already done in the case of Charlemagne by granting him the kingdom of Jerusalem, granted to the Catholic Sovereigns 'the government and empire over the Western Indies and rights of navigation there, enjoying high, Royal and Imperial dignity'. More effective as an argument, however, than the baroque titles characteristic of that age, titles based on theory and erudition rather than on good sense, was Solórzano's conclusion: there should be an end to disputes as to the justice of titles; many evils had been committed during the conquest, but there was no point in subjecting to interminable scrutiny kingdoms that were already old; if the principal objective was sound and was achieved, 'one is not wont to inquire over-zealously as to whether some sins were committed in the means and manner of attaining that end' (*Politica Indiana*, I, 12, 24). At this point the positive good sense of this jurist is uppermost.

From Palacios Rubio to Solórzano, therefore, and taking account of the friars who argued that the king was the Pope's Vicar, we can trace an ideological development which we might describe as theocratic or neo-Guelph. One contributing factor was, of course, the need to construct a theoretical basis for the Bulls and for the political and religious supremacy of the king in the Indies. In addition to this, however, it is legitimate to conceive of this process as a prolongation of earlier theories – a living tradition maintained by the jurists and canon lawyers of a nation whose most vital ideological cohesion had always been based on the notion of a Holy War.

After Solórzano, with the end of the era of the Counter-Reformation and the *de facto* and *de jure* acceptance of the presence of other colonial empires in America, the Bulls ceased to have effective force. The writers on canon law hardly made any fresh contribution to the debate, being fully preoccupied with the question of patronage and the theoretical and practical problems derived therefrom. The *Thesaurus Indicus* (1668), written by the Jesuit Diego de Avendaño, asserted that those who regarded the Bulls as making a merely tutelary concession had never read the texts concerned, and that the real basis of the Papal donation was St Thomas's doctrine that war is lawful not to impose the Faith by force but to prevent missionary activities being hampered (*Summa Theologica*, II, II, q. 10, a. 8). Furthermore, he considered that Papal authority over spiritual and temporal matters to be incontrovertible, in accordance with the definitions of Boniface VIII (Egaña, 1949). There still remained a faint echo of interest in the Bulls at the beginning of the eighteenth century: Prudencio Antonio Palacios, the author of *Notes on the Clauses and Laws of the Compilation of the*

Indies (MSS., Library of the Royal Palace, Madrid), after asserting that the discovery of America was the most important event since the Creation and the Incarnation – quoting the well-known affirmation originally made by López de Gómara in his dedication – declared that the Bulls provided a more firmly established title than any other argument, and that, thanks to the discovery, the task of combating the Antichrist had fallen to the Spaniards and the Portuguese.

Thus, from 1492 and until a date which we can establish as being between 1670 and 1713, Spanish America was integrated into the juridical cosmos of the West: at first this happened in accordance with notions based on the concept of Christendom, and later it was incorporated into the system of national monarchies, after innumerable doctrinal debates and phases of transition from one order of things to the other. The Bulls of Alexander VI, quite apart from their practical repercussions, are a supremely important symptom of this incorporation into Christendom, a notion which was still in force as late as the end of the seventeenth century. 'Christendom' was essentially a system unifying the spiritual and the temporal; modern thought shattered that solidarity and tried to create a new juridical and ideological unity, ignoring both Papal and imperial power, to which the national States were to be subordinate: a unity based on reason and customs, the *Jus Gentium*, which had now evolved into international law, which had full validity within the 'concert of European nations' and which also, in theory, was valid in other continents. The struggle between the powers obliged Spain, the last nation to believe in 'Christendom' – even though, ironically, it had in the sixteenth century foreshadowed in theory the idea of a corpus of international law based on Natural Law – to submit to the new consensus, which was broadened to include the Americas. A thinker such as Saavedra Fajardo, in the 1640s, no longer theorised within the context of Christendom but within that of the European monarchies; and his ideas on the American colonies already foreshadowed the criticisms voiced by the economists during the following century.

It appears to us to be essential to an understanding of the history of the Americas to bear in mind that their discovery and settlement were not merely 'events' taking place in seas and 'lands belonging to nobody', but were immediately made the subject of legal interpretations of world-wide scope, and gave rise to the most complex theoretical problems at the highest level. This incorporation into the context of world ideas was due to the Spanish monarchy and the Papacy – that is to say, to the 'Roman' powers, accustomed to thinking of political problems in juridical terms.

CHAPTER 3

THE INSTITUTIONS AND FOUNDING
IDEAS OF THE SPANISH STATE
IN THE INDIES

In describing the institutional framework of the Spanish Indies, one must
take as one's starting-point the fundamental fact of the Conquest and the
society that was formed as a result of it, with its hierarchy based on ethnic
stratification; then one must consider the effects of geographical influences – the ocean separating the metropolitan country from its colonies
– which imposed a specific pattern on maritime traffic. Such basic factors
as these obviously influenced the structure of the State. Nevertheless,
they do not provide a sufficient explanation of it, because the pattern
itself had its origin in other structures which were gradually formed in
Spain during the Middle Ages and the sixteenth century, and which
preserved both their coherence and their durability in the Americas.

In order to describe as concisely as possible the Spanish State in the
Indies, one must concentrate one's attention on the period of its foundation, when the bases for all subsequent development were established. It
may be asserted that the decade of the 1570s marks the end of this period;
in those years Juan de Ovando and Francisco de Toledo were active, and the
outlines of a unitary political structure are already discernible. However,
this new order of things made a systematic impact on the consciousness of
governors and jurists only half a century later, thanks to the American
jurists – particularly Solórzano – who wrote their works during the early
decades of the seventeenth century. Even the *Compilation of Laws of the
Indies* of 1680 was mostly drafted around 1640 by Antonio de León Pinelo
(Manzano, 1956). Therefore, any examination of these institutions and the
fundamental underlying trends must be based on a general survey of the
first one and a half centuries of Spanish conquest and settlement in the
Americas (1500–1650).

Moreover, around 1650 there took place in the Spanish political conscience a process of internal mutation which was to reach its apogee in the
eighteenth century, as a consequence of military defeat and internal
exhaustion. The guiding principles underlying the monarchy and, to a
certain extent, its overseas empire, were affected by this process. However,
other fundamental structures of the Spanish Indies and of the peninsular

State were able to resist this trend and, to a certain degree, assert their durability. The task of historical research is to define, in each case, the duration of the institutions, systems of values and collective attitudes, when they were in full force as historical factors.

In this chapter, which may be described as a historical survey of institutions and of society, we will attempt to point out certain prominent characteristics of the Spanish American State, basing our approach on certain central themes: the king as a lord in possession of his patrimony and as the centre of legitimate order; the 'realm' in the process of bureaucratisation; the subjection of the Church to the State through the patronage system; the trend towards urbanisation on the part of both Spaniards and Indians; the mutual relationship of the social classes and races, orientated towards the social model of the '*caballero*', a concept which permeated the entire social structure. Another fundamental institution, the university, will be considered in a later chapter.

The king and the fundamental objectives of the State

The fact that the Indies had been acquired by kingdoms that were already 'modern'; that the 'realms' had been settled under the general direction of the Crown, and that all authority emanated from the king; all these characteristics of an already 'founded' State resulted in the situation being different from that which prevailed in Castile. However, certain fundamental concepts of the Castilian Middle Ages formed the context within which the events of Spanish American history made their own impact; without due consideration of these concepts, the events cannot be properly understood.

The king of Castile was, in the first place, 'natural lord' (*señor natural*) by virtue of a 'natural' order which, in this context, meant the right of dynastic succession, a 'lordship of flesh and blood', as Sancho IV, the Brave, was to put it. Moreover, on the basis of that same authority, he was lord of the 'land', of the environment in which the kingdom was established, as lord of the realm itself. This 'natural lordship' was the aspect of kingship that enjoyed the most deeply rooted popular appeal; it was a lordship both dynastic and patrimonial. It was a lordship orientated, like all political institutions in the Middle Ages, to the upholding of the law. The cardinal virtue in a king was held to be the dispensing of justice.

On the basis of this traditional notion, the *Partidas* elaborated a system both more far-reaching and more eclectic in origin. The jurists working in the reign of Alfonso X gave explicit form in one great corpus to ideas derived from the jurists of Bologna, schooled in Roman law, and the Papal canon lawyers, without departing entirely from the ancient '*Fueros*' which embodied the traditional law of Castile. The underlying ethical and political ideas were derived principally from the ancient world, either through such intermediaries as St Isidore or through the Scholastics. When the *Partidas* attempt to unite in one legal system 'the good life according to God's precepts' and 'the good life in the terms of this world', one can detect the influence of Aristotle's political thought and its evaluation of nature and of the State. Moreover, dogmas, sacraments and canon law form the entire subject matter of the First *Partida*. Alfonso X's work does away with any dividing line separating legal precepts and advice concerning the good life and right doctrine; it is, at the same time, a legal code and a manual for the education of princes and peoples. The internal subdivisions of the work are based on the number seven, and there is a plethora of Biblical, historical and astronomical allusions, based on symbolist and exemplary notions (Dempf, 1937; Berges, 1938). Divine wisdom, will and power serve as a model for human authorities; but justice, on the other hand, plays a part as a metaphysical intermediary between divine and human things, assuming the function of the inspiring principle of the State (Ferrari, 1934). On these premises there is based the idea of the king as God's Vicar, placed in office to keep peoples 'in justice and truth in temporal matters' (II, 1, 5); this 'vicarial' theory was divided from ecclesiastical law, and, originally, from the Roman system of administration.

However, this vicarial idea and this exalted conception of royal dignity – the king was 'emperor in his realm', as was the case in France – does not imply an unlimited absolutism. He can modify laws and *fueros*, but he cannot alienate portions of the 'land', which in this context is identified with the Latin word *patria* (Maravall, 1965, 248). Natural Law and Divine Law impose limits which must not be overstepped; the king cannot be a 'tyrant'. Above all, his power is conditioned by one ubiquitous objective, the 'common weal' of the land, both in spiritual and in material matters, 'common weal' in the Aristotelian and Scholastic sense of the term, which also embraces his own honour and that of his subjects, indeed the entire sphere of 'justice and truth' in the metaphysical and ethical sense. Thus, even though royal power was a condensed expression of the entire strength of the newly established national state, an entire corpus of ideas based on Christianity, Roman law, Scholasticism and Castilian common law embodied ethical principles which placed limitations on that power and assigned certain obligations on the State.

In 1500 the *Partidas* were still in full force, both legally and doctrinally, in the monarchy recently strengthened by the Catholic Sovereigns, and they constituted the theoretical justification of the State, and the fundamental corpus of ideas which inspired the earliest legislation affecting the Americas. But the renaissance of Thomism in Salamanca between 1520 and 1540, when Francisco de Vitoria held the chair of theology there, gave rise to a more explicit theoretical interpretation of the State ('the Republic'), which was to be continued by theologians and jurists belonging to that school or influenced by it: Domingo de Soto, Martín de Azpilcueta (the 'Dr Navarro'), Diego de Covarrubias, Fernando Vázquez de Menchaca, Luis de Molina, Francisco Suárez and so on. Whereas the *Partidas*, as might be expected from the date of their compilation (the mid-thirteenth century), show the philosophical influence of Augustinian, neo-Platonising and Aristotelian ideas, all absorbed into an 'exemplary' mode of expression with strong theological tendencies, the Spanish school of the sixteenth century deliberately based its reflections and attitudes on unambiguously asserted Aristotelian and Thomist principles, which enjoyed a validity independent of revealed truth. In this sense, Vitoria and his followers are representatives of Renaissance humanism, with which they were also connected by way of their neo-Stoic conception of *Jus Gentium* or international law.

Sánchez Agresta (1959) has given an excellent summary of the essential facets of the teachings of this school: (1) humanity is a plurality of States, each one of which is an entirety in itself; (2) this whole is conceived as an organic unity, hierarchically structured, a 'mystical body' based on a moral unity, and not simply on submission to power; (3) the royal power is an 'office' which gives expression to the general power of the *res publica* in order to achieve the common good; (4) common allegiance to a political system is a natural necessity – the power of the State is derived in this sense from the Creation, and is 'divine' but natural; it may, ostensibly, abrogate some of the precepts of the Decalogue (that forbidding the taking of life, for example), but with a view to the common weal; and (5) the State is an ethical and teleological entity, based on the common weal; its power is supreme in its own sphere, but it is indissolubly connected with its own end, which is precisely that common weal.

These doctrines found concrete expression in more precisely defined juridical concepts: 'majesty', 'principality' and 'mere *imperium*'; in the submission of the prince to the law as a general guiding principle, but without his being subject to actual legal coercion; the doctrine of the 'just war'; the pact of submission, whereby the community transfers its authority to the prince, but in the sense that the power of the latter derives from Natural and Divine Law, rather than being an arbitrary concession on the part of the community (this idea is expressed very explicitly in Vitoria, and it differentiates his doctrine from the modern democratic theory).

When Juan de Ovando, during his tenure of office as Visitor and President of the Council of the Indies, published his *Book of Spiritual Governance of the Indies* (1571), which was to be his first contribution to the full-scale corpus of legal theory which he felt to be necessary, he defined in his preface the overall objectives of what that very text was already referring to as the 'State of the Indies'. In this book the King of Spain recognised 'the obligation which God has laid upon us in giving us so many Realms and Kingdoms, and miraculously giving and entrusting to us the kingship and overlordship and discovery, possession and conversion to the Holy Catholic Faith and incorporation into the bosom of the Holy Church of all this New World of the Western Indies, which was unknown and outside the law of His chosen people and the law of His Grace, proclaimed by His Only Son...', until in 1492 its existence was revealed to the Catholic Sovereigns, and the Pope entrusted and granted to them 'the kingship, sovereignty and rights of discovery of that new and unknown world, and the conversion of the barbarous peoples and nations which might be found there'. The Sovereigns had sent clergy and ecclesiastics to preach 'to govern men's souls in spiritual matters, and Viceroys, *Audiencias*, Governors and judges to govern the land and uphold justice there, and providing, and arranging to provide, both Spaniards and Indians with bread, wine, oil, cloth, silks, linens, horses, cattle, arms and tools, to work and cultivate the land, and crafts and industries and all other things needed for the sustenance and recreation of men'. As a result of the enterprise of the Sovereigns, according to this classic exposition of the theoretical foundations of the Spanish State in the Indies, more than 9,000 leagues of the coastline of the mainland had been discovered, quite apart from the islands, and the natives had been liberated from the tyrannies to which they were subjected, especially the tyranny of idolatry (which was interpreted as the work of the Devil), and from sins, unnatural vices, cannibalism and human sacrifice. The Crown had established, the text went on to say, four archbishoprics, twenty-two bishoprics, many collegiate, parish and votive churches, monasteries, mission centres and convents, two viceroyalties, ten *Audiencias*, many governorships, *corregimientos*, and major and ordinary *alcaldías*; many cities of Indians and of Spaniards had been founded, with their *Cabildos*, and all this formed a real 'republic'. The text ends with the words: 'Seeing that in all of them [the Indies] or in the greater part of them there is a properly established and political republic, both in spiritual and in temporal matters, and since in all this area there is one Church, one Realm and one Republic, we desire that throughout the Indies the same Law shall be observed, so that it shall everywhere display the same consistency and uniformity' (published by Maurtúa, 1906).

The extension of the Spanish monarchy to the New World, which is here celebrated as a deliberate design of Providence, was originally connected with the discovery, evangelising mission and administration of the new lands for the common good of Indians and Spaniards: these were, in short, the objectives of the 'State of the Indies'. This conception of the 'common weal' embraced various different matters. In the first place, there was the spiritual common weal in the religious sense, especially the evangelisation of the natives, which was regarded as the most important obligation affecting the king's conscience. The second aspect was the 'upholding of justice'. It must not be forgotten that the primary function of the medieval State was to uphold the law and the traditional prerogatives, whether these were established in writing or had simply been handed down from time immemorial; the king who was 'just' was the one who paid regard to the faithful maintenance of those '*fueros*' and sound customs. This judicial notion of the State persisted throughout the colonial centuries as a basic and ineluctable principle. The captains of the conquistador bands had to be judges of the conflicts that arose among their men and acted as arbiters and administered summary justice: Pizarro obtained from the King express authorisation to do so. But it was, above all, the *Audiencias* which had to realise the ideal of 'just judges', impartial and exercising a protective role, particularly with regard to the Indians and the weak.

In the last resort, the 'common weal' in the code of Ovando and in the laws of the Indies in general was what in the language of the humanists was called 'policy' and what we would today call 'civilisation'. The code implied the suppression of customs deemed to be inhuman or unnatural, and the introduction of the European way of life in spheres where it was considered to be most obviously beneficial, such as agriculture, cattle-raising, craft industries and trade in goods. Ovando's book enumerates with satisfaction all that has been transmitted to the Indians in these respects, both in the islands and on the American continent – throughout the 9,000 leagues of coast so far discovered, as he takes care to emphasise (it was in those years that Ovando has sponsored geographical surveys in each province, and drafted the 'Ordinances for Descriptions', and it was in those same years that there were published the Reports on the Cities of Spain, which are of such importance for our knowledge of contemporary Castile, so that the metropolitan country and the colonies were engaged in this task of geographical description simultaneously).

It has been said that there are different types of State: some States are legislative, some administrative and some judicial, depending on where the centre of gravity may be said to lie (Carl Schmitt). The State in the Indies was no longer a merely judicial State, as it had been in the Middle Ages; it was, above all, a legislative State. In pursuit of the ethical and political ideals derived from the *Partidas* and from Scholasticism, it made efforts, from afar, to implant justice by promulgating general or specific laws, and entrusting their enforcement to the bureaucracy and the ecclesiastics, in the forlorn hope of imposing certain ideal canons of behaviour, which would also redound to the profit of the Treasury.

The legislation of the Indies does not contain any explicit formulation of a doctrine concerning the basic principles of the State: civil power, the pact of submission, the rights of the prince and so on. Usually, only the specifically 'American' objectives of the State find expression in legal texts; their most solemn and detailed enunciation is contained in the passage of the code of Ovando which has been quoted above.

However, Spanish and 'American' legislation formed part of the same legal corpus, and were based on the same fundamental doctrines, so that it is a mistake to consider the legislation affecting the New World in isolation from that of the peninsula. The *Audiencias* – according to the Ordinances of 1528 – were obliged to enforce the Hispanic laws, in addition to ordinances applying only to the region. Among these Hispanic laws was an order of precedence which had been established only recently in the Cortes of Toro in 1505, by virtue of which priority was given to laws promulgated in the Cortes by the kings; next in order were the *fueros* (which in America had hardly any validity, except in so far as they concerned the status of *hidalgo*); and the Seven *Partidas*, which in their turn were the source of all the doctrinal foundations to the laws. In addition to this, however, although the trend was sometimes recognised and sometimes rejected by the Spanish Cortes (Madrid, 1499; Toro, 1505), the way was left open for the operation of an overwhelmingly strong tendency – the application of the doctrinal teachings of the masters of Roman and canon law, whose works were known through university teaching and published literature: this was the so-called 'law of the jurists', which tended to give a unitary and 'Roman' spirit to the interpretation of the laws. In Spain, the comments of Gregorio López on the *Partidas* (from the edition of 1555 onwards) acquired an immense authority, and in them he makes copious use of the great Roman law commentators such as Bartolus and Baldus, and also of St Thomas, St Gregory the Great and Aristotle; he thus combines professional traditions and authorities with ideas of a philosophical or theological origin. The

73

fundamental notions of learned men concerning the Spanish State in the Indies were derived, then, from these sources, which were the same as those employed as authorities in Spain.

With regard to the limitations placed on royal power and the right of resistance to it, there is a marked difference, in the history of Spanish America, between the era of the Conquest, which ended around 1550, and the period which followed. This is, of course, due, in the first place, to the difference that is obviously discernible between periods of foundation, during which rule is established by military action – and in this case by warfare carried on by armies recruited by improvised leaders – and periods of settled legal organisation and administrative order. This is the fundamental difference between the two periods to which we refer as the 'conquest' and the 'colonial period'. What is under examination, however, in this paragraph is whether there was also a theoretical change in the actual conception of the limitations placed on the power of the State and in the legal possibilities of resistance to abuses of that power.

In the Middle Ages and the sixteenth century, there was not only a right to resist 'tyranny' or specific unjust commands, but also commands which ran contrary to the common weal or the welfare of the subjects. Law, justice and the common weal are so closely interconnected in the medieval outlook that the right of resistance resided ubiquitously in all authorities and communities. In the first place, there was always the possibility of preventing the enforcement of an unjust or inappropriate ordinance of the king or his delegates, and this recourse was fully institutionalised, and at the disposal of an authority – this was the maxim, so often misunderstood, 'we obey but we do not comply', or, in more technical language, the right of 'suspension' or 'stay of execution'. On many occasions, viceroys, *Audiencias* or governors had suspended laws deriving from Spain because they ran counter to the common weal of the new territories and, more especially, of the new powerful groups that had arisen there, which, generally through the *Cabildos*, drew up a 'supplication' to submit to the king reports and petitions to justify the suspension. Ovando and Diego Colón, as Governors of Hispaniola, suspended grants of *encomiendas* which had been made by Ferdinand the Catholic, in order not to disappoint the expectations of the *vecinos* of the island; Cortés declined to enforce the royal order forbidding the incorporation of Indians into *encomiendas*; he was persuaded – 'almost forced', he states in the Third Letter – by the conquistadors and the royal officers. Pedrarias Dávila, accused of not having punished certain crimes, as he was obliged to do by law, replied that he had decided against doing so 'because they are things and occasions of great substance and crimes

74

affecting the greater part of the inhabitants of the land, and because they are matters about which it was necessary to consult Your Majesty...' In a work published in 1951 the author made a detailed study of this institutionalised non-fulfilment and the juridical principles on which it was founded.[1]

However, another phenomenon that occurred in the Americas in the sixteenth century was armed resistance or *de facto* disobedience to an authority or to a legal measure; this was frequently done by the *Cabildos* in the name of the bulk of the Spaniards: governors were often 'required' to use the money from the Royal Treasury on the pretext of the 'law of necessity'; or they were required to distribute Indians as vassals among the conquistadors; or the authority of a governor was rejected and the leader of some faction was 'required' to assume the appointment. The requirement and 'force' applied to the governor were often merely feigned, being a device to deny the responsibility of the person who appeared to be condoning the abuse of power. The Crown usually overlooked such acts, and only later – after the moment of crisis had passed – would initiate proceedings against those responsible; it did not, however, undo what was a *fait accompli*. The armed 'supplication' led by Gonzalo Pizarro was quite evidently an act of defiance of the Viceroy, but Charles V tempered his wrath, writes Gómara (*General History*, 265), when he learned that the rising had been accompanied by an appeal to him, and that the Viceroy Núñez de Vela was responsible because he had not accepted the supplication (even though in rejecting it he was, in fact, merely acting in strict accordance with the New Laws): the Emperor was, in other words, satisfied with the formal recognition of his authority, and blame fell on the man who had carried out his commands in too rigid and indiscreet a manner. His Peruvian subjects, on their part, insisted on the legitimacy of their attitude: when La Gasca, writing from Panama, offered them a pardon, they answered, according to Gómara (*ibid.* 266): 'None of us is asking for pardon, for we have done nothing wrong, but we have served our king, preserving our rights, as his laws permit.' These sources, therefore, show that in the first half of the century there was a period of total flux in the transition of juridical attitudes from the medieval framework to those associated with absolute monarchy. The principles remained ambiguous, and legitimacy was decided, to a great extent, according to the political circumstances prevailing in these 'new lands'; but the ultimate principle, that of obedience to the king, was always respected, at least formally. The definitive victory of La Gasca was undoubtedly due to the fact that, besides softening the rigour of the New Laws, he was capable of appealing to that underlying sentiment of obedience against a chieftain whose associates had already exceeded those bounds.

Even on the occasion of the rebellion of the city of Quito against the imposition of the *alcabala* tax in 1592–3, we find the *Cabildo* protesting on the grounds that 'to conquer these realms of Peru His Majesty did not have to make any contribution from his own patrimony; on the contrary, the land was won by those who came over at their own expense'; and it went on to mention the donations made and services rendered against the English corsairs. The same pattern was repeated. The excessively intransigent policy of the President Barros was abandoned; negotiations were initiated with the *Audiencia*; and then came the final repression, carried out by forces dispatched by the Viceroy Cañete which put an end to the rebellion. Even a decade later, the viceroys of Peru were to contrast the discontent of those under their administration with the obedient behaviour of other provinces.

Don Antonio de Mendoza, in his instructions to his successor, asserted that it was an easy task to govern the Spaniards of Mexico, 'if one knows how to handle them'. What was necessary, therefore, was a policy based on prudence, tenacity, concessions on points of detail and occasional rigour, for the impulses of the conquistadors to be gradually brought under control by the bureaucracy. In the seventeenth century there were sometimes disturbances in Mexico itself and even attempted rebellions, but the authority of the Crown and its representatives was consolidated, and there was no repetition of the Civil Wars of Peru. Depositions of governors took place only rarely: when this happened in Chile in 1655, the movement was led by the *Cabildo* of the frontier city of Concepción and the army itself, but it was disowned by the *Cabildo* of the capital, and, in the absence of any external support, the frontier authorities reinstated the deposed Governor. The nerve of the right of resistance had been broken by the gradual strengthening of the Crown's bureaucracy.

In the field of legal theory there was also a development, which corresponded closely to the transformation of the Castilian monarchy. Whereas Aragon, Catalonia, Valencia and Navarre were better able to preserve their *fueros* and traditional prerogatives until about 1700, Castile, after the defeat of the *Comunidades* and the reduction of the *Cortes* to a purely passive role, increasingly became a unitary and administrative monarchy. Philip has been called the 'king of paperwork'; but 'paperwork', as Braudel (1965) has pointed out, 'is a sign of the new times, and the consequence of government from a distance'.

At the same time as this concentration of political forces, the Scholastic theory of the State, based on rational and teleological premises, gave way to the voluntarist notion of 'sovereignty', as a 'power not bound by the laws', according to Bodin's famous definition, which found widespread acceptance in Spain after the translation of his work in 1590 (Maravall, 1944). Without completely abandoning political Aristotelianism, the Spaniards of the seventeenth century came to accept an extraordinary or 'absolute authority', subject to the untrammelled will of the prince – even though this did not provide any justification for tyranny – an exceptional power, which did not eliminate the 'ordinary authority' regulated by the laws. The writers of treatises on the royal authority still recognised the 'pact of submission' as the origin of the State; by virtue of this pact the authority of the king did indeed derive from the people, but now more emphasis was placed on the role of the people as merely instrumental than had been the case with the Scholastics: power was derived immediately from God, through the will of the community as a whole (González de Salcedo).

This notion of sovereignty acquired its fullest importance in the systematic negation of the right of resistance. The king was subject to Natural Law, but not to specific laws and customs; even though it is reasonable to expect his government to be legal and just, tyranny cannot be punished by the people, since punishment is a prerogative of sovereignty; all one can do is obey and pray for better times, in accordance with the counsels of the New Testament. It is true that Fr. Juan de Mariana, in his *De Rege et regis institutione* (1598) asserted that tyrannicide was justified (Book I, VI); but this was an exceptional position, made necessary by the need to justify the assassination of Henry III of France and the policy of the Catholic League in general, which enjoyed such strong support from the Jesuits. This combination of historical circumstances was only short-lived and was at all times quite irrelevant to the real situation in Spain.

The great intermediary between the thought of the seventeenth century and the juridical theories being developed in Spanish America was Solórzano. In his writings it was possible for the *letrados* to observe the aggrandisement of the royal authority, the reaffirmation of the symbol of the king as Vicar of God (a conception expressed in the *Partidas* and derived from an apocryphal work of St Augustine) and the immediate origin of the royal power in God Himself (*De Indiarum Jure*, I, II, 3–4); this entire line of thinking, however, was eclectic, and did not clash directly with doctrines derived from Roman law and Scholasticism. Carlos de Sigüenza y Góngora (*Theatre of Political Virtues*, Mexico, 1680, 53 ff.) still felt able to affirm with complete certitude the superiority of the people over the king, on the grounds that the people constituted his authority, and he quoted in support of this thesis Covarrubias, Vázquez de Menchaca and the great

German jurist influenced by the school of Salamanca, Johannes Althusius. However, there has not yet been sufficiently detailed research to achieve a precise evaluation of the influence of the thought of this Mexican writer. In any case, it is legitimate to suggest that this theme was no longer a topic of controversy at the time he wrote. It is possible to find in libraries copies of Suárez' book attacking James I of England and defending the Scholastic theories against the ideal of the Divine Right of kings, but this does not mean that this doctrine was widely taught, because the syllabus of the Jesuit colleges and the universities did not include the subject of political philosophy. The assertion that Suárez' theories prevailed in this field (Furlong) is lacking in sufficient proof, particularly as regards the seventeenth century. The elimination of the right of resistance, when the period of the Conquest had ended, had undermined the bases of the juridical convictions prevalent in the Middle Ages and the sixteenth century; the era of the 'bureaucratic monarchy' caused the *letrados* to exercise a considerable degree of eclecticism in their thinking; they were wont to quote, in swift succession, authorities deriving from the most diverse sources of inspiration. Heated controversy was restricted to problems of less wide scope and of more practical character: the patronage system, appointments to public office, the demarcation of spheres of competence between organisations and institutions and so on. Only in the second half of the eighteenth century and at the beginning of the nineteenth was there a revival of theoretical and ideological debate about these problems.

Nevertheless, the right of resistance by the legal methods of 'supplication' and the suspension of laws by local authorities was still an important factor in the seventeenth century (an example of this was the incident arising out of the collection of tribute in Chile in 1639, in Góngora, 1967). There has been a lack of sufficient research into the question of how far recourse to these legal methods survived hereafter.

To summarise, it may be asserted that there always existed in the Indies a very firmly based notion as to the ultimate objectives of the State, which embraced the preservation of the legal and customary rights and privileges of individuals and groups; and, connected with this notion, the preoccupation with the spiritual and temporal 'common weal'. The *Partidas* contain eloquent passages summarising the ideas relating to the notion of 'common weal', with all the consequences implied in that notion. The laws of the Indies are imbued with these underlying presuppositions. As regards the problems connected with the origin and sources of political power, these received great emphasis at times of crisis and discord, but were not prominent in the day-to-day life of the institutions of the Indies. The suspension of the laws by the authorities representing the king, at the instance of the *Cabildos*, constitute the most noteworthy form of legal limitation of the central authority by the interests and the sentiments of the Creoles. It is superfluous to point out that, in any case, the natural respect felt in any traditional society for royal authority was, generally speaking, maintained throughout the colonial period, and it was reinforced by the ritual of everyday political life.

The Indies as appendages of Castile

By virtue of the Papal Bulls, Ferdinand and Isabella became the personal overlords of the new lands, but from 1516 onwards the latter were definitively incorporated into the realms of Castile. Since 1493, however, the administrative process of assimilation had begun, with the appointment of Juan Rodríguez de Fonseca, who the following year was to be Bishop of Badajoz and also Councillor of Castile, to hold overall responsibility for the administration of the Indies. The Council of Castile had juridical competence, and a Lieutenant of the Chief '*Contador*' of Castile had jurisdiction over financial matters. Gradually there was formed a group of councillors of Castile who had some knowledge of the new lands, and this led to the definitive establishment, in 1524, of the Council of the Indies, as part of a process well described by Schäfer. The Provisions of 1519, 1520 and 1523 were the expression of a solemn promise that the recently discovered islands and continents would not be alienated from the Crown. The few private fiefs in the Americas soon passed to the control of the *Audiencias*, and that of Hernán Cortés was the only one of any real importance. The cities and the *vecinos* living in them preferred to be subject to the direct jurisdiction of the king; to belong to the 'royal estate' was synonymous with increased liberty. Mexico City, in a lawsuit initiated against Hernán Cortés over certain forests and pastureland, used as an argument the Provision of Inalienability of 1523.

Castile, in the sixteenth century, was a monarchy incorporating many different 'realms', which were enumerated in the king's full title: Castile, Leon, Toledo, Córdoba, Seville, Granada, Navarre and so on; the last title to be mentioned was the Lordship or Realm of the Islands and Mainland of the Ocean Sea. All these ancient political units were more closely connected with Castile than were the realms of the Crown of Aragon, which all enjoyed a greater measure of autonomy; the Castilian realms, according to Ramos (1967), were 'interlocked'. The Indies were mentioned in the *Cédula* of 1556 in which Philip II announced the abdication of his father: 'the

Kingdoms and lordships of Castile and Leon and others dependent thereon, among which those states of the Indies are included'. The act of annexation, in the lawsuit with Columbus's heirs, was to serve as a basis for the assertion that in 1524 the laws of Castile were in full force in the Indies (Góngora, 1951, 39). Haring (1947, 7), therefore, is incorrect in stating that the Indies were incorporated into the Crown, but not into the realms of Castile: such a contraposition of concepts is appropriate only to the Crown of Aragon with its four dependent realms; in Castile there was no such clear demarcation between the kingdoms and the Crown, either in theory or in practice. It is perfectly true that the Creole lawyers, at the time of Independence, made this distinction, but this was an argument employed for political ends and it did not reflect the historical truth. Although annexation implied a communication of laws and institutions, this did not signify, in the sixteenth century, a systematically unitarist policy, as it did in the eighteenth century. The monarchy was an agglomeration of realms, each enjoying a certain autonomy, although to a lesser degree than in Aragon. The Council of the Indies was, for the time being, 'Supreme', and that of Castile was not supplied with information about developments in the New World.

This problem ceased to be merely juridical, and acquired a political character, in the years of the government of the Count-Duke of Olivares (1621–43), when the problem of the relative degree of unity or diversity assumed the utmost importance for the Spanish monarchy (Jover, 1950; Elliott, 1963). The disturbances in the Indies, which did recur with some frequency, cannot, however, be compared with the Catalan, Portuguese, Sicilian or Neapolitan insurrectionary movements of the 1640s. As it happens, it was at that very time that Juan de Solórzano Pereira was establishing a clear distinction between political realms united to Castile as appendages, such as the Indies, and other realms united to Castile 'with equal principality', and preserving their own laws, examples of which were Flanders, Portugal, Navarre, Aragon and the Italian realms (*Política Indiana*, III, xxxii, 23; IV, xix, 31 and 37; V, xvi, 12). The realms 'with equal principality' were to be governed, in his words, 'as though the King who rules them all together were King of each one of them separately', and public appointments should be filled only with natives of the realm concerned. The concept of 'each realm by itself' had already been defended by the Licentiate Francisco Falcón at the Second Council of Lima in 1567, as applying to the Indies.

Theoretically, it is obvious that the Indies did not enjoy this status, even though they were governed by a Supreme Council, because those parts were governed by the laws of Castile, except where these conflicted with special laws promulgated for the New World, of which there was a very much smaller number. The problem of appointments to public office constitutes, as everybody knows, one of the most disputed and vexed questions of colonial history. There were innumerable royal ordinances which stipulated that the *beneméritos*, the descendants of the conquistadors and the early settlers, should be rewarded with *encomiendas* and public appointments. The legislation with regard to benefices in the ecclesiastical *Cabildos* ordered preference to be given to the 'sons of the patrimony', that is to say, to the descendants of Spanish *vecinos* and settlers who had made their abode in those dominions or 'patrimonies' of the king (Konetzke, 1950). At the same time, however, because those territories were part of the realms of Castile, the natives of the metropolitan country enjoyed the same rights as those born in the Americas, and both groups were referred to as 'Spaniards' in official documents. The attempts of the Creoles to exclude completely the Spanish-born from economic and administrative appointments in the new land were doomed to failure, and the same was true, in any case, in the Aragonese realms, when there were attempts to exclude Castilians from office. Resentment was especially strongly felt, in the seventeenth and eighteenth centuries, among the members of the religious orders, and it led, in 1622, to the system of alternating, in election to episcopal office, between the Spanish-born and the Creoles. The Indies were, therefore, appendages as realms, but they aspired to the status of 'kingdoms in themselves', particularly with regard to appointment to public offices, ecclesiastical benefices and privileges of the 'sons of the patrimony' and the *beneméritos*.

Solórzano used the terms 'kingdoms', 'provinces' and 'lands', virtually as synonyms, when writing of the Indies. The term 'colonies' in the classical Roman sense of nuclei of settlement established in other lands can be found in Solórzano (*Política Indiana*, III, III, 16; III, xxvII, 6; IV, v, 3). Of those writing in the 1630s and 1640s, Jover (1949, 212) distinguishes between those who regarded the Indies as mere outposts of Spanish power (Saavedra Fajardo, in particular), and those others who, like Pellicer or Jáuregui, had a more ecumenical outlook and did not consider Ormuz or Mexico to be in any way inferior in status to the Italian realms; they praised the purity of the Christendom to be found in the Spanish dominions, in contrast to 'heretical' France. Moreover, the word 'colony' did not then have a merely mercantile sense; for this reason we consider, *pace* the emphatic assertion of Ricardo Levene that 'the Indies were not colonies', that they quite evidently were, in the sense that they were colonies for settlement and, like those of Rome, organically connected with the institutions of the metropolitan country and participating in them. The word 'colony' did not acquire the other connotations until the eighteenth century.

The bureaucracy

In the form of government transplanted to the Indies by Spain one can observe the paradox of a traditionalistic society and a State whose central controlling principle was monarchy and which nevertheless, by reason of the distances involved, which were incomparably greater than in Castile, was conditioned by the inescapable fact that the king was invisible and inaccessible. The traditional modes of conduct of the Middle Ages had been based on geographical proximity, almost on the immediate presence of the king's person; in America, however, this presence was always indirect and vicarious, and the effective 'form of government' came to be the bureaucracy. The sociologist S. Eisenstadt is correct in including Spanish America in his category of 'historical bureaucratic societies'. But there were, of course, very different types of bureaucracy: a governor or *Adelantado* in a recently conquered country and a very different approach to the political situation from that of the president of an *Audiencia*. The term 'bureaucracy' is used here in a broad, generic sense of delegated forms of legitimate authority.

In the first place, one must consider the institutions in Castile itself which were responsible for the administration of the Indies. After the tenure of office of Bishop Juan Rodríguez de Fonseca and of a group among the members of the Council of Castile which specialised in American affairs, the Council of the Indies was first established as an independent body in 1524. The system in force in the preceding years had really been government by one person (and of the clique of secretarial and financial officials described by Giménez Fernández, 1953, 60). What was now established was a collegiate system of government, which was to be dominant for about two centuries. It was mostly composed of jurists, and the members also included a few prelates and grandees; the numerical representation of the latter group was greater in the seventeenth century than in the sixteenth. The president and the *Fiscal* were usually the most prominent figures in the long list of councillors. Because they were appointed by the 'Chamber of Castile', a small group within the Council of Castile, those proposed by it for appointments in the Council of the Indies were generally officials of metropolitan Spanish chanceries and *Audiencias*, or members of governmental institutions; only rarely were they officials who had seen service in the Indies. According to the calculations of Schäfer (1935), only one *Oidor* who had served in the Indies was appointed to the Council of the Indies in the sixteenth century, six between 1600 and 1629, and no more were appointed for the rest of the seventeenth century: so that it was not easy for the supreme organ of government to become familiar with the problems with which it had to deal.

By examining the Ordinances of the Council (1542, 1571, 1636), it is possible to get a detailed picture of its functions and activities, although these can be adequately summarised as coinciding with the fundamental objectives of the Spanish State itself, in their particular application to the region. Its jurisdiction, in the strict sense of the term, although it was at first very extensive, was limited after 1542 to taking cognisance of final judicial appeals and cases of notorious injustice, in order to confine its functions more strictly to the sphere of actual government. The perusal and circulation of reports from the New World was deliberately systematised during the tenure of office of Juan de Ovando, in order to acquire fuller information on American affairs; it was further provided, in 1571, that the Council should take measures to collect geographical descriptions, cosmographical tables with details of latitude and longitude, a general history of the natives and a natural history. A fuller knowledge of American affairs and a careful examination of the resorts were to serve as the foundation for sound legislation: the Council was to draft the new decisions made necessary, and consult the king on the matter; and it was to confirm the ordinances and statutes which were promulgated by the authorities established in the colonies. It would take measures to achieve the appropriate and mutually consistent demarcation of administrative, jurisdictional and ecclesiastical provinces. Questions arising out of the *encomienda* system came to the attention of the Council on the occasion of the royal confirmation of grants of *encomienda* and when a final decision had to be made in disputes arising out of claims to *encomiendas*. Proposals for appointment of senior secular officials, and to important ecclesiastical posts, for submission to Rome, were embodied in 'consultations', a procedure whereby the king chose names from a list of candidates which included details of their past careers. A close relationship between the place-seekers and the councillors was, in these circumstances, inevitable, and the consequence of this was an increase in the power of the councillors; this explains the tenacious struggle of the Council against the establishment of a more restricted 'Chamber of the Indies', which enjoyed a monopoly of such 'consultations' between 1600 and 1609, and achieved definitive control of this process in 1644 (Schäfer; Phelan, 1967). Apart from the right to put forward candidates for ecclesiastical appointments, as provided for in the patronage agreement, the Council took cognisance of all other matters connected with religion – the approval of documents emanating from the Pope and the generals of the orders, the construction of churches and monasteries and so on. Matters connected with war and with the Royal Treasury were, of course, of special concern to this body. The reports arising out of royal 'visits' and the *Residencias* of the higher officials made it possible for the Council to exercise supervision over administrative discipline and the moral conduct of officials in the colonies. In general, therefore, the Council, especially after the crisis provoked by years of reform (1542 and 1568–71), might be described as a legislative and supervisory body, acting by means of general and special legislation appointments to public office and the judicial supervision of officials. This ideal conception, however, was inevitably attenuated in the course of the years, on account of the difficulties of governing a whole new world from a distance, from a country which in Europe was subjected to immense military and financial strain.

The crucial problems, which arose at times of reorganisation and crisis, were resolved, not by the Council of the Indies but by large-scale extraordinary *Juntas*, in which the president and the councillors sat with the members of other Councils of the Crown, prelates and prominent men who enjoyed the king's confidence. This procedure was used to decide, in Burgos in 1512 and in Valladolid in 1513, the first important laws governing the *encomienda* system, and plans were made for the expedition of Pedrarias, which was the first time that the '*Requerimiento*' was used. The *Junta* held in Saragossa in 1518 was attended not only by Fonseca and the usual group of councillors and bureaucrats, but also Peter Martyr of Angleria and, apparently, Las Casas. The *Junta* of Barcelona of 1529 reorganised the system of government of New Spain, and the meeting was attended by members of the Councils of the Indies, of Castile and of the Treasury. The Valladolid *Junta* of 1542 drafted the New Laws: in addition to the President of the Council of the Indies, Cardinal Loaysa, who was shortly afterwards to be convicted of peculation, there were present the former President of the second *Audiencia* of Mexico, Ramírez de Fuenleal, Bishop of Cuenca, and the *Fiscal* of Castile, Gregorio López, the great commentator on the *Partidas*, who was to be the second *Visitador* sent out by the Council of the Indies and who was to prove the allegations of corruption. At the *Junta Magna* of 1568, which imparted instructions to the Viceroys Toledo and Enríquez, there were present the President of the Council of Castile and the Grand Inquisitor, Cardinal Espinosa, the

Visitador of the Council of the Indies Juan de Ovando, the Prince of Eboli, members of various Councils, three theologians, and the future Viceroy, Toledo. The famous *Junta* of Valladolid of 1550, the purpose of which was not legislation but theoretical controversy, is known to us in detail through the documents in which the theologian Domingo de Soto summarised the propositions and replies of Las Casas and Juan Ginés de Sepúlveda.

The *Casa de Contratación* was established in Seville in 1503, and by that date Seville's monopoly of trade already existed in practice (Chaunu, 1959, 109), both as regards the export of merchandise to the Caribbean and the reception of imports, the appointment of ships' captains, instructions and reports: these were the functions established in the first Ordinances, which appeared in the same year. Its members – the treasurer, the *Contador* and the factor – also exercised jurisdiction over maritime matters until they were replaced by judges versed in that branch of the law, in 1584. The character of the institution thus became more complex: on the one hand, there was the *Audiencia*, responsible for deciding questions relating to mercantile law, which was governed by the laws of the merchants of Burgos concerning companies, all types of marine contracts, freights, insurance, legal disputes between merchants and their factors, litigation involving ships' crews and so on. On the other hand, there was the administrative department, which was always headed by the treasurer, the *Contador* and the factor. In the ordinances of 1503, which were still influenced by the notion of the 'entrepôt', the most urgent problem was state commerce for the maintenance of settlers and soldiers in Hispaniola. By the time of the Ordinances of Monzón (1510), colonisation and private commerce were more fully developed, and the *Casa de Contratación* exercised official supervision over ships and passengers, of the Customs, and the receipt and recording of precious metals dispatched to private individuals or the king. It would be superfluous to describe here the procedure for the registration of ships and their cargoes, the mechanism of registration and the statistics which were compiled, all these matters being of fundamental importance for the study of the history of maritime traffic with the Indies, after the studies of this matter by Chaunu. In addition, it was responsible for the supervision of the payment of the *almojarifazgo*, the *alcabala* and the *avería*, or contribution to the costs of military defence against hostile navies. This supervision, however, was not confined to Customs matters, but also, as has been observed by Puente y Olea (1900), involved tutelary functions appropriate to medieval commerce, and in this field the *Casa de Contratación* recorded its most positive achievements, in arranging for training in seamanship by the chief pilots and, after 1552, by the establishment of a chair of cosmography to instruct those who embarked on a career as ships' pilots. The early years of the *Casa de Contratación* were, therefore, marked by the activities of Juan de la Cosa, Américo Vespucio, Vicente Yáñez Pinzón and Alonso de Santa Cruz. Finally, mention must be made of another important function of this institution, the maintenance of the register of passengers to the Indies; this included details of each individual, together with his family and domestic servants, on evidence supported by sworn witnesses, and it also recorded the place of origin of each passenger, his social rank or occupation and his credentials as an 'Old Christian'; this category excluded recent converts to Christianity, Jews and Moors, and those who had at any time been convicted by the Inquisition. In this way, the overall supervision established by the *Casa de Contratación* embraced not only technical and financial matters, but was also designed to reinforce that unanimity of consensus characteristic of the Spain of the time with regard to the 'Old Christian' caste, based on the exclusion of the 'New Christians'; this was one of the most important underlying assumptions of that century in Spain, and the authorities wished to apply it to the New World as well.

The basic administrative unit in the Indies was the local governorship. However, the governors headed institutions of widely differing type and origin. One characteristic they had in common, however, was that they always exercised judicial functions of first instance and certain governmental prerogatives which (to dispense with a more detailed definition) embraced all matters concerned with the common weal of the territory under their control, including the power to legislate by means of ordinances. Government and justice were always functions which had to be exercised in different ways, because of the instrinsic distinction between them, even though they were exercised by the same authority. Thus, the governor himself did not intervene directly in legal actions but left this to the 'lieutenant-governor', who was usually a *letrado*.

The specific characteristics of the governor varied greatly, depending on the historical context in which he operated. In the case of Christopher Columbus, the viceroyalty and the governorship had been granted as hereditary offices; they were revoked, but the Council of Castile, which was more traditionalistic in its outlook than the representatives of the Crown, ratified the hereditary titles in its judicial decisions of 1511 and 1520, and the Kings had to accept these decisions, and re-acquire their title to these offices in 1535. The real position of Diego Colón and, later, of his widow, was that they were purely and simply powerful figures in the colonial territories, surrounded by a small court but always subject to the supervision of royal officials and judges.

Only after the conquest on the Mainland, which was definitely outside the sphere of jurisdiction of the Columbus family, did there first appear – the obvious example being Balboa – governors in the strict sense of the term, and their authority was to be definitively established from 1510 onwards. In some cases they were designated by the conquistadors themselves (Balboa, Cortés, Valdivia, Martínez de Irala and others); on other occasions they had come from Spain after being directly appointed by the king (for example, Pedrarias Dávila); on still other occasions, their appointment was included in a *capitulación* (Montejo, Pizarro and others); but the decisive characteristic that united them all was the impulse to conquer or to colonise, and their basic assumption was that the newly won land was a 'patrimony' which the king was obligated to grant them. The salary received was the least important part of the governor's emoluments: what was far more important was the power to assign Indians to *encomiendas*, and this included the right to create *encomiendas* for oneself. Nevertheless, governorships were offices tenable for the life of one man only, for the Kings never again promulgated legal instruments similar to the *Capitulaciones* of Santa Fé. However, many of them received, more as an honour than as an additional responsibility, the title of *Adelantado*, and this was sometimes hereditary. The governor as a characteristic type – the conquistador and *encomendero* – should, theoretically, have disappeared after the promulgation of the New Laws, but the figure persisted in the poorer lands, which were incapable of financing any other sort of government. Thus Tucumán, in 1550 and 1560, had governors who received 3,000 pesos per annum, accruing from the small sums collected by way of tithes, fines inflicted by the *Cámara*, and the property of deceased persons; whereas the services of the Indians in their *encomiendas* were valued at 4,000–5,000 pesos. In Chile, a governor of the *encomendero* type such as Pedro de Valdivia received a salary of 2,000 pesos; a governor without Indians assigned to his service, and whose sole remuneration was the salary paid by the Crown, such as Don García Hurtado de Mendoza, received from his father, the Viceroy, an allowance of 12,000 pesos. It is understandable that the Council, in 1558, should have preferred to designate an *encomendero* as governor, and that this system should have continued in Chile until 1592.

Finally, there was another variety – the administrative and bureaucratic governor, who was not involved in the process of conquest. Examples of this type were, in a sense, Bobadilla and Ovando in Hispaniola, although the subordinates of Ovando undertook military expansion in the direction of

Puerto Rico and Cuba. After the promulgation of the New Laws, this new type gradually prevailed over the others; this process coincided with the ending of the phase of Conquest. Even though the governors were generally soldiers who had seen service in Europe or the Indies, their outlook reflected the overall bureaucratic tendency of the colonial era, except in places where continual warfare caused the persistence of a more military system. The governors of more bureaucratic mentality received no legitimate emoluments apart from their salary, and remained in office for, at the most, ten years.

From the time of Columbus himself, in 1493, the governors usually held the appointment of Captain-General – sometimes merely 'Captain' – and this conferred military command and jurisdiction. Furthermore, Columbus himself, who was hereditary Viceroy and Governor by virtue of the *Capitulaciones* of Santa Fé, was able to exercise those authorities only over the entrepôt and nascent colony for the space of seven years, and he always preferred to use his other title, that of Admiral, which conferred rights over ships, seamen, goods in transit and even over the coastal areas, in accordance with the prerogatives of the Admirals of Castile. The simultaneous tenure of the offices of the governorship and of the captaincy-general had the effect of increasing the governor's prestige.

In conjunction with the governorship, which was the basic political entity, there arose, as new territories were settled or conquered, the *Audiencias* and the viceroyalties. When the first *Audiencia* was established in 1511, in Santo Domingo, and Diego Colón succeeded in re-acquiring his title as Viceroy of the Indies, in the same year, uniting this appointment with those of Governor and Captain-General which he already possessed, this meant the establishment in the Indies, for the first time, of an administrative apparatus of a high level of complexity. A similar system was to come into force in Mexico (the first *Audiencia* being established in 1527 and the Viceroyalty in 1535) and Peru (where the *Audiencia* was established by the New Laws of 1542 and the Viceroyalty in the same year). A similar system, though on a much smaller scale, came into force wherever *Audiencias* were established within the territories of governorships, whether the *Audiencia* itself directly assumed the responsibility of government (as in Mexico before the arrival of the first Viceroy, in Panama in 1538 and so on), or there was an individual as governor, as occurred more often.

Lalinde Abadía (1967) has termed this complex system 'viceregal-senatorial' or 'gubernatorial-senatorial', and has emphasised two important aspects: (1) the origin of the system was the Crown of Aragon, as has already been observed by other writers, and this is explained by the fact that

88

in Aragon, as in the Indies, the king, who was not resident in the territory he ruled, wished to have personal representatives of high rank, with such titles as viceroy, governor-general, lieutenant-general and so on; this hardly ever occurred in Castile; (2) in the Indies, however, just as in Castile, the *Audiencia* specialised in the dispensing of justice and the viceroy or governor in the tasks of government, independently; this tendency may possibly be explained by the considerable power of the jurists in Castile, whereas in the Aragonese realms the justice dispensed by the *Audiencia* proceeded, theoretically, from the viceroy himself.

The complex superior governmental structure which thus arose in the Indies emphasised, quite naturally, the representation of the king vis-à-vis his subjects. The acts of the *Audiencia* were under royal seal, and the Provisions which they promulgated were headed with the name and titles of the monarch. The viceroy was usually a nobleman or, on more rare occasions, a *letrado* or a prelate, and he represented the king's person in an even more evident manner. He possessed, for example, sweeping authority to grant pardons. The reception of the royal seal by the *Audiencia*, which in the case of Santo Domingo happened fifteen years after its establishment, and which made the institution equal in rank to the chanceries of Spain, was one of the important acts of the political ritual of colonial times, and represented a symbolic attempt to compensate, albeit only partly, for the permanent absence of the king.

In broad outline, the system is easy to describe. The *Audiencias* functioned, above all, as courts of appeal; the viceroy or governor dealt with government, war, the supervision of the Royal Treasury, and ordinary justice (exercised by the lieutenant-governor, who was a *letrado*). The viceroy was also president of the *Audiencia*, but he was not permitted to intervene directly in specifically judicial matters; these were left to the *Oidores*. The *Audiencia* sometimes operated as an ordinary law court of first instance, especially in litigation between natives and Spaniards, which were considered privileged 'court cases'.

This brief description does not, of course, cover all aspects of institutional activity; this embraced all the important problems that arose in the bigger colonial centres of population. The *Audiencia* was not, of course, only a law court, in the strictly judicial sense of the term. The Castilian monarchy placed its trust in the *letrados* and made them the preferred instruments of its activity. In the Indies, through the *Audiencias*, the Crown confided to their sense of justice – which it desired to maintain as an impartial authority vis-à-vis the conquistadors and the colonists – all the problems arising out of the juxtaposition of different races; measures to ensure fair treatment, the enforcement of the laws designed to protect the natives, the punishment of offending *encomenderos*, and the official approbation of those who had complied with the laws in order that they should receive *mercedes* in Spain. The direct correspondence carried on by the *Audiencia* with the Council of the Indies made it possible for it to give all kinds of advice and opinions on general aspects of government, as well as specific recommendations. Moreover, the *Audiencia*, in common with all the other governmental institutions, was empowered to promulgate legislative Ordinances. The defence of the Crown's jurisdiction against that of the Church endowed it with authority in its dealings with the Church; its ability to ratify the Ordinances of the *Cabildos* and the tributes established by the latter, gave it a similar power in its dealings with the Spanish *vecinos*. This tribunal, therefore, displayed all the virtues and defects of men with legal training. Legislation was designed to isolate them, at any price, from the influence of the environment in order to safeguard their impartiality. The members of the first *Audiencia* of Mexico were dismissed from office on the grounds that they had usurped the lands of the Indians and made the latter work for their (the *Audiencia* members') profit; its President, Nuño de Guzmán, who had been both Governor and Conquistador of Pánuco, had made a business of the capture of slaves in that territory for sale in the islands. The second *Audiencia*, however, staffed by men of the calibre of Ramírez de Fuenleal and Vasco de Quiroga, adhered strictly to the legal framework. The visits and *Residencias* of the *Oidores* usually provide abundant proof of the ineffective nature of many of the controls; but they also show that the theoretical level of standards and of ethical judgment remained intact, and that corrupt practices were never sanctioned by law (Góngora, 1951, 56–62).

During the sixteenth and seventeenth centuries, the *Oidores* were usually Spanish, rather than American-born. Solórzano attempted to secure the appointment of Creole lawyers, but these men had to be appointed in a province other than that of their birth, abandon their property and former connections, and this in many cases made the prospect of appointment unattractive. The Spanish-born were more easily able to obtain expeditiously the favour of the Council or of the Chamber of the Indies, but their children found it easy to acquire connections with the Creole aristocracies and settled down in their new places of residence, and this circumstance sometimes influenced the behaviour of their fathers. Despite all the lapses in the fulfilment of the ethical precepts enjoined by the law, as has been observed by Phelan (1967), the Spanish bureaucratic system, the models *par excellence* of which until the end of the eighteenth century were the *Oidores* and *Fiscales* of each *Audiencia*, possessed many 'rational' values (in the sense in which Max Weber uses the term): a scholarly professional training based on the heritage of Roman law, a vision of society as it should ideally be, which reflected a coherent conception of the world enshrined in natural and divine law; there was a tendency towards systematic organisation in the appointment of officials, with provision for their retirement at a certain age; salaries were fixed, even though insufficient; and there was supervision of their private lives in order to ensure the fulfilment of their public duties – in other words, to realise the ideal of the bureaucracy as an institution.

All the attributions of the governor were possessed, to an even greater degree, by the viceroy. These were formally summarised in the provisions governing his appointment: the service of God, the conversion of the natives, the maintenance, colonisation and betterment of the land. The Instructions which were given to them when they were appointed to their posts were very much more detailed, and became stereotyped by the end of the sixteenth century. Don Antonio de Mendoza, in 1535, was entrusted with the building of churches, the supervision of missionary centres in Indian lands, the study of the *encomienda* system as a whole with a view to deciding whether to make it hereditary, the system of revenue-collection and general matters connected with the Royal Treasury, the Mint, fortresses and garrisons and so on. The Viceroy Cañete took to Peru, in 1555, one 'Instruction' for peacetime use and another for wartime, because that country was still threatened with insurrection: these Instructions included authority and advice for the encouragement, by all possible means, of the colonisation of the land, the consolidation of the *encomienda* system as a means of collecting tribute, the measures to stamp out vagrancy and other activities prejudicial to Spanish society, authorisation to draw on funds from the Royal Treasury for the purposes of pacification and so on. In all cases, the keystone of the power of the viceroy (or of the governor, in the smaller territories) in the sixteenth and seventeenth centuries was his power to assign Indians in *encomienda* and to make grants of land. It was through these acts that the social force of the aristocracy was decisively established; for this reason the latter depended, fundamentally, on the bureaucracy.

If the viceroy enshrined what might be termed the nobiliary ideal of the Spanish State (as did the governor, in the same way, in a less sophisticated environment), and the *Audiencia* enshrined the juridical ideal, the two institutions were united in their acceptance of another fundamental aspect of this system of government, that is to say, the notion that all important decisions should be taken 'in council' – they could not be derived from the exclusively personal initiative of one man. The king governed 'in council' throughout medieval and modern Europe, and this was a guarantee that a decision was arrived at with deliberation, even though such a decision was, in the last resort, taken by one man. This principle was reflected in the colonies in two ways. One of these was the duty of the viceroy to solicit the opinion of the 'notables' when really difficult problems arose; this category of people usually included the bishop, the canons, the superiors of religious orders, the *letrados* and old-established and meritorious *vecinos*. There was, however, a 'council' of a more technical nature, formed in the governorships by the officers of the Royal Treasury, and, in places where such an appointment existed, by the *Alcalde Mayor* (a *letrado*) or the lieutenant-governor who acted as legal adviser to the governor. In the viceroyalties and headquarters of the *Audiencias* there arose, separately, two types of council or '*Acuerdo*': the *Oidores* discussed matters pertaining to government, and the royal officers matters pertaining to finance. There was a sharp distinction between a council with 'consultative opinion' and the decision of the viceroy or governor, who, moreover, convened these councils at his absolute discretion. One of the principal accusations, enjoying unanimous support, against Blasco Núñez de Vela was that he had enforced laws without conferring with the *Audiencia*.

In this way, the underlying unity of the problems to be resolved resulted in the laws of the Indies entrusting in some way, not always with specific and detailed demarcation, the cognisance of the same matters to various authorities. This was to ensure, as far as possible, shrewd judgment of the issues and a mutual equilibrium of interests. A problem such as the protection of the natives, for example, was entrusted to all the secular and ecclesiastical authorities, the intention being not so much to ensure the formal demarcation of spheres of juridical competence as to achieve an overall consensus along the same general lines. This represents a 'material' rather than a 'formal' conception of law (Góngora, 1951, last chapter). In other fields, however, where the protection of the legal rights of the Spaniards was the first priority and it was desired to place some limitations on the arbitrary power of the government, it was necessary to establish an extremely fine demarcation between the sphere of government and that of justice. The fulfilment of the precepts of sound government might be prejudicial to one party: an injunction ordering a *vecino* to remove his cattle from some place in order not to prejudice the natives, for example, or the incorporation of an *encomienda* into the Crown. A series of *Cédulas Reales*, from 1552 onwards, made provision for a plea of unjustifiable injury against acts of the viceroy, to be submitted to the *Audiencia*, in order to prevent the infringement of private rights; but, in order not to paralyse the governmental procedures, this plea had only a returnable effect, and did not stay the execution of the viceregal order. There was an increasingly specific definition of the supremacy of the government as regards ordinances designed for the common good, and also, to counterbalance this, of the superiority of the *Audiencia* in matters concerned with justice and the safeguarding of acquired rights; in such cases, the plea of the injured party had the effect of suspending the viceregal decree. When there was a conflict of opinion as to whether the matter in hand was a matter for justice or for government, the final decision rested with the viceroy, but he informed the Council of his decision.

The *Audiencias* achieved their maximum influence when they were simultaneously exercising the governorship on a corporate basis, as was the case with the two Mexican *Audiencias* between 1527 and 1535, or the first *Audiencia* in Chile in the period 1567–75, even though in both cases the captaincy-general was exercised by a separate authority – in Mexico by Hernán Cortés, and in Chile by the president of the *Audiencia*.

The 'superior government' of the viceroy was exercised, in the first place, in the *Audiencias* of which he was president and the seat of which was the capital of the viceroyalty (Mexico City or Lima); but he also exercised authority over other governorships and *Audiencias* within the bounds of the viceroyalty. The viceroy of Peru was governor and captain-general of the *Audiencias* of Quito and Charcas and even, in the early stages of colonial rule, the president of those bodies, in spite of the distances involved, but he was soon deprived of this last attribution, though still retaining the other appointments. Panama and Chile, which were governorships and captaincies-general enjoying a greater degree of autonomy, and where the governors were presidents of the respective *Audiencias*, nevertheless were obliged to obey, in questions of war, finance and even government, the orders of the viceroy in Lima. This connection was flexible, and, by virtue of the very nature of the factors and problems involved, subject to a wide measure of discretion in its actual application. It was precisely this 'discretional' factor, however, which was one of the most marked characteristics of the Spanish system. There was an analogous relationship between the viceroy of New Spain and the *Audiencia* of Nueva Galicia.

Viceroys, *Audiencias*, governors and *Cabildos* had legislative powers; even though their ordinances required ratification by the Crown, they acquired force immediately and for an indefinite period, except when expressly revoked by the Council. The mere act of refraining from ratifying a local law, on the part of the central administration, allowed the ordinance concerned to remain in force. This degree of autonomy constituted a considerable counterweight to the centralising tendencies inherent in the

Castilian monarchy (Altamira, 1945). Another juridical institution which also had this effect was the refusal to enforce laws originating from metropolitan Spain, which has been discussed earlier in this chapter; this tendency was particularly important in the governorship territories, rather than in the seats of the viceroyalties, because of the lesser degree of control from the metropolis in those parts.

Also belonging to the higher bureaucracy were the extraordinary judges of various kinds. There were, among others, investigatory judges, such as Bobadilla in Hispaniola, who in that capacity deprived Columbus of office; specially commissioned judges, such as the Jeronymites sent by Cisneros to carry out a complete reform of the government of the islands; *Residencia* judges who investigated the conduct of government officials; specially commissioned judges sent to Peru, with wide powers, such as Tomás de Berlanga and Vaca de Castro; the *Visitador* Tello de Sandoval, who took with him to Mexico the New Laws and, acting in conjunction with the Viceroy, contributed to attenuating their enforcement. In all such cases, the extraordinary judges were empowered to revise ordinary judicial acts and to legislate, particularly through the mechanism of the *Visita*, or to judge officials after their tenure of office had expired (*Residencias*). They represented one aspect of the power of supervision that the administrative centre held over distant provinces and over all kinds of institutions. The Council of the Indies was itself the subject of a secret inquiry in 1542, and as a result two councillors and the President himself were found guilty of receiving bribes from conquistadors; the *Visita* of Juan de Ovando, from 1567 onwards, provoked a complete overhaul of the system of government in the Indies, which the Viceroys were to put into effect.

Among the subordinate jurisdictions, mention must be made of the minor governorships, which were not held in conjunction with a captaincy-general, and were completely subject to viceroys, *Audiencias* or to some governor who combined that rank with that of captain-general.

All the governmental districts, whatever the designation of the person heading them, were formed by cities and towns which embraced, in addition to the actual built-up areas concerned, their *términos* or jurisdictional territory – the area that in Castile was called the *alfoz*. Within these areas, jurisdiction might be in the hands of the respective *Alcaldes Ordinarios*, or subject to royal officials, appointed by the king or by the governors, and this had the effect of limiting municipal autonomy, in accordance with a practice dating from fourteenth-century Castile. These officials were called *Alcaldes Mayores* in Mexico and Guatemala, and *Corregidores* in almost all the other American territories. Whatever their designation, they were justiciars-in-chief and 'captains of war', and this gave them jurisdiction of second instance over the *alcaldes* and command over the militias. They were appointed by the king from Spain, usually at high salaries and with their residence in the larger administrative centres; or they might be appointed by the viceroy or governor from among the rich *vecinos* of the city concerned. The former group were of the more bureaucratic type, whereas the latter were usually *vecinos* and *encomenderos*. The simultaneous tenure of an *encomienda* and a *Corregimiento* was forbidden by the Ordinances of the *Audiencia* of 1563 and by a *Cédula* promulgated in Peru in 1569. In Chile, however, there is evidence that the *Corregidores* were normally *encomenderos* in the districts under their jurisdiction, and an attempt to abolish this duality of function was circumvented by the governor in 1638.

The appointment of *Corregidor* of Natives (*Corregidor de Naturales*) arose from specifically American circumstances and situations. The forerunners of these officials were, according to Simpson (1950, 86), the 'administrators' provided for in the Instructions imparted by Cisneros to the Jeronymite Friars in 1516; these men were supposed to be 'old-established settlers of upright moral conduct, who have treated their Indians well'. In 1530 the second Mexican *Audiencia* put forward the same plan, but stipulated that the office-holders should not be *encomenderos* but poor *vecinos*, appointed for a period of one year, renewable for a further year, and subject to a *Residencia* inquiry at the expiration of their tenure of office. The Crown and the *Audiencia* envisaged an official whose function it was to protect the Indians, and for this reason the system was first tried among the Indians who were direct vassals of the king, in Mexico in 1530, and later among those assigned to *encomenderos* (1550). In Peru the institution was established by the President Lope García de Castro, who in 1565 described the objectives of the system as follows: the officials were to ensure the loyalty of the Indians, concentrate them in urban centres of population and dispense justice to them; they were to act as a brake on the attempts of the missionaries to constitute themselves as a secular authority among the natives and make use of their services; they were also to restrain abuses of power on the part of the *curacas* and *caciques*. A special responsibility of the *Corregidor* was that of visiting his district and compiling a register of tribute-payers; he was paid a fee for each Indian included in the register (Lohmann, 1957, 49–51). Subsequently, this arrangement apparently led to abuses, and the officials were paid a government salary, under Viceroy Toledo; this was financed from the tribute revenue, as was the case in Mexico. The *Corregimiento* normally included several *pueblos*, with jurisdiction over them, but subject to that of the nearest Spanish-inhabited city and to the *Audiencia*.

This original tutelary concept was soon replaced by the objective of rewarding those *vecinos* who had been left without *encomiendas*. Another problem that arose, however, was that of the right to nominate persons to these offices: the Crown appointed Spanish-born claimants, who had managed to gain the favour of the Council, and came to the Americas with the very definite objective of enriching themselves during their short term of office, which was normally about three years. The viceroy and the Creoles naturally protested against competition from this quarter; the viceroys saw it as an abridgment of their right to reward *vecinos* or their own servants and retainers. In Peru, around 1670, there were up to 85 vacancies for the office of *Corregidor*, of which the Viceroy appointed 52 from among about 600 candidates, after holding prior consultations with the *Oidores* 'in council' (Lohmann, 1957, 124).

The lower-level and ill-paid bureaucracy in each territory became the mouthpiece, quite openly from the end of the sixteenth century in Peru, and almost certainly in Mexico at about the same time, of complaints regarding illicit trade carried on by the *Corregidores* with the Indians and the Spaniards in their districts, especially on the part of those who had come from Spain and incurred great expenses to make the journey, and re-covered this outlay during their short term of office. The *Corregidores* and the suppliers who made available for them resources in money and in kind (the *aviadores*) exploited their monopoly of the Indian market, selling cloth (both Castilian and local), cattle and alcoholic drink. The *repartimiento*, a term which Lohmann (1957, 427) maintains was used for the first time in this sense in 1676, consisted not only of the mere exercise of commercial activities but also in a coercive supervision of the distribution of goods and raw materials for manufacture among the Indians, through the *caciques*. The prices of manufactured goods, the wages of the weavers and other workers who received raw materials, or of the muleteers who transported goods with their drives, were arbitrarily fixed by the *Corregidor*, who used his jurisdictional authority for the purpose. All competition with other merchants was eliminated, and this consideration played an important part in contributing to the abolition of the office during the era of reforms inspired by the Enlightenment. However, in the time of Archbishop Mogrovejo and the Second Viceroy Cañete (the 1590s) and throughout the seventeenth century, there was a chorus of condemnation of the business dealings of the *Corregidores* and of the sufferings of the Indians that resulted from them.

There has not been sufficient historical research to give a detailed description of the characteristics of the class of military officers commanding the small regular forces that were maintained in the sixteenth and seventeenth centuries in the fortresses, garrisons (*presidios*), ports, vice-regal capitals and on the Araucanian frontier.

The financial bureaucracy comprising the Royal Officers (which had already taken shape in Columbus's time) and the officials of the Tribunals of Accounts (which were established in Mexico City, Lima and Bogotá only in 1605) is now well known, as far as its organisation and functions are concerned, as a result of the researches of Sánchez Bella, 1968. However, the social and political situation and status of the Treasurers, *Contadores*, Factors and *Veedores* of the Royal Treasury have not been, as far as we know, the subject of detailed research. Such a personality as Gonzalo Fernández de Oviedo, the *Veedor* of Mines in Darién, was exceptional; but it is of interest to observe his activities in the pearl trade (Otte, 1958) and, in general, the commercial bent of the Royal Officers of that time, which gave rise to *Reales Cédulas* prohibiting these activities (Pérez de Tudela, 1959). For the greater part of the sixteenth century the Royal Officers belonged wholly to the world of the conquistadors and the *vecinos*, as is shown by documents of the time of Hernán Cortés and the Civil Wars in Peru. They participated in the proceedings of the *Cabildo* with the same right as the *Regidores*, and were advisers to the governor. Their appointment as *Regidores* in perpetuity lasted, according to Solórzano, until 1621, from which date these offices were sold for the benefit of the Royal Treasury. However, since 1560, when they were granted jurisdiction over financial matters – at a time when all the *vecinos* were in some way connected with the Treasury – they developed closer connections with the bureaucratic milieu (Sánchez Bella, 1968). Solórzano deplored the arrogance and striving after ceremonial honours displayed by these officials; this was a sure sign of the rivalry existing between them and the *Audiencias*. They were appointed from Spain, and most of the appointments were filled by the Spanish-born.

It is possible, therefore, to distinguish different levels of importance within the bureaucracy established at the time of the foundation of the new realms. The highest level, viceroys, governors of the administrative type, the *Oidores* and *Fiscales* of the *Audiencias*, represented the Spanish State in the strictest sense, both according to 'nobiliary' and to legalistic concepts. In contrast to this group, the *Adelantados*, governors who were also captains-general, ordinary governors, military officers, *Alcaldes Mayores* and *Corregidores* having jurisdiction over Spaniards, were usually drawn from the caste of conquistadors and rich *vecinos*. The Royal Officers, the *Contadores* of the

Tribunals of Accounts, the middle-level officials of the *Audiencias,* had a situation intermediate between that of the more skilled citizens and the more honourable status of the members of the *Audiencia.* Finally, the *Corregidores* having jurisdiction over Indians reflected the concept of public office as a mere profit-making activity or a sinecure, suitable for *vecinos* of limited prestige or upstart Spaniards aiming to get rich quickly.

It may be observed that the moral standards of the bureaucracy declined in proportion to the effective absorption of that body into the 'Creole' environment. The viceroys and the judges of the *Audiencias* constituted the highest model of that bureaucracy, the one that most faithfully reflected the 'State'; it was assumed that they displayed the highest standards of decorum, impartiality and integrity; they were forbidden to possess *encomiendas* or land, to engage in trade, to accept gifts, to contract marriage with a woman belonging to any of the families of the district concerned, to stand as godfather to the children of the local inhabitants and so on; they were paid the highest possible salaries. The *Residencia* inquiries re-established the ideal concept of administrative order, even though this might have been violated by particular officials. Consequently, the Creoles were admitted to appointments in the bureaucracy only in provinces other than those of their birth and upbringing, in order to maintain those standards. This was the origin of the complaints, whether founded or unfounded, the increasing tension throughout the seventeenth and eighteenth centuries between the desire for promotion within the bureaucratic structure on the part of some individuals, and the greater possibilities of obtaining such promotion by the exercise of influence in Spain, on the part of others. The very concept of an exemplary administrative order, which was part and parcel of the Spanish system, was always extremely difficult to carry out in practice.

Cities, Cabildos, *estates, militias; the two republics*

The entire system of defence of this small number of Europeans living among an aboriginal population which overwhelmingly outnumbered it made concentration indispensable. The fortresses, in early times, were precarious, and developed into more monumental structures only when they began to suffer the attacks of other European navies. The American 'cities', the number of which increased with the growth of colonisation and settlement, were open to the surrounding country: it was a renaissance of the ancient city, in contrast to the fortified city of the Middle Ages (Braudel, 1967, 401). Ovando and Velázquez played important parts as founders of cities in Santo Domingo and Cuba. Of later foundation were the cities on the mainland, in places determined by the earlier Indian centres of population, or in places corresponding to the new pattern of commercial and administrative relationships. The colonists were obliged to concentrate in order to preserve their entire system of ecclesiastical, judicial and political organisation. The cities were predominantly 'agro-administrative' in character, according to Morse (1971): to possess the political status of *ciudad* or *villa*, to be the seat of authority and have a territory under its jurisdiction, was essential; moreover, the dominant social strata derived their income from mining and later from livestock raising and agriculture – in any case, from the surrounding country, and not from trade, as was the case in the cities of northern Europe. Furthermore, this characteristic emphasised by Morse was also predominant in the centre of Spain, between the Duero and the Guadiana, according to the description given by García de Valdeavellano (1960): the cities were military and agrarian in character, and thus differed from both those on the Pilgrim Road to Santiago and the great Muslim cities of the south.

The Spanish medieval city was based on notions appropriate to an urban civilisation, inherited from the Ancient World, especially from Aristotle's *Politics*. The latter and the political writings of St Thomas and Egidius Romanus were the basis of the thought of Rodrigo Sánchez de Arévalo, who wrote his *Suma de la Política* in 1454 or 1455. Maravall (1960, 236–44) has noted that the term 'citizen' became fashionable during the reign of the Catholic Sovereigns, and occurs in contemporary literature; it was also used, later, at the time of the War of the *Comunidades* in Castile, and by Fray Alonso de Castrillo, the author of the *Tratado de la República*. The latter author distinguishes three units of social life – the home, the city and mankind – paying particular attention to the city. Although it is based on the premise, formulated by St Augustine, that the origin of political domination is tyrannical, the city or republic constitutes an attempt to harmonise natural liberty and equality with social obligations; it is 'the noblest of all companies'. It appears to us that there is some significance in the conjunction of home and city in the writings of Castrillo; for in the European city, before life became wholly orientated towards the market economy, the home was the basic framework of life, with its characteristic combination of production for domestic consumption and for the market, a system having its roots in the village mentality (Otto Brunner, 1958). The home had a patriarchal constitution: it was formed by the children, poor relations, servants, slaves and so on, all subject to the authority of the *paterfamilias*.

The city, in its turn, was thought of as a large-scale and self-sufficient home. In addition to the actual buildings, it included – both in Spain and in the Indies – the cultivated plots of the *vecinos* (called *chácaras* in the Indies) in the suburbs; communal lands for the grazing of cattle for domestic use and as places of recreation for the *vecinos*; pasture-lands for cattle-raising, under the supervision of herdsmen paid by the proprietors; woodland for the supply of firewood for the community; and *Propios* (lands to provide income for the *Cabildo*). Even within the built-up areas, the houses had vineyards and orchards adjoining them. Notions derived from village life persisted in the city.

The word 'republic' in the Indies recurred frequently in official documents. The term 'a good republican' was applied to the *vecino* who had acquitted himself well in the discharge of appointments in the *Cabildo*. The 'two republics', that of the Spaniards and that of the Indians, were considered, in the *Libro de la Governación Espiritual* of Juan de Ovando, the mainstays of the 'state of the Indies'; for the latter, even though its apex was the king, admitted of an organic differentiation between two distinct 'republics', similar to the distinction recognised between the spiritual and the temporal orders.

The city was supposed to have a *Cabildo*. From 1507 onwards the *vecinos* of Hispaniola elected their *alcaldes*, but the rest of the *Cabildo* was constituted by *Regidores* appointed by the Crown and by officers of the Treasury. There were timid attempts to establish a system of election of *Regidores* to fill vacancies, in accordance with a concession granted to the Mainland in 1513. The *alcaldes* administered justice, and the government of the city was in the hands of the *Regimiento*, that is to say, of the *Regidores* under the chairmanship of the *alcaldes*: this was the basic conception of municipal government. As a result of their lawsuit with Diego Colón, the *vecinos* also managed to elect a *procurador*, designated by acclaim in open *Cabildo* by all of them, as a delegate of the 'commonalty' vis-à-vis the representative institution, the *Cabildo*. In the lands subjected to the Conquest, from Mexico and Peru, the appointment and composition of the *Cabildos* underwent changes of which there is no need to give a detailed description here. The *caudillo* who had been appointed governor or *Adelantado* intervened in the appointments and acted as a counterweight to the opinions and interests of the conquistadors; however, the king continued to make use of his royal prerogative, and appointed *Regidores* (see Góngora, 1951, 69–86). It may be asserted, as a general rule, that from 1540 onwards the prevailing system was that established in Santo Domingo – that is to say, the annual election of *alcaldes*, *Regidores* whose tenure of office was for only one year, and of the *procurador* of the commonalty, apart from other less permanent appointments, such as *Alguacil mayor, Alférez mayor, Fiel ejecutor* and so on. These officials were not, however, elected by the *vecinos* as a whole but by the *Cabildo* of the preceding year. In other words, the principle of popular suffrage had been replaced (except in exceptional areas such as Paraguay) by that of co-option. The open *Cabildos* were held only on special occasions – for instance, when the problem of a successor to the governor arose, or new laws had to be promulgated or new tribute raised, or there were decisions to be taken over vital matters concerning, for example, mining or the payment of the Royal Fifth, and finally (and most important of all) during times of rebellion.

The division of the *vecinos* into *encomenderos* and other citizens influenced the *Cabildos,* and it became the custom to appoint to office only men holding *encomiendas.* A *Real Cédula* promulgated in Chile in 1554, at the request of the conquistadors, made it clear that to be a *vecino* was a sufficient qualification for appointment, a *vecino* being understood to be a person with a settled household; this definition was quite clearly in accordance with the traditional Castilian *Fueros* and the original basic intentions of the legislation applying to the Americas, which envisaged the granting of privileges to all the colonists. In two cases – Peru and Chile – the *Cabildos,* composed of *encomenderos,* delayed for as long as possible the enforcement of the provisions of 1554 and 1564 (the latter stipulated that only half the *alcaldes* and only half the *Regidores* should be drawn from the ranks of the *encomenderos,* while the other half was to be composed of ordinary citizens). Finally, however, the law was enforced.

The *Cabildo,* the members of which were drawn from the newly arisen local aristocracies composed of *encomenderos* and 'honourable' citizens, had control not only over the jurisdiction exercised by the *alcaldes,* but also over the entire administration of the city (the 'polity'): the drafting and enforcement of municipal ordinances, the fixing of prices and wages, the supervision of pasture-land, woodland, communal grazing lands, and the *Propios* belonging to the *Cabildo* (that is, property whose purpose was to bring in income to defray the expenses of the institution), the regulation of commerce, transport and industries. In addition to all these activities, however, the *Cabildo* granted the freeholds of urban and suburban houses and smallholdings, and, in early times, also the tenure of completely rural properties, until, by legislation, the latter sphere of jurisdiction was transferred to the governors and viceroys, in order to prevent the unrestrained exspoliation of the lands of the natives. The *Cabildos,* especially in the earlier periods when there was still no *Audiencia* in the province concerned and as a result the bureaucratic structure was still not firmly consolidated, were the natural advisers of the governor and the bodies responsible for making reports on all kinds of different subjects to the Council of the Indies. Wherever an *Audiencia* was established, these overall political functions were progressively curtailed. But whenever there occurred any extraordinary or unforeseen vacancy in the governorship, or there arose a spirit of resistance to some new legislation relating to taxation or Indian affairs, the *Cabildos* in the sixteenth century – and, much more rarely, in the seventeenth century – recovered their importance and resurrected the spirit of the civic independence of the medieval *Ayuntamientos*. On such occasions, the aristocratic factor increased in strength owing to the popular support embodied in the open *Cabildos*, because then the *vecinos*, of whatever status or condition, felt themselves to be allied against the bureaucracy or the legislation of the Crown.

The political governors appointed by the Crown at times found it advisable to place limitations on the liberty of the elections for councillors, and thus allowed intervention in the sessions by the viceroy or the *Oidores* or the *Alcaldes Mayores* and *Corregidores*. Voices were raised in favour of the Indians and against the judicial measures of the *alcaldes* who were simultaneously *encomenderos*. The correspondence of the viceroys of Peru in the late sixteenth and early seventeenth centuries reveals, on numerous occasions, an attitude of reasoned opposition to the *Cabildos* and the continual petitions of the latter to safeguard the liberty of their electoral processes, incorporating requests that the viceroy should not intervene in them. The city of Quito, as a punishment for its insurrection against the *alcabala* tax in 1592–4, was governed for many years by a *Corregidor*, with no *alcaldes*.

The Council of the Indies, faced with the problem of resolving these tensions, was reluctant to go so far as to abolish municipal liberties altogether. It often imparted orders that the king's representatives should not attend the sessions held at the end of each year, when the incoming *Cabildo* was elected; it stipulated that the sphere of the administrative functions of the *Cabildo* should be respected, and forbade the *Audiencias* to intervene in urban administration; and, although it withdrew from them the right to grant the freehold of rural properties (in Mexico in 1559 and in Chile in 1573), it really took this measure in order to save the lands of the Indians. This preservation of municipal liberty, though subject to certain limitations, is an indication that there still persisted the notion that the Americas were 'new lands', and that colonists had to be attracted there by all kinds of concessions (Góngora, 1951, 84–6).

The meetings of representatives of the cities of a province – the 'general *Ayuntamientos*' or 'congresses', that were inchoate forms of a *Cortes* system which was never properly institutionalised – were another manifestation of municipal liberty in the Indies. Of great importance was the meeting held in Santo Domingo in 1518, which lasted for a month and was attended by the *procuradores* of the city and of the ten other towns in the island, being authorised by the Jeronymite Commissioners and the Chief Justiciar. Of more significance than the sixteen petitions, which were unanimously accepted, and included the expected requests for exemptions from tribute, are the instructions imparted by each city or town to its *procurador.* These instructions are a clear expression of the 'popular voice' of the colonists twenty years after the great Spanish enterprise had been commenced. They demanded communal liberties and guarantees vis-à-vis the bureaucracy and the tendency to incorporate all authority into the Crown; they displayed hostility towards the converts and the foreigners who had acquired a reputation as usurers, but accepted the others; they demanded freedom of commerce with Spanish ports, and freedom of movement and of traffic in Negro slaves; they supported the granting of *encomiendas* in perpetuity to resident colonists, though subject to limitations as to the size of the *encomiendas* (Góngora, 1951, 86–8; Giménez Fernández, 1960, 147–76).

At later dates, *Ayuntamientos generales* were held in other provinces: in Mexico, for example, during the expedition of Cortés to Honduras; in Lima, in 1544; in Chile, during the vacancy of the governorship, in 1555, and for the purpose of commuting the obligation of military service into monetary payment, in 1568. At times attempts were made to give institutionalised form to these congresses, and to accord a privileged rank to the most important cities, such as Mexico City (1530) and Cuzco (1539), within their respective provinces. During the movement in Peru to establish the perpetuity of grants of *encomienda,* there were proposals for the formal establishment of a *Cortes,* or Parliament (Lohmann, 1947). As late as 1611, the Viceroy Montesclaros, in a letter dated 12 April of that year (*AGI,* Lima 36), argued against the acceptance by the Council of the idea of a *Cortes* for the viceroyalty, to be held every three years, which somebody had suggested. Montesclaros argued that such representative institutions would be dangerous in 'provinces subject to such disturbances', and pointed out that all the rebellions had begun by using this pretext. The rebellion of Quito, twenty years before, was still causing the Viceroys to be hesitant. In 1635, the Count-Duke of Olivares considered the possibility of giving a vote in the first *Cortes* to be held in each reign to the cities of the Indies, in accordance with his plans for giving a unified structure to the Empire (Ramos, 1967). All these projects, however, were always shelved as a result of the natural mistrust felt by the upper bureaucracy towards *Comunidades*, as they had been called in the sixteenth century.

The *Cabildos* underwent a structural transformation when the system of selling public offices began to take root. In the early years of the settlement of the Indies, according to León Pinelo, all the offices were granted by royal favour, 'because the kings, either to reward services rendered, or to encourage discoveries newly attempted, granted such offices to their vassals'. However, this seventeenth-century jurist adds, expansion led to an increase in public expenditure, so that it was necessary to have recourse to a number of arbitrary measures, especially after the national bankruptcy at the beginning of Philip II's reign, and one of these was the sale of public offices. This system was merely a logical corollary of the concept of the king's royal patrimony and of his authority to grant public offices. France adopted the same system from the beginning of the sixteenth century and even earlier, and went to greater lengths: offices in the judiciary and in finance and public administration were sold. In Spain, between 1559 and 1591, legislation was passed providing for the sale of various types of notarial appointment, miscellaneous offices remunerated from the proceeds of customs tariffs, and appointments in the *Cabildos* (Parry, 1953). None of the monarchies renounced, at least in theory, the right to investigate the suitability of the appointee or his successors; this preserved the notion of the 'public' character of the office, despite its having become, in effect, an adjunct of the royal patrimony.

In sixteenth-century Spain, the principle was staunchly maintained that there should not be any sales of offices that directly implied jurisdiction, in order to prevent the degradation of the judiciary. However, the Count-Duke of Olivares, when in office, proceeded to sell appointments of Officers of the Royal Treasury, who did exercise jurisdictional powers, despite the determined opposition of the Council of the Indies. The same thing happened in the case of the *Contadores* of the Tribunals of Accounts, during the last years of the Habsburg dynasty, and in that of several governorships and occasional appointments as *Oidor* of an *Audiencia* (Parry, 1953, 51–8). The legislation itself, however, never gave sanction to the corrupt practices of the seventeenth century.

The *Audiencias* were affected by the new system only as regards appointments of *Escribanos*, receivers, *procuradores*, and the office of *Alguacil mayor de Corte*, who was responsible for the execution of sentences and ordinances. The *Cabildos* underwent many more changes as a result of the growth of venality. All appointments to the office of *Regidor* were sold, excepting only the case of the very impoverished towns, where there were simply no *vecinos* capable of paying the required sums. The same thing happened in the case of the *Alguaciles mayores* of the *Cabildo,* the royal standard-bearers (*Alféreces mayores*) who carried the royal standard on ceremonial occasions, the receivers of fines of the chamber, the General Depositaries of the property of deceased persons, the *Veedores* of weights and measures who supervised weights and measures within each city, and, in the seventeenth century, the *Alcaldes provinciales de la Santa Hermandad,* who were responsible for the suppression of banditry. The office of *alcalde,* because it implied jurisdictional authority, escaped from this tide of venality. As a whole, however, the *Cabildos,* which in the sixteenth century had achieved a degree of freedom of electoral procedure no longer enjoyed by the great Castilian municipal corporations of the time, because this was a special concession granted to 'new lands', later tended to become increasingly assimilated to the system prevailing in metropolitan Spain, and to decay in vigour as institutions. The same process was evident in the system of tribute collection, in which the exemptions of earlier times were gradually whittled away.

The case of Santiago de Chile is interesting in this connection, and was, perhaps, similar to what was occurring in other cities. Merchants and men of wealth were interested in the acquisition of honorific titles and of offices remunerated through special levies, which in addition were usually accompanied by such honours as a seat in the *Cabildo.* The *Cédula* of 1606, which applied throughout the Indies, allowed the passing on of offices which had been purchased, so long as this were done at least twenty days before the incumbent's death, and this measure opened the way for the establishment of a municipal and bureaucratic minor nobility which occasionally acquired a hereditary character (in cases where the successor was related by blood to the office-holder). In Santiago, in 1612, six appointments of *Regidor* and that of *Alférez mayor* were sold to landed proprietors, merchants and craftsmen, all 'new men' who had become rapidly enriched in recent years, and who were thus acquiring honorific appointments. There soon followed an aristocratic reaction, led by the *Cabildo*: a subscription was raised among the *vecinos* in order to offer to the Royal Treasury a sum of money equivalent to that demanded for the offices concerned, so that the latter should continue to be elective; this was achieved, and the system survived for several decades after the event (Góngora, 1970, 77–87, 94–8). Thus the elective and aristocratic principle was safeguarded, even to the detriment of fiscal income, because the argument was used, as it was so often used in Chile, that it was a 'land at war' and impoverished. Furthermore, a *Cédula* of 1607 lent legal force to their argument, because it stipulated that

Cabildo appointments should not be sold to persons who lacked the required 'parts and qualities'. A provincial city in Chile, La Serena, maintained the elective character of these public appointments as late as the eighteenth century; Santiago proved unable to do this except in the case of the *alcaldes*.

The sale of public offices, with its complicated system of legislation drafted with fiscal aims, made the State in the Indies even more patrimonial in character. But there has not been sufficiently detailed research into this subject to establish whether this system of venality had any effect on the social composition of the *Cabildos*, except in certain centres of population. In Upper Peru, where the 'fiscal' criterion prevailed decisively, no objection was raised to particular applicants for public office except on financial grounds, and the attempts of some were fruitless; nevertheless, the new system brought to the forefront, in addition to the now decadent class of *encomenderos*, that of those engaged in the quicksilver industry of Potosí – that is to say, the most wealthy and powerful citizens, and in La Plata that of the *chacareros*, or medium-scale proprietors (Inge Wolff, 1970, 98–136). In other areas, we have no knowledge as to whether the sale of public offices contributed to social mobility, or whether the 'old rich', to preserve their social prestige, imposed their collective will on the occasion of such sales. The only thing that can be definitely asserted is that the poorer and more remote centres of population, where the Royal Treasury had no practical interest in selling public offices, were probably more successful in preserving the aristocratic character of their municipal institutions.

The *Cabildo* members were at all times a select sample of the Spanish population in the Indies. In order to analyse the social stratification of that population, one must bear in mind, first of all, the legal dichotomy prevailing in the sixteenth century: the *vecinos* were divided into *encomenderos* and *moradores*, a distinction which approximately corresponded to the medieval one established between *caballeros* ('horseman' or 'gentlemen') and *peones* ('foot soldiers'). The *encomendero*, who at first had been a colonist endowed with the privilege of employing Indian labour, with a corresponding obligation to encourage the conversion to Christianity of the natives, also acquired, from the time of Hernán Cortés onwards, well-defined military duties in connection with the defence of the city and the land, including the furnishing of horses, arms and retainers. Their monopoly of appointments in the *Cabildo*, which at first was absolute and later was shared with the more prominent of the *moradores*, made them a real estate of the body politic, enjoying a strong economic base on account of their near-monopoly of Indian labour. During the earliest period of settle-

ment what prevailed throughout the Indies and within each of the provinces was the notion that the *encomenderos* were the principal estate of the
body politic, and excelled all others in power, wealth and prestige.[2] The
duration of *encomiendas* for two natural lives guaranteed the stability of this
social group.

However, the *encomenderos* were never able to constitute themselves as
a hereditary estate enjoying full possession of their privileges, nor achieve
the status of a real feudal nobility. Naturally, royal legislation substanti-
ally modified their economic strength by the gradual abolition of the
encomienda based on personal service, by stipulating in the New Laws and
in subsequent ordinances (in 1543, 1549 and 1551) that the natives should be
subject only to a monetary tribute; their economic relationship with their
overlords thus resembled that of the peasants of Castile. The system of the
encomienda based on payment of tribute was, by implication, an institution
entirely different from the earlier one, because it was no longer based on the
value of the labour performed. Subsequently, the various attempts made
at least to compensate the *encomenderos* by giving them the security of
hereditary succession and concomitant powers of jurisdiction were uni-
formly unsuccessful. In 1559, at an extremely critical moment for the royal
finances, Philip II decided to send commissioners to Peru with orders that,
in collaboration with the Viceroy Nieva, they should make legislative
arrangements providing for perpetuity, but excluding any jurisdictional
powers. The Report submitted by Nieva and the three Commissioners
(Levillier, *Gobernantes,* I, 395–471) emphasised the value of the *encomiendas,*
'the nerve-centre, treasure and strength of the realm', and recommended
that perpetual tenure should be granted in the case of a third of them,
leaving another third for the duration of two natural lives, with the
remaining third being incorporated into the Crown. However, the Crown's
categorical refusal to grant jurisdictional powers led to the entire plan being
abandoned. A few years later, in 1567, the jurist Juan de Matienzo once
again stated the arguments in favour of what would have been the
coherent establishment of a semi-feudal order or state: the *encomendero* who
was certain of being able to bequeath his Indians to his heirs would treat
them better than did the present *encomenderos,* they would defend them
against other Spaniards as they would defend their own property, the land
would become more stable because the *encomenderos* would have a greater
stake in it, and this would in turn have a beneficial influence on the
prosperity of the merchants and other citizens. However, he rejected the
proposals for conferring civil and criminal jurisdiction, because the attempts to introduce this, on the occasion of the visit of the Commissioners

in 1562, had caused resentment and irritation among the other *vecinos*, who feared that by these means the *encomenderos* would acquire control over the communal lands of the Indians (*Gobierno del Perú*, 93–113).

However, the proposals for the perpetuation of *encomiendas* always found adversaries among the upper bureaucracy of the Council and among the viceroys, who felt that in this way they would lose their power to distribute favours. The regular clergy, who were attacking the proposals around 1560 and persuaded the Indians to offer a pecuniary tribute to the King to ensure that the proposals were not accepted – this was one of the last gestures made by Las Casas – had changed their thinking on this subject only towards the end of the century, because by then the Indians had other problems and other dangers to deal with. In any case, by that time inertia itself weighed against introducing variations into the system, in order not to strengthen an institution both decadent and diminished in importance. The second Viceroy Cañete recorded, around 1590, that the *encomenderos* of Peru were indebted and impoverished, and that most of them derived their principal income not from their *encomiendas* but from cultivated land, flour-mills, mines, workshops, cattle-ranches and so on. The prohibition against residing in the Indian *pueblos* where their vassals lived further diminished their authority (Mörner, 1964; Góngora, 1971, 9–15). Moreover, once the period of the Conquest was over, the military duties involved in their status lost importance; and when they were called upon to serve outside their cities of residence against wild Indians (such as the Chiriguanes in Upper Peru in the time of the Viceroy Toledo, or the Araucanians in Chile during the second half of the sixteenth century and throughout the seventeenth century), the *encomenderos* doggedly refused to lend their services personally.

For these reasons, there never took place the systematic establishment of a feudal and hereditary constitution of the estate on the basis of hereditary succession, based on primogeniture, of Indians held in *encomienda*, according to the terms which the *vecinos* of Peru around 1560 wanted to see enforced, because 'they are Spaniards born in these kingdoms, where there is no question of feudal tenure but of entail (*mayorazgo*)'. The *encomenderos* were left in a halfway house between tributary feudalism and a patrimonial and bureaucratic State. With regard to their actual social and political influence, this varied from one province to another. Chile was a country at war, and personal service was never abolished there; in Venezuela, Tucumán and Paraguay, where the tribute system was established at a very late date, if at all, the *encomenderos* continued to exist as a political stratum at least throughout the second half of the sixteenth century and the first half of the seventeenth century; nevertheless, the real basis of their power shifted from their tenure of power over men to their ownership of land. In the viceregal centres and the mining regions, however, as early as the second half of the sixteenth century the *encomienda,* though still a source of income and of social prestige, was certainly no longer the basic element in the structure of the State, as it had been in the decades immediately following the Conquest.

Those *vecinos* without an *encomienda* were usually referred to as *moradores* (or exceptionally, as in the viceroyalty of Peru, as 'soldiers', although this was certainly a misnomer). They constituted a social category defined solely by their lack of *encomiendas,* and included extremely diverse social groups. At first, the *caudillo* distributed *encomiendas* among his comrades according to his own appreciation of their deserts, and, of course, depending on the number of Indians in the region concerned. Subsequently, according to Lockhart (1968), priority in the assignment of *encomiendas* – in Peru – was based on such criteria as length of service in the country, social origins and participation in military actions occurring after the Conquest. By 1560 the granting of *encomiendas* had become very selective, and they were never granted to craftsmen. If one fell vacant, owing to the completion of two natural lives, the new holder was chosen from among the ranks of the more prominent *moradores,* the 'honourable men'. Membership of the *Cabildo* was also drawn from this group, after it ceased to be a monopoly of the *encomenderos.*

The minimum requirement exacted of these prominent *moradores* was that they should have a freehold house and property in the city, and, in addition, should be men of wealth, a factor which of course depended on the economy of the region concerned. In Upper Peru, they were mining entrepreneurs, especially those engaged in the quicksilver industry, and the owners of ore-crushing mills. However, the risks inherent in mining operations, the fluctuations in price-levels and dependence on a usurious system of credit made this social sector extremely unstable (Helmer, 1956; Inge Wolff, 1970). During the seventeenth century this area was wracked by bloody ethnic strife and by struggles for power within the *Cabildos,* because of the rise to power and wealth of the Basque immigrants, who acted as a united clan. The mine operators, as a group, were fundamentally dependent on the power of the State, which dispensed the *mita* and the mercury for the refining of silver. Their position was, in some respects, similar to that of the owners of textile workshops in Quito.

The factor that ensured aristocratic rank almost throughout Spanish America, in later times, was ownership of land, which rose slowly in value as a result of local commerce and the export trade. The more prominent *vecinos* usually possessed smallholdings and vineyards in the suburbs; and, in the extensive countryside subject to the jurisdiction of each city, they owned plantations in the tropical areas, and cereal-growing and cattle-raising properties in the temperate zones. As the *encomienda* lost its value as a source of labour and became a system based on tribute payment, the centre of gravity of aristocratic power became the ownership of land well situated with regard to the ports of export or the great consumer markets. The demographic catastrophe which overtook the aborigines of the Americas favoured the migration of labour from the mines to agricultural and stock-raising activities, which required a smaller labour force. The land-owners settled the Indians assigned to them in *encomienda* on their estates, or obtained Indian labour by other legal means (*repartimiento, mita, concertaje,* peonage, *yanaconaje* and wage-labour) or bought Negro slaves (and Indian slaves, in places such as Chile, where the enslavement of Indian prisoners of war persisted). In this way, large landholdings became the necessary basis of political power, not only in the case of the more eminent *moradores* but also that of the *encomenderos* themselves, who as a social sector were simply absorbed into this 'class of possessors' (*Besitzerklasse*), to use the term employed by Max Weber. Nevertheless, this class was still characterised by factors typical of a system of manorial overlordship in its relations with the rural labour force, and its entire behaviour was impregnated with ethical and conventional values characteristic of an aristocratic system. Gentle-manly decorum and the social and human model of the *caballero* were held in universal esteem among all social classes. Romances and books of chivalry had been the favourite reading of the conquistadors (Irving Leonard, 1953). There is not, perhaps, apart from Hispanic Catholicism, a historical element of longer duration in Spanish America than this social model; its influence continued after the achievement of Independence.

This system of values based on the concept of nobility did not, of course, diminish the commercial spirit, which was also common to the upper nobility of Andalusia (Konetzke, 1963). The export of the products of their estates, plantations and workshops brought this aristocracy into contact with the entire system of maritime commerce. At times it encouraged entre-preneurial developments in overland commerce: for example, the trade between Argentina and Chile and Upper Peru, where the silver from Potosí was 'invested' in a variety of merchandise or in slaves. The professional merchants were obliged to face competition. The Viceroy Velasco re-ported that in Peru 'commerce and profit-making...is indulged in by all the nobles who do not have private means, and they are not thought of as merchants nor advertise the fact' (*AGI*, Lima 34, letter of 10 October 1603). The 'harvesters' of Santiago de Chile used to sell bread, wine, tallow and candles from their smallholdings in rooms in their houses in the city, thus avoiding the taxes levied on shops. Financial contracts – principally those involving rentals and loans – introduced into this social sector all the notions connected with the monetary economy. The habit of doing business and the contacts with the government that this necessarily involved existed side by side with notions based on the concept of nobility. This led to the rise of the '*Indiano*', or person who made his fortune in the Indies, as a figure. In Mexico, a merchant wrote that 'from the Viceroy to the poorest official they are all merchants, without excepting friars, *Oidores*, or ecclesiastics, even though they be princes of the Church; and he who is not a merchant is a nobody. And so honourable an occupation is it, that he who does not do business as and when he can is not accounted an honourable man' (Otte, 1969, 17). But there still persisted, implacably, the obsession with 'purity of blood' which, originally based on the exclusion of those of Jewish descent, was now used to exclude the members of the coloured castes from all honorific offices and even from membership of the guilds; even though the strict application of these measures was impracticable, nevertheless they subsisted as important principles. There was still contempt for 'tradesmen' and for Spanish upstarts who came to dispute the profits of the land with the Creole nobility (Durand, 1953, II, 74 ff.)

On occasion, the rank of *hidalgo* was conferred, in the *Capitulaciones*, on all the conquistadors who participated in an enterprise – this was the case, for example, with the companions of Pizarro – but more usually it was promised only to the leaders of the expeditionary force, as was stipulated in the Ordinances for Discoveries of 1573. This rank did not, in fact, confer many material advantages in the Indies, where everybody was exempt from the personal *pecho* (poll-tax). However, the status of *hidalgo* was undoubtedly a mark of honour in the sixteenth century, and was mentioned in all the testimonies of merits and services; nevertheless, it was never a required qualification for the grant of *encomiendas* and other economic concessions. Although the *Cédula* of 14 August 1509, addressed to Diego Colón, established a gradation in the size of *encomiendas* according to an order of priority in which the royal officials came first and were followed by the *caballeros*, squires and small farmers, this provision remained a dead letter. For eligibility for membership of the *Cabildo* of Cuzco the Viceroy Toledo stipulated that the *alcalde* nominated to represent the *moradores* should be an *hidalgo*.

The Council of the Indies stubbornly refused to concede, on an automatic basis, the status of *hidalgo* to the descendants of the conquistadors, considering them to be 'men of low degree', according to its pronouncement of 1556; and, although in the sixteenth and seventeenth centuries recourse was often had to the sale of the rank of *hidalgo*, of the habit of the Military Orders, and of Castilian titles, this at no time implied a truly 'imperial' fusion with the Spanish nobility. Such sales were the consequence of the chronic financial predicament of the Crown. The titles of duke, marquis or count, more frequently granted in the viceroyalties than in the territories ruled by governors, did not imply jurisdictional overlordship, except in certain cases. The only overlordship that was politically important, and even potentially dangerous to the Crown's authority, seems to have been that of Hernán Cortés when he was Marquis of the Valley of Oaxaca; but the *Audiencia* of Mexico took deliberate measures to restrict his jurisdictional powers. In short, therefore, as Konetzke (1951) has rightly observed, the administration in metropolitan Spain, despite its financial difficulties, always attempted to confine the American nobility to the overseas sphere of influence, and this class had to content itself with *encomiendas*, succession in strict entail on the basis of primogeniture, or titles which conferred no real overlordship, but at least conferred social prestige within their immediate environment. And their most persuasive title of legitimacy was always that of being a *benemérito* – of being the real or presumptive descendant of the conquistadors and the earliest settlers. On the basis of this descent, they clamoured for concessions and honours.

In contrast to the aristocratic stratum, which was partly a 'class of possessors' and partly an estate of the realm, the merchants clearly constituted an urban 'guild', and are referred to as such in the documentary sources. They were an intermediary stratum, not classified as being of 'low degree' in the scale of honours, but still not aspiring, despite their economic power, to political or social supremacy; on the contrary, they accepted their place in the stratified social structure dominated by the aristocracy and the royal bureaucracy. One contributory factor in this situation was the imbalance between power, wealth and prestige, which, in the view of Eisenstadt (1963), was one of structural characteristics of 'historico-bureaucratic' societies.

Within the mercantile guild one can, of course, observe a stratified distinction between the more wealthy importer – the *cargador* of Lima, who was usually also a ships' outfitter (Helmer, 1967) – and the merchants who owned general stores, down to the small-scale traders with their stalls in the main square. In Lima the big merchant might have a general store, though in the principal quarter of the city (Rodríguez Vicente, 1960, 65 ff.); this was not the case in Mexico City, which followed the pattern of Seville more closely. Lima was well known for displaying a more marked mercantile consciousness, revealed by the fact that the merchants tended to form dynasties and established business associations with their relatives, and showed no desire to abandon commerce and invest their capital in land. As an extreme contrast to this, the merchants of Chile usually possessed smallholdings and estates, and one rarely finds dynastic continuity in their business relations. Lockhart (1968, V), in his studies of the merchant class of Peru, emphasises their lack of interest in the acquisition of *encomiendas,* whereas in Chile the merchants, being landowners, tended to make efforts in that direction.

Although the merchants did not possess a closed guild organisation, in the form of a 'university' (*universidad*) such as prevailed in Europe, they occasionally attended open *Cabildos,* where they staunchly defended their interests. What really gave them a coherent corporate structure was the establishment of the Tribunals of the *Consulado,* which were inaugurated as a result of the *Cédulas* of 1592 and 1593 in the two great viceregal capitals, and thereafter at various dates in the less important provinces. The *Consulado* was an institution with mercantile jurisdiction, principally in an arbitral capacity, but it was above all an organisation designed to represent commercial interests vis-à-vis the Crown, the bureaucracy and the *Cabildo* in the numerous matters which might directly or indirectly affect its members; it also had connections with religious and charitable organisations. The *Consulado* was, above all, the representative institution of the most powerful importers and exporters. In Mexico City the smaller shopkeepers were excluded from the election of the Prior and the Consuls; in Lima, the Ordinances of 1613 granted them the right to participate in these, but these privileges were again subjected to limitations thirty years later. The members with full voting rights were, in Peru, the *cargadores* who engaged in the commerce of the South Seas as far as Panama, the owners of general stores in the streets near the main square, the shipowners, and the factors who were in business on their own account (Rodríguez Vicente, 1960).

There have not been any detailed studies of mercantile families after the period of the Conquest (although research on this topic has been carried out by Lohmann, 1967), so that it is difficult to make assertions apart from overall generalisations with regard to the social mobility of the merchants. We do know that in the case of Santiago de Chile the practice of the sale of public offices played a part in the social rise of certain individuals, as did appointment to the *Cabildo,* rank in the militias, and marriages into prominent families (Góngora, 1970).

A small, though important, group among the prominent *moradores* were the lawyers. Their influence in intellectual and political life was decisive in colonial times, as it was to be later, in the nineteenth century, on account of the importance of juridical notions in the entire social life of the period, and the professional standing of the lawyers, especially in cities which were the seats of *Audiencias*. They were sometimes to be found occupying appointments in the *Cabildo* or the office of judicial assessor or, at a higher level, making their career as officials of the *Audiencias*; in the latter case, however, they were given employment in a province other than that of their origin. In contrast to this group, the *Escribanos* had lower social prestige. Doctors of medicine were too few in number to constitute a recognisable social stratum.

Craftsmen, in the period of the Conquest, went to the wars, were granted small *encomiendas* and became landowners. However, pacification brought in its train a more rigid stratification, and the craftsmen were relegated to a lower social status, not being eligible for appointments in the *Cabildo* and enjoying no political influence; nevertheless, they might be householders, with a Negro slave for domestic tasks, and they were able to contract apprentices and subordinate employees. The most serious problem with which they were faced was competition from *encomienda* Indians who engaged in craft industries and, after the abolition of the *encomienda* based on personal service, competition from free Indians and half-castes. In Mexico, the Indians learned European crafts extremely quickly, and formed their own guilds; this process, however, was soon replaced by the procedure of incorporating them into the guilds controlled by the Spaniards, although they were not allowed to achieve the status of master-craftsman (Gibson, 1964). The Guild Ordinances sometimes included a ban on the admission of coloured men; in some cases to all grades and ranks, and in others only to that of master-craftsman (Konetzke, 1949; Carrera Stampa, 1954, VII).

Despite all these obstacles, the European guild system was transplanted to the Americas, although without its usual overall coherence and, more especially, without the political influence in municipal affairs which it achieved in Europe. However, the existence of *Veedores* who investigated and judged lawsuits arising from professional conflicts provides evidence of at least a certain autonomy. The religious sodalities, the *Cofradías*, constituted nuclei of popular life, and played an important part in religious and charitable activities.

The ideal notion of the 'republic of the Spaniards' embraced all these socio-political and professional groups. As time went on, however, there appeared other groups that were not based on Indian membership either statutorily or ethnically, and were exempt from the obligation to provide personal service or to pay tribute, and that were also exempt from slavery, that nevertheless did not belong to the 'republic of the Spaniards'. These were the so-called 'castes', the *castas*, a category which included Negros, mulattos, *mestizos, zambos* and other ethnic groups, and sometimes also free Indians exempted either in practice or in law from the payment of tribute to the king. These groups were, in effect, outside any institutional structure. Moreover, within the Spanish population, there were strata existing outside the recognised estates of the realm and professions. In the sixteenth century, there were the 'servants' or 'soldiers' who were contracted by the conquistadors or rich *encomenderos* for military expeditions, and also innkeepers and domestic servants. There were also many 'orphans' or illegitimate children, poor relations and retainers, who lived in the big houses; there were the foremen in the mines and on the big estates and, finally, the vagrants. All these categories, however, though important as social types, are of little importance in a discussion of the institutional structure; they were not provided for in the founding ideas, which is the subject of our study in this chapter.

Of great interest to the social historian are the militias, which were founded towards the end of the sixteenth century in Spain and the Indies to defend the cities, coastline and the conquered and settled territories (Góngora, 1970; McAlister, 1957). Cities usually maintained a 'battalion', with a prominent *vecino* as commanding officer (*Maestre de Campo*), and regiments and companies of cavalry and infantry. In principle, all *vecinos* were liable for military service. The officers were appointed by the viceroy or governor. There was a company recruited from the commercial sector, which included merchants of all sorts and conditions, a 'coloured' (*Pardos*) company, formed by free Negroes and mulattos and officered by them; and various other companies recruited from the *vecinos*. On feast-days these units held parades or reviews, and practised arms drill. Their organisation closely reflected the social structure. Officers continued to use their rank even when they were no longer in command of troops, and therefore such rank was eagerly sought after because of the high status it implied; it came to have the prestige of a minor noble rank and, especially for the merchants, conferred social prestige. Positions in the ranks of the militias, however, were by no means enviable. The infantry in the cities was responsible for guarding the prison, providing escorts and taking part in construction works, and the parades became increasingly burdensome and vexatious, as did, to an even greater extent, the expeditions to territories at war, although in the latter case the militiamen received small amounts of pay. The result of this was that the majority of the wealthier *vecinos* evaded conscription by one method or another, and those who were subject to it were chiefly the craftsmen, small farmers and unskilled labourers. The number of deserters among the militiamen, when military actions took place, was very high. Thus this organisation – which made its appearance at a very early date, parades and reviews being held in Lima in 1596, and in Chile from about 1608 onwards, this custom becoming increasingly widespread in the seventeenth century – displayed more coherence in its officer corps than it did where the troops were concerned. The militias, rather than being an effective military instrument, were a means of disciplining the population and of according status to the officers. As was the case throughout the period of the absolute monarchies, the rank of officer implied prestige and that of soldier a burdensome obligation and ignominy (Góngora, 1970, 98–102).

The notion of a 'republic of the Indians' also signified an urban mode of existence. The Indians of Tenochtitlán who continued to live there when it became a Spanish city lived in special quarters under an urban form of government, with their own officials (Gibson, 1964). As for those who lived in the rural areas, they had to be concentrated in an urban system of life, with a church, *Cabildo* and hospital, according to provisions of a very early date such as the Instructions imparted in 1503 to Nicolás de Ovando; in other words, even before the formulation of mission policy, the Crown envisaged the need for urbanisation. Cisneros included in his Instructions to the Jeronymites, issued in 1516, the idea of free communities of natives, a notion derived from Las Casas; but the epidemics of smallpox ravaged these communities (Giménez Fernández, 1960, 495–503). Ten years later, the most persevering and exemplary attempt was made to put into effect a policy of urbanisation by the missionary friars of Mexico, who considered that proper religious instruction was quite impossible without the establishment of properly constituted villages. There has been a good description of these by Robert Ricard (1933, 169–185). In Acámbaro (Guanajuato) in 1526, the first step was the erection of a wooden cross, then the streets were laid out, a chapel with a belfry was built, and then land was distributed among the Indians of both persuasions (*parcialidades*) who were to live in this 'reservation'. Finally, the *Cabildo* was elected. The basis of the economy were the *milpas*, that is to say, cultivated plots of which the majority were privately owned, although some were held on a precarious tenure. Pastures and woodland were used in common for the livestock. In addition to maize, the friars developed the cultivation of wheat, irrigated orchards and mulberries for silk production. The community chests (*Cajas de comunidad*), supervised by the clergy, helped to finance the payment of tribute.

The system prevailing in Mexico, the details of which have been most intently studied by Ricard (1933), Kubler (1948) and Gibson (1964), constituted a model for New Granada. In 1560 instructions were given to a *Visitador* to Pamplona to concentrate the natives 'in the same manner as the Spaniards' in permanent villages. Throughout New Granada, by the end of the sixteenth century, the 'protected areas' (*resguardos*) had been established; in 1623 orders were given by a *Visitador* that these should be organised 'in the same way as the villages of Mexico' (Colmenares, 1970, 52; M. González, 1970; Friede, 1944; Ots Capdequí, 1946). However, these social areas did not, in general, offset the dispersion of the population in the rural zones, and the natives probably went to the village only on feast-days (Mörner, 1970, 282–5).

The urge towards urbanisation in the viceroyalty of Peru came from officials and jurists rather than from the regular clergy. Juan de Matienzo, in his book, expounded an entire programme of settlement in villages, with five hundred families in each one, with streets laid out according to a regular pattern around the Main Square, which was to contain the church, the offices of the *Cabildo*, the *Corregidor, Doctrinero* and the judge responsible for tax-collection; in addition, the inn, the prison and the cattle-pen. This plan was the basis of the famous 'reservations' (*reducciones*) established in the time of Viceroy Toledo (Duviols, 1971).

The Jesuit missions, which were first established in Juli (Echánove, 1955) and developed on a greater scale in the vast territory of Paraguay – which included the entire River Plate basin – differed from the Mexican model and from the mission station which prevailed throughout the Indies, in so far as the natives under the supervision of the Jesuits avoided *encomienda* service and were subject to only a moderate tribute to the king; neither did they pay tithes, nor even the *alcabala* tax on their considerable volume of commerce. *Yerba mate,* mules and cattle constituted commercial resources that underpinned most satisfactorily the secluded life of those peoples. The internal organisation of the latter differed from the prevailing legislation in that land cultivated to feed the family was held on a life tenure, instead of being a hereditary property; and collective cultivation for the purposes of trade in foodstuffs occupied a considerable part of the time (on this point see Pablo Hernández, 1913 and Mörner, 1953).

One cannot really speak of 'missionary States' of the Jesuits (or of other Orders). However, the province of Paraguay was a genuine military frontier vis-à-vis Portuguese expansion, especially from São Paulo, and a peculiar characteristic of it was the existence of Indian militias equipped with firearms, instead of garrisons of Spanish infantry as was the case on other frontiers.

Urbanisation, in the Mediterranean and Aristotelian sense of the term, was a project rather than a reality in the case of the Indians. The political liberty of the citizenry could quite obviously not be established in practice because, even though isolated from the Spaniards, the Indians were always 'infants in law' in the eyes of the clergy. There were scant native clergy, so that as a political foundation it was incomplete (Ricard); there could not, therefore, be genuine urban self-government. The *Cabildos*, nevertheless, were of some importance. In Mexico the Indians elected governors (who were usually *caciques*), two *alcaldes*, four *Regidores*, a variable number of *Alguaciles*, a scribe conversant with the Nahuatl or Zapotec language, and *fiscales* responsible for concentrating the Indians in the mission area. These officials acted as the legal intermediaries between the Indian masses and the Spanish political régime, and it was they who first designated Indians for the *repartimiento*, collected the money for the community chest, were responsible for the enforcement of the Ordinances and so on. The *alcaldes* carried a symbolic staff of office, and had power to inflict minor penalties (Chevalier, 1944).

Gibson (1964) has emphasised the important role played by the old Indian nobility in the sixteenth century, the men generally referred to as 'caciques and prominent men' (*principales*). At first exempt from labour and tribute payment, Hispanicised as regards their clothing, with the right to use the title *don* and wear swords, they often filled appointments in the recently established Indian *Cabildos*. However, as a result of the *repartimiento* system which gradually replaced the *encomienda* based on personal service from 1550 onwards, and which involved increasingly burdensome labour obligations, the ordinary Indians (the *macehuales*) came into contact with the *Corregidores*, judges in charge of the *repartimiento*, notaries, interpreters and other agents of the Spanish socio-political stratum. The functions of the Indian *Cabildo* were progressively curtailed, and with them there decayed the organically assimilated manifestations of Spanish culture: weights and measures, the writing of the native languages in the European alphabet and so on. This led to a 'deculturation' of the Indians and to the fall of their nobility. The uniform system of tribute payment established around 1560 granted exemption only to the *caciques* and to their eldest sons, and the other dignitaries and members of the old aristocracy fell to the same level as the *macehuales* (Cook and Borah, 1963). Furthermore, the cattle owned by the Spaniards and grazing in the surrounding countryside, as Simpson (1952) has observed, did damage to the communal pastures and cultivated land of the Indian *pueblos*, so that the natives very often found it to their advantage to leave their homes and settle on the big Spanish estates, where they became tenants without any independence.

The background of this entire process was, of course, the demographic collapse caused by the epidemics, which hampered the establishment of villages. There were, indeed, chroniclers such as the Dominican Dávila Padilla, who considered that urbanisation was detrimental, because it helped the spread of contagious diseases; but the majority of the friars continued to support, in principle, the system of villages. In any case, these survived in the succeeding centuries with their *Cabildos*, now much diminished in power and status and really dominated by the governors, or even by the local landowners, and with their religious and charitable sodalities and similar organisations, which continued to have an appreciable role.

In Peru, too, we have evidence of the decline of the Inca or regional nobility through the pathetic lamentations and eulogies of its representatives, the Inca Garcilaso de la Vega, Guamán Poma de Ayala and Santa Cruz Pachacuti.

Ecclesiastical patronage

Finally, it is worth emphasising here that one of the fundamental characteristics of the Spanish monarchy in the Indies was the right of patronage over the Church; this was an entire system of political and ecclesiastical law, by virtue of which the Spanish Crown mitigated the influence of Rome in its dominions; it constituted in its own way, on the basis of orthodox and missionary principles, an equivalent of the trends of ecclesiastical and nationalistic thought which, in all the Western monarchies, placed limitations on Papal power. This was the period in which the Spanish Inquisition, with the support of the king, both challenged the institutions of Rome and claimed a monopoly of the struggle to safeguard religious orthodoxy.

After the concession of the tithes, in return for the obligation to build and endow churches and hospitals throughout the new lands (1501), Ferdinand the Catholic obtained from Pope Julius II, in 1508, the Bull *Universalis Ecclesiae*. By virtue of this document, the King and his successors would have in perpetuity the exclusive right to found cathedral and parish churches, mission stations, monasteries and hospitals, and to submit, in accordance with canon law, the names of candidates for ecclesiastical appointments and benefices, from those of lowest ranks to bishops and archbishops. The Kings also acquired, as a concomitant of this basic privilege, the right to establish the geographical extent and boundaries of dioceses (1543), and to restrict the bishops to receiving no more from the revenue of the tithes for themselves and their dioceses than the sums stipulated by the Crown (1510, 1511). In other words, what occurred in this case was a legal reversion: in 1501 the King received from the Pope the tithes collected, but returned to the churches a proportion of them fixed by himself. This practice was officially sanctioned by the Agreement of Burgos entered into between the King and the first bishops of the Antilles, in 1512: tithes were to be paid on agricultural and livestock products, not on ore production; half of this revenue was to go to the bishops and cathedral chapters; the other half was to be divided, in fractions of one-ninth, between the upkeep of the fabric of churches, the hospitals, the clergy with the cure of souls, whereas two-ninths went to the Royal Treasury (Leturia, 1927; Gómez Hoyos, 1945; Borah, 1941).

However, this system of politico-ecclesiastical relations was not confined to the exercise of this prerogative; this system of universal and perpetual patronage – an inalienable prerogative of the Crown, in the words of the *Cédula* of 1 June 1574 – incorporated numerous other elements. For example, the approval or *exequatur* of the Council of the Indies was required by all ecclesiastical documents emanating from the Pope or the generals of the religious orders, and also by all correspondence written from the Indies and addressed to Rome. This prevented the direct communication which had been carried on by St Toribio de Mogrovejo, Archbishop of Lima (Leturia, 1940). The Council might also withdraw Papal edicts which it had not duly approved, as happened in the case of the Bull of Paul III which proclaimed the liberty and rationality of the Indians in 1537 (de la Hera, 1956). The nuncios in Madrid were systematically prevented from having any direct communication with the Indies (1605, 1607). Judicial appeals to the *Audiencias* against sentences or measures of ecclesiastical courts (*recursos de fuerza*) caused continual friction among jurists who jealously defended the State's rights and ecclesiastics who equally jealously defended the prerogatives of their respective law. The clergy, as an estate of the realm, and the lawyers, as a united profession, were in constant conflict in the jurisdictional and intellectual struggles to which problems in this field gave rise, the hidden background of which was the entire problem of the sovereignty of the State. Although, in accordance with the Spanish tradition of juridical argument, recourse was always had to the Papal concessions as an ultimate justification, this in no way prevented the incessant increase of the attributions embodied in the patronage system. From Solórzano to Ribadeneyra, the Regalist thinkers steadily advanced towards the complete incorporation into the State of the original Papal grant. The independent republics of the nineteenth century were to follow the same course.

It is important to realise that the king of Castile did not succeed, until the Concordat of 1753, in eliminating Papal influence in the appointment of clergy within metropolitan Spain; the kingdom of Granada had preceded the Indies in the process leading to universal patronage. A new type of power could be implanted in the newly conquered lands before this could happen in the mother country. It is true that the royal power was subject to all kinds of practical limitations in the Americas, derived from the difficulties inherent in government from a distance, but it was not offset on a theoretical level by any other power – Papal, imperial, municipal or feudal – similar to those with which the king had to contend in his European dominions. The colonial environments where this power was first 'founded' at a particular moment in time were the forerunners of the modern uniform system.

One important factor in the constitution of the Spanish State in the Indies, especially in the first century after the Conquest, was the rivalry between the secular and the regular clergy, which to a certain extent reflected the polarisation between Spanish and Indian forms of Christianity.

With regard to the religious and cultural insignificance of the secular clergy, the *Cabildos*, the parishes, secular mission stations and minor ecclesiastical benefices, there is abundant evidence of this (Lopetegui-Zubillaga 1965, 564 ff.); this was true both in the case of the Creole 'native sons', who were to be given preference in appointment to benefices, according to the Agreement of Burgos of 1512, and in that of clergy who had come from Spain, but who had speedily been absorbed into the colonial network of interests. The 'smallholder-cleric' was a well-known figure. The admission of *mestizos* to Holy Orders, despite the objections which it provoked, nevertheless took place, to a certain extent, from the middle of the century onwards (Lopetegui, 1942, XIII). The reforms decided upon by the Council of Trent were introduced slowly and partially; seminary training, the educational system of the Jesuits, and the influence of the American synods and of the bishops modelled on the image of Trent, such as St Toribio de Mogrovejo in Lima, gradually made an impact on the clergy. There is no question, however, as to the superiority of the regular clergy in every field, especially in the first two centuries after the Conquest.

Hernán Cortés, in his Fourth Letter, asked for regular clergy for the mission stations, because the presence of the secular clergy would provoke scandal among the Indians, 'on account of their vices and immoral behaviour', according to Cortés, and also because the former Mexican priesthood had led lives of seclusion. The secular clergy could fill appointments in the cities where the Spaniards lived. Cortés even requested that the Pope appoint two subdelegates, one Franciscan and one Dominican, as superiors of their respective Orders in New Spain, 'because these lands are so far distant from the Church of Rome, and the Christians who are residing or may reside there are so far from the remedies for our consciences and, like all human beings, liable to sin'. These proposals were never put into effect, but the words of Cortés are valuable evidence of the moral authority of the newly arrived friars – who were usually connected with movements of Observant reform within their Orders, and some of whom achieved a high degree of spirituality – on that world of conquistadors and Indians. The Franciscan Archbishop, Fray Juan de Zumárraga, hinting at the moral deficiencies of the secular clergy described by Cortés, suggested that the canons in Mexico should be obliged to lead a monastic life in common, bound by vows of poverty, following the practice of the Canons Regular of St Augustine (Bataillon, 1953).

The entire missionary operation carried out by the mendicant friars was always liable to attacks from the secular clergy. Archbishop Montúfar of Mexico reproached them for their opposition to the Indians' paying tithes, a practice which worked to the detriment of their payments of fees for priestly functions, and emphasised the fact that the Indians before the Conquest had been accustomed to making gifts and oblations. As far as he was concerned, this was merely a stratagem employed by the friars in order to preserve their absolute control over the Indian *pueblos* and their access to the *Cajas de communidad*, which enabled them to live on the Indians' tribute. The *Audiencia*, for its part, was hostile to a form of Christianity not juridically and linguistically Hispanicised, of the kind which the friars desired to establish and preserve. However, the friars had the support of the governors and viceroys; this was the case from the time of Cortés onwards. It was a different situation in Peru, where the Viceroy Toledo was to reproach them for their inveterate tendency to interfere in all questions of government.

The *Junta Magna* of 1568 and Juan de Ovando restated, in a different form, the arguments of the conquistador of Mexico. Ovando's idea was to establish, in places where there was an Indian majority, dioceses in which the bishops and the *Cabildo* members would be drawn from the regular clergy, so that their evangelical poverty would attract and benefit the natives and also save money for the Treasury. All were to pay tithes, including the Indians, but in the distribution of the tithe-revenue priority would be given to the mission stations, and also to the parishes where Spaniards lived, by reducing the percentage due to the bishop and the *Cabildo*. He was thus stating a preference, in the words of Leturia (1928, 75), for 'the dynamic character and consolidated structure of the parishes and mission stations rather than the static splendour of the *Cabildos*'. Furthermore, the nationalistic and Regalist tendencies of the Spanish jurists and ecclesiastics manifested themselves in the Junta in the proposals for the creation of a patriarch of the Indies and commissioners-general for each of the Orders, who were all to reside in Spain. On the one hand, this measure would eliminate the remnants of Papal influence exercised through the nuncio at the Court of Spain; on the other hand, however, it would mean giving supreme control over ecclesiastical affairs in the Americas to the priesthood, rather than to the jurists of the Councils and *Audiencias*. All that came of these proposals, some years later, was the appointment of a Franciscan commissioner for the Indies, and a certain degree of judicial autonomy vis-à-vis Rome. The most significant development, however, was this forging of an alliance between the upper echelon of the bureaucracy and the friars, which had already been prepared by the Papal Brief *Omnimoda* of 1522, according to which the selection of missionary friars was to be carried out by the Orders and the King in conjunction. The missionaries' urge to achieve autonomy vis-à-vis the institutional apparatus of the Church and the episcopal hierarchy coincided in this way with the Regalist ideas of the *letrados* and the bureaucrats.

This alliance, however, became more difficult to maintain in being after the Council of Trent ordered that the regular clergy working in parishes were to be subject to the jurisdiction of the Bishops. From 1583 onwards *Cédulas reales* were published to the effect that, as soon as there were secular clergy suitable for the task, they should reassume control of the mission stations and parishes, although no immediate changes were envisaged. The Crown was therefore able to delay this transfer of power and continue its support for the friars, but Solórzano regarded this policy as destined to disappear (*Política Indiana*, IV, 16). In fact, in the middle of the seventeenth century there were heated disputes between bishops and friars in Puebla de los Angeles, with Juan de Palafox, and in Asunción, with Bernardino de Cárdenas; there were especially violent attacks, in both cases, on the powerful Company of Jesus. The right of the bishops to visit the mission stations and parishes under the control of the regular clergy, and the stipulation that the Jesuits' estates should pay tithes to the episcopal sees were perhaps the most typical problems, though not the only ones, that arose out of this conflict of jurisdictions; an additional factor, in the Paraguayan case, was the struggle of Bernardino de Cárdenas against the 'Guaraní Catechism' of the Jesuits. It was not until 1746 that the resolutions of the Council of Trent were put into full effect.

The alliance between the Crown and the friars gave rise to the ideological formulation of the 'Royal Vicariate' in the Indies (Leturia, 1929; Egaña, 1958), which implied a theoretical development of the attributions of the king in matters connected with the missions, on the basis of concessions granted in the Bulls of 1493 and 1522 and later documents. Juan Focher, Alonso de la Veracruz, Manuel Rodríguez, Juan Bautista, Luis Miranda and other friars developed the idea of a jurisdictional delegation of spiritual authority by the Pope to the King of Spain, who thus became 'attorney-general, patron and, as it were, legate in spiritual matters', in the words of Juan de Silva; the Pope had 'discharged his conscience' on the kings of Spain. Solórzano adopted this theory and developed it into a baroque reinforcement and re-emphasis of the patronage system itself; he used this technique, according to Egaña (1958, 114, 125), not so much to reach fresh practical conclusions as to assert that the position of the king in the Indies was equivalent to that which the kings had enjoyed in Sicily as pontifical legates, and to the position enjoyed in past Spanish history by the Visigothic monarchs. Even though these passages of Solórzano's writings were placed on the Index, the theory continued to be developed. The twin concepts of patronage and of vicariate lent the Spanish monarchy in the Indies a militant and missionary character, though not specifically 'Roman Catholic' in the canonic sense.

Summary

The institutional characteristics of the State in the Indies, between 1570 and 1700, were not very different from those of the Spanish State. At the apex of the pyramid there was an absolute monarch, not subject to the laws, but in practice restricted by factors derived from religion, ethics, Natural and Divine Law, and inviolable traditions. His power was based, ultimately, on the dynastic right of succession; he was the 'natural lord', but within the framework of Public Law, not as the possessor of a proprietary right. The patrimonial prerogative which he had over his realm coexisted with a corpus of Political Law that was derived, above all, from the *Partidas*, which, from the time of the Catholic Sovereigns onwards, were given an increasingly monarchical and centralistic interpretation. The Neo-Thomist political philosophy of the School of Salamanca, though never explicitly rejected, became subordinated during the following period to the Regalism of the kind expounded by such jurists as Solórzano Pereira. The ecclesiastical hierarchy accepted the patronage system; the friction and disputes that arose did not destroy this system. The king governed the Indies through an upper bureaucracy of nobles and *letrados*, and this constituted the authentic and permanent form of government in the Indies, after the initial heroic era of the *caudillos* and the conquistadors. The collegiate institutions (the Council of the Indies, the *Casa de Contratación*, the *Audiencias* and the judicial and financial committees) and the officials wielding personal authority (the viceroys, presidents, governors and *Corregidores*) were the executive organs of this legislative and administrative monarchy and were all, to a greater or lesser degree, a reflection of the principles that inspired it.

The 'kingdoms' of the Indies never had the consistency of those of Navarre or those of the Crown of Aragon because they lacked *Cortes* and estates of the realm at the general and provincial level, and in them the laws of Castile were in force as subsidiary law. They were, more exactly, provinces with the status of appendages, though possessing a somewhat higher comparative status when they were governed by viceroys or *Audiencias* – in other words, the status accorded to them depended on the rank in the bureaucratic structure held by the local representatives of the king. The lack of properly constituted estates of the realm, because there did not arise a nobility composed of *encomenderos* holding their *repartimientos* in perpetuity, and the lack of authentically free cities, prevented the development of powerful 'realms' that might have acted as a counterweight to the bureaucracy. The Church alone was an estate enjoying regular development. The *Cabildos*, despite everything, always preserved some importance, on account of the system of concentrating the population in urban centres. Whether the *Cabildos* were elective, or the system of the sale of public offices prevailed, the *Cabildos* still provided a representative forum for the *encomenderos*, the landowners, the merchants and the lawyers, and preserved a certain degree of local autonomy vis-à-vis the bureaucracy.

This entire system resembled the Spanish State of that period. The one authentically 'American' factor was the impossibility of a thoroughgoing enforcement of the underlying legislative notions and of the Spanish conception of the State, on account of the immense distances involved, ethnic diversity and the tendency in the colonial environment to evade legislative provisions that proved burdensome. What developed was a characteristic peculiar to the Americas – a form of liberty existing outside the framework of the State, in contrast to the liberty within the State existing in the European Middle Ages. Liberty in the Americas was not based on any well-defined notion nor on any new concept of the State: it was rooted in laxity: it was, in other words, essentially 'colonial'.

TRENDS IN COLONIAL HISTORY AND CHANGES IN THE FOUNDING IDEAS: THE CASE OF THE NATIVE LABOUR SYSTEM

The colonial empires founded after 1500 were characterised by all sorts of tensions and conflicts between the imperial authorities in the metropolitan countries and the discoverers, colonists and conquerors. In the case of the Spanish Empire these acquired especial importance in the sixteenth century and in the late eighteenth century, that is to say, at times when the metropolitan authorities were most active and had most clearly defined ideas regarding the foundation or the reform of the Empire, and were thus more vulnerable to the reactions and criticisms of the 'colonials' or 'Creoles', whose interests, convictions or aspirations were affected. However, throughout the periods when the metropolis played a passive role – the situation which, in the history of the British Empire, was known as 'salutary neglect' – and which, in the case of the Spanish Empire, was the century and a half between 1600 and 1750, there was a more peaceable and less dramatic development of the colonial world.

In the sixteenth century, up to 1570, the basic underlying cause of the tensions was the Indian problem. The Spanish Crown, though subjected to constant pressures on account of the financial penury which impelled it to encourage the exploitation of the precious metals that were the source of the Royal Fifth, was never prepared to yield entirely to the demands of the conquistadors and their descendants by giving them complete dominion over the indigenous population. This attitude was, of course, influenced by the reluctance of the Crown to allow the establishment of a new order of nobility when this had disappeared, in practice, in the peninsula itself: even in 1559, when the national bankruptcy of the early years of Philip II's reign induced the Crown to offer *encomiendas* in perpetuity and even to establish the Cortes in Peru, the Crown nevertheless still declined to invest such *encomiendas* with jurisdictional powers. Moreover, attitudes towards the Indian problem were influenced by ideas derived from Natural Law, the principal exponents of which were the ecclesiastics and the jurists, who formed the backbone of the Crown's administration. The obligatory personal service imposed in the colonies was incompatible with the juridical liberty of the king's Indian subjects in the light of these notions; and it also stood in marked contrast to the degree of liberty already achieved in the course of history by the peasants of Castile, both those living on royal property and those subject to feudal overlords. This series of conflicts began with the legal decision given at Granada in 1500, which set at liberty several hundred Indian slaves brought to the peninsula by Columbus. Thenceforth, the struggle between the idea of the natural liberty and juridical capacity of the Indians and the need to maintain a system of colonisation based on Indian labour continued without remission for three hundred years. From this tension there emerged a system of labour and of organisation of the Indian centres of population which was, quite evidently, very different from the Spanish ideal of the 'two republics' living in freedom under the sovereignty of the same king; it was not, however, purely and simply a reflection of the desires of the conquistadors. The extensive vicissitudes undergone by such institutions as Indian slavery, the *encomienda* system, *repartimiento, mita* and so on constituted a veritable 'political history' in colonial times. The colonial period was not merely an era of vegetative growth, of interest only from the standpoint of economic, social, demographic and cultural history; it was also genuinely *political* history, a history of contests and decisions, especially in the earliest and latest stages of Spanish domination, when parties and policies contended for mastery.

Indian slavery

The fundamental juridical concept of the era was the Roman notion that slavery, even though it had no basis in Natural Law, was nevertheless sanctioned by the general usage of nations, in other words by the *Jus Gentium*; and it could, in any specific case, be justified on the grounds of possession in good faith since time immemorial, of legitimately effected purchase, and of the capture in battle of 'barbarians', a term which in Christendom came to denote the infidels (Verlinden, 1955).

None of these grounds of justification could be shown in the case of the Indians sent home by Columbus to be sold in Andalusia, and this was the reason for the judicial order to manumit them issued in 1500. In the years that immediately followed, however, those criteria were employed to justify the enslavement of the rebellious Indians captured in Higüey and in Puerto Rico, and of the cannibalistic Caribs of Venezuela. The peaceable natives of the Lucayas and the Gigantes, brought in chains to Hispaniola by gangs of *rancheadores*, were eventually granted to their captor as *naborias* in perpetuity, their legal status being similar to slaves in every respect, except that they could not lawfully be sold (Zavala, 1938). Ever since the *Requeri-miento* of 1513, which in practice made it possible to justify any and every conquest, enslavement through warfare became a general practice throughout the Main, Venezuela, Central America, northern Mexico and elsewhere. Expeditionary forces consisting of small numbers of Spaniards, which set out from the settled towns with the intention merely of engaging in barter-trade with the Indians, often behaved in a similar manner to the major expeditions, and indulged in war and slave-raiding. Thus, in one case that occurred in 1529, an expeditionary force of about nineteen men set off from the town of Acla, on the Spanish Main, in a small fleet consisting of two ships; it began by trading axes for gold artifacts which the Indians brought to the sea-shore; they also purchased babies still at the breast from their mothers; later on, however, they would fall on a settlement, capture Indian women and boys, clothing and even a certain amount of gold (Góngora, 1962, 27–9). Isolated incidents of this nature recur constantly throughout the phase of conquest.

From 1530 onwards, the denunciations of the atrocities committed by *rancheadores* and conquistadors, such as those of Nuño de Guzmán in Pánuco, gave rise to legislation designed to prevent them. This series of legislative measures, after many vicissitudes, was to lead to the definitive abolition of slavery by the New Laws in 1542. During the previous decade, the most interesting document concerning this subject is the judicial Report submitted by Vasco de Quiroga in 1535; this was based on the knowledge which that official had acquired of Indian law: it points out that the Aztecs had never had slavery in the strict sense of the word, although they did have bond-servitude in perpetuity, without the right to alienate the bond-man; slavery, he maintained, had been introduced only recently, owing to the cupidity of the Spaniards, of which the Indian chiefs had caught the contagion (Zavala, 1941).

The abolition of slavery by the New Laws was one of the occasions when notions deriving from Natural Law enjoyed the most resounding victory, because it not only made provisions for the future but, in practice, had a retroactive effect. In fact, by means of a *Cédula* promulgated for Santo Domingo, the Crown decreed the immediate manumission of women and children, and also of all adults whose enslavement could not be proved by the necessary legal document: brand marks on the arms, legs or face would not be sufficient proof. When instructions were given for the enforcement of this order in Guatemala, the *Audiencia* petitioned the King to the effect that this would inevitably lead to total abolition, because no one possessed legal documents proving enslavement, and that this measure in effect abolished a patrimonial property acquired by virtue of earlier concessions. They pointed out in addition the ill effects it would have on the economy of the land and the revenue from the *Quinto real*, because a tax of one-fifth of the value was payable when slaves were captured. The *Audiencia* would have preferred due legal processes to be followed in each case, and immediate steps taken to prohibit the alienation of slaves, thereby following the behests of Bishop Marroquín, who had threatened to deny the Sacraments to anyone refusing to comply with the order. However, the Crown insisted, and continued to insist, on complete abolition (Simpson, 1940). This is one of the most obvious instances, in the legal history of colonial times, of certain positive rights, with a sound basis in law, being set aside in deference to a theoretical law, by virtue of the principle enshrined in Roman and in canon law of always interpreting a doubtful case in favour of increasing natural liberty (Góngora, 1951, 272–3).

After 1542, enslavement in war continued in only a few regions – those inhabited by hostile Indians. The Caribs of Venezuela were still regarded as slaves in 1756, and they themselves sold captured slaves from the banks of the Orinoco to the Spaniards and Portuguese (Arcila, 1957, 37–41). The Pijaos of Popayán, who made war on both Spaniards and other Indians and practised cannibalism, were reduced to slavery for ten years (Konetzke, 1958, 51) at the end of the sixteenth century. The Araucanians on the Chilean frontier, after the great insurrection of 1598, in which the Indians destroyed all the settled towns of southern Chile, were enslaved when captured in battle. This practice continued from 1608 to 1674, save for a brief interregnum in the period 1612–25 resulting from the policy of 'defensive warfare' advocated by Fr. Luis de Valdivia. Another Jesuit, the chronicler Diego de Rosales, in the long run achieved the abolition of Indian slavery in 1674: this measure applied to prisoners of war, children captured and indentured for a period of twenty years (*Indios de servidumbre*), or sold into servitude by their parents (*vendidos a la usanza*). In the *Cédula* abolishing slavery one can detect the influence not only of ethical scruples but also of the phenomenon denounced so vehemently by Rosales, and by so many others, namely that the Spanish soldiery of the regular army garrisoning the Chilean frontier in 1601 considered slaves to be their rightful booty of war. The slaves were captured in the course of forays or *malocas*, for sale in Lima or in northern Chile. The soldiers regarded this practice as a legitimate perquisite of their occupation, and as a result had no real interest in putting an end to enemy resistance. War itself provided the fuel for further war, and the Royal Treasury was the loser, because it was obliged to maintain an army two thousand strong. A similar connection between the ingrained habits of the soldiery and the institution of slavery may be observed in the case of northern Mexico, on the Chichimeca frontier. In that case, however, it appears that there was never any question of permanently legalised slavery; what happened was that the big mining centres, or the landowners of Sonora, bought captive hostile Indians and had the benefit of their services for a ten-year period. In 1671–2 there were 202 captive Indians labouring in the mines in Parral, and 702 in those of Zacatecas, in addition to children employed in domestic service. During the big rising in Nueva Vizcaya in 1680, the Governor of that district decided to sell all prisoners of war into slavery for a period of ten years, and this measure received the royal assent (Navarro García, 1967, 164–7). The soldiers who captured Indians in Venezuela, Chile and northern Mexico therefore recruited part of the native labour force for the Mexican mine-owners or Chilean, Peruvian or Venezuelan landowners. These incidents were *cabalgadas* of a new kind, similar to those of the era of the Conquest, when the aborigines had been captured for use as slave-labour in the plantations and mines of the Antilles.

Personal service under the encomienda system

Slavery, however, could be no more than a partial solution, because the vast mass of the indigenous population could not all of a sudden be uprooted and resettled on the lands already colonised by the Spaniards. The labour of the natives was organised through another institution, the best known of all those established during the centuries of Spanish rule.

Columbus was the first to institute (in 1497) the forced labour of the Indians in farms and gold-washing plants, the profits of this labour being reaped by the colonists, apart from the tribute in gold and cotton due to the king, which was a fixed cost. From that date until 1503, when colonisation in the sense of settlement became definitely established, there was a situation of uncertainty as to the eventual orientation to be adopted by the entire enterprise of colonisation. In 1501, the Crown reiterated its instructions to Governor Ovando that the natives of Hispaniola should pay their tribute to the King in the form of service in the mines and other enterprises being carried on in his name. The lengthy Instructions issued in Madrid in 1503 included prohibition of obligatory service to private individuals; the latter were to contract Indian labour on a voluntary basis and to pay wages. Furthermore, this measure embodied the earliest proposal for a general-ised policy of concentration of Indians in *pueblos* organised on the basis of urban concepts, the fundamental purpose of which was conversion to

Christianity and coexistence 'in accordance with the customs and usages of those people who live within our realms'. Nine months later, however, on 20 December 1503, the·Crown, acting on information supplied by Ovando, effected a radical change in its Indian policy. The Indians, in the words of this royal document, were not prepared to work voluntarily even for wages, and tended to live apart from the Castilians, thus impeding conversion to Christianity. In future, the Governor would grant to certain Spanish *vecinos* the power to dispose of the labour of the Indians assigned by the *caciques*, in gold-mining, building work or labour on arable land or cattle-ranches, paying them daily wages. The Indians were to perform this labour 'like the free persons that they are, and not as serfs'. On holidays, the natives living at their places of work were to be given instruction in the Catholic faith.

This was the first statutory instrument establishing the *encomienda* based on personal service, which was to be extended throughout the Indies, as a general rule, in the course of the ensuing half-century. The medieval Castilian *encomienda* was essentially connected with the notion of military defence, in conjunction with jurisdiction over a given territory: this might take the form of the defence of the domains of a monastery, or perhaps of certain communities or 'lands', and it conferred the right to exercise jurisdiction and to collect revenues. The commanders of the Military Orders would receive the grant of an *encomienda* unconditionally – and this eventually became a grant in perpetuity – and were obliged to maintain squires, horses and arms: this conferred the right to collect a number of the taxes payable by the population of the territory subject to the *encomienda*, the most important of which was the tithe. It is possible that the notion of 'defence' became transmuted in the Indies into the duty to give religious instruction and fair treatment to the natives, because the term applied to the metropolitan Spanish institution was adopted perhaps with this idea in mind.

The statutory basis of the *encomienda* (the royal decrees of 1509 and, above all, the Laws of Burgos of 1512) provide an insight into the institution, in its American form, as it had already been elaborated after so many initial experiments. The assumption was that the natives owed the king service, and that the king ceded that service to a Spaniard, as a privilege which remained legally guaranteed and was to last for two natural lives. The concession was explicitly restricted to productive works – one-third of the Indians were working in the mines, while the rest were employed on cattle-ranches and arable farms – and wages were to be paid in the form of clothing and a ration of food. Labour in gold placer-mining, which was the keystone of the economy of the Antilles, was to be performed by natives working for a period of five months at a time, after which they were entitled to a furlough of forty days to work their own plots of land, whereas the Indian slaves did not enjoy this remission. A decree of 1512 granted exemption to women during pregnancy and immediately after child-birth, and in the following year this exemption was extended to all married women in the case of gold-panning labour. Stock-herding and agricultural labour was to be performed on ranches in the vicinity of the *pueblos*, because the Laws of Burgos attempted, by means of various provisions, to encourage the concentration of the population in these *pueblos*, as had been commanded from 1503 onwards.

This concession granted to the *encomenderos* was not, therefore, a fief, but rather the usufruct of a royal prerogative – the service which the natives owed to their new sovereign in commutation of the tribute normally owed to kings and lords. This usufruct of the personal service of the Indians was strictly regulated, in the sense that it was imperatively restricted to labour in the mines and in agriculture and animal husbandry; it was not allowed to be substituted by domestic service of a greater or lesser degree of ostentation, in the style of a true nobility – for example, employment as pages or squires; this was stipulated in a *Cédula* of August 1509. It was strictly a concession granted to meet the needs of the colonisation and economic exploitation of new lands. However, in the *encomienda* (in its Caribbean form), this juridical arrangement was not entirely homogeneous, because it was often accompanied by the payment of wages in kind and therefore, in essence, with the notion of an obligatory labour contract.[1]

The introduction of the *encomienda* into the Antilles, and all the legislative vicissitudes undergone by that institution in the first twenty years of the sixteenth century, have been described in detail by Silvio Zavala (1935, 1938) and by Manuel Giménez Fernández (1960), and there is no need to provide a further description in this study. The most far-reaching structural innovations were introduced at the time of the conquest of New Spain. Hernán Cortés stipulated in detail the military obligations of the *encomenderos*, to which reference has already been made in the previous chapter; he envisaged the American *encomenderos* as having a status similar to the commander in the Spanish Military Orders, a type that he knew very well in his native Extremadura. Labour was to be performed on the same land where the natives lived, in the form of agricultural tasks regarded as composition for the payment of tribute to the *encomendero*, as far as this was possible, and strict controls were established over migration from the territory concerned – such movement was inevitable in the case of certain economic activities. Payment of wages fell into desuetude, because labour was envisaged strictly as the fulfilment of a tributary obligation. President Ramírez de Fuenleal, in a Report submitted in 1532, emphasised that the Indians had formerly paid tribute in the form of taxes and services to Montezuma, to the city of Tenochtitlán and to individual overlords of various kinds, the legitimate heirs of whom were now the King and the *encomenderos*; this was subject to the proviso that the latter were not exorbitant in their exactions, and service and tribute were to be properly regulated; this also applied to the relations between the natives and their new overlords. Fuenleal and the other members of the Second *Audiencia*, and also the more prominent friars and Bishop Zumárraga, came forward around 1530 – and again in 1544 (except, on this occasion, for Fuenleal, who was by this time a member of the Council of the Indies) – as advocates of the system imposed by Hernán Cortés, in all its essential features. They all, in common with Cortés, defended the hereditary *encomienda* system as being the most effective method of avoiding the destruction of the Indian masses by unbridled exploitation, such as had happened in the Antilles as a result of the behaviour of absentee and transitory *encomenderos*. The Crown, both in 1534 and on the occasion of the more authoritative *Cédula* promulgated on 26 May 1536, ordered an assessment to be made of all the forms of tribute hitherto paid by the *caciques*, to serve as a basis for the proposed new system of revenue collection; furthermore, it established the principle of hereditary bequeathal for the term of two natural lives; each *encomienda* was to pass to the children or the widow of the original beneficiary. The principles laid down in 1536 became generally accepted throughout the Indies (Zavala, 1935; Simpson, 1950). Although the new type of overlordship was always to remain subject to limitations, owing to the absence of jurisdictional powers and of perpetuity, it preserved, under the influence of the traditional European notions of protection and defence, the new obligation to make efforts to give the natives instruction in Christianity, and the duty of supplying arms and men for the defence of the towns and districts concerned.

The basic presupposition underlying the system of the *encomienda* based on personal service was that Europeans were not to perform labour on the land or in the mines. It was on this point that Las Casas based the greater part of his arguments: in contrast to the arrogant claims advanced by the Spanish immigrants, even those of the lowliest origin, to their right to live off the labour of the natives, he would have preferred, as did so many other reformers and visionaries of that age, a scheme of colonisation carried out by settlers prepared to work for themselves, who would people the lands left uninhabited by the Indians, and who would coexist with the latter on the basis of free contractual relationships. All the ambitious proposals put forward by Las Casas between 1516 and 1521 and the political ups and downs of those same years – the reformist notions of Cardinal Cisneros, the Jeronymite Commission, the support given by Charles V's favourites to reform, and so on – might have modified that fundamental trend, but all the vested interests became aligned against it: this is the view advanced by Giménez Fernández (1953, 1960); the failure of the experiment inspired by Las Casas on the coast of Paria was the last significant episode of this experimental phase. Colonisation by settlers prepared to work turned out to be, in the long run, merely another Utopian scheme. One may quote in this connection a much later testimony, that of the Viceroy of New Spain, Luis de Velasco, in 1554:

there is a great number of Spaniards who are unwilling to serve, or to work, and go around trafficking with the Indians, and the natives derive no good example or profit from this...and of these the greater part are peasants and people of low degree who have come from Spain to avoid both tribute and service, and over here they are not prepared to work, and they will not put their hand to plough nor to hoe, regardless of any reward or punishment offered them...and as these people do, so will the same be done by any peasants who come here, even though they are accustomed to the work and bring their tools with them. Moreover, the temperate zones and the irrigated lands that are well watered are so thickly peopled with Indians that there is not room for one person more, and on the coast, both northwards and southwards, there are uninhabited lands in abundance, but these lands are so hot and sickly that they are not fit for habitation by Spaniards...And since they have been granted lands near Mexico City and other towns peopled by Spaniards in this region, one may well ask who is going to build their houses for them and furnish them with oxen and ploughs, and ox-carts, for with two hundred ducats a small farmer would not be able to purchase what he needed, and there are few of them that arrive at the port with even one ducat...And even when they do till and sow the land, if there are no Indians to weed it, they get no bread therefrom. There are so many problems, that one would go on for ever if one tried to enumerate them all (Mariano Cuevas, *Documentos inéditos del siglo XVI para la Historia de México*, 189).

This was the interpretation given by an efficient administrator like Velasco to the Spanish colonists' attempts to rise in the social hierarchy.

An interesting case in the social history of Mexico is that of Puebla de los Angeles, a city without *encomenderos*, where the landowners had properties of only moderate size, but had Indians assigned to them as labourers (Chevalier, 1947).

However, the power of the Mexican *encomenderos* suffered a significant abridgment as a result of the process of tribute assessment initiated by the Second *Audiencia*; moreover, this measure was also applied to the communities which were direct fiefs of the Crown and were administered by *Corregidores*. In the same way as medieval customary law had established the contributions payable by the peasants, and those customs subsequently assumed the form of written laws, from 1530 onwards the notion of a just and moderate tribute gradually gained acceptance. Previously, the amount of the tribute had been decided by the governor in each particular case, and it also varied greatly depending on the arbitrary whim of the *encomendero*. Very often the latter also declined to pay the stipends of the clergy, so that this additional burden fell on the natives. As a result of the *Cédula* of 1536, the *Audiencia* was obliged, as a preliminary measure, to hold an inquiry into the numbers of the population, the quality of the soil, the tribute formerly paid by the natives to their Indian overlords and the tribute now levied; it then had to fix a rate of tribute that was as acceptable and light as possible for the natives, leaving a record of this decision in a registry containing details of the *pueblos*, their inhabitants and the tribute assessment. This institution had, in any case, been engaged on this task for some years.

The tribute assessments, carried out with the co-operation of Bishop Zumárraga, varied greatly from one locality to another, and took account of payments both in labour and in kind. The latter varied from one *encomienda* to another: thus, in the examples quoted by Miranda (1952), one finds woven cloth, blankets, poultry, cacao, honey, baskets of maize, quantities of *ají* and so on. Among the services due, the principal one was labour in the mines and another closely connected activity, namely, the transport of maize for the feeding of the gangs of mine-workers, or providing for the sustenance of the latter by sowing and harvesting plots of maize and beans near the mine-workings. These mine-workers might be either Indians assigned under the *encomienda* system or slaves (also Indian). Other Indians worked as cowherds or shepherds, in the growing of maize for pig-food, in the cultivation of cereals or market-gardening, on sugar-cane or cacao plantations or in the transport of merchandise from the *pueblo* to the city. The arable land lay within the jurisdictional area of each *pueblo*, or on the *estancia* of some *encomendero*. The Indians subject to the marquisate of the Cortés family worked in sugar-mills and shipyards. The cultivation of silk-worms and woad was carried out through commercial

136

partnerships between the *encomendero* and his Indians, and the tribute assessments took account of these arrangements. The *pueblos* which were fiefs of the Crown were subject to similar provisions (Miranda, 1952, 185–223). The assessments of the Second *Audiencia* remained, generally speaking, static for the space of about two decades, except where commutation took place by agreement between the two parties. Basically, these provisions left intact the pre-Hispanic system of assessment of tribute due to the Indian central and local authorities, except where such continuity was not feasible on account of the introduction by the Europeans of new goods and services (Borah-Cook, 1960, 10). The fundamental cause of this instability and disturbance was the demographic catastrophe, which altered the real value of the assessments; of particular importance were the epidemics of 1545–7 and 1576–9.

Around 1542, all the conquered parts of the mainland displayed characteristics reminiscent of the stage through which Mexico passed before the Second *Audiencia* – that is, before 1530. There was no general legislation, in the strict sense of the term; instead, there were internal regulations within each governorship which varied greatly and which left wide scope to the arbitrary behaviour of the *encomenderos*. The Crown made an attempt in 1542 to secure the eventual abolition of the *encomienda* system, but it withdrew from this extreme position in 1545, accepting the principle of the transmission of the *encomienda* for two lives (the *Cédula* of Malinas). On 22 February 1549, however, the Crown promulgated, for the whole of the Indies, a new assessment which eliminated personal service entirely; and, by the terms of the Provision of 4 June 1551, it was ordained that the new tribute should be less than that previously paid to the Indian overlords, leaving a margin for the needs of each family. It is possible, therefore, to assign to this date so important a structural reform as the principle of tribute assessment, first conceived twenty years earlier.

The new policy affected not only the *encomenderos* but also the Royal Treasury, for obvious reasons in the case of *repartimientos* vested in the Crown, but above all because it tended to curtail the yield from the mines, owing to the abolition of forced labour, and this would inevitably imply a decrease of the Royal Fifth. 'The essence of this land is its mines', asserted Viceroy Mendoza. However, despite the protests and the problems encountered, in the course of the 1550s the *Visitadores* carried out this reform on the central tableland of Mexico and in Pánuco. The problems that arose had important repercussions on the economy of the viceroyalty – for example, the question whether the Indians could pay their entire tribute in cash rather than in kind involved a risk of shortages in the urban areas; for this reason, the Viceroy placed restrictions on this form of commutation. The question of whether taxation should be on a collective or a *per capita* basis had more critical effects on the social structure of the communities concerned. The *Visitador* Valderrama, in 1554, finally decided that payment of tribute was to be on an individual basis, usually in the form of one gold peso and half a *fanega* of maize, if the Indian concerned was a married man, and half this sum in the case of bachelors or widowers. Decrees of 1558 and 1578 legally defined the tax-paying stratum: the lower and upper age limits were fixed at 18 and 50 respectively. The *Oidor* Zurita, in a letter of 1560, gave a description of the procedure that was already in force: after a perfunctory survey of the land and the compilation of a census of the Indian population, declarations were taken from the natives and from the *encomendero* (or *corregidor*); the *per capita* tax due was multiplied by the number of tax-payers; three-quarters was set aside for the King or the *encomendero*, depending on the circumstances; the remaining quarter, plus the yield from the communally owned arable land and the excess taxes paid, was ear-marked for the stipend of the missionary priests or friars, the building of churches, charitable works, and the salaries of the Indian *alcaldes* and of the *cacique*.

When the old collective tribute was abolished, Valderrama and the tax-collecting authorities had an obvious interest in increasing the number of tax-payers. This meant that the Indian lesser nobility were now made subject to tribute, except for the *cacique* and his eldest son; moreover, there were now included in the category of *macehuales* or ordinary tax-payers members of social strata which had previously been exempt, for example, those destined to work on the lands of the nobility as serfs or *terrazgueros*, in accordance with the pre-Hispanic stratification (Borah-Cook, 1960, 1963). Gibson (1964) believes that in many cases the uniform system imposed by the Spaniards was evaded in the hinterland of the Indian communal areas, as far as the internal distribution of the tax burden was concerned; but on the whole he concedes that the loss of the personal service previously performed by these lower strata meant a loss of income, power and prestige for the Indian nobility (156–65).

The transformation of the *encomienda* based on personal service into the *encomienda* based on tribute signified a very radical change, and, in theory, it brought the situation of the Indians into line with the legal status of the European peasant. At once, however, other legal devices were found to reintroduce obligatory labour. All the same, from the point of view of the *encomenderos* it meant a real change in the nature of the institution. This development took place much later in provinces other than Mexico. The

Civil Wars in Peru prevented the new tribute assessment from being put into effect until 1550, twenty years after this happened in Mexico. Three years later, when the abolition of personal service was decreed, this still provoked the abortive insurrection of Sebastián de Castilla and Hernández Girón. During the 1560s, the problems arising from the Indian policy were the subject of heated discussions among the jurists (Hernando de Santillán, Polo de Ondegardo, Juan de Matienzo and Francisco Falcón). Polo de Ondegardo was anxious to maintain the desired continuity with the Inca system, which, thanks to their rotation of the labour force, ensured an equitable organisation of collective life; he emphasised the need for an assessment which would have permanent validity, and would not be subject to 'reassessments', for this practice encouraged idleness; he attacked the idea of individual assessment, because this led to the dispersal of activities; 'what we must do is to act in accordance with their customs, and base our system on those customs, so that their rights are safeguarded,' he wrote in his report of 1561. Juan de Matienzo, likewise, supported the idea of obligatory labour, in order to avoid dispersal of activities and idleness; however, he disapproved of both the Inca system and the *cacique* system in force in his own day; he maintained that collective assessment led to abuses on the part of the *caciques*, and he preferred individual assessment as being a surer way to safeguard the property rights of each Indian. The ideas of Matienzo regarding Indian *pueblos* were the basis of the policy adopted by Viceroy Toledo (Góngora, 1951, 129–30, 212–15).

The question of whether tribute assessment should be on a collective or an individual basis might be a very serious matter for the Indians during the times of depopulation, when the tribute originally assessed on a collective basis became an intolerable burden for the survivors. In many such cases the Indians petitioned for a reassessment and thus obtained a reduction, and Peru, in contrast to Mexico, opted, from the time of Viceroy Toledo, for the collective method of assessment (*Cédula* of 28 December 1568).

In 1550 and 1560 there were similar modifications in the *encomienda* system in New Granada, with the introduction of mixed assessments based on labour performed in growing and harvesting cereals and on the delivery of cotton blankets. The *visita* of Tomás López, sponsored in Popayán by Bishop Juan del Valle in 1559, was of great importance, both because it initiated the concentration of Indians in *pueblos*, and also because it assessed tribute on the basis of cotton blankets, chickens, and the cultivation by the whole *pueblo* of maize, beans and yucca on the lands of the *encomendero*. Subsequent assessments maintained this element of personal service, but the new tribute applied only to the area of land capable of

139

producing one *fanega* of maize. In Bogotá, from 1565 onwards, there were examples of tribute reduced to a fixed amount of gold and blankets. Collective assessment still occurred as late as 1593, despite the depopulation; but in 1597 the *Audiencia* decided in favour of individual assessment (Hernández Rodriguez, 1949; Friede, 1963; Colmenares, 1969).

This process, of which are mentioned only the principal stages relevant to this study, took place in a very broad context. Recent research into the history of ideas has made possible the abandonment of many previously accepted generalisations. An important contribution is that of Zavala (1944), who has pointed out that the theory of 'natural servitude' did not imply legalised slavery, but rather suggested, in the minds of John Major, Palacios Rubio, Matías de Paz and the learned Aristotelian humanist Juan Ginés de Sepúlveda, a paternal tutelage exercised by the wiser over the more ignorant, in accordance with the well-known theory of Aristotle. Rather than a justification of slavery, this was the true theory of the *encomienda*: it affirmed juridical liberty, while limiting the use of it on the grounds that the Indian was a 'miserable sinner' who had to be guided and kept in protective custody. The real, and very different, day-to-day operation of the *encomienda* system in the Caribbean gave rise to the controversy which Hanke has recounted as the 'struggle for justice' (1949). In connection with that controversy, research concerned with Las Casas has been developed into a specialised field on its own account by such writers as Bataillon, Hanke, Giménez Fernández and Pérez de Tudela.

Another great contribution made by historical research, concerning the problem of personal service, has been made by the school of historical demography of Berkeley, represented by Borah, Cook and Simpson. Of cardinal importance is the theory of an extremely large and dense pre-Hispanic population in the Caribbean and in Aztec Mexico, based on the cultivation of maize, beans and other crops; this population, by about 1500, had passed its optimum level in relation to the natural resources available, and was already condemned to ruin when the Spanish Conquest accelerated this process (Borah-Cook, 1962, summarising earlier monographs, and 1971). In contrast to the calculations of Rosenblat (a population of 5,600,000 in North America and the Caribbean in 1492), they give an estimate of 7 to 8 millions as a probable figure for the population in 1492 of the island of Hispaniola alone; this figure far exceeds that given by Las Casas, which had been thought to be exaggerated. The influence of European factors in the demographic decline of Mexico was such that, according to these historians' most recent studies, from a total of 25.2 million in 1519 the population fell to 16.8 million in 1532, 6.3 in 1548, 2.65 in

1568 (this is the most accurate figure, being based on the *Visitas* of that time), 1.9 in 1585, 1.375 in 1595 and, finally, 1.075 in 1605. These figures refer to the total population, calculating 2.8 persons per tribute-payer on the basis of the exact figures for 1568 (1960, 1963, 1971). The regions which suffered most from the European impact, both in Mexico and in the Americas as a whole, were the coastal regions, where the indigenous population was almost entirely replaced by Negroes.

Chaunu (1959, 495–510 and 803–9), basing his calculations on the sources and research of the Berkeley historians, had described and analysed the effect of European influence on the depopulation of the Caribbean, emphasising the epidemics stemming from a diet poor in nutritive qualities and deficient in milk, the transfer of labour from traditional activities to gold placer-mining, with the consequent breakdown of traditional social equilibria, and the practice of employing women in gold placer-mining, which obliged women who had recently born children to wean them prematurely, since the Laws of 1512 and 1513 came too late to remedy this evil. In Mexico, the impact of the epidemics, particularly that of 1545–7, was really devastating. An additional factor, of greater importance in Mexico than in the islands, was the presence of large numbers of European livestock of all kinds; they altered the ecological balance, they strayed into the Indians' arable land and destroyed their crops. Moreover, the very decrease in the numbers of the natives favoured the granting of land as *mercedes* to the Spaniards, who grazed their animals on their new property, steadily drawing nearer to the Indian *pueblos*, despite the voluminous legislation prohibiting this practice (Simpson, 1952). Finally, there was the factor described by Kubler (1948, I, 48–9 and 66) as 'psychological unemployment'. The traditional connection between labour and sacred and ritual activities, and its ancient ceremonial character, were shattered by the 'profane' labour imported by the Spaniards, the rhythm of which was interrupted only by idleness, dissipation and drunkenness. European secularisation destroyed the traditional concept of labour as a religious act. The friars realised this and, at least in part, compensated for the loss by music, pilgrimages, processions, dancing, sacred drama and religious confraternities, to help the Indians forget 'heavy labour and the lure of their pagan ways' (Alonso de Veracruz).

Although the abolition of the *encomienda* based on personal service marked a temporary victory of the Crown over the colonists, it must be remembered that this provision could not be applied to the provinces that were poorer and more involved in warfare. As late as 1600, Comayagua, Nicaragua and Costa Rica (all subject to the *Audiencia* of Guatemala),

Venezuela (subject to that of Santo Domingo), Trujillo, La Grita, Pamplona, parts of Tunja and other districts of the *Audiencia* of Santa Fé de Bogotá, Popayán and Salinas (subject to the *Audiencia* of Quito), and the governorships of Santa Cruz de la Sierra (Paraguay), Tucumán (subject to Charcas) and Chile (subject to Lima), all still maintained the system of the *encomienda* based on personal service, according to the report of Fray Miguel de Agía.

In Venezuela, where *cabalgadas* and slavery continued for a long time and the *encomienda* was introduced only at a late date, personal service persisted until 1686, with the difference that in this area the womenfolk had to lend service in cotton-spinning (Arcila, 1957), in addition to the labour provided by the men in gold placer-mining, sugar-mills, textile workshops, forestry and so on. In Chile, the *encomenderos* always pleaded the fact that they were giving service in the Araucanian war – a service that was at first military and later economic – to obtain suspension of the tribute assessment; there was a partial attempt to introduce this between 1580 and 1584. During the period when the gold placer-mines were booming (1541–90), the pacified Indians worked in them on a *mita* system – for the profit of the *encomenderos*; however, they received as payment a sixth part of the gold extracted. This was a sort of obligatory partnership, as a result of which the Indians acquired ownership of a significant number of sheep and goats, in which their share of the gold was invested; as time went on, however, this capital came to be invested in credits to the Spaniards through the 'census-contract', the *censo*, and ceased to be of any benefit to the natives (Jara, 1961). The system of tribute assessment imposed by the provincial legislature in 1580 was radically changed from 1584 onwards, when the authorities decided to solve the problem by commuting tribute into daily labour performed for the *encomendero*, in the mines, textile workshops, agriculture or stock-herding. The *encomienda* Indians worked on a *mita* basis for a third of the tribute-payers, returning afterwards to their *pueblo*; they received as wages, in the form of clothing, the difference between the days worked and the tribute which they owed to the *encomendero*. Between 1590 and 1620 the *encomienda* became definitely rural in character, and was especially orientated towards the raising of livestock for the trade with Peru. Although the *Tasas* still laid greatest emphasis on the tribute, they provided for its commutation into labour performed in return for low wages, and this commutation came to be the general rule, except when the Indian entered the service of another landowner, who then profited from his labour but paid the tribute in cash to the *encomendero* (cf. the Ordinances of 1620, 1622 and 1635). Furthermore, the *pueblos* in the

Repartimiento, mita *and* concertaje

pacified zone were left desolate because their inhabitants settled on the estates of the Spaniards, despite the efforts to concentrate the Indians in reservations made by Jesuits, bishops and *Audiencias* (Góngora, 1970). In the River Plate region, Tucumán and Paraguay, one also finds the persistence of domestic or rural service. The Ordinances of the *Oidor* Alfaro (1611–18) established a monetary tribute but were obliged to make provision for the optional commutation of this for labour, which continued to be the most widespread method of payment. The pretext invariably advanced was the poverty of the Indians (E. Service, Gandía, Zorraquín Becú).

Repartimiento, mita *and* concertaje

As soon as work began on the construction of towns, churches and highways, this inevitably gave rise to forms of obligatory labour quite independent of the *encomienda* system, and Simpson (1934) has drawn attention to certain Ordinances of Viceroy Mendoza concerning public works and the transport of merchandise; these stipulated payment for such labour, but insisted that it was to be performed. Since the abolition of Indian slavery in 1542 and of personal service to the *encomenderos* in 1549, the Spanish authorities were faced with the alternatives of free labour or compulsory labour, which were really a reflection in the practical sphere of the great theoretical debate over the capacity and liberty of the natives. The Instructions given in 1550 to Viceroy Velasco for his government of New Spain left the new incumbent free to use both methods: he was to encourage a system of free wage-labour, but he was to impose concurrently an element of obligation, though within the context of administrative regulations and independently of the *encomienda* system. The fundamental justification was the public benefit derived from the labour performed – namely, the common weal – but over and above this the Instructions emphasised the Viceroy's duty to take measures to counter the sloth and idleness of the Indians who had no employment. Mention was also made of vagrant Spaniards as a potential source of labour – later this was to be extended to include the *mestizos* and similar 'castes' – but the authorities were powerless to act in this sphere, and their most pressing concern was always the natives. The struggle to mobilise the idle poor had been a recurring feature of the legislation of every nation in Europe since the fourteenth century. The new system, whereby the Viceroy and the *Jueces repartidores* in each region decided the beneficiaries of the labour, the hours of work and the numbers of workmen required for the various tasks, came to be known as the *repartimiento*, and the fundamental difference between this system and the previous one was that the new dispensation provided for temporary assignment of workers, which did not constitute a privilege and was effected for public works or private undertakings which the Viceroy considered to be beneficial for the community as a whole. It was a system eminently appropriate to the increasingly bureaucratised monarchy of Philip II and his successors, to the extent that the two Viceroys who established the new system, Enríquez and Toledo, based their legislation on the *Junta Magna* of 1568, which decisively consolidated the legislation concerned with the Indies.

Verlinden (1970) has described the practical working of this system in Mexico in the late sixteenth century. One *Juez repartidor* in charge of several *pueblos* assigned the Indians on a weekly basis; each Indian had to work three times a year for a week, for a wage of half a peso for the six days. The Indian 'foreman' was responsible for seeing that the Indians turned up for work; both he and the *Juez repartidor* received a fee for each Indian assigned for labour; in most cases, it was the *Juez repartidor* who fixed the amount that the beneficiary designated by the Viceroy was to receive. The quota of assigned Indians, in relation to the total number of tribute-payers, varied according to the region and the season of the year, but tended to be between 4 and 8 per cent of the total, depending on the calendar of agricultural tasks. Despite the short duration of the system of *repartimiento* in Mexico, deportation from one locality to another and the consequent upheavals served to aggravate the process of depopulation. The Franciscans, especially Mendieta, waged a heated struggle against the system from 1565 onwards; they alleged that the Indians were being forced to wear themselves out for the benefit of upstarts, and they refuted the accusations of Indian idleness by citing the example of those of Mexico City and Puebla, who worked for wages quite willingly. To till the sown land of the *vecinos* of the capital, according to the *caciques*, four or five hundred Indians went out every week, carrying their own food and being assigned a short working day. The *Oidor* Zurita (quoted by Simpson, 1934, 19–20) reported that the Spaniards had increased by tenfold the old forced labour of the Aztec *cuatequil.* Construction work and labour in the textile workshops were the activities which provided the Indians with most grounds for complaint. Churches and convents, *doctrineros* (for the building of their residences) and the Jesuits (for their plantations) also demanded Indians assigned in *repartimiento.* The mining regions of northern Mexico, however, which were able to offer high wages, only required Indians assigned in *repartimiento* in one or two mines, and these went on working with this system until the beginning of the seventeenth century; in general, the labour force in the mines was provided by captured Indians from the hostile northern tribes, or by Negro slaves, or by the mass of free workers of varying ethnic origins, who were entitled, in addition to their wages, to issues of silver ore which were their customary right and which they could sell. This was, in particular, the system in operation in Zacatecas and Parral (West, Bakewell).

In New Granada, the gold and silver mines were worked by Negroes and Indians, mostly the former. The gold mines of Pamplona and the silver mines of Mariquita used the *mita* system to the greatest extent, though never on the scale that was common in Peru. President Manso de Velasco reported in 1729 that the natives fled rather than be conscripted for *mita* labour, and preferred to work as boatmen on the River Magdalena. The gold mines of Chocó were usually worked by gangs of Negro slaves (Jaramillo Uribe, 1964; Colmenares-Melo-Fajardo, 1968, 130–64). The rural *mita* or *concertaje* was subject to regulations promulgated by President Pérez Manrique in 1657. One-quarter of the able-bodied Indians were to be distributed among the landowners nearest to them, in preference to those living farther away. The *encomendero* himself and the *cacique* might be beneficiaries, if they were landowners. The regulations of Pérez Manrique laid down the working hours and the food ration. The landowners who were not beneficiaries under this scheme had to hire free wage-labourers, and this was more expensive (Hernández Rodriguez, 1949; Colmenares-Melo-Fajardo, 293 ff.).

In Peru, as in Mexico, one can observe a similar extension of the regulations of 1549 and subsequent years, which originally provided for only a limited system of compulsory labour. The colonial authorities, under the pressure of regional interests, rapidly developed a great variety of systems of *repartimiento*. A description of these can be found in the work published by Matienzo in 1567; he describes the situation of the *tindaruna*, who offered themselves for employment in the main squares of the cities, and of the various *mitayos* employed in the cultivation of cereals or coca, in stock-herding, on public works, the building of wayside inns and churches and so on (I, 9–11). The 'main square *repartimiento*' was the system which best guaranteed the Indian's freedom of contract of employment, because, although he was obliged to go to the city, he could hire out his labour in the main square to anyone he wished, and then work in domestic service or in the vineyards and arable land. In 1562 the *mita* system was already in force in the mines of Guamanga, but its legality was being questioned. President García de Castro, in a letter of 1567 (Levillier, *Gobernantes del Perú*, III, 220–1), justified the compulsory labour system on the grounds of the idleness of the

Indians and the need to maintain commercial ties with Spain: '... and of course they will not send goods from there in exchange for the maize and potatoes and *ají* and sweet potatoes which we produce here, but only for gold and silver, and these cannot be produced without mines, and the mines here cannot be worked by Negro labour because they are all in the cold regions.' The increase in silver production and the discovery in 1560 of Huancavelica, the mercury from which was to make possible a further and very marked increase, naturally lent an added seriousness to this question. Juan de Matienzo justified the practice of making the Indians travel long distances to labour in the mines, on the grounds that otherwise the nearest mines would enjoy an unfair excess of labourers; he did not consider, however, that they should have to travel to an area which was climatically different, and he thought that this might easily happen in the territory subject to the *Audiencia* of Charcas (Levillier, *Gobernantes*, I, 9). He described the life of Potosí, which had attained great complexity even in his time, with a thousand different trades and occupations engaged in by Indians and Spaniards: 'There is, in short, a very great confusion, and there are few who understand it; the only thing really agreed upon is that one should not introduce any innovation into that place, but simply bring in more Indians, for that never does any harm, but on the contrary is always useful' (I, 40). A century later, Viceroy Lemos reported (in 1669) that 'the *mita* system in Potosí, with the variety of interpretations to which it has given rise, has become incomprehensible' (quoted in Lohmann, 1946, 245).

At first the *mita* in Potosí, organised by Viceroy Toledo on the basis of previous experience and official recommendations, including those of Matienzo himself (Lohmann, 1967, XXXVI), conscripted 4,500 Indians who worked for a tour of duty of four months, in other words 13,500 Indians a year, a seventh part of the 94,000 Indians living in the sixteen provinces affected by the *repartimiento*, stretching from Cuzco to Tarija. Distributed among the 'quicksilver-operators', the owners of ore-crushing mills or ordinary mine-owners, they were paid a much lower daily wage than the free wage-labourers or *mingados*. Every Indian, therefore, was obliged to go to work in Potosí once every seven years, in some cases travelling as far as 200 leagues; payment for the return journey was one of the numerous problems frequently discussed. Many studies have described the weekly descent to the ore-face, the labour of the gang by the light of a tallow candle, the various categories of workers in the mines and ore-crushing mills, the forms of evasion developed in the seventeenth century (for instance, the 'money-bag Indians' who bought their freedom for cash, and who by 1654 constituted one-quarter of the *mitayos*), the relationship of the labourers with the *mita* foremen, the encampments where the families of the *mitayos* and *mingados* lived and so in (Alberto Crespo, 1955, based chiefly on the description by Pedro Vicente Cañete in his *Guía Histórica, Geográfica, Física, Política, Civil y Legal del Gobierno e Intendencia de la provincia de Potosí*, written in the late eighteenth century). There is no point in entering into a more detailed description in this present study.

The Potosí *mita*, like the other *mitas* in mining regions – the harshest and most dangerous of which was that organised for the extraction of mercury in Huancavelica – had the effect of provoking the demographic collapse which is such a well-known historical phenomenon. From the early seventeenth century onwards, the official reports are concerned with the decrease of the labour force, the increase in the period of compulsory labour and the desertion of the *mita* Indians, who stayed on in Potosí as free wage-labourers. Viceroy Lemos was the first to propose a general reform of the system, and then its complete abolition (1670). Viceroy de la Palata attempted to reorganise the system and succeeded in increasing the numbers of *mita* Indians to 2,821, working for two periods each year; this was all that remained of the *mita* of 4,500 Indians recorded a century earlier by Toledo. The sixteen provinces concerned, according to his Official Report of 1689, contained 64,000 Indians, of whom 16,000 lived in Spanish settlements, while 31,000 were outsiders from other districts. The Viceroy bitterly concluded that 'this republic is falling to pieces'.

The *mita* for the textile workshops, where women and boys also worked at spinning and weaving, and which was of such importance in the presidency of Quito, was abolished by law in 1659.

Personal service given under the *repartimiento* system also provoked, as has been mentioned above, moral and legal criticisms which were initiated by the Franciscans in Mexico, and which resulted in the *Cédula* of 1601, which abolished the institution entirely, on the grounds that it hindered both the work of evangelisation and the maintenance of the Indians' families. The new regulations established, as the normal method of recruitment of the labour force, the system of 'main square *repartimiento*', whereby the Indian could seek employment with any employer he wished and receive a just wage fixed by the authorities; this took place in the Spanish *ciudades* or *villas* nearest to the Indian *pueblos*. Viceroy Velasco, however, was unable to comply with this law, as he stated in his Report, 'because all things in this realm have been so arranged from the beginning that, from the greatest thing to the smallest, they depend on the labour and service of the Indians', and the latter were averse to work. It was then that the Franciscan Miguel de Agía wrote his extensive treatise *Servidumbres personales de indios*, with the approval of the Viceroy and all the 'notables'. This study includes a very detailed description of the labour system; it recognises the justice of the royal law in that it supports the principle of natural liberty, but in conclusion it advances all the arguments of a practical nature which justified the position of the Viceroy, who, according to the author, is not a mere executor of the law but an 'arbitral judge', who is empowered to alter the law if this is advisable for the public weal. The public need for productive works justified the labour system; nevertheless, the author pleads for the closing of the main shaft at Huancavelica, because it is a hazard to health, and condemns all the numerous remaining forms of personal service to the *encomenderos* which still persisted. The Crown retracted its position to some extent in 1609, and permitted *repartimiento* in mining, agriculture and stock-raising, in the cases where this system was already in force, but it attempted to achieve a systematic reduction as far as this was possible, and set its face against any extension of the system for the benefit of private employers. In Mexico, where the new labour system based on *peonaje* was already highly developed, the abolition of the agricultural and stock-raising *mita* was carried out without provoking any protest in 1632, as was the mining *mita* in the mid-eighteenth century. In Peru, the mining *mita* persisted until the Cadiz Cortes of 1812, but on a much reduced scale.

In short, the history of this form of compulsory native labour reflects in its development the fundamental tension between the interests of the 'land', that is to say the productive activities developed by the Spaniards, and the Crown, which was in its turn obliged to reconcile ethical motivations with financial requirements. For example, one provision of the *Cédula* of 1601 expressed disapproval of the planting of vines and olives in defiance of the legal prohibitions dictated for the benefit of Spain, and forbade the assignment of *repartimiento* Indians for this work. The equivocal nature of the Crown's motives is quite apparent in this case, and Agía was speaking for the Creole interest when he maintained that this cultivation was in no way contrary to Divine Law, and that the common good of the land should be given priority over the interests of individual Spaniards. The attitude of Solórzano Pereira towards the compulsory labour system reveals his perplexity, and no doubt reflects the struggle between his scruples of conscience – he was for many years in charge of the official *Visita* in Huancavelica and knew all about the 'mine sickness' – and his official and political responsibilities. In conclusion, he was in favour of abolishing the *mita* in the mines, in coca cultivation and in the textile works, basing his arguments, fundamentally, on moral objections; however, he considered the system acceptable for agricultural and stock-raising tasks, where there was no danger to the health of the natives.

From the standpoint of social history, the replacement by about the mid-sixteenth century of the *encomienda* involving personal service by the system of *mita* and *repartimiento* is extremely important, because it demonstrates the strength of the Crown's reluctance to permit the growth of a feudal nobility, a reluctance displayed by its tendency to supply a labour force for landowners, mine-owners and operators of textile works through the medium of administrative arrangements, without conferring any permanent or hereditary privileges. The Crown thus transformed the upper strata of society, and placed the *encomendero* who occasionally benefited from the *repartimiento* on the same level as any other miner or landowner; institutions that still bore traces of medieval concepts of overlordship were replaced by others more firmly based on the ownership of land or of a business enterprise; this did not mean, however, that there was any diminution of the caste distinction existing between the Spaniards and the native population.

The trend towards ruralisation in the seventeenth century: Yanaconas, estancia *Indians, peons*

In the sixteenth century the cities were at first supplied with food from the smallholdings in their suburb and by means of the tribute brought by the Indians to their *encomenderos*, in the shape of the product of the gold placer-mines, maize brought by the natives, and meat from the pigs raised by the *encomenderos*. Only later did the Spaniards acquire an interest in obtaining grants (*mercedes*) of land in places farther from the towns, for the rearing of all kinds of livestock, plantations of sugar, cacao, dye-plants and other tropical crops, as well as the cultivation of wheat and barley. These *mercedes*, granted by viceroys and governors, were principally orientated towards the export trade with Spain and other regions of the Americas, between which a sort of complementary commerce took place (thus, Chile exported to Peru hides, tallow and wheat, in exchange for manufactured products from Spain and Peru, and also sugar; Venezuela exported cacao to Mexico in exchange for precious metals, and so on). The demand for food of the large capital cities and of the silver-mining centres also increased the hunger for land: mining often acted as the incentive for agricultural and stock-raising colonisation. What were at first moderate grants of land grew in size and eventually became vast *haciendas*; this process has been very fully described, in the case of Mexico, by Chevalier (1952). In other cases, as in

Chile from 1580–90 onwards, the exhaustion of the early gold placer-workings led the *vecinos* to devote themselves to agriculture and stock-raising, as long as there was a remunerative market to which to export their produce, because the white population of the small towns did not provide sufficient incentive.

In the sixteenth century, the land was worked in accordance with the systems described above, that is to say the *encomienda* and the *repartimiento* or *mita* which replaced it, often under the supervision of Negro or Mulatto foremen. In the rural areas, however, there were other categories of Indians permanently dependent on some Spaniard – whether or not the latter was their *encomendero* – and who no longer had connections with *caciques* or *pueblos*. In the Antilles these were the *naborias* or *tapias*, and they were also to be found on the mainland; they were of servile status, but inalienable, unlike true slaves. The *naborios* or *laborios* who were later to be found in New Spain enjoyed, despite the similarity of name, a freer status. The *yanaconas* already existed in the Inca Empire as servants of the nobles, and were exempt from the obligation of belonging to communities. After the Conquest these men and, no doubt, a great many others who had not been *yanaconas* at all, fell into the hands of the conquistadors and soldiers, and accompanied them as body servants in the civil wars and new *entradas* into hostile territory. Juan de Matienzo describes them as completely lacking in juridical capacity and subject to the legal tutelage of the *Audiencias*, which assigned them to a variety of tasks. Some worked as domestic servants in the houses of Spaniards, and had very unstable employment; some worked in the big silver mines, and delivered a fixed amount of metal each week to their master, but this system was abolished in 1567, to prevent the *mitayos* escaping from their onerous predicament and entering into similar arrangements. Others worked on the coca plantations in the Andes and, finally, there were those employed by the Spaniards in the *chácaras*, the most important agricultural holdings destined for this purpose being in the viceroyalty of Peru and, more especially, in the district subject to the *Audiencia* of Charcas. On these farms, the Indians had their huts and their small plots of land for growing food to support their families. Viceroy Toledo, in an attempt to increase the food supply of the big mining towns, issued a series of Ordinances in 1572; according to these, the Indian who had worked on a smallholding for four years could not be dismissed, but neither could he leave his employment, except in cases of ill-treatment duly attested before the *Audiencia*. The Indians could sell their surplus production in the mining centres. They were to work five days a week for their employer, but the latter was to leave them one day free for their own work; he was also obliged to lend them oxen and ploughs, pay for their medical treatment and instruct them in Christianity. The *yanacona* was to pay a tribute of one peso, as opposed to the six pesos paid by the ordinary Indians (*Ordenanzas de Toledo*, Levillier, 1929). The similarity between this institution and the various forms of servitude resulted in the *Cédula* of 1601, which abolished personal service, prohibiting this system as well and forbidding any mention of *yanaconas* resident on an agricultural holding in deeds of sale or donation of the land. This *Cédula*, however, was never enforced, and in 1648 Solórzano, in his *Política Indiana* (II, IV), was still deploring the quasi-servitude which the *yanacona* system involved.

This institution, however, was to be in many regions the typical manifestation during the seventeenth and eighteenth centuries of the general onslaught of the *haciendas* against the Indian communities, and of the struggle between the Hispanic and the pre-Hispanic rural worlds. In the late sixteenth and early seventeenth centuries the Creoles in Chile tried to have the Indians already settled on their estates reduced to the status of *yanaconas*, in accordance with the system in force in the territory subject to the *Audiencia* of Charcas, but they were unable to do this by legal methods. Moreover, the term '*yanacona*', which at first was applied only to the Peruvian Indians, was used in Chile to describe all the Indians who no longer owed allegiance to any Chilean *cacique* and had entered the service of a Spanish master, though the term never acquired an exclusive and unequivocal meaning. Nevertheless, there was formed in this way a class of Indians who worked on the estates, and this became increasingly more numerous than that of those living in *pueblos* and assigned to labour through the *mita* system; by 1614 the former group far outnumbered the latter. The *estancia* Indians worked for their *encomenderos*, but with the passing of time one finds cases of them being settled in other *estancias* themselves, and paying their tribute to the *encomendero* in cash; sometimes, there is no longer any recollection or mention of their ever having belonged to any *encomienda*. The Ordinances issued by Viceroy Esquilache in 1620 were the first attempt to regulate the status of these Chilean Indians; these provisions left them in a more favourable legal situation than was the case with the Indians subject to the *Audiencia* of Charcas, because they were free at all times to return to their *pueblos* of origin, or simply to the nearest *pueblo*, if they so wished. However, because most of them were by now definitely settled on their respective *estancias*, the Ordinances regulated their working conditions there, giving them the usufruct of a plot of land and the right to hire out their labour within a radius of four leagues once they had fulfilled their labour obligations to the landowner. In 1634 the

Fiscal of the *Audiencia*, Pedro Machado de Chávez, who had consistently championed the liberty of the Indians, considered that residence on the *estancias* was more beneficial for them than in the *pueblos*, where *Corregidores, Administradores* and passing soldiers subjected them to all kinds of abuses. The patriarchal system which was being built up in the rural areas came to be a new factor in the relations between Spaniards and Indians, and the loss suffered by the Indian who left his *pueblo* was now to some extent offset by his enjoyment of protection and security.

In a regulation concerning the wages of the Indians of Peru promulgated by Viceroy de la Palata in 1687 (quoted in Mörner, 1967, 96), there is less use of the traditional term '*yanacona*', which is now confined to the coastal areas of Peru, and more frequent references to '*agregados*'; one noteworthy feature of these regulations is that, in addition to the right to their own plots of land, the Viceroy ordered that they should be paid the same wages as the *mita* Indians. In south-eastern Peru the *agregados* were more usually referred to as '*arrenderos*'.

The system of *peonaje* prevalent in Mexico has been described by Zavala (1944) and Chevalier (1952), and its general features are to be found in many parts of the Americas. The free Indians (*naborios, laborios, gañanes* and *peones*), who could hire out their labour to any Spaniard except during the times when they were conscripted for labour under the *repartimiento* system, soon tended to settle on some *estancia* or *hacienda*, where the owner granted them the use of a plot of land. This was not a legalised *yanacona* system but a mechanism sanctioned by civil law, and arising purely from the traditional usages of the rural areas: the method consisted of advancing the wages due for an entire period, account being taken of the tribute-payment due and, when appropriate, the costs of medical treatment, thus burdening the peon with a debt which he had to pay off by labour, without being able to leave the *hacienda*. Zavala quotes a number of viceregal Ordinances which tried to place limitations on this practice. In 1629 the maximum period for which wages could be paid in advance was fixed at four months; in 1634 and 1635 it was stipulated that the Indians could pay off this advance in cash instead of labour. Increasingly, however, in the course of the seventeenth century, the Indian became tied to his place of work, and, if he returned to his *pueblo*, the owner of the *estancia* would go there and demand that the Indian governor hand over the debtor. The advances of wages were made in the form of merchandise sold in stores which were often situated on the *hacienda* itself – the kind of shop which subsequently became known as a *tienda de raya*. In the seventeenth century one finds debt-peonage on the Jesuit plantations in Mexico (Berthe, 1966), and in

Yucatán the *peones acasillados* (Mörner, 1967, 97), and also in the silver mines of northern Mexico (West, 1949, 51; Bakewell, 1970, 126). In the eighteenth century it was still the most widespread labour system on the *haciendas*. In 1769 José de Gálvez introduced the clearance-certificate system; this document certified that the peon had no outstanding debts and could therefore seek employment with another landowner. In 1784 his brother, Matías de Gálvez, issued detailed regulations for the peonage system. These still recognised the peon's freedom to move from one *hacienda* to another, but made the possession of the clearance-certificate obligatory. In order to increase this freedom of movement, the regulations reduced the amount of wages that could be advanced, and allowed a landowner to assume responsibility for the past debts of a peon without the latter's having to go back to a creditor for whom he no longer wanted to work; furthermore, the local judicial authority took a hand in the issue of the clearance-certificate. The most obvious purpose of this legislation was the protection of the Indian peons, not the white or *mestizo* ones; this was a reflection of the paternalistic approach of the old laws of the Indies towards the native population (Zavala, 1944, 346–7).

Debt-peonage existed in many parts of Spanish America, although our information on this subject is fragmentary. The Mining Ordinances of New Spain authorised the practice, and this legislation served as a model for other regions. Carmagnani (1963, 57–63 and 107) has proved that it existed in the gold and silver mines of Chile from 1690 at the latest, with a system of clearance-certificates similar to that in force in Mexico; one also finds examples of this sort of indebtedness in the *haciendas* of the Norte Chico mining region of Chile. Macera has drawn attention to the existence of this type of worker on the *haciendas* of Peru. Colmenares (1969, 87–8) has observed that in Quito this system of 'assistance' was often used on the Jesuit estates in the eighteenth century; one administrator of the Jesuits' temporal affairs considered that these advances of wages were inevitable, because otherwise the Indians abandoned themselves to drunkenness and idleness. 'They die without settling [their debts]', is a phrase that occurs in the accounts of the Ibarra College.

In the late seventeenth and early eighteenth centuries many old-established colonial institutions came to an end, either being abolished outright, like the *encomienda* in 1720, or losing all relevance, like the *mita*, which survived only in a few mining centres. The Indians were legally exempt from personal service, and hired out their labour as *gañanes, peones, jornaleros* or (in Peru, according to Macera, 1966, 26) *alquilas*, and so on. They were, however, bound to the *estancias* where they worked by such systems as *yanaconato* or *concertaje,* or as *indios de servicio* or *asituados* (in Quito, according to Colmenares, 1969, 88–9). Others did not actually live on the *hacienda,* but came to seek employment on a daily or seasonal basis from the nearest *pueblo* or *villa* (Chevalier, 1952, 384).

One also observes, however, the development of systems of employment based on the renting of small plots within the *hacienda.* Chevalier (1952, 373–7) records the existence of *terrazguero* Indians, and of *rancheros* who did not belong to any definite caste, in Mexico. The *arrenderos* of La Paz were Indians who paid a rent in maize for the use of a plot of land. Examples of forms of ownership exercised by people other than Indians were those of the *arrendatarios* in Chile, Peru and elsewhere, the *inquilinos* in Chile, and the *vivientes* in Boyacá (Góngora, 1960; Fals Borda, 1957). All these different categories of tenants were poor Spaniards, *mestizos,* free Negroes and Mulattos, and Indians not subject to compulsory residence in a particular place. To judge from the Chilean process, it would appear that initially they received a plot of land as a 'loan' or as 'alms', and with time this became subject to a rent in cash; however, one decisive factor was that in addition to the monetary rent or instead of it, these tenants helped to guard the remote frontiers of the *hacienda* and to round up the cattle – that is to say, their conditions of employment were freer than those of the peons. They had complete freedom of movement and received no wages. In the eighteenth century, when there was considerable development of these varieties of what Mörner (1970) calls 'colonato', there was also, owing to the increase in the commercial value of land, a diminution of the liberty traditionally associated with the 'colon's' status. In Chile, at least, the tenants or *inquilinos* found themselves increasingly obliged to work on the tasks of the *hacienda,* and gradually lost their status as independent smallholders. It would be interesting to compare their condition with that of the peasantry in other regions.

The most intensely ruralised period of colonial history was accompanied by the compulsory attachment of the Indians to the farm or mine where they worked, through the system of debt-peonage, which had originated in the sixteenth century. However, this process of ruralisation reached its apogee in the seventeenth century (which many modern economic historians consider as extending from 1610 to 1690), and its characteristics can be studied today principally with reference to the Mexican model. Chevalier (1952) has published an excellent description of the origins and growth of the typical large *hacienda* in Mexico, and of the way in which it attracted the population of the Indian *pueblos,* which were already in decline. The collapse of the large-scale silver-mining industry caused a decline of the rest of the economy and society, partially stifling ordinary commercial trade and transforming the *hacienda* into a unit with autarchic tendencies, especially in the northern region, which has been more fully studied in this respect than have the centre and south of the Mexican tableland. Borah (1951) has emphasised the Indian demographic catastrophe of the previous century as the most important causative factor in the depression of the seventeenth century:[2] the growing Spanish population could no longer supply its needs on the basis of a native mass living in *pueblos* with a sharply reduced population, which was scarcely able to supply the necessary manual labour through the *repartimiento* system. One solution to the problem was, in fact, the expansion of the *haciendas*, where the Indians were subject to compulsory labour in a system of commercialised agriculture, under the direct control of the Spanish owners or of their bailiffs and foremen. Moreover, similar causes probably produced similar effects, in the opinion of Borah (*ibid.* 29), in Guatemala, Quito, New Granada and Upper and Lower Peru. Chaunu (1959) has studied the depression in relation to the trade between the Americas and Seville, but does not neglect its connection with the demographic catastrophe and the collapse of mining: the era of vast treasure and of the great mining boom had been made possible, he asserts (VIII, 1423), thanks to the labour of an Indian mass which suffered an abrupt decline over the course of a century; after this period there supervened many years of exhaustion and of the employment of Negro labour on the plantations. It must be remembered, however, that the decline of the trade with Seville did not provoke a collapse of commerce in general: inter-provincial trade was flourishing at this time, for example between Chile and Peru and between Venezuela and Mexico (Arcila, 1950).

From about 1685–90 onwards there was a period of stabilisation, and around 1730 a general economic expansion took place. But the agricultural and mining workers were still bound by the system of peonage and indebtedness. The Chilean *inquilino*, now that agriculture was more commercialised, had increased labour obligations and less freedom. Compulsory labour, which previously had been based on institutions deriving, to a greater or lesser extent, from notions of feudal overlordship, or the concept of the common weal, became based in the eighteenth century on premises deriving from civil law (indebtedness, or the usufruct of land), which were explicitly recognised by the colonial authorities – the legislation of Spain itself took no account whatever of such institutions. The new relationship between the Spaniards and the Indians was theoretically freer than had been the case under previous systems, but the peon's compulsory attachment to the land he worked was a glaringly apparent feature of the new social order. Systems of 'colonato' were, however, more flexible. Yet, it appears quite evident that eighteenth-century society cannot be described as 'bourgeois' in any sense of the word, if one bears in mind, for example, that in addition to this more or less compulsory attachment to the land Negro slavery still persisted as an institution; this had its origin in the remote past and remained intact throughout the colonial era. Furthermore, there is a vast difference between the bourgeois mentality and the aristocratic mentality prevalent in eighteenth-century Spanish America. What really happened was that the most varied systems of labour and of land tenure coexisted and supported each other within a predominantly aristocratic social structure.

The caste society established in the sixteenth century still persisted in the eighteenth century. The principal difference was, perhaps, that there had been in the interim a certain downward social mobility among the whites; the 'poor Spaniards' had moved closer to the subordinate ethnic strata. The Indians were still differentiated from the rest of the population by their liability to tribute and by the restrictions placed on their freedom of movement. The marginal castes of *mestizos*, Mulattos and so on, maintained their identity and increased in numbers. Miscegenation of every kind had eroded the dividing lines between the basic castes and had destroyed their ethnic consistency (Mörner, 1967, 1970). As this writer observes, the castes were still the basis of social stratification, owing to the important role they played in collective sentiments and attitudes. The entire corpus of written and unwritten social norms maintained this hierarchy based on caste-differentiation, however much miscegenation and social mobility might blur the formerly rigid dividing lines.

During the 'era of foundation', the Indians had been concentrated in *pueblos* in order to evangelise them and raise their standard of living in accordance with Spanish models. These *pueblos*, however, by the very reason of their being an attempt to establish an ordered society, presupposed a restriction of the Indians' freedom of movement. Zavala (1948) has proved, in the case of Mexico, the degree of vacillation evinced by the Spanish authorities in the face of the contradiction between the liberty of the Indian to work and pay tribute to his *encomendero* or the king in any place and the system of protection constituted by the reservations or *pueblos*. Solórzano, who was against the *yanaconas* being compelled to reside on the *estancias*, nevertheless advocated their concentration in the *pueblos*, in other words a 'conditional liberty'. The era of the Enlightenment displayed less vacillation than did that of the rule of the House of Austria, because the royal finances were now on a more rational basis. Gálvez, basing his reasoning on the need for a more efficient collection of the tribute, tried to attach the Indians more systematically to their *pueblos* and *estancias* (on the latter, the landowner was responsible for payment of the tribute owed by the peons and *terrazgueros*, according to the Ordinances promulgated in Mexico in 1770). Gálvez, in a document published in 1771, also supported the idea of establishing compulsory residence of the Indian mine-workers, for the sake of a more efficient collection of the tribute. He also tried to put an end to the deportations that habitually took place along the northern frontier of Mexico. However, as Zavala himself points out (1948, 414), not even the Bourbon zeal for orderly revenue collection went so far as to abolish all liberty of movement and provoke in the Americas a situation similar to the 'second serfdom' described by writers on the history of eighteenth-century Russia. The Spanish authorities hesitated to take this step, owing to the influence of the legal texts inspired by Natural Law and gathered together in the Compilation of 1680; these were to some extent reinforced by a certain sensitivity on this matter typical of the Enlightenment, so that officials did not allow themselves to be swayed exclusively by the economic interests involved, but partially attenuated the harshness of these factors. The *Audiencia* of Mexico, in its actual enforcement of the laws, showed a reasonable attitude in acquiescing in liberty of movement so long as the payment of the tribute was guaranteed in any particular case. The persistence of certain legalistic scruples, though these were often at variance with the real situation prevailing, was a marked characteristic of the history of Spain and Spanish America, and is a tribute to the strength of the principles derived from Natural Law and Catholicism.

Nevertheless, as a situation discernible by the historian within the context of society as a whole, one can observe the tendency to attach the Indian compulsorily to his place of residence, whether that were a *pueblo* or an *estancia*. Compulsory residence was one of many aspects of the structure of a caste society, established in the sixteenth century on the basis of the concept of 'the two republics'.

However, what was thought of in the sixteenth century by missionaries and jurists as an 'order of society', based on the intention of protecting and civilising the natives, according to the Spanish model, became steadily transformed into a simple racial differentiation devoid of any idealistic purpose. In the mission territories, the racial division always maintained its original character – the system was a bulwark against the intrusion of whites or *mestizos* who might hinder the entire labour of evangelisation. In the open colonial societies, however, the notion of 'the two republics' was gradually transformed into a fiction, and the Indian and *mestizo* sectors came to be regarded as inferior racial strata; this process became increasingly apparent in the course of the seventeenth and eighteenth centuries. In a sense this was inevitable, because the Spanish colonists brought with them their notion of a hierarchy based on distinct estates of the realm, and they superimposed this on the system of ethnic differentiation (Mörner, 1967, 54): in so far as they conceived of society as a unity, their hierarchical valuations were bound to assume an ethnic or racial content.

THE ENLIGHTENMENT, ENLIGHTENED DESPOTISM AND THE IDEOLOGICAL CRISIS IN THE COLONIES

Continuity with earlier colonial history

It would not be correct to classify the entire development of the eighteenth century as representative of the 'century of Enlightenment'. In addition to the processes which began around 1700 or 1750, the actual situation also included the continuance of structures established at the time of the Conquest, and modified to a greater or lesser degree in the course of the seventeenth century. Besides the emergence of new processes, one can observe the traditional structures, either in decline or flourishing as vigorously as ever.

The total population of the Americas, according to the calculations of Rosenblat, increased between 1650 and 1825 from about 10,459,000 to about 21,619,000. The Indian population always comprised a considerable percentage of these totals, although it was declining in proportion to the whole: in 1650 it comprised 3,950,000 people, or 80.5 per cent of the total; in 1825 it had grown to 6,830,600, but by then it constituted only 45 per cent of the total, because the greatest increases had been among the white, Negro and *mestizo* sectors. In 1650 the number of whites was about 659,000, and in 1825 it was 4,349,000, that is to say, it had increased by more than sixfold. In this absolute, though not relative, increase in the Indian population – which eventually began to grow again after its long decline – one can observe the influence, as Chaunu (1964, 106–7) points out, of such factors as the appropriation of European livestock, which now came to constitute an asset to Indian agriculture, and also the Indians' acclimatisation to imported diseases and medicines. The general ruralisation of life had the effect of attenuating the destructive impact of mining operations.

The white population owed its increase, apart from natural growth and miscegenation, to the considerable current of immigration in the eighteenth century; this was predominantly composed no longer of Andalusians and Extremadurans, but of emigrants from the northern realms of the peninsula (Navarrese, Old Castilians, Basques, Cantabrians and Asturians) and from the Canaries; the former group brought with them attitudes and customs different from those which had shaped early colonial society. A much more numerically important factor, however, was the increase in the biological and legal assimilation to the white sector of Indians, *mestizos* and Mulattos. The Indian who had escaped from his *pueblo* or his *encomienda*, the second-generation *mestizo* who used Spanish dress and a Spanish surname, were already generically classified as 'Spaniards', on a level of equality with the Creoles. In countries of intensive miscegenation, such as central Chile, Carmagnani (1973) has observed that only the figures for the white and *mestizo* populations showed an increase. In the city of La Serena, both groups together increased from 64.3 per cent in 1777 to 76.2 per cent in 1813; and in Santiago, from 78.5 per cent to 84.9 per cent during the same period.

The population was stratified, as has been observed above, in accordance with the model of a caste society. Even when identity of occupation tended to blur caste differences, there still persisted differentiation based on the social prestige which the individual enjoyed; this happened, for example, among the craftsmen, as is clear from the guild ordinances (Konetzke, 1949). A clear demonstration of these notions of prestige (or lack of it) based on ethnic origin is provided by the judicial objections filed by fathers of families against the proposed marriages of their children under the age of legal majority to persons of Negro, *mestizo* or Indian blood: this legal recourse was employed even by craftsmen. This racial taboo was accompanied by notions about the supposedly servile nature of certain occupations – an objection that was raised against craftsmen of the most varied kinds and against domestic servants. Commerce, however, even the retail trade, apparently did not by the end of the eighteenth century involve any social stigma (Vial, 1965). Notions based on caste and on the functions of the various estates of the realm were, therefore, in greater force than ever at the end of the colonial period. It should, incidentally, be added that the Royal Pragmatic Sanction of 1776, which established the judicial objections to marriages described above, stipulated that the father's consent was needed for the marriages of children under the age of legal majority, and supported a refusal when the latter was based on the honour of the family: this legal provision shows the degree to which the policy of Charles III, far from being bourgeois, was still inspired by notions based on status and honour. It is not, therefore, surprising that in the Americas these attitudes should have persisted in all their intransigence, in spite of miscegenation and the practical problems that often arose in determining ethnic origin, for the parish priest baptising an infant or the official responsible for classifying the population of a given locality; these were often obliged to accept the declaration of the interested party or of some witness (Mörner, 1967, 53–70). Despite this blurring of the lines of ethnic differentiation, as Mörner emphasises, 'it was the caste system which continued to furnish the social valuations in force and which received the support of the law until the end of the period' (*ibid.* 54). Only in the frontier regions, apparently, was this rigidity attenuated. Félix de Azara, in his *Memoria sobre el estado rural del Río de la Plata*, published in 1801, asserted that even though most of the peons engaged in stock-herding and agriculture were legally Spaniards, 'they do not hesitate to work as day-labourers, on a par with the Indians, blacks and slaves, either out of simplicity, or because rural work has less witnesses that can put them to shame, or because such tasks are appropriate to their inclinations and habits, which make them reluctant to be at hand and give direct service'. These very words of Azara show that he is describing a problematical situation, which he seeks to explain in terms of the honour of particular social classes; but in fact such behaviour was quite consistent with other characteristics of the River Plate region, which differed in this respect from the other provinces of the Americas.

A peculiar feature of the caste society, as it was conceived in the sixteenth century, was the preservation of the Indian languages. The missionaries attempted, in accordance with their overall conception of society, to evangelise the natives using the medium of the aboriginal languages, the learning of which they considered to be one of their first duties: it is to the missionaries that we owe the earliest grammars, vocabularies and catechisms in these languages, and they taught Nahuatl and Quechua in the universities of Mexico City and Lima to train the catechists. This policy was deliberately continued by the Mendicant Friars and later by the Jesuits and even by the secular clergy. However, peaceful coexistence at every level led to bilingualism, even though in the remote regions, as the Viceroy of Lima testified in 1682, there were Indians who could not understand Spanish. The Crown intended to establish a voluntary system of instruction in Spanish, but did nothing to create adequate educational means, so that in the eighteenth century the linguistic barriers were as formidable as ever. Archbishop Lorenzana of Mexico, a typical representative of the Bourbon clergy, suggested in 1769 that the Indian languages should be suppressed, because they were the source of hatred of the conquistadors and of idolatry, in his view. The *Visitador* Areche, after the insurrection of Tupac Amaru, made the same suggestion, but the authorities succeeded in maintaining the *status quo*, which left both Spanish and the Indian languages to thrive as before (Ricard, 1961; Konetzke, 1964).

At the end of the colonial period, society displayed a broad spectrum of ethnic and social strata: these were social barriers and notions, rather than any differences strictly measurable according to the criteria of physical anthropology. At the bottom of the scale there were the Indians; those belonging to the free 'castes' (*mestizos*, Mulattos, *zambos*, quadroons, *quinterones, moriscos, cholos, chinos, pardos, morenos* and other picturesque designations); finally, the Negro and Mulatto slaves. That is to say, that in addition to strata previously defined by legislation and with a strictly regulated status (for instance, Indians and slaves) there were the marginal ethnic strata, the offspring of illegitimate unions, which were so frequent on account of the general context of race relations and the scarcity of Spanish women in early times. The Governor of Buenos Aires wrote on 20 May 1599 that in his domains there were two groups, 'one composed of Spaniards born in Spain of a Spanish father and a Spanish mother, and the other of the so-called *mestizo* natives' – *los dichos naturales mestiços* – and later in the same letter he uses these last two terms as synonyms (quoted in Zorraquín Becú, 1961, 116). Church and Crown advocated segregation of the races and disapproved of miscegenation, because it was illicit on religious grounds and conflicted with the overall concept of 'the two republics' (Konetzke, 1946, 1960). Documentary evidence and ecclesiastical disapproval can be found, for example, in the regulations and controversies over the admittance of *mestizos* to Holy Orders (Lopetegui, 1942, 379). However, all the Spanish officials, priests, soldiers and travellers acted as agents of biological miscegenation and of acculturation (Borah, 1954). The 'war frontiers' were especially favourable to miscegenation, because of the relationship there with friendly Indians and with prisoners of war, and because the Spanish environment in those areas was less aristocratic (Navarro, 1964, 117, for northern Mexico; Góngora, 1966, for southern Chile).

The *encomenderos* ceased to have legal existence in the Indies after the laws of 1718–20, apart from exceptional areas like Chile, where the institution survived until 1789. The Creole upper stratum was composed in the eighteenth century basically of the landowners, who absorbed within a couple of generations the newcomers who had made their fortunes in commerce, mining or public office. The planters of sugar, cacao, indigo, cochineal, cotton and tobacco in the tropical regions; the landowners engaged in cereal-growing and cattle-raising on the Mexican tableland, in the central valley of Chile or the inland provinces of the River Plate area; the owners of vineyards in Chile, Cuyo, the Peruvian coastal areas or the north of the viceroyalty of Mexico; all these, despite the considerable differences in income levels, could be regarded as belonging to the 'possessing class', to use the term coined by Max Weber, and they had many of the genuine characteristics of an aristocratic class.[1] Typical of this class were the *mayorazgos* (estates bequeathed in strict entail according to primogeniture) and the Castilian titles, the sale of which increased in the eighteenth century, when increased wealth demanded the adornment of a noble title.

Mayorazgos and titles of nobility conferred great social prestige, but it must be remembered that they did not imply any 'overlordship' over men or land, nor did they confer powers of jurisdiction or signify any special exemption from taxation. In the sphere of private law, Spanish legislation, which had been unified by the Seven *Partidas* and by Roman law, did not tolerate the growth of any particularist law in this sphere. It is, however, true that such honours played an important part in appointments to public offices of all kinds. Konetzke (*Documentos para la historia de la formación social de Hispanoamérica*, III, I, 208, 299) records the establishment of genuine overlordships over vassals in Havana and Caracas, in 1732 and 1761 respectively; but these were obvious exceptions which had no effect on the situation as a whole.

The social status of the mine-owner varied enormously from one province to another. The mines in Peru, according to Humboldt, were the worst worked in all the Americas; so that it is possible that the mine-owner was always harshly exploited by the money-lenders or *aviadores*, just as he had been in the sixteenth century (Helmer, 1956). However, Humboldt himself has given us a most eloquent description of the wealth, nobility and distinction of the mining magnates of Guanajuato and Real del Monte, in the middle and late eighteenth century, when silver mining was enjoying another boom, and mining operations were carried on using the techniques of the Freiberg school, thanks to the mission of Fausto de Elhuyar, and the 'mining estate' had its own tribunal and its own school (Howe, 1949; Whitaker, 1951).

The most important innovation in the social stratification of the whites was the rise of a new type of merchant, above all the Basque, Cantabrian or Navarrese immigrant, hard-working and thrifty; rather than compete with these newcomers, the old-style Creole merchants withdrew, and diverted their capital to investment in land or mining (Brading, 1971, for Mexico). The Basques and Montañeses formed two parties in the *Consulado* of Mexico, each of them with a consul; the others were obliged to enlist in one or other of these factions. The merchants' guild often became a preserve of the *gachupines* or *chapetones* (the Spanish-born); this circumstance reinforced the contempt they felt for the idle and spendthrift Creoles. It was a guild united by blood relationship and by the ties between fathers and godfathers, where merchants were initiated into their profession as apprentices or cashiers in the shops of their relations, and went on from there to engage in all kinds of commercial activities. In Mexico, in addition to managing their shops in the capital, they bought large quantities of goods at the fairs in Jalapa or the north or Acapulco, and also distributed their wares in the provinces; they even financed mining concerns or the *repartimiento* business carried on by the *alcaldes mayores* among the Indians. In the case of Chile, Villalobos (1968, 204 ff.) has observed the same lack of specialisation and the same adaptability to all types of business, with Chilean and Peruvian merchants competing in the markets of the viceroyalties of Peru and of the River Plate, making plans for trade with the Philippines or with Britain, and even establishing themselves in Cadiz and acquiring merchant ships. In contrast to the situation in Mexico, in Chile both Europeans and Creoles were members of the guild and the *Consulado* (though both groups tended to be of Basque or Navarrese extraction).

Throughout the Americas, these merchants, even though they continued to manage their shops, were passionately interested in acquiring titles of nobility and were full of enthusiasm for genealogy, a habit in full accord with the *hidalgo* tradition typical of northern Spain, and they frequently acquired titles of nobility or the habits of the military orders. The 'bourgeois' life style was still alien to their collective consciousness. Their habits of thrift and diligence were at all times typical of an immigrant class, and never, in our opinion, developed the characteristics which would make it possible for us to describe these merchants as a 'bourgeois class'. At the most, as Kossok (1965) observes, they displayed the purely mercantile element of bourgeois consciousness, and this had no effect on the overall structure of society, which still maintained as far as its internal market was concerned a predominantly 'natural' economy (as suggested by Romano, 1962). The merchants were, undoubtedly, an important guild, but they did not aspire to play a dominant role in the structures of a society based on castes and estates of the realm, and in essence aristocratic (not 'feudal' – the author considers this term to be utterly inappropriate, both on account of the objective content of the word itself, and in the light of the system of values which any feudal order presupposes; such a system never existed in Spanish America, except in the case of the military *encomienda* at the time of the Conquest).

It is a well-known fact that Buenos Aires always constituted the exception as far as the merchants were concerned. Its geographical situation far from the Andes, which were the central axis of the pre-Columbian empires and also of the Spanish viceroyalties, and the scarcity of Indians and precious metals, made this region, from its first settlement, the centre of legal and illegal trade between the mining regions of Upper Peru and the commerce of the Atlantic. Moreover, the River Plate region became, in the seventeenth and eighteenth centuries, a typical cattle-raising frontier territory, exporting cattle on the hoof to Upper Peru and hides to Europe. There is no need to recapitulate here the research that has been done on this historic role of the region (by Levene, Céspedes del Castillo, Kossok, Mörner and others). What should be emphasised at this point, as far as the mercantile stratum is concerned, is that both contemporary observers – for example, Concolorcorvo in his description of Buenos Aires – and the historians mentioned above draw attention to the exceptionally important role played by the merchants and the insignificance of the aristocratic element. The landowners, who were cattle-owners and exporters of hides rather than agriculturalists, were admitted to membership of the Tribunal of the *Consulado* after 1797 on a basis of equality. 'Here every man of substance is a merchant, and he who boasts the proudest title of nobility spends the day with a tape-measure in his hand', wrote one witness in 1750 (Furlong, 1953). Concolorcorvo asserts that there was not a single *mayorazgo* in the city. One edict of the *Cabildo* enumerated the 'estates' of which the population was composed in 1775, namely the clergy, the armed forces, the merchants, the farmers and the craftsmen. The *Cabildo* was so thoroughly controlled by the merchants that the latter did not show any interest in establishing their own *Consulado* until the last decade of the century (Céspedes del Castillo, 1947, 14, 16). The foreigners were very numerous at the beginning of the nineteenth century, especially after the repeal of the prohibition against commerce with neutral countries in 1797.

Below the merchants in rank, in the system of social stratification in force in Spanish America, were the farmers, both proprietors and tenants (of the type described as *colons*), and in the city the craftsmen, in so far as they were all legally 'Spaniards' and had not been assigned to the inferior castes. The growth of the population in the course of the eighteenth century was reflected in the increasingly dense occupation of land. Wherever agriculture or stock-raising was possible, one finds small farmers or tenants settled. The royal authorities in the eighteenth century no longer favoured vast grants of land for the purpose of large-scale cattle-raising, and everywhere, especially after an important edict published in 1754, followed the policy of selling off Crown lands or of legalising occupation without title on payment of a 'composition fee'. It was thus attempting both to fulfil the needs of the Royal Treasury and to obtain the general economic benefits deriving from more intensive agricultural colonisation, normally giving preference to those who were already proprietors. The rural areas were now no longer the preserve of the Indians and wild cattle; they now belonged to the small farmer, the tenant, the *inquilino* or rancher, and they were also the home of the vagrants and bandits, who were now more numerous than ever (Góngora, 1966; Ots Capdequí, 1946).

However, another fundamental sixteenth-century notion was still in force – that of the predominance of urban life. The trend towards ruralisation led to the deterioration of the entire jurisdictional, administrative and ecclesiastical system established in earlier times. Moreover, colonisation of the rural areas by the Spanish and *mestizo* sectors acted to the detriment of the *pueblos* of the Indians, whose lands were invaded and whose way of life was violently upset. Mörner (1970, 212 ff.) quotes several cases in Quito and Guatemala where towns were founded or planned with the object of preserving the segregation of the Indians then living in the *pueblos* of a particular region. In Chile a *Cédula* issued in 1703 at the instance of a governor and a bishop marked the beginning of a policy of founding urban settlements which were to last throughout the century: towns and cities were established with the object of concentrating the scattered Spanish and *mestizo* population. The nuclei of settlement established as a result of this policy (a study of them may be found in Guarda, 1968) were surrounded by rural properties, and had only enough space for a small built-up area, some suburban smallholdings and a common; they did not have communal grazing lands and forests like the old-established cities. The city was no longer conceived as a self-sufficient unit, but was merely a rural market town supplied by the owners of the surrounding properties. The big landowners were generally hostile to these projects, and did not take any part in the life of the new towns until many years later, so that economic standards there remained very low. However, research into the situation in Mexico at the regional level (A. Moreno Toscano, 1970) has made it possible to assert that in that country the provincial towns founded in the eighteenth century often reached a high level of prosperity, thanks to their local industries or to agricultural commerce.

That other expression of the urbanising ideal of the sixteenth century, the Indian *pueblos*, survived and grew in number in the eighteenth century only in the great mission territories, often misnamed 'mission states'. At that time there still existed the Jesuit missions of the province of Paraguay, and those of Maynas in Quito, Mojos on the River Mamoré, Chiquitos to the east of Santa Cruz de la Sierra, those in California and so on; there were also missions organised by Catalan Capuchins and Aragonese Franciscans in the Orinoco-Guianas region. In addition to being the expression of the missionary spirit and contributing to the preservation of the Indians, these mission territories were responsible for the military defence (against raiders from São Paulo, the English, the Dutch and even, occasionally, the Russians) of the frontiers of the Spanish Empire in places where Spanish settlement had not taken place, either on account of geographical remoteness or because they were low-lying areas without reported mineral wealth (Quelle, 1934). Some of these military frontiers were defended only by Indian militias, while others had Spanish garrisons.

Any description of the social strata which persisted in colonial society would be incomplete without at least a passing mention of the great institutions which were not, strictly speaking, social strata: the Church, the universities, the civil service and the still very small standing armies of the time; in other words, everything that in medieval terms stood for priesthood, empire and learning.

The concept of colonial empire and reformist policies

The gradual decline of the universalist notion of Christendom and its swift collapse around 1650, coinciding as it did with the end of the power of the House of Austria, paved the way for the rise of nation states as the fundamental pillars of the European system, and of their offspring, the concept of mercantilist colonial empires. The loss of Italy and the Low Countries, and the abolition of the traditional liberties of the Crown of Aragon under Philip V, were decisive steps towards the establishment of a unitary national state: the privileged commercial companies, created in imitation of the policy pursued in France by Colbert, and the gradual process of the recovery of overseas commerce by Spanish ships were expressions of this new colonialist policy, after the second decade of the century. As Chaunu has observed (1964, 198, 203), Spain lost the commercial control of the Indies between 1630 and 1660, and for the following century Spanish America was a condominium shared by the maritime powers in proportion to the size of their navies and the productive forces of their industrial capitalist system, Spain being left only with the burden of administration. The Bourbon politicians fully realised this situation, and also the military threat posed by the rival empires on the various fronts in the Americas, and they tried to preserve Spain's imperial power by imitating the methods of its enemies.

It is true that the Crown in the sixteenth and seventeenth centuries was aware of the possibilities of protectionist measures for the benefit of the metropolitan power (for example, the legislation concerning vineyards and textile works), but these were isolated and fruitless decisions, for the edicts always had loopholes (Konetzke, 1965, 308, 322ff.). In general, the Indies were colonies based on settlement, and were self-sufficient in foodstuffs and in the products of local industries, with a certain amount of inter-provincial commerce (for example, the textiles of Mexico and Quito); although in qualitative terms industrial products from Spain and other European countries completely dominated the consumer market consti-tuted by the wealthier Spanish population. In exchange, the Americas exported precious metals and the products of tropical agriculture.

The systematic mercantilist conception of the Spanish American Empire found its principal expression in the 'New System' advocated by Campillo, Philip V's Secretary of the Treasury; this treatise was written in 1743 and circulated widely in manuscript form before it was printed in 1789, becoming so well known that the *Proyecto económico* published by Ward in 1779 is largely derived from it. Artola (1952, 1969) has observed in the writings of Campillo many of the ideas that inspired the reforms of Charles III: the demand for the industrialisation of Spain and free trade with the Americas, without excessive duties, and without permitting the establishment in the New World of competing industries in the textile and metallurgical spheres; the definitive abandonment of the exaggerated evaluation of mining operations (the mines had been useful when Spain had had goods to exchange for the gold and silver); the economic evaluation of agricultural settlement and colonisation; the reform of commerce, and the abandonment of the convoy system, which encouraged contraband. 'It can be said', he asserts, 'that we have closed the door of the Indies to the products of Spain and invited the other nations to carry them off to their realms.' It was necessary to examine the methods employed by the English and the French, 'and to adopt any advances they may have made in this sphere'; the *Visitadores generales* who were to be sent to the Americas to inquire into the population, administration and economic resources should be acquainted with the methods of other European nations. There are, above all, two well-defined viewpoints regarding the Americas in the writings of Campillo: on the one hand, the area should be a market for goods and merchandise; on the other, the Americas were an important domain of the Spanish Crown. If the first of these considerations was provided for by the mercantilist concept of complementary economies, Campillo also made an important observation regarding the political importance of the Americas. 'The surest policy', he wrote, 'would be to establish there the same form of government that we have in Spain: that is to say, to appoint Intendants in those provinces.' This is a clear expression of the reasons underlying the administrative uniformity that was to charac-terise the introduction of the Intendant system in the Indies.

A report made by Campomanes and Floridablanca in their capacity as

Fiscales of the Council of Castile – submitted in March 1768 as a result of disturbances in New Spain (and studied by Konetzke, 1950) – makes it clear that, despite the mercantilist conception of the colonial empire, some of its supporters (including Campomanes himself) did not for that reason neglect the more strictly political notion of an imperial community. The American countries, in the words of this statement, cannot be regarded 'as a mere colony, but [should be looked upon] as powerful and important provinces of the Spanish Empire' (an expression which calls to mind that of the Minister Carvajal y Lancaster, 'America, which is the heart and soul of our greatness'). In order to eliminate 'the spirit of independence and aristocracy', Campomanes and Floridablanca, who had always been opposed to the insubordinate aristocracy of Spain, devised a number of political concessions to put an end to the ever-present grievances of the Creoles over the lack of public rewards and offices in their own countries. They suggested, for example, giving high offices in Spain to Creoles, while maintaining the policy of sending out Spanish-born officials to the Americas, in order to preserve the principle of impartiality in the granting of public offices. They also suggested appointing at Court deputies to represent the three viceroyalties and the Philippines, founding a regiment and a college for Spanish Americans in Spain itself, granting Creoles commissions in the Army, and so on. By means of all these calculated concessions the *Fiscales* hoped, in the spirit of the rationalism predominant in that century, to form 'a Nation as one united body'.

As Konetzke has observed, the results were very meagre. The Extraordinary Council to which this report was submitted accorded it its unanimous approval. The *Cabildo* of Mexico at once raised objections with regard to appointments to posts in its cathedral chapters, and refused to be content with anything less than a monopoly for the Mexican-born. A Submission by the same *Cabildo* in 1771 reiterated the eternal Creole grievances over the lack of secular and ecclesiastical offices, using arguments which echoed, among others, those of Solórzano, León Pinelo, the 1667 Report of Bolívar de la Redonda. The *Cabildo* reminded the Crown of the fidelity of Mexico during the piratical invasions and wars of that century, and of the continual rivalry between the European- and the American-born for public and ecclesiastical offices, the important posts in the religious orders and in commerce. It is true that a College of American Nobles was founded in Granada in 1792, and the following year Spanish Americans were permitted to form a company of the Royal Bodyguard. In contrast to this trend, however, during the last decades of the century the Spanish authorities greatly increased their opposition to the establishment of industries in the Americas. Such opposition was expressed, for example, in 1786 by the Council of the Indies, on the grounds of the supposedly complementary nature of the economies of the different parts of the Empire. Even a viceroy as concerned for the welfare of his territory as the second Viceroy Revillagigedo stated in his Instructions of 1793 that Mexico was a colony and should therefore give a certain amount of profit in return for protection; this arrangement for mutual benefit would cease only when the European manufactured goods distributed by Spain ceased to interest the consumers.

Contemporary observers, however, by no means regarded as completely intractable the tensions and problems involved in the task of reconciling these two conceptions of empire – the colonial-mercantilist and the political – based as they were on premises so different from the ones originally accepted in the sixteenth century. Only at a much later date, when it was possible to look back on the unpredictable catastrophe of 1808, did all this appear to be part and parcel of an inevitable process. The idea of a confederation of kingdoms under the rule of Spanish princes, all acknowledging the imperial supremacy of the king of Spain, still seemed to many intelligent contemporary observers a wise arrangement which would solve the many problems involved. This was the solution proposed in the famous Secret Report of the Count of Aranda, which has come down to us in a distorted form, but is authentic as regards its content, to judge from other letters of the same writer; this plan was discussed again, on various occasions, during the last years of the reign of Charles IV (Ramos, 1968). The eighteenth century, with its characteristically naïve confidence in political rationality (conceived of, of course, in rationalistic terms), gave birth to a great many projects, and also effective reforms of every kind, all designed to reaffirm the power of the Spanish Crown after a century of impotence (1630–1730).

An essential component of Spanish Enlightened Despotism was military reorganisation, the advocates of which found it perfectly compatible with the precepts of enlightened philanthropy. It was the urgent problems of foreign policy that were the immediate cause of reforms of every kind. The viceroyalty of New Granada was established, tentatively in 1723 and definitively in 1739, to combat both contraband and the English threat in the Caribbean; that of the River Plate was established in 1776–77 to contain Portuguese encroachment – the latter was supported by British interests, which also posed a threat from the Falklands. The capture of Havana by the British in 1762 provoked the *Visita General* of O'Reilly to the island of Cuba, and subsequently that of Juan de Villalba and José de Gálvez to New Spain.

The reorganisation of the militia and veteran forces, and also the creation of Intendancies, took place first in Cuba and then was extended to New Spain. The famous *Visita* of Gálvez by no means confined its inquiries to administrative and fiscal problems. Gálvez became enthusiastic over the possibilities of maritime expansion in the Pacific, the discovery of fresh sources of mineral wealth in Lower California, the settlement of Upper California by soldiers and missionaries, and, finally, by the prospect of creating a new and vast administrative system destined to guarantee the presence of Spain from Texas to the Californias – what was to be, from 1776 onwards, the Commandancy-General of the Interior Provinces. The north of Mexico, which since the second half of the sixteenth century had been a mining and cattle-raising frontier, and also a zone of continuous warfare against the Chichimeca Indians (Powell), acquired in the eighteenth century the additional characteristic of being a line of defence against the expansion of the British, the North Americans and occasionally the Russians. Gálvez himself, this time as Secretary for the Indies, signed the decree providing for the creation of the viceroyalty of the River Plate, another vast military, cattle-raising, mining and missionary territory which also possessed, as a unique feature, a port suitable for international trade. This new administrative unit attempted to contain both the Portuguese advance and the British expansion towards the Pacific from the Falklands. The older large viceroyalties were thus left weakened, and the Spanish-Indian administrative units were relegated to second place in comparison with the great frontier zones. The personality of José de Gálvez, whom Navarro (1964) considers to be the successor, in some respects, of Hernán Cortés, was not merely that of a staunch representative of Enlightened Despotism, but that of a man with far-ranging geopolitical vision.

Apart from these vast reorganised frontier regions, on which there exists a copious historiographical literature (Bolton, Priestley, Powell, Hernández Sánchez-Barba, Navarro, Levene, Ravignani, Céspedes del Castillo, Gil Munilla), the other important manifestation of the military conception of the State was the reorganisation of the militias. Originating, as has been observed above, in the last decade of the sixteenth century as an expression of the citizen's duty to contribute to the defence of the land, they survived for a further century and a half of the Indies, on such a reduced scale that they came to be little more than devices for awarding ranks to the officers – these ranks were greatly coveted by the Creoles, especially the merchants; while the Negroes formed companies employed on various subordinate tasks (Góngora, 1970, 98 ff.). After the Seven Years'

War they underwent a thorough reorganisation. The plan was to make liable for military service all males between the ages of sixteen and forty capable of bearing arms, the period of service being ten years. One innovation introduced in Mexico was the division of the entire population into five categories, and the selection of those liable for service by a system of ballot among those categories, in such a way that the men most likely to be called up for service were those with few family and economic commitments; this was done to remedy one of the defects of the early militias, which had been almost exclusively recruited from the craftsmen. Rank as an officer was socially attractive, not only because of the titles and honours which accompanied it but also because it conferred immunity from criminal proceedings, which extended to troops while on service; this immunity had existed from the earliest times, but it became important in society towards the end of the colonial era precisely because of the expansion of the militias (McAlister, 1957). These militias were militarily inefficient (except, to a certain extent, those trained by veteran officers), but were nevertheless influential in society (Velázquez, 1950).

The traditional political units dating from the sixteenth century had always reflected the greater degree of independence enjoyed by the governorships which were simultaneously captaincies-general vis-à-vis the viceregal authorities: Guatemala, Puerto Rico, Cuba and Florida, Venezuela and Chile were now made more directly responsible to the authorities in Spain. Within the internal sphere of competence of each viceroyalty, there was also a change in the nature of the office of the viceroy himself, because from now on he lost much of the direct contact which he had formerly had with the *Audiencia*, as there was now interposed between them a purely judicial official, the Regent (1776). The judicial aspect of the viceroy's office suffered a certain abridgment in comparison with early days: from now on the office was less judicial in character, and more executive and military.

This same schism between the old upper bureaucracy, with its ceremonial and judicial character, and the new concept of an executive bureaucracy was also reflected in the metropolitan Spanish institutions responsible for the administration of the Americas. After 1717, the Council of the Indies was deprived of responsibility for the matters which at the time were considered to be the most vital: the Treasury, the Navy, commerce, war and even appointments to public offices became the responsibility of administrative secretaries, in accordance with a system of division of functions derived from the French monarchy; the Council only retained certain responsibilities in the sphere of ecclesiastical patronage and other departments of government and justice. The *Casa de Contratación*, which ceased to serve any useful purpose after the abolition of the convoy system and the introduction of free trade, survived until 1790.

The significance of the intendancies as the prototype of the new executive bureaucracy in the Indies has been studied in great detail by modern historians, who have investigated both the basic presuppositions of the system and its actual functioning in the provinces concerned (see Lynch, 1958; Navarro, 1959; Acevedo, 1965; Deustúa, 1965; Hamnett, 1971; and others). The concept of public appointments of the 'commissary' type, without permanence of tenure and with their terms of reference not defined by any administrative statute, in contrast to the 'official', who displayed both these characteristics (a vitally important distinction in the history of European administration, as has been pointed out by Otto Hintze, 1910), was in no way alien to Spanish or Spanish American law. The 'judges of commissions' and the *Visitadores* constituted examples of this type of appointment as early as the sixteenth century. However, the term itself, and the actual office of 'intendant', is quite clearly of French inspiration, having arisen in the sixteenth century in France as the instrument of the Crown to control and counterbalance the ordinary officials; the intendants had become permanent officials by the end of that century. Even the Spain of Charles II had used French terminology when it created the offices of superintendents of the Treasury and of the Provinces (Navarro, 7), which shows that the spirit of imitation of French institutions was present even before the change of dynasty; but it was, as everyone knows, the Ordinances of 1718 and 1749 which – apart from the purely military intendancies of the War of the Spanish Succession – definitely established the offices of intendants of the Army and of the Provinces throughout the Iberian Peninsula.

In the Indies, too, the intendancies were at first purely military and naval appointments in Cuba and Louisiana, established immediately after the disastrous end of the Seven Years' War, as an indication of the will to recover, in the place where Spain had suffered its worst defeat, the capture of Havana. However, the fundamental ideas that inspired the new institution first appeared in the Plan published by Gálvez in 1768 when he was *Visitador* in New Spain, and in the subsequent Instruction of 1774, issued when he was a member of the Council of the Indies. Of decisive importance was his desire to replace the *alcaldes mayores* and *Corregidores* and their control of the '*repartimiento*' (their monopoly of trade with the Indians) by a system of free internal trade and a bureaucracy of higher status and greater efficiency. The viceroys and governors had administered territories far too big for intensive administrative control. The intendants were to be responsible for smaller districts and, within the bounds of these, for justice, finance, war and general policy, and by virtue of the attributions inherent in this last responsibility, which constituted the greatest innovation, they were to take steps to put into practice the projects of agricultural colonisation formulated by the Spanish economic writers. The encouragement of agricultural colonisation, the distribution of land to the Indians, the provision of facilities to the latter to engage in free internal trade, and new missions and mining operations, were all manifestations of this new responsibility for 'general policy'. The intendant was also to act as vice-patron in ecclesiastical affairs. Directly below him in rank were the subdelegates, who were responsible for collecting the tribute from the Indians, being paid a small commission or salary: this was to be one of the weakest of all the measures of reform, for it meant, once again, entrusting direct dealings with the natives to subordinate officials who were usually rapacious. However, the ideas of Gálvez found expression, albeit with modifications, in the definitive Ordinances for Intendants issued in the 1780s, despite the sceptical attitude of many viceroys and ministers, who preferred instead to reform and improve the existing system, or who put forward sound practical arguments for doubting the effective possibilities of a system of free trade which would really replace the '*repartimiento*' (on this last point, see Hamnett, 1971, for a description of the actual results of this new system in Oaxaca).

The intendant system was designed, generally speaking, to replace the viceroys, whom the *Visitador* Areche had seen as one of the causes of the ills of the Americas (Palacio Atard, 1946). During the early years of the reform, in fact, a superintendent-general of finance took over responsibility for financial matters from the viceroy, but in 1787 this measure was rescinded. However, the new system had the effect of weakening the traditional Spanish American institutions, and, far from implying any process of decentralisation, meant a more intensive control of each territory by these agents of the central authorities; it only had a decentralising effect as far as the viceroys and governors were concerned, according to Lynch (1958, 287–8) and Navarro (1959, 98). However, Lynch rejects the traditional theory that the intendants had the effect of asphyxiating the *Cabildos*: the latter were in a state of considerable decay by the eighteenth century; what in fact happened was that the intendants called for the active collaboration of these bodies; this interpretation is in general supported by Acevedo (1965, 183–92), in the case of Salta.

Militarisation and the rise of an executive upper bureaucracy at various levels of the administration were the principal characteristics of the policy of Enlightened Despotism in the Americas, apart from the new economic policies. The secretaries partially replaced the Council of the Indies, the intendants abridged the authority of the viceroys and governors, and the *Audiencias* became more strictly judicial institutions. The principal mechanisms of the traditional system were left partially dislocated. Moreover, the new intendants did not usually have legal training, but were recruited from the Army or from the new branches of the civil service created in the eighteenth century, which were more specialised in character than the appointments of the older royal officers, for example the Accounts Department, the Royal Treasury, the Tobacco Monopoly, the Customs, the departments responsible for administering various revenues and so on (see Lynch, 1965, 290 ff., for a list of the intendants in the viceroyalty of the River Plate). Furthermore, they were nearly always Spanish-born: Creoles were excluded from public office, according to one Intendant of Cochabamba, because they were accustomed to disregarding the law (Lynch, 1958, 79). The clashes of personalities and of views between the new and the old upper bureaucracy, the older group being more flexible, more easygoing, more tolerant, and better acquainted with the American environment, and at times more corrupt, make an interesting chapter in the history of administration and political life: examples of such clashes are the conflicts between Gálvez and Bucareli and between Areche and Guirior. The harshness of the punishment meted out to Tupac Amaru and the question of the Indian languages were aspects of the policies of Areche which demonstrate the rigidity of the new bureaucracy and the opposition this provoked among the tolerant and the 'enlightened' (Palacio Atard, 1946). The creation of fresh tributes and the rationalisation of old ones set off a wave of insurrections and disturbances: the rising of the *Comuneros* of Socorro in New Granada is only the most famous example of these. Although the abolition of the '*repartimiento*' system controlled by the *Corregidores* remedied one defect of the previous régime which had offended sentiments of justice and provoked hatred of the Spanish-born upstarts, nevertheless the subdelegates soon became the object of similar criticisms and attacks. On the whole, therefore, the policies of Enlightened Despotism provoked in Spanish America – even among officials of the older type that were most sympathetic to the ideas that inspired those policies – feelings of hostility or at least of bewilderment. The American milieu, accustomed as it was to 'salutary neglect', was obviously not prepared for a more rationalised and intensive policy, which was more methodical in fiscal and military matters, less influenced by Creole opinions, and more intent on reserving public appointments and trade for the Spanish-born. The American environment had been shaped in the course of the sixteenth and seventeenth centuries, and was obviously not readily compatible with the new forms which it was desired to impose upon it.

Finally, one important aspect of the new régime, which it is not intended to discuss in detail here, was its commercial and fiscal policies. Of particular importance was the ending of Cadiz's monopoly of trade, from the introduction of the system of registered ships (which operated from 1720 onwards) to the legislation permitting free trade from 1778, with all the repercussions that these measures had on contraband, on American industries, on inter-provincial traffic, on the favourable or unfavourable balance of trade of each region, and so on. These problems have been described and discussed in great detail: the works of Levene, Hussey, Arcila, Céspedes del Castillo, Muñoz Pérez, Villalobos and others provide analyses of eighteenth-century trade in various regions, and there is no need to summarise their conclusions here. It is, however, important to emphasise the fact that free trade often meant the destruction of inter-provincial traffic and its replacement by new commercial ties with Spain (see Arcila, 1950, for a study of the trade between Venezuela and Mexico); many local industries were ruined, but in the long run others arose in their place, thanks to new incentives, as happened with the textile and gold-working industries of Mexico (Hernández Sánchez-Barba, 1963). In agriculture, the increase in the circulation of goods and the development of a more commercial outlook led, at least in the wealthiest and most densely populated parts of Mexico, to an increase in the number of rural properties and in the intensity of their exploitation (Chevalier, 1963). However, it would not be correct to assert that this was generally true throughout the Americas, for it appears that internal trade continued to be sluggish in comparison with transoceanic and inter-provincial trade; as a result, the original agrarian structure remained intact. In addition to the Spanish American exports such as precious metals and tropical fruits which had been important in previous centuries, new exports, such as hides from the River Plate region and Mexico, achieved prominence as a result of the economic policies of the eighteenth century.

At the same time as commercial contacts increased between Spain and its overseas provinces, administrative uniformity was intensified. The Secretariat of the Universal Office of the Indies, created in 1717 and made responsible for all essential matters, was abolished in 1787; but in 1790 matters relating to war, finance, commerce and navigation, justice and ecclesiastical affairs were delegated to the five respective secretariats of State and of the Spanish Office. Only the Council of the Indies, now shorn of many of its attributions, preserved in the peninsula a recollection of the ancient concept of the 'realms of the Indies'.

The crisis in the ideological foundations of the Catholic monarchy

The basic presupposition of Western society had been, from perhaps the ninth until the seventeenth century, the notion of Christendom as a political and religious unity. From 1300 this notion was beginning to lose its original force, firstly because of the new self-assertion of the national monarchies vis-à-vis the supremacy of the Empire and the Papacy, and secondly because of the attacks of the Humanists and the Protestant Reformers. Even the School of Salamanca, represented by Vitoria and his successors, had lent its support to the negation of the Empire and the abridgment of the power of the Papacy. However, long-established ideas have a great capacity for survival: the fifteenth-century Papal Bulls in favour of Portugal and Spain, which expanded the frontiers of Christendom, are proof of this. Later, the expeditions of Cisneros and Charles V to North Africa, the Holy League against the Turks in the time of Philip II, the alliance of the two branches of the House of Austria during the Thirty Years' War, are further proof of the persistence of the notion of Christendom.

Spain had been, until 1492, the march of Christendom against Islam; after that date, however, it adopted a more complex role. On the one hand, the Italian conquests and the connection with the House of Austria transformed Spain into a great European power, closely linked to the Empire and the Papacy (despite occasional disagreements with the latter). At the same time, it became a monarchy with an overseas missionary empire. In the expansion of the known world, which might have led the Church to have doubts about the universality of her mission – in the view of Dupront (1971, 437) – she found, on the contrary, an opportunity to recover her strength. Spreading beyond the bounds of her established world, she became a missionary Church; the new missions replaced the Crusades. In the realm of ideas, Spain committed itself whole-heartedly to this new role as a missionary monarchy, now no longer medieval in character, but projected in 'modern' terms as far as the Atlantic and the Pacific, and symbolising the supreme unity of the spiritual and the temporal – Christendom, however far removed this guiding concept often was from the realities of daily life.

However, after the Peace of Westphalia and the establishment of French hegemony, and later under the British system of the balance of power, the national states came to constitute the new context of political life. Saavedra

Fajardo – according to Jover (1949) – had already hinted, in his work published in 1634, at the transition from the great 'monarchies' (that is to say, the historic universal powers) to 'states' which were smaller, but could still be quite influential within the limitations placed on their powers. The Spanish mercantilist writers of the seventeenth century (a summary of whose thought can be found in Hamilton, 1932) had initiated the critique, from an economic point of view, of Habsburg Spain, and this was to be expanded in the eighteenth century, being accompanied, from 1700 onwards, by the centralism of the Bourbon monarchy and, from 1760, by an undisguised Enlightened Despotism. The Count-Duke of Olivares himself, echoing these criticisms, wrote: 'and if the great conquests (even though they meant conquering and winning victory and acquiring those domains for ourselves) have reduced the Monarchy to so miserable a state, that it can be said with some justice that it would be more powerful if it did not have that New World...' (quoted in Aldea, 1961, 23). The Spanish State was, therefore, beginning to abandon its intentions of unlimited expansion and to concentrate instead, at least from 1700 onwards, on the rationalisation and intensification of its administration.

Moreover, the policy of Enlightened Despotism, when carried to its logical consequences by the senior officials, meant setting aside the personal and charismatic aura of royalty, and instead emphasising the role of the king as the representative of the power of the State, and of sovereignty (Palacio Atard, 1947). It is true, however, that the dynastic concept and the doctrine of the Divine Right of Kings had the effect of attenuating this tendency.

The Catholic monarchy had inherited from the Middle Ages an intellectual universe in which the highest theoretical points of reference had been Latinity, Scholastic philosophy and theology, and Roman and canon law. However, after 1680–90, through academic circles, the new images of 'modernity' and Enlightenment began to penetrate this universe. First Copernicus and Gassendi, then Descartes and finally Newtonian physics became part of the cultural patrimony of all the readers of learned periodicals from beyond the Pyrenees or of volumes of the *Teatro Crítico* or the *Cartas eruditas* of Feijóo, from 1726 onwards. The reception of modern philosophy and science (which had been known, in isolated instances, to some seventeenth-century writers, as Menéndez y Pelayo has observed), began to take effect in academic circles at the end of that century (Quirós-Martínez, 1949), and made its impact on the reading public with the writings of Feijóo. As a vulgariser of Benedictine critical historiography, and also of the great post-Cartesian systems of philosophy and of Newtonian physics, this considerable literary figure set his seal on the Spanish

Enlightenment (Delpy, 1936). After the important event of the expulsion of the Jesuits in 1767, the Spanish State officially abandoned its previous ideological posture of harking back to the Counter-Reformation and the Baroque Age, and adopted the new 'enlightened' ideologies. From this date, it is possible to speak of a genuine Enlightened Despotism in Spain.

This Enlightenment – the best historical account of which to appear in recent years has been, in the opinion of the author, that of Sánchez Agesta (1953)[2] – was fundamentally eclectic in its approach. It was both unable and unwilling to embark on a direct critique of Christianity or adopt a Deist position; but it was able to overturn accepted Catholic historical interpretations. What was attacked was the traditional alliance of Catholicism with philosophy and above all with Aristotelian physics; the object of these attacks was to clear the way for the reception of the science and philosophy of the eighteenth century. Attacks were also levelled against the baroque spirit, in all its religious, rhetorical and artistic manifestations, and these attacks tended to favour the incipient vogue of neo-classicism. The 'modernisation' of philosophy replaced the integrated scholastic curriculum with an eclectic approach which inevitably resulted in the new curriculum consisting of academic instruction in the history of philosophical systems: this led to the current fashionable preference for vast encyclopaedias of the history of ideas such as that of the former Jesuit Juan Andrés, which enjoyed such a wide circulation in Spain and the Americas. In any case, the interest of the reading public was really being reorientated towards the 'useful sciences', a trend which reflected the reformist and educational ambitions of the State and of the Economic Societies, which were typical centres of social life in 'enlightened' circles.

In addition to its 'modernisation' of the sciences, the Spanish Enlightenment manifested itself in the fields of historiography, criticism and erudition. The negation of the past was principally directed at the era of the House of Austria and the Baroque Age. On the other hand, the history of Visigothic Spain, of the Middle Ages and of the Catholic Sovereigns, and the literature of the sixteenth century, aroused passionate interest, from Macanaz and Mayans at the beginning of the century to Jovellanos and Martínez Marina at the end. This interest had a partly pragmatic motive: the rights of the Visigothic kings over the Church and the much later manifestations of Regalism were studied in the hope of finding a historical precedent for the anti-Papal policy of the time (this was the tendency termed by Menéndez y Pelayo 'Hispanism', by analogy with Gallicanism). On other occasions, however, scholars were motivated by a genuine antiquarian passion for the past and the intellectual urge to achieve a critical understanding of it. Nationalist feeling thus acted as a counter-balance to the process of reception of foreign models.

The Spanish Enlightenment and the Spanish American one had, of course, a natural connection. The eighteenth century was a period of intensive communication between the Americas and Spain, particularly as regards the circulation and reading of books. The works of Feijóo and Campomanes, and such journals as the *Semanario erudito* or the *Espíritu de los mejores diarios* were to be found in all good colonial libraries in the eighteenth century. The diffusion of the knowledge of the great post-Cartesian philosophical systems and of the 'useful sciences' (physics, chemistry, mineralogy, botany, natural history, medicine and so on) spread extremely rapidly from Spain to the colonies, through the medium of the reformed university curricula, the learned journals and the Economic Societies. The Spanish naturalist José Celestino Mutis wrote in 1802 to the Viceroy of New Granada that the curricula had been reorganised in accordance with 'the ideas of the men of Spain', and there would be no going back to the old system 'as long as there continues to be untrammelled communication with their metropolis and with the learned world'. All recent research has proved that the old theory of 'French books' smuggled into the continent as being the sole source of the Spanish American Enlightenment was defective, because it took no account of the fact that there had been an officially accepted and propagated Spanish Enlighten-ment which acted as an intermediary, both through original Spanish books and through the innumerable translations (some of them expurgated) made of foreign works in the seventeenth and eighteenth centuries.

Having said this, however, one must emphasise one important difference between the Spanish and the Spanish American Enlighten-ments – a difference which does not find direct expression in the writings of the period, but which is nevertheless apparent enough to the present-day historian. In Spain itself, the reception of 'modern' thought was accom-panied by a certain development and selection of pre-existing national traditions, even though, of course, this did not prevent the ideological schism between the 'two Spains', which had its origin in the eighteenth century. Nevertheless, such thinkers as Mayans, Jovellanos and Martínez Marina managed to preserve an internal balance between traditionalism and modernity which in itself is enough to refute the disparagement of such men as mere 'imitators', in the crude sense of the term, which was certainly justified when applied to the 'parlour philosophers' ('*filósofos a la violeta*'). In Spanish America, however, there is no doubt that this 'reception' was of a much more one-sided and even uncritical nature, and constituted a much more violent break with the past than was the case in Spain. The author does not share the opinion of Picón Salas (1944, 163) that between the preceding theological literature (for example, Avendaño's *Thesaurus Indicus*) and the Enlightenment there was no break in continuity, because such themes as the Social Contract are to be found in both sources: it is a well-known fact that the Scholastic 'pact of submission' had theoretical premises and a conceptual function very different from the Social Contract as conceived by Rousseau. It is also true that in 1690 the Mexican Carlos Sigüenza y Góngora published his *Libra Astronómica*, refuting astrological beliefs and quoting Kepler, Galileo, Gassendi and Descartes, and even admitting, as a hypothesis, the Copernican theory. But this author was, above all, a disciple of the seventeenth-century Jesuits, particularly of Athanasius Kircher, representative of the baroque school of 'physicotheology'. The work of Sigüenza y Góngora, viewed as a whole, shows him to be a typical baroque 'polyhistorian', rather than an 'Enlightened' or neo-classical thinker; and much the same can be said of the Peruvian thinker Peralta y Barnuevo, who wrote nearly half a century later and corresponded with Feijóo. Both men were teachers of mathematics, but within the context of the seventeenth-century university curriculum.

It is, however, possible to discern a new generation, 'enlightened' and neo-classical in outlook, in some Jesuit writers of Mexico, Quito, New Granada, the River Plate and Chile; these men obtained teaching posts shortly before 1767, and later produced copious works in exile in Italy. Nor was this, of course, a spontaneous movement: the Jesuits of the Seminary of Nobles in Madrid and of the University of Cervera had already adopted an eclectically 'enlightened' outlook at the beginning of the eighteenth century (Casanovas, 1953). After 1767, the bulk of the reorganised curricula incorporated in their entirety the orientation and the textbooks which were being recommended in those same years in the universities, colleges and convents of Spain: it was these writings which inspired the most characteristic reformers in Spanish America, Gamarra, Goicoechea, Caballero y Góngora, Pérez Calama, Espejo, Rodríguez de Mendoza, Funes, Maciel, José Agustín Caballero, among others.

However, this almost literal 'reception' of Spanish reforms had one characteristic which limited its profundity. This was the fact that at the time Spain was not the mistress of Europe, but the disciple. Feijóo himself was an important agent of this transmission of culture, as is shown by the checklist of his foreign sources, which have been traced by Delpy (1936). The curricula followed as 'models' by the Spaniards were those of Mabillon, Rollin and Fleury, which constituted a summary of French culture, particularly ecclesiastical culture, of the seventeenth century; Mabillon's *Traité des Etudes Monastiques* was one of the books most frequently quoted by Feijóo, and it had been translated in Madrid very early in the century, in 1715. To these books must be added the *Verdadero método de estudiar para ser útil a la República y a la Iglesia*, by the Portuguese Luis Antonio Verney, Dean of Evora, 'o barbadinho' (1746, Spanish translation 1760), which provoked a reply by the Spanish Jesuits and which was read in Spanish America, being most frequently quoted in Mexico. The Oratorian Friar Gamarra, who modernised the philosophy curriculum in New Spain, made great use of this work (González Casanova, 1948); the future revolutionary leader Miguel Hidalgo, when he wrote a short work sponsored by Pérez Calama, *Sobre el verdadero método de estudiar teología escolástica*, in 1784, based his ideas on those of Feijóo and the 'Barbadinho', almost copying the title of the latter's work. Apart from the changes in university curricula, French, Italian and Portuguese works which were influential in the Spanish Enlightenment circulated widely in Spanish America, as can be seen, for example, if one examines the contents of the libraries in Chile and the River Plate region in the colonial period; this was particularly true of works of an encyclopaedic or vulgarising character, such as Pluche's *Spectacle de la Nature*, the works on physics of the Abbé Nollet, the *Recreaciones Filosóficas* of Almeida, and the *Memorias de Trévoux* of the Jesuits. School textbooks in Latin, too, were usually the works of foreign philosophers, theologians and writers on canon and Roman law. The dominant ecclesiastical culture was represented, apart from the Scriptures and the writings of St Augustine and St Thomas, principally by Bossuet, and, to a lesser degree, by the other sacred orators of the century of Louis XIV and other French and Italian authors. Although not in such great quantity, these libraries included some of the great works of the seventeenth-century philosophers and scientists, and also of the eighteenth-century *philosophes*, even though the latter generally ran the risk of condemnation by the Inquisition.[3] The Spanish American Enlightenment, like the Spanish one, on account of its eclectical and academic character, required for its sustenance a considerable volume of contemporary literature, duly translated and adapted. Foreign theories normally reached the reading public in manuals from which the anti-Catholic implications had been expurgated. This was the case, for example, with the *Historia del Derecho Natural y de Gentes*, written by the professor of that subject in the Royal College of San Isidro in Madrid, Joaquín Marín y Mendoza; this served as a standard textbook in this field, being one of the works most widely read and esteemed by jurists towards the close of the century, until the suppression of the chair as a result of the alarm aroused by Revolutionary propaganda. The Netherlands and German jurists (Grotius, Pufendorf, Thomasius and Heinecius) thus contributed to the development of a new mentality among jurists, which was at variance with the old theories based on Natural Law, Roman law and Scholasticism, despite the efforts of Marín y Mendoza to achieve a synthesis of the two systems.

The educated classes in Spanish America were obliged, therefore, to abandon their exclusive orientation towards Hispanic thought, under the influence of this mass of literature which was either translated or was serving as a vehicle for the transmission of culture. Spain was no longer the standard-bearer of a universalist corpus of thought, developed through classical antiquity and the Middle Ages, when Spain itself had made a partial contribution, for example through its theologians and jurists. On the contrary, in the eighteenth century the cultural situation was quite different from that which had prevailed for the preceding two centuries: Spain was now the disciple of contemporary science and philosophy, and of competing national cultures. The reaction of Spanish America to this situation, therefore, differed from that of Spain. Creole resentment found expression in such phrases as that which Humboldt heard in Mexico: 'The cultivation of the intellect makes more rapid progress in the Colonies than in the Peninsula.' The Spanish American Jesuit writers who published apologetic works on their homelands in Italy contented themselves with a few sentences in their prologues in praise of Spain, and would then wax eloquent in their eulogies of Creole intelligence, and indulge in idyllic descriptions of nature and the pre-Columbian cultures or the present-day customs of the Indians. Fr. Clavígero's *Historia antigua de México* was attacked by his Spanish fellow-Jesuit Caballero on the grounds of its excessive Mexican nationalism. Only one Jesuit, a native of Guayaquil, undertook an apologetic defence of both Spain and Spanish America, in a work attacking Raynal (Batllori, 1953, 106; 1966, 581–2).

Of course, this process of negation of Spain was not without significant exceptions. José Antonio Alzate, defending himself against the accusation of being a slavish imitator of foreign models, in an article published in the *Gaceta de México* on 28 December 1772, asserted that he admired the political and military glories of Spain, and also the humanists, theologians and mystics of the sixteenth century – for example, Nebrija, the editors of the Complutensian Polyglot Bible, Vives, García Matamoros, Melchor Cano, Soto, the Spaniards who took part in the Council of Trent, Arias Montano, Azpilcueta and so on – and that he felt a similar admiration for the era of Philip V, Feijóo and Charles III. This affirmation of a balanced admiration for Spanish culture – which was, in any case, a reply to an accusation, and not a spontaneous act – is couched in the same terms that would have been employed by any 'enlightened' Spaniard, in its attempt to achieve a synthesis between the contemporary age and the sixteenth century.

More common in Spanish America, however, was the uncritical acceptance of 'modernity', without any perception of the totality of the spiritual evolution which preceded it; this acceptance was, therefore, often accompanied by a Utopian radicalism. The course followed by the Enlightenment led the Spanish Americans to regard Spain as, culturally speaking, a mere province, and to have little respect, therefore, for the historical role formerly played by Spain or the value of its achievements of conquest and colonisation. Condemnation of the atrocities committed by the conquistadors became a frequent topic in writings, and praise was reserved for the Indian cultures, which were compared with those of classical antiquity; writers denied the Satanic character of the Indian religions – a denial already formulated by Las Casas in his *Apologética Historia*. Praise of the natural environment of the New World, written in refutation of denigrations of it, was another important *Leitmotif* in the writings of the Spanish American Enlightenment (Zavala, 1949; Villoro, 1950; and, more especially, Gerbi, 1960). The more learned and temperate of the exiled Jesuits adopted an interesting position in this respect. Arnoldsson (1960, 33–7) has observed that Clavígero, Cavo and Molina did not by any means adopt a consistently anti-Spanish attitude, and showed a high appreciation of the founders of nations such as Cortés and Valdivia – in their writings, these warriors are recollected, together with the Indians, in a chorus of praise of their respective nations. Nevertheless, they display a much greater esteem for the great indigenous cultures, in the case of some nations, and, in the case of others, for the martial bravery of the hostile Indians, because of the contribution this made to the sense of nationhood. Clavígero uses the term *mexicanos* of the Aztecs and also of the present-day inhabitants of the country; and to Molina, the words *chilenos* and *araucanos* are synonymous; this usage implied a revolution in the understanding of history, even though this was never explicitly stated.

During the sixteenth and seventeenth centuries, the Creole had enjoyed a feeling of cultural security in the environment created by Hispanic ideas and forms of the Renaissance and Baroque Ages; literature, art, thought and the outward manifestations of religious feeling all bear witness to this. The aristocracy boasted of being descended from the conquistadors. However, the ideological schism that took place in eighteenth-century Spain naturally produced effects which one is unable to analyse in due detail, because for the most part they belong to the category of things left unsaid. The theoretical bases of the State originally established in the sixteenth century were forgotten; they ceased to form part of the collective consciousness. Neither the Spanish Middle Ages nor the Golden Age were considered to be of any value in themselves by the 'enlightened' Spanish Americans (apart from such isolated testimonies as that of Alzate), and in this respect they differed from the 'enlightened' Spaniards. The remains of older structures survived in society, but they were no longer values justified by any theoretical concept. There is some significance, of course, even though it was an exceptional case, in the fact that the Peruvian agitator and ex-Jesuit, Juan Pablo Viscardo, felt a sense of solidarity with the conquistadors against the absolutism of the sixteenth-century monarchs. It is also of some significance that Fray Servando Teresa de Mier, in Book XIV of his *Historia de la Revolución de la Nueva España* (1813) and in other writings published subsequently, should have elaborated his theory of a Magna Carta of the Indies, deriving from a 'pact of the conquistadors' between the Crown and its military commanders, which around 1550 was, so to speak, a Constitution, a bulwark of the liberties of both Spaniards and Indians; later, however, this was violated by the forces of despotism (Góngora, 1965). This interpretation, fundamentally traditionalistic and pro-Hispanic, was employed on this occasion to justify the rebellions which were breaking out in the Americas at the time, and was analogous to the ideas of the later Jovellanos and of Martínez Marina, by whom it was quite possibly influenced. Mier was, however, too inconsistent for his theories to be taken very seriously: even in the later volumes of that same *Historia*, the anti-Spanish diatribe reaches a level of virulence too pronounced for him to be classified as a 'traditionalist revolutionary' in this sense of the term. His pro-Indian stance was much more consistently maintained.

When considered in its totality, the homogeneity of university curricula and of other forms of divulgation of the Enlightenment, in Spain and in Spanish America, can be seen to be superficial; beneath this surface there was a growing separation between the two cultural spheres. A similar process appears to have taken place in the case of administrative unification and other measures resulting from the projects of the mercantilist writers and of José de Gálvez. The plans themselves, drawn up in such elaborate detail – for example, those of Campomanes and Floridablanca or that attributed to the Count of Aranda – are an indication that the more perceptive politicians were aware that imperial unity did not really exist. At the end of the century, according to Humboldt, one could hear the phrase,

'I am not a Spaniard, I'm an American'. The conflicts of ethnic and regional interests, which are a feature of every empire and which existed as early as the sixteenth century (with all its rebellions and conspiracies) became exacerbated towards the end of the eighteenth century. The Enlightenment, by explicitly rejecting the conception of the world on which the Catholic monarchy rested in both continents, inevitably provoked a qualitative increase in previous schisms; and it was not possible to recreate a sense of unity on a new basis – that of the community of interest implicit in a 'colonial pact', or that of mere ethnic and linguistic ties.

The Enlightenment also provoked, in Spanish American society, a schism between the strata educated in an atmosphere of reception of 'modernity', and the popular strata, in the correct sense of this last term – that is to say, all those sectors whose historic development derived from the Indian past or the Hispanic-Indian amalgam of the sixteenth century. The process of repulsion and attraction that took place between the 'enlightened' and the 'popular' – which was to be described with such perception, at times, by Domingo Faustino Sarmiento – was to constitute one of the most important strands in the history of the nineteenth century.

Moreover, the Enlightenment led in Spain, as it had in Spanish America, to an ideological schism within the educated classes and the socially dominant strata, concerning the content and the speed of the process of reception of 'modernity'. Menéndez y Pelayo has recorded the names of the opponents of *Encyclopédisme* in Spain; among them were one perceptive writer, Forner, the Peruvian convert Olavide and, above all, Jovellanos, who gradually adopted this position from the 1790s onwards. In Spanish America, the controversy had already begun around 1760, when Rousseau, Feijóo and modern philosophy in general were attacked by some writers who have been studied by González Casanova (1948), who has applied to them the polemical term 'misoneístas' (anti-innovators). The most important of these was, without a doubt, the bibliographer Juan José Eguiara, who perceptively observed that 'change in philosophy imperceptibly introduces change in theology'. The expulsion of the Jesuits in 1767 – the irony of the situation being that this was the Order which was then making most efforts to be receptive to the currents of the Enlightenment – constituted, as Mörner (1963, 3) has observed, not only a historical event but the subject-matter of numerous myths forged by the victims and by their adversaries. The expulsion of the Order which most effectively embodied the spirit of Catholic expansion, the Counter-Reformation and world-wide Mission – that is to say, the most prominent objectives of the Catholic monarchy of the Baroque Age – did, of course, appear as profoundly symbolic.

Unfortunately, most research into this subject has concentrated on the pragmatic course of immediate causes and effects, rather than on the significance of the expulsion from a long-term historical point of view. Anyway, this royal decision provoked, in the short term, a division of opinion among the clergy, and this division only became more pronounced in the following decades. The struggle in favour of or against the 'Enlightenment', in its broad acceptance of modernisation, was to determine, at the beginning of the nineteenth century, conservative and liberal positions among the politically conscious Creoles of the Independence period and, later, in the new national republics. At times these conflicts assumed the character, as they did in Spain, of veritable wars of religion. Very often, the anti-Enlightenment party would not confine itself to rejecting modernity as being in conflict with tradition, but would seek other cultural and ideological supports contributed by the contemporary political currents of Europe (for example, French Traditionalism, from the 1820s onwards); thus both extremes, despite their ideological enmity, were often inspired by contemporary European notions.

Reforms in the academic curriculum

Universities had been founded in the Indies for the very specific purpose of training priests for the missions, canons for the cathedrals, lawyers to plead before the *Audiencias* and one or two doctors of medicine; in short, servants of Church and State. The bigger cities aspired to be the seats of universities because this satisfied their civic pride and provided them with a student population. The academic degrees of Bachelor, Licentiate, Doctor and Master constituted the qualifications for ecclesiastical and judicial posts which the Creoles found attractive; thus the Creole demands for a greater share of appointments and benefices were always connected with the academic qualifications of the petitioners. Moreover, the university reinforced the urbanising concept which was a central feature of the Spanish system. A defender of the University of San Marcos in Lima was to say, in 1620, that when students went to the city of Lima 'they awoke and began to develop, escaping from the confinement and narrowness of their villages and being taught good speech, urbanity and manners, and being weaned from the breast and made to forget the habits of speech and tone of voice of the Indians, among whom those of the better class have been brought up' (quoted in Eguiguren, II, 83ff.). The Spanish American university also enjoyed at times an arbitral role similar to that of the universities in the early Middle Ages: Archbishop Zumárraga requested the foundation of a university in Mexico City in order to have the benefit of its opinion on questions concerning the Indians: 'every day fresh problems arise, and there is no university of men of letters to consult, and those in these parts are so far distant, that before we can receive information from them we have already committed errors in our dealings' (quoted in Ajo, II, 159).

It is not necessary, for the purposes of this study, to trace the history of each of these academic foundations, from Santo Domingo, Mexico and Lima in the sixteenth century to the numerous universities and colleges which owed their foundation, to a great extent, to the initiative of the religious orders (especially the Dominicans and the Jesuits), and which arose throughout the continent during the seventeenth and eighteenth centuries, in addition to the new universities subject to the royal *Patronato* (see Medina, 1905, 1928; Eguiguren, 1940, 1949; Lanning, 1955; Leal, 1963; Konetzke, 1968; Salazar, 1946; and others). The universities subject to the royal *Patronato* had a corporate system of government and jurisdictional autonomy, like those of the Middle Ages. The rector was empowered to deal with minor offences committed within the university precincts, and to decide questions connected with studies and discplinary problems; in the case of serious offences, his powers were limited to making a preliminary judicial report and handing over the culprits to ordinary justice. The cloister (of doctors) and the students took part in the designation of rectors, members of the council and professors. In the Pontifical universities, which functioned in the houses of religious orders, the respective order enjoyed more authority in appointments, and the jurisdiction of the cloister was more limited. The colleges, particularly the *Convictorios* run by the Jesuits, were institutions with only a few dozen students, drawn from the sons of the local aristocracy, and these came to be centres of education *par excellence*, where not only the curriculum but the entire rhythm of student life acquired a distinctive character.

It has already been emphasised that the content of the curriculum was fundamentally the medieval plan of studies, with certain modifications introduced in the sixteenth century. The 'minor faculties', or course of general studies, consisted of Latin grammar, in accordance with the methods of Nebrija and Vives, followed by a three-year course in Aristotelian philosophy, with an emphasis on logic. On completion of this course, the students were distributed among the 'major faculties' – theology, law and medicine. In the first of these faculties, students imbibed the teaching of the great churchmen drawn from the various orders – St Thomas Aquinas, Duns Scotus and Suárez – often using the *Sentences* of Peter Lombard as a textbook. The Scriptures received much less attention than

Scholasticism in the theology course. In the course on Roman law, students read the Institutes and certain chapters of the Pandects or of the Code of Justinian; and in that on canon law, the Papal Decretals. Medical education was based principally on Galen; but this faculty was the least renowned and the least well attended, even in the great universities in the viceregal capitals, until in the seventeenth and eighteenth centuries these studies were improved and diversified. The first proposals for a university in a mission territory gave rise to a project, which denoted a certain Erasmian influence, whereby the teaching of logic and theology should be purged of 'subtleties' and schoolmen's disputes, and there should be good chairs of Holy Scripture (Bataillon, 1952, for a description of a project for Guatemala). But the vested interests of Scholasticism based on traditional logic easily frustrated this change of orientation. The reading of textbooks was supplemented in the course of studies by frequent exercises in logic and dialectics, which were a basic feature of university life and were also an essential part of graduation ceremonies and of the procedure for appointment to chairs. There remained, however, of the original missionary projects, the plan for the creation of chairs in the 'general languages' – that is to say, Nahuatl and Quechua, in Mexico City and Lima respectively.

The report of an official *Visita* to San Marcos in Lima in 1581–2 throws some light on the actual character of the classes themselves. The professors of law, according to one student, 'put their case in Latin and then, after making comments, draw conclusions from the text and often while away their time with doctoral disputes...' (Eguiguren, II, 83 ff.). They would read in Latin, but occasionally quote certain examples in Spanish.

In the courses on logic, dialectics, physics, heaven and earth, generation and corruption, the soul and metaphysics – that is to say, the entire corpus of Aristotelian philosophy which formed the curriculum of the faculty of arts – studies were based on printed textbooks which achieved a wide circulation, such as that of the Augustinian Alonso de Veracruz and the Jesuit Antonio Rubio, who both held chairs in Mexico City (Gallegos Rocafull, 1951). In theology, however, the teachers preferred the system of dictation, in order to gain continuing support for their own opinions or the views of particular schools of thought regarding current topics of controversy (grace, *Scientia media* and free will, for example).

Latin was never a colloquial language, but it was used as a medium of academic instruction, and in provinces such as New Granada it attained a certain degree of rhetorical excellence (Rivas Sacconi, 1949). Jesuit teachers often added courses in rhetoric and poetics, and sponsored theatrical works in Latin verse on subjects from antiquity or the lives of the saints, designed to inspire the students with the Jesuits' aesthetic notions and ideals.

The seventeenth-century Spanish Amercan universities, despite their strong attachment to formalism and dialectical 'subtleties', nevertheless received some innovatory influences, which almost certainly stemmed from the 'Realia' which predominated in the Imperial College in Madrid, an institution independent of the universities and organised for the education of nobles (Góngora, 1959). In the two great universities in the viceregal capitals, chairs of medical method, anatomy and surgery were founded; in the same centres of learning there were established chairs of mathematics, chiefly orientated towards cosmography. The two famous holders of these chairs in Mexico City and Lima, Sigüenza y Góngora and Pedro de Peralta, were also fortifications experts (Leonard, 1933, 1959). There has not yet been adequate detailed research on the characteristics of Hispanic Scholastic education in the seventeenth century, and that of the eighteenth century, according to Ceñal (1961), was inferior to its predecessor. The new intellectual possibilities opened up by the thought of Suárez, which caused his philosophy to be so widely received in Germany, do not seem to have been noticed in Spanish America.

This type of university, closely orientated towards professional training, which formed people but was itself imprisoned by formalism, was subjected to a process of criticism which was bitter and at times crude (as, for example, in the attacks on Aristotle), the general course of which has been described above. The Jesuit *Convictorios*, which were now renamed *Convictorios* of St Charles, and the new royal universities, which sometimes replaced those founded by religious orders, were the chief vehicles of the reforms. Their proponents were often ecclesiastics: José Celestino Mutis, who defended Copernicus' theory in Bogotá in 1774; the Oratorian Friar Gamarra in Mexico City; the Franciscan Goicoechea in Guatemala; José Antonio Caballero in Cuba; the Viceroy-Archbishop Caballero y Góngora in New Granada; Bishop Pérez Calama in Quito; Toribio Rodríguez de Mendoza and the *fraile de la Buena Muerte* Isidoro Celis in Lima; Canon Maciel in Buenos Aires; and Dean Funes in Córdoba; and everywhere, until 1767, the 'modernising' Jesuits. Sometimes they were lawyers, like Juan Egaña, a Peruvian who established in Chile the teaching of literary history (in the sense in which Juan Andrés had used the term, that is to say the history of ideas). Occasionally they were members of the *Audiencias*: Villaurrutia in Guatemala, Moreno y Escandón in Bogotá, Cerdán y Pontero and Rezabal y Ugarte in Lima, and so on. There were some doctors of medicine, such as Esparragosa in Guatemala and Unanue in

Lima. Especially noteworthy was the *mestizo* Eugenio Espejo, a physician, who in his *Nuevo Luciano de Quito* copied Verney's plans for the thorough-going reform of academic curricula. Centres of ecclesiastical studies – both seminaries and novitiates – were often vehicles of the Enlightenment; in addition to their usual academic disciplines they taught law, mathematics, experimental physics and medicine. Of course, not all the ecclesiastical colleges and universities accepted the innovations, but the circulation of textbooks printed in Spain gradually replaced the system of dictation and, in the long run, encouraged the uniformity of studies.

The Enlightenment was brought to Spanish America by Spanish officials and ecclesiastics, with whom Creoles associated themselves; enthusiasm for 'enlightened' thought crossed the lines of ethnic origin. The Enlighten-ment led to the abolition of Latin as the language of academic instruction, and it became simply another university subject. The study of Spanish was introduced, and this was to flourish during the nineteenth century.

In the faculties of arts, Aristotelianism was replaced by eclecticism ('elective philosophy'), which was, to all intents and purposes, the history of philosophy. Aristotelian physics was replaced by modern physics and cosmography. The Spanish texts of Tosca and Bails were used in the advanced courses in mathematics.

In the faculties of theology, the teaching of the Scriptures, which had fallen to a very low level in the colonial period, was given greater pro-minence, and the courses of Scholastic theology were based on the text-books of Thomist or Scotist authors, the thought of Suárez being elimi-nated from the curriculum. In moral theology, the anti-Jesuit offensive went to even greater lengths, with the obligatory introduction of textbooks of more rigorist moral theology, especially those of the probabiliorist school.

The national State, which encouraged the vernacular language, also insisted on the systematic study of national law (both Spanish and Spanish American), the knowledge of which had previously been acquired merely through practice. Roman law, which traditionally had been conceived as a 'formative' discipline *par excellence*, was relegated to a purely propaedeutic function. The Enlightenment almost entirely abandoned the idea of humanist 'formation' of the student in all subjects, and sought instead to impart an encyclopaedic knowledge of the natural world.

Canon law, in university studies, became orientated towards Gallican doctrines of an increasingly Regalist emphasis. Moreover, the newly founded chairs of Natural Law and the *Jus Gentium* were the vehicles of a moderately absolutist teaching derived from the principles of Natural Law, in accordance with the thought of Pufendorf, Wolf and Heinecius, through the medium of Marín y Mendoza, whose textbook influenced even the generation which carried out the struggle for Independence (Zorraquín Becú, 1962); this chair, however, must have become the vehicle for the propagation of politically dangerous ideas, because it was suppressed in the years following the French Revolution. The teaching of medicine also incorporated the new scientific discoveries (Lanning, 1956).

There is no need to embark here on a monographic study of this process of renovation, which has been studied in special detail as far as the field of philosophy is concerned (Parra 1934; Gaos, 1945; García Bacca, 1956; Furlong, 1952; Navarro, 1948; Zuretti, 1947; Lamadrid, 1955; Pueyrredón, 1953; Hanisch, 1962/3; and others).

Apart from the universities and the colleges, there appeared towards the end of the century the 'patriotic schools', often founded by an 'Economic society of Friends of the Country' – Sociedad Económica de Amigos del País. The Basque Society, a discussion circle composed of young noblemen influenced by French ideas, was the earliest example of a type of society which appeared in a great number of Spanish American capitals from the 1780s onwards (Shafer, 1958). These were centres of propagation of the Enlightenment formed by groups of distinguished men, who championed these new ideas not merely as academic theories but as the embodiment of the civic aspirations of adult men important in society. The Basque Society had inspired the foundation of two types of educational institution: the seminary for young noblemen, such as that of Vergara, and the 'patriotic schools' for the instruction of craftsmen, along the lines suggested by Campomanes in his *Educación popular*. In both types of institution, teaching was orientated towards the 'useful' sciences and the realistic type of education which the European bourgeoisie was demanding at the time.

In Spanish America, some societies encouraged the foundation of elementary schools for the Indians, as in Guatemala; this elementary instruction, however, was often combined with languages, mathematics and technical skills. The Patriotic School in Veracruz, in 1787, taught Christian doctrine, Spanish and French grammar, history, geography, arithmetic, handwriting, drawing and music. The classes in drawing had as their objective the training of mechanical and architectural draughtsmen. In Chile, where the Academy of San Luis, founded by Manuel de Salas, was maintained by the *Consulado*, because there was no Economic Society, education consisted of reading and writing, grammar, arithmetic, geometry and drawing. In Havana, botany and chemistry were taught, because of the interest in these subjects aroused by the sugar-cane industry, and attempts were made to found a botanic garden, in imitation of the one in

Mexico City directed by the naturalist Mociño. Other educational measures of this nature included – although in this case it was not sponsored by any Economic Society, but by the Mining Institution and Tribunal – the School of Mines of Mexico City, which has already been mentioned. The director of this was Fausto de Elhuyar, who had studied in the famous Freiberg School, thanks to a scholarship from the Spanish Government. In this way, independently of the universities, rudimentary primary and technical education was established. The traditional Spanish concept, based on Scholasticism and humanism, had conceived of education 'from the university downwards' by virtue of its organic conception of men's participation in society, leaving the problem of practical training to the crafts themselves or to everyday life. The European Enlightenment, however, was based on a more empirical and utilitarian approach.

The Economic Societies and the journals sponsored by them, or which had close links with their leading spirits, came to be, in the last two decades of the colonial period, the propagators of an Enlightenment which was more Europeanised than that of the generation of 1760 or 1770. The use of words like 'patriotism', 'humanity' and 'felicity' in the constitutions of the Society founded in Peru in 1792 and in the speeches of its first President, Baquíjano, words which were, moreover, frequent in the intellectual writings of the time, bear witness to a more direct influence of eighteenth-century literature. By 1808 their vocabulary had become more overtly inspired by Rousseau's thought or by Revolutionary ideas from France. The naturalist Francisco José de Caldas, a disciple of Mutis, writing in the *Semanario de Nueva Granada* of February 1808 an article entitled 'Discourse on Education', in addition to formulating a plan for the 'patriotic schools', called for a common, egalitarian and uniform educational system capable of regenerating his country in accordance with the model of the republics of antiquity. Similar aspirations were held by Juan Egaña in Chile in 1811 (Góngora, 1964); he was deeply influenced by his reading of Mably, Rousseau, Filangieri, and such authors as Daunou and Condorcet, who had influenced the French Revolutionary laws concerning education. An idealistic and revolutionary spirit of neo-classicism became predominant in the generation of the contemporaries of Independence, and led them to have a rooted belief in 'national' and 'philosophical' education, which was to be imbued with the Republican spirit. The moderate eclecticism of the Spanish Enlightenment, which had encouraged a process of reception of 'modernising' influences, now yielded ground, in accordance with its own principles, to the reception of a new 'modernity'.

Gallicanism and Catholic Enlightenment

The era of the Enlightenment and of Enlightened Despotism coincided in Spain with the zenith of Gallicanism and of Catholic Enlightenment, which brought about a significant transformation of Hispanic ecclesiastical culture, accompanied by a serious internal crisis; and ecclesiastical changes were, of course, closely connected with analogous movements in secular culture.

One aspect of Gallicanism, and the one which was of most interest to the State, was the doctrine of the Divine Right of Kings. Medieval theories, as has been pointed out above, were based on the political ideas of Aristotle, with its emphasis on the importance of the political community or 'republic' in the transmission of monarchical power. To the seventeenth-century Regalists like Salgado, González de Salcedo and Solórzano, power was derived directly from God, 'even though these same Princes and Monarchs are borne to the summit of power through human agency and institutions' (Solórzano, *De Indiarum Jure*, I, II, 3–4). But it was, above all, the jurist from Saragossa who became a senior official in the viceroyalty of Peru, Juan Luis López, a contemporary of Bossuet, who was to develop fully, and as a polemical thesis, the idea of the immediate Divine origin of the royal power, basing his argument on the Biblical passages which asserted that 'all power comes from God', and on texts from the Fathers. The philosophical basis of the argument in Scholastic terms, and the legal basis derived from Roman law, should yield first place, in the view of López, to the Biblical texts. His thesis was formulated in the course of the lengthy polemics between Viceroy de la Palata and the Archbishop of Lima and other bishops arising out of the usual controversies concerning the immunity of ecclesiastical buildings. Having formulated this theory, López had no hesitation in drawing from it conclusions favourable to the power of the Crown. The kings are completely independent in temporal matters and recognise no superior in this sphere; moreover, by virtue of the resolutions of the ancient Visigothic councils, they are the protectors of Divine Worship and the custodians of canonical discipline. The Regalists of this new Gallican type continued to develop the argument along these lines in the course of the eighteenth century. As Leturia (1926) has observed, the totality of the specific powers which the king already possessed in matters of canonical discipline in the Americas by virtue of the *Patronato*, or by the 'Vicariate' which had been attributed to him by a succession of writers, were as broad, if not broader, than the powers over the Gallican Church exercised by the king of France. The objective of the Gallican jurists of the first half of the eighteenth century was, rather, to find a theoretical justification for these powers in the intrinsic authority of the kings in their capacity as 'Protectors' of the Church; they no longer desired to base these powers on Papal concessions, as Spanish jurists, without exception, had done formerly. Macanaz, Alvarez de Abreu, the learned Jesuit Burriel, Ribadeneyra, Campomanes, the exiled Jesuit Juan Francisco Masdeu and others, all made their successive contributions to the development of this theory. In 1753 the King succeeded in acquiring the rights of patronage over all the churches in Spain – the same rights which he already possessed in Granada and the Indies – and with this measure a considerable part of the specific aspirations of Regalism in Spain was satisfied. Of more importance than these factors, however, was the spread and development of a theory that had originated in France and that everywhere, either through imitation of this theory or by way of reaction against it, had the effect of exacerbating nationalist sentiments (as Hazard has observed). The nationalism of the eighteenth century – the phenomenon which Menéndez y Pelayo termed, in the case of Spain, 'Hispanism' – had a Gallican basis. And, as in France, jurists and ecclesiastics who supported the new theory used Biblical and historical sources to magnify the royal power, which was the core of the sentiments of nationhood and was, by implication, anti-universalist and anti-Roman.

It is easy to understand how the expulsion of the Jesuits, when a single historical event symbolised a considerable spiritual break with the past, unleashed an offensive against Papal Ultramontanism (which the Jesuits, apart from significant exceptions which we have mentioned above, had championed), and caused the Gallican doctrine, in its various manifestations, to receive official approval. The Company of Jesus was accused of having defended tyrannicide and, in consequence, the political theories which could serve to justify such an act. Such theories might be either the doctrine of popular sovereignty or that of the indirect power of the Pope in temporal affairs. The attitude of the Jesuits at the time of the Catholic League in France, around 1590, and the writings of Bellarmine and Juan de Mariana could be used as remote evidence of the truth of these accusations, and more immediate evidence was provided by the supposed implication of the Jesuits in the conspiracy of 1759 against the King of Portugal. A consequence of this was the interminable series of official and doctrinal writings in defence of the Divine Right of Kings published from 1767 onwards. In Spanish America, this propaganda was intensified after the insurrections of Tupac Amaru and of the *Comuneros* of New Granada, in 1780/1. Mention may be made of the *Catecismo Real* (1786), by the Bishop of

Córdoba, José A. de San Alberto, and of the *Breve Cartilla Real* (1796), by Lázaro de Ribera, Governor of Paraguay. Both works expound, in the form of questions and answers, the theory of the Divine origin of the king's power: there is no appeal from his decrees, his power is indivisible and cannot be shared with the people, there is no legal possibility of resistance, there is a moral (not merely physical) obligation to pay tribute and denounce conspiracies and so forth. This is not, however, a eulogy of tyranny: the king must act in accordance with justice and protect the poor, writes San Alberto; the king's power is sacred, paternal and absolute, but subject to reason, according to Ribera. To the Spanish Enlightenment there was no incompatibility between the words 'absolute' and 'rational'. However, Ribera explicitly states that, although the king is subject to certain norms, his failure to observe these norms does not give the subject the right of resistance (Furlong, 1954). Similar ideas can be found in academic theses, in documents for internal circulation among the members of religious orders and, at a later date, during the struggle for Independence, in edicts promulgated by bishops and inquisitors against the Patriots. The great doctrinal source of Divine Right was, at that time, Bossuet, particular use being made of his 'defence' of the Four Articles of the Gallican Church published in 1682 (Góngora, 1957; 1969, 53).

It is, nevertheless, surprising that Enlightened Despotism as conceived by, for example, Campomanes – and he was its most brilliant expositor – should have accepted both the theories based on Natural Law and a moderate version of the Social Contract, as developed by Pufendorf, and also the doctrine of the Divine Right of Kings. The idea that peoples have a right to rise against those who govern them is sacrilegious, for it means subjecting the Lord's Anointed to the judgment of private individuals; and such theories have been developed into dogmas since the time of Mariana, asserted the powerful *Fiscal*, on the occasion of the trial of the Bishop of Cuenca in 1767. 'The genius of sovereignty', he wrote in *El Juicio Imparcial*, 'is scrupulous; it does not share its supreme power in this world, nor should it permit any external act within the Realm which it does not examine and sanction'. Campomanes's ideas were, therefore, contrary to both popular sovereignty and Papal power, since he categorically affirmed the Divine Right of Kings, although this did not prevent him sponsoring, in the curriculum of the College of San Isidoro, the teaching of the Social Contract in accordance with modern theories derived from Natural Law. In the opinion of Krebs (1960, 91–6), Campomanes made use, on a pragmatic basis, of either theoretical position as the needs of the moment dictated. Sánchez Agesta (1953) and Ricard (1957) consider that almost all the

Spaniards of the Enlightenment had a somewhat esoteric (though rationalist) attitude, a certain caution in their use of the media of propagation of their ideas, motivated by the fear that these ideas might be abused by 'the ignorant'. When viewed in this light, the Divine Right of Kings appears as a good theory for official adoption, and Natural Law a more appropriate doctrine for the purposes of study. This would explain why in Spanish America it was precisely the 'enlightened' reformers such as Pérez Calama, Maciel, Rezabal y Ugarte, Moxó, Abad y Queipo who were the propagators of the Biblical basis of the doctrine of the Divine Right of Kings, which was adopted as the official ideology of the State.

Were the Jesuits expelled in 1767 in fact, at that time, militant defenders of the doctrines of the Social Compact and of the right of resistance, basing their arguments on Mariana and Suárez? This opinion has been maintained by Giménez Fernández (1946) and Furlong; in the author's view, they have done this without sufficient documentary proof and with too many conjectural suppositions. According to them, the problem of the origin of power, which was a topic of heated controversy in the sixteenth century, was the accepted doctrine throughout the seventeenth and eighteenth centuries. The author considers that what in fact happened was the reverse process: there was a revival, and an application to contemporary questions, of Scholastic doctrines of the Social Contract at the end of the eighteenth century among the ecclesiastics writing in Italy, such as the ex-Jesuit Hervás y Panduro or the secular priest Nicolo Spedalieri (the author of *I Diritti dell'Uomo*, 1791). In order to oppose Enlightened Despotism of the kind represented by the Emperor Joseph II, or perhaps to provide themselves with weapons adequate to deal with those of their French Revolutionary adversaries, these writers revived the medieval theories of the social pact and the right of resistance, although they emphasised, as a basic presupposition, the natural and organic foundation of political society, in accordance with the thought of St Thomas Aquinas. Furthermore, they made far more use of the latter's (unassailable) authority than of that of Suárez, whose name had been taboo since the dissolution of the Company. They thus arrived at a neo-Guelph position – an anti-absolutism based on Scholastic premises. Some traces of this re-interpretation can be observed during the Wars of Independence, both in Spain and in the Americas. Joaquín Lorenzo de Villanueva and Francisco Martínez Marina tried to achieve a synthesis of Liberalism and Thomism in the Cadiz Cortes. Fray Melchor de Talamantes, a Peruvian Mercedarian friar resident in Mexico, who was inconsistent but extremely influential, as is well known, in Mexico in 1808 asserted that 'the sovereignty of the People is an idea derived from St

Thomas, and can be found in a work of his commonly called the *Government of Princes'*. Mier was maintaining, as late as 1823, the right of the People to depose tyrants, and quoting St Thomas in support of this principle. In a document written by the Dominican Friar Pedro de Arce (quoted in Hanisch, 1964, 273), St Thomas, Cajetan, Vitoria and Soto are quoted as authorising the freedom of peoples to give themselves the type of government they deem most appropriate. However, evidence such as this (and one could add many similar documents) does not make it possible to assert categorically that Thomist doctrines were the most influential in the Independence movement, as has been maintained by the 'populist' school of historians led by Giménez Fernández. What happened was that the Creoles made use, without excessive theoretical distinctions, of all the theories of popular sovereignty based on the Social Contract which might be mobilised for their struggle: they used both those of St Thomas or Suárez, and those of French philosophy (particularly Rousseau); and also those theories based on Natural Law and derived from Grotius and Pufendorf, which had been the official teaching in the chairs of Natural Law and the *Jus Gentium*. If any of these ideas had an opportunity of exercising a wide influence, it would probably be the last-named (Zorraquín, 1962). Besides the problem of sovereignty, the Creole jurists were obliged to justify the existence of the Indies as separate States, and they deliberately examined the Laws of the Indies to find evidence to support their thesis and ignored evidence which contradicted it (this was done by Talamantes in 1808, by Mier in his *Historia* published in 1813, and by Egaña around 1818, quoted in Hanisch, 1964, 263).

What still remains unresolved, therefore, is the historical problem of whether, between 1620 and 1767, during the period of decline of Scholasticism, the question of the origin of power was still being thought of in these terms. There do not appear to be any extant sources that can definitely decide this question. As has been observed above, the absence of any crisis which made urgently necessary a definition of the terms used in these controversies – in contrast to the situation in the sixteenth century – led to a marked degree of ideological eclecticism in the following centuries. A good example of this is Sigüenza y Góngora's *Teatro de Virtudes Políticas*, published in 1680. He repeats time-honoured phrases such as 'the Prince is the Vicar of God' and '[the Prince] is a living image of God, like a God on Earth' (p. 6). He asserts (p. 53) that it is not his intention to establish the sources from which that authority emanates: 'I take this for granted, with the respect and veneration due to such authority.' However, he then goes on to quote Vázquez de Menchaca and other supporters of the theories derived from the German jurist Johannes Althusius, who maintained that the People had a constituent power; in other words, it had pre-existing and princely authority, and was superior to the prince. It is not possible to establish with absolute certainty Sigüenza y Góngora's final conclusions on this subject.

Gallicanism, in addition to re-examining the problem of political power, sought to make the power of the Papacy once again subject to its early limitations; this attempt involved a return to the sources of canon law of the first millennium of the Christian Era, before the centralising tendencies of Rome gained the upper hand. The Spanish writers developed their own variant of this position, laying particular emphasis on the recorded practices of the Visigothic kingdom and councils, the core of Spain's national tradition; in that age, Spanish monarchs and bishops had governed a Church enjoying considerable autonomy vis-à-vis the canonical discipline of Rome. As early as the seventeenth century, admiration for Visigothic culture had been the expression of this desire for a national Church and of the ambition of the kings to acquire the rights of patronage over all churches in Spain, because in that way they would also have the right – enjoyed by the Visigothic monarchs – of choosing the bishops (Aldea, 1960, 65 ff.). Those who wrote treatises in the eighteenth century on the *Patronato* in the Indies, such as Alvarez de Abreu, Ribadeneyra and Manuel Josef de Ayala, ceased to base their arguments on the Papal concessions, and instead justified the *Patronato* on the grounds of the king's royal prerogative and majestic authority, supported by historical documentary sources (de la Hera, 1963; Giménez Fernández, 1950). Denunciations of the False Decretals and of Ultramontanism became part of the stock-in-trade of these writers, from Macanaz to Martínez Marina, Llorente and Villanueva. The historical criticisms of the Maurinos made erudition a powerful weapon which could now be used against the power of the Papacy. Gallicanism of the moderate kind, expressed within the limitations imposed by a deeply felt sense of the unity of the Church, like the Gallicanism of Bossuet, was carried beyond these limits by van Espen, the lower clergy influenced by Richer, Febronio, Pereyra, Ricci and Tamburini, whose development of this theory eventually led to a position of full support of Joseph II of Austria. In Spain, Campomanes was the most prominent representative of this new type of Regalism, which differed from the earlier type not so much in its practical application as in its doctrinal presuppositions (contrary, in the author's opinion, to the view held by Rodríguez Casado, 1948, 21). There thus arose a type of Catholicism which has been called 'Jansenist', but which it would be more appropriate to call 'Gallican', because in fact it had very little in common with the piety of Port-Royal and the Jansenist doctrine of Grace. This movement was, on the contrary, almost entirely absorbed by ecclesiological problems concerned with the structure of power in the Church: the powers of the bishops and councils, the limits of Papal power, the rights of the Crown with regard to the external discipline of the Church, the rights of the clergy vis-à-vis the bishop, the subordination of the regular clergy to the bishops and so on. To these tendencies, however, one must add (and in this respect it is more proper to speak of 'Jansenism') the offensive against all traces of Jesuit teaching, such as probabilism in moral theology and the baroque style in sacred oratory and devotional practices. The victory of this new ideological trend in the universities and ecclesiastical colleges was ensured, after 1767, by the bestowal of official approval. The new chairs of ecclesiastical history, Councils and ancient Church discipline, the holders of which lectured to students of canon law and theology, and also the printed books prescribed for all ecclesiastical studies, all implied criticisms of the existing structure of the Roman Catholic Church (see Góngora, 1957, II). Reorganisation of the curricula and the approval of a high proportion of the bishops appointed by the king provoked, in Spanish America as well, a change in the outlook of part of the clergy. The conception of the *Patronato* as a royal prerogative based on sound historical evidence was transmitted, as the legacy of Enlightened Despotism, to the new republics established in the nineteenth century, and a consequence of this was the crisis in the relationships between Church and State.

Furthermore, Campomanes and, in general, other champions of Enlightened Despotism wished to undertake the reform of the Church in Spanish America, both through Provincial Councils and by means of official *Visitas* to inquire into the state of the religious orders. The *Tomo regio* of 1768, which convened the Council of New Spain, and the Instructions imparted to the *Visitadores* in 1769 are the most important documentary sources for the study of this attempted reform. The *Tomo regio* signified, quite unambiguously, that the King was assuming the right to convene Councils, being represented at them by a 'Royal Attendant'; at the Mexican Council, this official was Ribadeneyra, the author of the *Manual Compendio del Regio Patronato Indiano* published in 1755. Both the Councils and the *Visitas* have traditionally been considered as mere attempts at enslavement of the Church in the name of absolutism and as part of the offensive against Jesuitry (Giménez Fernández, 1939; Vargas Ugarte, 1954; Lopetegui-Zubillaga-Egaña, 1965–6). However, Rodríguez Casado (1951) has drawn attention to the presence, side by side with exaggerated Regalism, of the long-standing aspirations towards ecclesiastical reform, particularly reform of the regular clergy, which could be traced back to the Council of Trent and the age of Philip II. It must be remembered that the Tridentine reforms took a long time to be put into effect, even partially, in the Americas, owing to the naturally easygoing character of the Creole environment. Denunciations of moral laxity in particular religious houses of men or women continued without cessation during the colonial period. Monastic life in common – which the reforms of 1768–9 were intended to make obligatory – was in many cases extremely difficult to put into practice, on account of the excessive numbers of religious in relation to the income of the convents, which meant that the religious had to earn their sustenance and clothing by means of activities greatly at variance with their rule. The Instructions of 1769 insisted on fulfilment of the vow of poverty, on the maintenance of good order in the elections of superiors, on obedience to the bishops, and on preaching in support of the king's authority. Both the *Tomo regio* and the Instructions insisted that moral theology should be taught with a more rigorist approach, and be accompanied by more thorough Biblical and historical instruction, and that preaching should be edifying and severe in tone, rather than a display of baroque rhetorical ingenuity (Rodríguez Casado, 1951; Góngora, 1969). Both documents were drafted by Campomanes himself, a fact that once again raises the problem of the personal motivations of this statesman, whom historians have constantly portrayed as being swayed by purely political considerations. However, his *Tratado de la Regalía de Amortización* (1765) is obviously a work inspired by economic motives: its intention was to put onto the market the lands then held in perpetuity by the religious orders, and to collect a lucrative land-tax on them (Krebs, 1960, 144–51). Campomanes's ideas were by no means new – they had been commonplace in the works of Spanish writers on economic matters since the previous century; in this work, however, they acquired greater intellectual force, because they were combined with ideological criticisms of the clergy, and it was for this reason that Campomanes was to be quoted as an authority at the time of the secularisation of ecclesiastical properties which took place during the reforms carried out after Independence in Spanish America (and in Spain itself, by the Liberals).

The period between 1760 and 1840 is a clearly perceptible unity in ecclesiastical history, as it is in the intellectual history of Spanish America as a whole. On the one hand, popular piety and practices remained virtually untouched, and the 'Ultramontane' clergy adopted an increasingly polemical stance, on account of the need to defend itself against attacks and the generally catastrophic events of the Revolutionary era. On the other hand, the currents of Gallican, Jansenist and 'Enlightened-Catholic' ideas, which during this period were barely distinguishable, for they overlapped to a great extent, were united in their opposition to traditional piety and practices, to the Jesuits and their legacy of ideas and sentiments, and to the absolute supremacy of the Papacy. There were concerted attempts at reform: that of the years following the expulsion of the Jesuits lasted for about a decade after 1767; the crisis provoked by the decree of the Minister Urquijo (1799–1801) concerning the devolution of power to the bishops during the vacancy of the Papal throne had fewer repercussions in the Americas than in Spain; but between 1795 and 1804 there was a considerable body of financial legislation concerned with ecclesiastical revenues, and measures were taken to secularise the *censos*, which gave the religious communities so much power over land. Between 1810 and 1830 virtually the whole of Spanish America underwent ecclesiastical reforms of an overtly Josephine character; these even included attempts to establish the popular election of parish priests, along the lines of the Civil Constitution of the Clergy. Gradually, as Rome recognised the independence of the new republics and reached a *modus vivendi* with them over the question of the *Patronato* (although the Papacy never recognised it as a prerogative), the interest of the national States in the reform of the Church began to diminish, and eventually it disappeared entirely. Moreover, in accordance with the general trend throughout the Church, from 1830 onwards the vast majority of the clergy adopted Ultramontanism. The internal reform of the Church by the State never took place.

Nevertheless, the part played during those seventy or eighty years by the currents of ideological innovation is of some interest from the point of view of the history of ideas, even though there was no necessary connection between such ideas and the political stances adopted by the clergy during the struggle for Independence; in the ideological sphere, the dividing-lines were different. Gallicans, Jansenists and 'Enlightened Catholics' were hostile to popular devotional practices, to festivals in the baroque style, and to the kind of preaching satirised by Fr. Isla in *Fray Gerundio*; they supported the authority of the bishops and the parish clergy, but had misgivings with regard to the power of the orders; in moral theology they were rigorist and anti-Jesuit. One aspect of their campaign coincided with a change of policy on the part of the Holy See, which authorised the reading of the Bible in the vernacular, as a result of which the translations of Scio and Torres Amat were published; the innovators insisted on the need for both people and clergy to receive sound Biblical instruction. They were opposed to Scholasticism, and supported the reformed curricula, but in dogmatic theology they still followed St Augustine and St Thomas. To these authorities they added, as an enrichment of their spiritual culture, the great French writers of the century of Louis XIV: Bossuet, Fénelon, orators like Bourdaloue and Massillon, the historian Fleury among others. This entire movement was, above all, anti-Roman and Regalist in outlook, although naturally the strength of these sentiments varied from a Gallicanism still within the bounds of orthodoxy to a more overt *étatisme* with Josephinist overtones, inspired by Febronio and Pereyra, or the Spaniards Villanueva and Llorente. Finally, it must be emphasised that this process of reception of modern thought in the ecclesiastical sphere was quite alien to popular piety and practices; indeed, the innovators were antagonistic towards the manifestations of that popular piety, which they described as 'superstition'. This attempted reform of the Church was, therefore, a highly 'intellectualised' movement.

As it has already been observed, it is not easy to distinguish in detail the various currents of thought which contributed to this movement of reception. When the Jesuits were expelled, the Pastoral Letters of such Mexican bishops as Lorenzana and Fabián y Fuero, and the statements made by the Franciscan Espiñeyra, Bishop of Concepción, Chile, at the Council of Lima (1772), concentrated their attacks on the alleged moral laxity of the Company and the Jesuits' probabilist approach to moral theology; Espiñeyra contrasted these with 'the pure doctrine of the Gospel'. Probabilism, he added, opens the door to evasion of the laws, and therefore it was in the interest of the State as well as of the Church to condemn it (Vargas Ugarte, 1954, III; Macera, 1963). However, the correspondence which took place between Bishop Gorrichátegui of Cuzco and Bishop Alday of Santiago in 1775 demonstrates the degree to which the rigorist approach, which approximated to the Jansenist position, encountered a contemptuous and hostile reception among other prelates who were learned men but opposed to innovations (Archivo Nacional, Santiago, Fondo Eyzaguirre, 25, 49). Exasperation with the Jesuits is clearly demonstrated in the Pastoral Letter of Abad Illana, Bishop of Tucumán, and in his correspondence with Bishop Alday in 1767–8. The antagonism of the other regular orders and of some bishops towards the powerful Company which had set its seal on the entire contemporary Church was, in many cases, quite undisguised. A good example of this is the anti-Jesuit campaign conducted in Rome by the Peruvian Francisco Javier Vásquez, General of the Augustinians. The Pastoral Letter written in October 1767 by Bishop Fabián y Fuero constituted a renewal of the offensive of his illustrious predecessor in the See of Puebla, Juan de Palafox, against the Company which – in the words of Fabián y Fuero – considers itself indispensable to the Faith and labels as 'Jansenist' anyone who opposes it.

It is, therefore, comparatively easy to identify Gallicanism, a theory which enjoyed official approval, and also a certain Jansenist trend in Spanish America – this was, of course, the Jansenism of the eighteenth century, characterised by moral rigorism, hostility to the Jesuits and a *de facto* alliance with Gallicanism, rather than by any definite theological interpretation of Grace, such as had characterised Jansenism originally. However, it is less easy to arrive at a precise definition of 'Catholic Enlightenment' (see Góngora, 1957, 1963, 1969; Appolis, 1960, 1966; Saugnieux, 1970; Sarrailh, 1954). If this term is taken to signify nothing more than an ideological *mélange* of the Enlightenment and Catholicism, one could in practice apply it to all the 'enlightened' thinkers who did not wish to abandon religious orthodoxy, and these constituted an overwhelming majority both in Spain and in Spanish America; but in that case the expression would contribute nothing to the task of analysis – the problem would be merely one of terminology. Recent historical research, however, even though at times it has been excessively partial towards this movement, has, nevertheless, made efforts to discern a recognisable style of thought and sentiments; this is more easily discernible in the case of individual personalities than when one tries to envisage the movement as a whole. In Spain the most obvious representative of this trend was Jovellanos, with his combination of sincere piety, moral rigorism, enthusiasm for the Enlightenment, and Gallicanism. It is very difficult to arrive at a general definition of this movement, for it implies a process of mutual attraction taking place between ideas as basically different as the Naturalism of the Enlightenment and Jansenism, which had its roots in a pessimistic view of human nature, derived from St Augustine: the alliance between these tendencies was paradoxical, but nonetheless very real, in the eighteenth century.

If one wished to name a Spanish American representative of this current of thought, perhaps the best choice would be Olavide in his later years, when he wrote his *Evangelio en triunfo* after his abandonment of the ideas of the *philosophes*, despite the doubts on his sincerity cast (without, in our opinion, sufficient evidence) by Sarrailh and Defourneaux, and taking due account of the undoubted influence of French Catholic apologetic writings of the eighteenth century. In the declamatory style characteristic of his age, he adequately expresses the attitude of 'enlightened' piety characterised by the repentance and polemical zeal typical of a convert, and a tone that is rhetorical, sentimental, moralising, unconcerned with metaphysics and imbued with the spirit of social and educational reform. The large number of editions of this book from 1798 onwards is a proof that it was attuned to the spirit of the age; copies could be found in many Spanish American libraries around 1800. It quite obviously influenced Juan Egaña's *El chileno consolado en los presidios*. Among the Patriots, one may consider as characteristic representatives of the Catholic Enlightenment certain individuals who combined deeply felt religious piety with the moral rigorism derived from Jansenism and with republicanism in the style of Rousseau, but who declined to adopt the new secularised outlook. One good example would be Juan Egaña himself; or Juan Ignacio Gorriti, the Dean of Salta, the author of the interesting work *Reflexiones sobre las causas morales de las convulsiones interiores en los nuevos Estados americanos* (1837); or so many others, throughout Spanish America. Not all ecclesiastics can be unhesitatingly classified in this way, because many of them were scarcely distinguishable from 'enlightened' thinkers of a more secularist outlook.

Among the Jesuits expelled in 1767, many maintained an eclectic attitude towards the ideas inculcated into them in their traditional education and the ideas of the Enlightenment; some became whole-hearted followers of the Enlightenment, and there were even a few revolutionaries (Batllori, 1966). It is not easy to find among them examples of 'Catholic Enlightenment' in the specialised sense of this term, for one would be unlikely to find among them the rigorist and Jansenist outlook, which was so essential a part of the Catholic Enlightenment. An exception which confirms this rule is the Chilean chiliastic Biblical scholar Manuel Lacunza, who, in the author's opinion, displayed some of the traits characteristic of this tendency (Góngora, 1969).

THE NEW WORLD IN ESCHATOLOGICAL AND UTOPIAN WRITINGS OF THE SIXTEENTH TO THE EIGHTEENTH CENTURIES

Edmundo O'Gorman has sharply criticised the customary assertion that Columbus 'discovered' the New World, analysing the internal logical contradictions inherent in attributing to him a project which he definitely never entertained. What remains undeniable is Columbus's certainty that he had reached Asia or lands adjoining it, and this is apparent from an examination of Columbus's writings as a whole. An intelligent observer such as Peter Martyr of Angleria used, in his letters of 1493, the terms 'new hemisphere' and '*novus orbis*', which were to achieve such wide currency. However, as O'Gorman observes, the sentence '*Colonus ille novi orbis repertor*' in his letter of 1 November 1493 does not have the significance commonly attributed to it: *novus orbis* is not capitalised, and merely means 'undiscovered world'. The third and fourth voyages of Vespucio and the famous letter '*Mundus novus*' were to make it clear that there was an *ecumene*, a vast and inhabited region distinct from Asia, which the well-known *Cosmographiae Introductio* printed in Saint-Dié in 1507 was to call America or the land of Americo.

However, the subject of this chapter is not this process of investigations and hypotheses, but another kind of notion inspired by the New World, which might be called eschatological or Utopian. Both kinds of notion can be found in the documents relating to Columbus.

Eschatological theories in the writings of Columbus and of the mendicant friars

The tendency to indulge in prophecies of an illuminist nature was a very important characteristic of the spiritual history of Europe from the eleventh or twelfth century onwards, and the last decades of the fifteenth century and the earliest ones of the sixteenth witnessed a wealth of eschatological theories. From the mid-thirteenth century onwards there was continual preaching of 'Joachimism', which announced a *renovatio*, a Third Age, that of the Holy Spirit, which was to achieve the definitive fulfilment, here on earth, of the promises of the Old and New Testaments. There was some connection between this trend and the political and spiritual movement led by Savonarola in Florence; it is a well-known fact, however, that the stronghold of Joachimist ideas was the Franciscan Order, which was to carry them to the Americas. The fall of Constantinople and the advances of the Turks, and Cisneros's expedition to North Africa were to revive the crusading spirit; and the reconquest of Granada was seen by contemporaries in the same light. Américo Castro (1949, 21–6) quotes fifteenth-century Castilian texts expressing Messianic impulses, including some lines of Gómez Manrique in which he calls on Prince Alfonso in 1468 to conquer 'the barbarous nations' both in Europe and overseas. Bataillon (1950), writing of Spain in Cisneros's time, E. Peuckert, describing pre-Reformation Germany, and M. Reeves, have all emphasised the vigour of eschatological sentiments during that period.

The case of Christopher Columbus is not, therefore, exceptional, save for the magnitude assumed by his ideas, which were commensurate with his vast enterprises. His Messianism (for a description see Phelan, 1956, 17–23) found expression in a few notions which were frequently reiterated. During the third voyage he formulated the theory according to which the Earthly Paradise was situated in South America, with the four rivers named in Genesis – of which he managed to see only the mouths of the Orinoco – forming a 'Land of Grace', in the centre of which was a protuberance like the small end of a pear; this was Paradise itself. He never repeated this assertion concerning the shape of the supposed Land, but he did refer again to the location of Paradise, in his letter of 1502 to Pope Alexander VI. The notion of America as the Earthly Paradise cannot really be classified as eschatological; it is, rather, the source and origin of the earliest Utopian theories. There was a connection between this and the impression caused by the first sight of the Indians of the Antilles, which at once suggested to contemporaries not only Paradise but the Golden Age of classical antiquity: the Indians were, Columbus wrote, unclothed, well-formed, unarmed and not practising idolatry, but prepared to believe in one God as Creator. This idyllic vision was to be transmitted to posterity by Peter Martyr of Angleria, and to achieve wide currency (Romeo, 1954; Elliott, 1970).

Of more frequent occurrence in the writings of Columbus is the idea of the recuperation and rebuilding of the Holy House in Jerusalem – the crusading impulse. On 26 December 1492 he noted that with the profits of his voyage Jerusalem could be reconquered in three years. In 1498 he bequeathed money in a will, to be deposited in the Bank of St George in Genoa, to contribute towards the liberation of Jerusalem. In his letter of 1501 or 1502 to Ferdinand and Isabella (*Raccolta Colombina*, I, ii, 79/83) he made an impassioned defence of the visionary outlook as compared with study and discourse, which, he said, had profited him nothing; for the former approach was based on the Prophets and on the sayings of 'certain holy men who, aided by Divine Revelation, have spoken of this matter'. However, he emphasised, in support of his theory, the learned astronomical calculations of Alfonso the Wise, according to which 5,343 years elapsed between Adam and Christ, to which one must add 1,501 years since Christ, making a total of 6,845 years, which was only 155 years short of the time established for the duration of the world, according to St Augustine's septennial interpretation of the history of mankind. This idea that the end is imminent finds particularly emphatic expression in the writings of Columbus in his zeal to restore Jerusalem as the centre of Christendom, for it was there that there would take place the eschatological events described in the Apocalypse and in the prophecies of the bliss and glory of the Holy City to which the Old Testament Prophets so often referred, together with the struggles against the Antichrist and the final triumph of God which the New Testament foretells. Columbus based his idea that the kings of Spain had been summoned by God to reconquer Jerusalem on the Book of the Prophecies (*Raccolta*, I, II, 148), especially on a saying of Joachim of Fiore which he repeated to the Catholic Sovereigns in 1492; and in the letter of 1501 or 1502 he quoted the same saying of Joachim of Fiore concerning Spain and Jerusalem. This saying cannot be authentic; it must have originated in one of the apocryphal works which circulated in such profusion in the later Middle Ages; Reeves (1969, 360) does not investigate the source of this saying. The best-known model of this project of the reconquest of Jerusalem by a Christian king was at that time the prophecy attributed to the Pseudo-Methodius, written in the Eastern Empire around the seventh century, and republished many times after being first printed at Cologne in 1475; according to this, a victorious monarch would subdue the Muslims, reign happily in Jerusalem, finally lay down his Crown and submit to the Cross, and this would be the signal for the immediate coming of the Antichrist and his brief reign of iniquity. This work, which had just been republished in 1498 by Sebastian Brant, may have provoked in Columbus a revival of the crusading ideal, which in any case had recovered strength during the early years of the war in Italy, with Charles VIII's enterprise. Columbus also quoted, as an additional source, the work of Pedro de Ailly – an authority whom he regarded as of great importance in all fields of learning – which sought to establish a connection between the revolutions of Saturn and the end of Islam and the coming of the Antichrist. In his letter of 1502 to Pope Alexander VI, he repeated the suggestion that the gold discovered in the new lands should be devoted to achieving the recovery of the Holy House (Navarrete, I).

The continuing vigour of the crusading ideal, which was fundamentally eschatological, was, therefore, an element in Columbus's discoveries, which were associated in this way with medieval Catholic notions of Christendom: in the early stages, at least, the Atlantic Ocean was a 'sacred sea', despite the contrary opinion of Dupront (1959, 103).

Equally apparent in Columbus was the conviction that, now that the Gospel was being preached 'in so many lands in such a short space of time', as he expressed it in the above-mentioned letter to the Sovereigns, the end was drawing nigh, as foretold in Matthew 24:14. He strongly emphasised on several occasions in his writings (such as his letter to the tutor of Prince John in 1500, in Navarrete, I) that he had reached 'the new heaven and earth foretold by Our Lord in the Apocalypse of Saint John, after being prophesied by Isaiah'. The entire compilation of Biblical and patristic texts made for the Admiral by his friend Dom Gaspar Gorritio in the 'Book of Prophecies' was directed towards proving that the newly discovered islands and countries could be identified with Tarshish, Ophir and the other 'Biblical' islands, and that their discovery by Columbus represented the fulfilment of the prophecies.

The Franciscan missionaries are a further source of eschatological notions in the New World, later than Columbus. This subject has been investigated in great detail by modern historians (Phelan, 1956; Bataillon, 1957). The latter author has pointed out the traces of Joachimist ideas among the French Franciscans from the northern regions, who set off in 1516 to evangelise the mainland; and this is most clearly apparent in Martín de Valencia, the monk of the Province of Extremadura, who belonged to a movement of 'poor evangelists' founded, along the lines of so many others in that same Order, at the beginning of the sixteenth century. Martín de Valencia was to be the leader of the twelve missionaries who went to Mexico at the request of Cortés, and he doubtless influenced the latter's Fourth Letter, in which the conquistador asked Charles V to establish a monastic and poor Church rather than one with bishops and prelates, as being more suitable for the mission territories. It is true that, as Bataillon (1957, 27) observes, these prophetically minded missionaries made no theoretical contribution to the complex problems of the theology of history such as had been made by men like Joachim of Fiore and his followers in the thirteenth and early fourteenth century; but they were enthusiastic over the prospect of the final conversion of the peoples of that new world, a process which some of them clearly considered to be a task appropriate to the 'end of the world'. In this connection, one can observe in them sentiments similar to those of Columbus, who, in any case, always maintained close relations with the Franciscans.

Motolinía, the best-known representative of the first generation of Franciscans in Mexico, was obviously speaking in earnest when he referred to the Age of the Holy Spirit and the other themes developed by Joachim of Fiore himself. His most famous historical analogy is that which he drew between the ten plagues of Egypt and the 'grievous plagues' – deaths, epidemics, heavy labour in the mines, work on the building of the great Spanish city of Mexico, and slaves who went to the mines 'like great flocks of sheep'. It must be admitted, however, that such writings are of a moralising character rather than the expression of a historical outlook (BAE, CCXL, 203–6). He was, primarily, a Franciscan with an idyllic outlook, filled with tender regard for the simplicity of the natives. 'These Indians', he writes in his *Historia de los Indios de la Nueva España* (ch. XIV), 'have almost no impediment to prevent them from attaining to Heaven, in comparison with the many obstacles which we Spaniards have and which we find so burdensome, for they are content with but little, so little, indeed, that they have hardly enough to clothe and feed themselves. They are not preoccupied with acquiring and laying up riches, nor do they kill themselves to achieve honours and dignities.' He goes on to give a forceful description of the daily customs of the average sixteenth-century Spaniard, by way of contrast. Franciscan veneration of poverty, as evinced by the Indian communities – the basic agricultural communities, of course, not the powerful and splendid Aztec imperial structure established in the city of Tenochtitlán – led to the missionaries' ideal of segregation of the *pueblos* and the division of colonial society into two 'republics'. Whereas the churches of the Spaniards were presided over by bishops and cathedral chapters, the Indian Christian communities were under the tutelage of the friars; and they even revealed their distinctive characteristics in the 'open chapels' described by Kubler (1948). Moreover, even though the missionaries wholeheartedly accepted the legitimacy of the Conquest as a fundamental premise of their entire system – as is shown by the forceful letter of Motolinía attacking Las Casas, written in 1555 – they would have preferred the temporal government of the entire Indies to have been left to a paternalistic viceroy, without the intervention of the *Audiencia*, which was legalistic and inspired by the urge to make profits (Maravall, 1949). Jerónimo de Mendieta was to compare Hernán Cortés with Moses, as the conquistador who opened for the missionaries the doors to the new Christendom; after his time, the Viceroys Mendoza and Velasco continued to show sympathy for the friars' labours; however, the Licentiate Valderrama, whose *Visita* in 1564/5 resulted in the modification of the entire Indian tribute system, was seen as the personification of the formalistic and unjust *letrado*.

The idea of a 'new Church' expressed in the Fourth Letter of Cortés merely means, in the author's opinion, the creation of a local ecclesiastical organisation (in contrast to the exaggerated interpretation which some have sought to give the adjective 'new' in this context). As a more positive term, however, in the writings of Martín de Valencia, Motolinía and, above all, Mendieta (who finished his labours in 1596), this concept approximates to that of the monastic and spiritual Church which would resemble the Primitive Church described in the Acts of the Apostles – a goal towards which all reformist movements since the eleventh century had striven; furthermore, this Indian Christendom could be imagined as the Age of the Holy Spirit, in the precise sense in which Joachim of Fiore had used this term. The loss which the Church had suffered as a result of Luther, wrote Mendieta, had been offset by Cortés in the New World; he was the New Moses who had opened the doors to the friars disillusioned with the corrupt Christendom of Europe, in order to establish a new and more pure Church, like that of the Apostles, but owing due obedience to the Pope (Phelan, 1956). The absence, during this process of evangelisation, of miracles, which had been so decisive an element in early Christianity, did not deter the friars: Zumárraga, the Franciscan Bishop, considered (as Erasmus would have done) that spiritual and moral religion was superior to that based on outward and visible signs (Bataillon, 1957, 451); Mendieta explained this absence on the grounds that miracles had been necessary to break down the hard-heartedness of the unbelievers, but they were of no use among such docile peoples (Phelan, 47).

This evangelism firmly grounded on spiritual foundations bears a certain resemblance to the outlook of Erasmus, but there are also obvious differences between the two approaches: on the one hand, there are the aristocratic and liberal attitudes implicit in Christian humanism, and the supremacy of individual spirituality; on the other, the strict paternal discipline to which the neophytes were subject. It is true that the idyllic outlook of such men as Motolinía had an overwhelming influence on the communications sent by the friars to the Spanish authorities, requesting defence and protection; but the internal organisation of the missions was severely authoritarian, and reflected the conception which the friars had of the natives as 'child-like' peoples. Martín de Valencia scourged himself in front of them, but he chastised them too. Mendieta, who stressed their wax-like pliability and simplicity, sometimes admitted that they indulged in heavy drinking, and that they were deceitful – they played tricks similar to those of the Gypsies; in conclusion, however, he resolved the contradiction by attributing their vices principally to contact with the Spaniards and *mestizo* sectors (*Historia Eclesiástica Indiana*, 500 ff.). The hostility of the friars towards the Indians' cult of the Virgin of Guadalupe, which was so warmly encouraged by the bishops (Ricard, 1933, 226 ff.), may be interpreted, as Bataillon (1950) suggests, as an attitude based on spirituality and indicative of Erasmian influence.

The resemblance to the Primitive Church and to the Twelve Apostles, explicitly suggested by men such as Motolinía and Mendieta, might be interpreted as yet another Franciscan 'reform', along the lines of so many that were initiated in the late Middle Ages, and lacking in explicit eschatological overtones. Mendieta, however, shows signs of a more positively eschatological outlook, as Phelan has emphasised. His outlook is not the idyllic optimism, related to an idealisation of the natural state of man, which one finds in Motolinía; although there are still many traces of this outlook, the friar who ends his book after the appalling demographic catastrophe which befell the Indians concludes his writings in a tone of denunciation and lamentation. He looks on death as a relief from their labours for the natives, and as a punishment for the Spaniards; he rejects the idea expressed by the Dominican, Betanzos, that the epidemics might be a punishment for the sins of the Indians. In the opinion of Mendieta, the Golden Age of the missions came to an end after the 1560s, and he attributed this decadence to the covetousness of the Spaniards, which was principally manifested by the *repartimientos* and their devastating consequences. Spain had already been punished by the rising of the Moriscos of Granada, by the conspiracy of Don Martín Cortés in Mexico and by defeats at the hands of the English. Here the eschatological outlook is sinister, rather than filled with hope. The prospect of the end of the history of salvation is expressed, above all, in Mendieta's interpretation of the parable of the banquet, from which all the guests in succession excuse themselves, and it is necessary to invite the poor and the maimed, and finally to approach those on the road and 'compel them to come in' (Luke, 14). As his final conclusion the missionary, despite all the disasters, looks forward to a Divine solution, and on this basis he justifies the Conquest.

It is possible, however, that there supervened a great sense of disillusionment, in comparison with the ambitious objectives originally pursued. Martín de Valencia, before his death in 1531, and Archbishop Zumárraga and his friend Fray Domingo de Betanzos ten years later, wanted to travel across the South Sea; the objective of the last two men was quite clearly East Asia. This might be explained as a manifestation of the unlimited spirit of adventure of the sixteenth century, or by the embittered feelings of the men concerned over their inability to put a stop to the exploitation of the natives by the Spaniards. Perhaps, however, what impelled those friars to continue their travels was their feeling of frustration when they compared the initial evangelism based on spirituality, and the conviction that they were witnessing a new epoch in the spiritual history of mankind, with the real state of affairs, arrived at after so much effort: Christian communities which needed constant compulsion and vigilance so as not to relapse into paganism, and evincing no obvious signs of the 'freedom' envisaged by St Paul and the Gospels.

In 1576 Sahagún made some important observations concerning the successive journeyings of the Church (these have been emphasised by Borges, 1956): the Church had moved from Palestine to Asia, Africa, Germany and the rest of Europe, a large part of which had now been lost to the Faith, with Italy and Spain being specially saved; from there it had crossed the Ocean to the West Indies. 'It seems to me that the Catholic Church cannot remain for very long in these parts...it is merely passing on its travels to hold conversation with those peoples who live in the region of China', where Augustinian missionaries had recently arrived and where there were 'most wise peoples, with a great polity, near the Spice Islands, where already the Gospel is being preached' (Book XI, chs. 12 and 13). History is conceived as a journey characterised by successes that are only partial but in the course of which there is a selection, in accordance with the ideas of St Augustine, of the elect for the City of God.

On a less exalted plane, theologically speaking, and, above all, complicated by factors connected with personal vices, there are the eschatological ideas discovered by Bataillon (1955) in the proceedings brought by the Inquisition of Lima against the Dominican Friar Francisco de la Cruz, burned at the stake in 1578. The movement investigated at this trial bore some resemblance to that of the Spanish *alumbrados*, and a pious woman ('*beata*') and certain friars were involved. The idea of a new Church in the Americas was connected with sentiments and interests which Bataillon considers to be the sublimation of certain typically 'Creole' aspirations: there were demands for the marriage of clerics and friars unsuited to their calling, for the granting of *encomiendas* in perpetuity, for fresh conquests to acquire rewards for poor Spaniards and soldiers, and for the acceptance of miscegenation; all these measures were to foreshadow the establishment of a 'Peruvian peace' presided over by Francisco de la Cruz himself and a son of his, holding sway over the mass of Indians, which was identified with the people of Israel (by means of linguistic arguments which were very common at the time); this would be the successor to the Church of the Gentiles. Also involved with this current of thought was the Jesuit Luis López, who harshly criticised the system of Indian reservations and the *Visitas* ordered by Viceroy Toledo; in his view, the entire Spanish régime was nothing more than a provisional tutelage, to last until such time as there appeared a Peruvian prince sufficiently staunch in the Faith (Duviols, 47). Both these clerics, therefore, represented the beginnings of a pro-Indian and pro-*mestizo* Americanist outlook.

By the end of the sixteenth century, as Bataillon (1952) has observed, 'modern Christianity was definitively established', and the Jesuits, who played a decisive role in this era, took the initiative in proposing a process of adaptation to the circumstances. José de Acosta, in his *De temporibus novissimis* (1590), declared that nobody knew whether there remained few or many lands to evangelise, for in that century more lands had been discovered than in the previous fifteen centuries. One cannot, therefore, say definitely that the process of preaching the Gospel to the whole earth has come to an end, nor that the time of the consummation of the Kingdom of Christ is approaching. Furthermore, preaching alone is not enough; it is necessary to achieve a real gathering together of the elect, and this takes time. Acosta has a reflective and reasoned approach, in contrast to eschatological visions, which in his writings are relegated to the role of a theoretical framework, without any degree of imminence. The same sober approach is apparent in his book *De procuranda Indorum salute* (1592), when he discusses the problem, which still aroused bitter controversies, of the lack of miracles during the process of evangelisation of the Indians. Acosta's explanation is a pragmatic one: miracles were not necessary, because it was not a question of converting cultivated and learned peoples, such as the Greeks, the Apostles being low-born and ignorant men and lacking in other methods of persuasion; in the New World, on the other hand, it was the Europeans who enjoyed cultural superiority, and the barbarians had shown themselves to be obedient and disposed to believe the Faith. Only one miracle was needed in these parts, he said pointedly: 'personal habits should be in accordance with the Faith that is preached' (II, chs. VIII, IX and X).

The reasonable explanations advanced by Acosta did not, of course, put an end to all eschatological speculations in the Americas. Eguiluz (1959) has published an account of a Franciscan, a native of the See of Quito, Gonzalo Tenorio (born 1602, died after 1675), whose voluminous unpublished work is an example of a form of chiliasm with a specifically American bias.

Tenorio was unable to publish his book in Spain, and attributed the objections to his work raised by the theologians in Spain to the contempt which they felt for the natives of the Americas. 'I would like to know', he writes, 'from whence cometh this hatred which the Spaniards feel for those whom they call *Indianos*, when we all have the same origin...but the Americans do not contradict the doctrines of the Spaniards; they received these doctrines from them; rather, they illuminate what they have received with admirable and solidly founded developments.' In his view, Spain is the new Israel, on account of its orthodoxy and devotion, but of late it, too, has shown weakness; the attacks of the heretics on the coasts of the Americas, the decline of trade and of the convoys, the avarice and ostentatious display of the Creoles, the internal feuds within the convents, and unworthy ministers in the Government of Spain – all these were manifestations of Divine punishment. However, this did not affect the Divine vocation of Spain, which was to consist, at the end of time, in announcing 'the Gospel of the Kingdom'. The Kingdom of Christ, *Paradisus restitutus*, would not be governed by Him directly; He would rule through a universal Monarch, the King of Spain, and the Pope, who would both be established in the Indies after being expelled from Europe by the heresies. The Messianic mission of Spain, therefore, lay in the Indies. That is to say, Tenorio was applying to Spain and the Indies the prophecies of the Pseudo-Methodius concerning the Messianic King and other spiritual chiliastic doctrines, which in his mind were closely associated with devotion to the dogma of the Immaculate Conception. His work contains, intermingled with his principal ideas, other interesting speculations concerning the early preaching of the Gospel by St Thomas, the Conquest as a punishment and purification for the Indians and so on.

Many thinkers emphasised the discovery of the New World, on account of the unparalleled importance of this event – it had been, as Gómara put it, the greatest event in history, except for the Creation, the Incarnation and the Passion – and incorporated it into their eschatological theories. The official theology of history in the Western Church had been for centuries that of St Augustine, who announced an undefined end of all things for the fulfilment of the eschatological events foretold in both Testaments. After 1200 there were new spiritual or chiliastic currents of thought, which put forward interpretations differing from St Augustine's teachings and which created, among fervent minority groups, a sentiment of the imminence of the End, whether their attitude towards this were optimistic or pessimistic. These apocalyptic interpretations of history were applied to the Americas, and above are examples of the resulting theories. They originated in

Columbus himself or the friars, influenced by their realisation of the grandeur, novelty and breadth of the possibilities which now lay open to their activity, or, perhaps, disillusioned by the collapse of those initial hopes. It was left to such men as Acosta to make a more reasoned analysis of the development of the mission, and to restore to its pre-eminent position a theology of history without eschatological overtones and more closely in accord the theories more generally accepted in Europe.

We have described eschatological schemes in which America enjoys a prominent place; during the colonial period, however, there were also interpretations of the Apocalypse in which the New World played no part. Gregorio López, the well-known mystic who was born in Madrid and settled in New Spain in 1562, where he lived the life of a hermit, wrote a treatise on the Apocalypse which has little originality. The exiled Chilean Jesuit Manuel Lacunza provoked a widespread propagation of the chiliastic theme at the end of the eighteenth century and the beginning of the nineteenth, with his book *La Venida del Mesías en Gloria y Majestad.* He may be justly regarded as one of the most significant Chilean thinkers, even though he makes no mention of America in his work, on account of the profundity and logical consistency of the Scriptural exegesis on which he based his eschatological fervour.[1]

The New World in the light of the Biblical account of the origin of man and the teachings of the Gospels

A problem which was of a more strictly erudite nature, within the terms of the intellectual outlook of the age, was that of the origin of the American Indian population. This had much less effect on the general historical outlook, although it is, of course, of great importance in the history of historical and ethnographic research. The intellectual curiosity aroused by the discovery of the American Indian cultures, and the need to reconcile them in some way with traditionally accepted historical and Biblical beliefs, provoked the tendency to construct ambitious schemes to explain the spreading to the Americas of the peoples described in the Old Testament. Theological teaching made obligatory the belief that the human race had descended from one couple, and had spread across the Earth from the time of those patriarchs of mankind recorded in the Mosaic tradition. The canonical and apocryphal books of the Bible, Plato's *Critias*, the pseudo-Aristotelian work *De mirabilibus auscultationibus*, Seneca's *Medea*, the historians of primitive Spain, who in the sixteenth century concocted lists of legendary kings and, finally, Indian accounts, speculations as to the relationship between languages, and the interpretation on the basis of analogy of remains, usages and customs – all these indications formed the subject-matter of the various 'opinions' advanced as to the origin of the Indians. The most complete inventory of these indications is found in the *Origen de los Indios de el Nuevo Mundo e Indias Occidentales,* published in 1607 by the Dominican Gregorio García; his own attitude was completely eclectic. Numerous researchers of the nineteenth and twentieth centuries have contributed, with fresh intellectual weapons, to this long-drawn-out controversy. It is not possible, in the space of this chapter, to summarise this line of inquiry: recently Huddleston (1965) has described the development of the controversy before the beginning of the eighteenth century.

García, quoting a vast number of authorities, expounded and analysed each of the theories: a deliberate voyage of discovery or a chance finding (Acosta had been inclined to believe the latter explanation); Carthaginian origins, Jewish origins, colonisation from the Biblical land of Ophir, and the Platonic myth of Atlantis; Oviedo's thesis of expeditions undertaken by the early Spaniards in the reign of King Hesperus, or during the era of Roman rule (in this connection, García made a comparison of the Roman and the Inca roads); and, finally, the possibilities of colonisation by the Greeks, Phoenicians, Chinese or Tartars.

Of these 'opinions', the most important in any consideration of American eschatological schemes and Utopias is undoubtedly the one of Hebrew origin, if only because, in the early seventeenth century when García was writing, this theory was the most widely held among the Spaniards in the Indies. As soon as it was discovered that the natives of Yucatán practised circumcision, the name of the area was connected with the Biblical Joktan, and observers emphasised numerous real or supposed analogies based on character, ceremonial customs, dress, infant sacrifice and so forth, which were held to apply to the American Indians in general. The actual origin of the population was held to be the migration of the ten tribes of Israel carried off as captives to Assyria and never returning to their homeland; instead, they crossed the Euphrates, and reached Arsareth, whence they would return at the end of time, according to the fourth Book of Esdras, which was apocryphal but always enjoyed great authority among the Jews of the later period and the Christians. On account of its connection with the eschatological belief in the return of the children of Israel to the Holy Land, the prophecy in the Book of Esdras was regarded as authoritative in northern Europe (being adopted by Johannes Fredericus Lumnius, the commentator on the Apocalypse, in 1567, and by the French cosmographer Gilbert Genebrard in the same year), and also by the Mexican chroniclers Juan Tovar, Juan Suárez de Peralta and Diego Durán, in the 1570s (Huddleston, 1967, 34 ff.). To such thinkers as Mendieta, the prophecy of the return in Esdras 4, considered in association with St Paul's predictions of the restoration of Israel within the Church, naturally signified the most authoritative possible confirmation of the hopes which he placed in the natives of New Spain. On the other hand, in the view of the Dominican Diego Durán, the punishments with which God so often threatened His people in the Old Testament on account of their idolatry were now being meted out, in the shape of the epidemics which, since the Conquest, had befallen the descendants of that people in the New World.

In this controversy, as in so many others, Acosta played the part of a demolisher of theories from a rationalistic standpoint. He rejected the theory of deliberate voyages of discovery, because such inventions as the compass had not existed in olden times and had been discovered by 'modern' man; and he rejected the theory of Hebrew origins, principally because of the absence of any system of writing among the Indians, and their lack of interest in money: both these played an important part among the Hebrews. He concluded that the most probable explanation was that the population was descended from wild races of hunters who searched for new lands because they were impelled by poverty. Nevertheless, he admitted that this did not explain the high level attained by the pre-Columbian cultures, and he suggested that after the original settlement there might have been certain cultural influences from the Old World.

The theory of the Jewish origin of the American peoples certainly gave rise to apocalyptic conclusions, for it implied that the Indians were God's people, and that their conversion heralded the consummation of all things. There was, however, another interesting theory, that of the early preaching of the Gospel in the Americas by St Thomas, and this assumed the character, from another angle, of an eminently 'Americanist' theory. The learned tradition according to which St Thomas had travelled to India – there were other, less widespread, versions, in which St Bartholomew was the protagonist – served as the basis for the assertion that, before the arrival of the Spaniards, the Indians had already received the Gospel, even though they had later forgotten its teachings. The Portuguese in India had been the first to learn of the tradition of St Thomas, and the first supposed testimonies of it to be found in the New World appeared in accounts of voyages to Brazil (Gandía, 1929, 228, quotes a German account published in 1510, which mentioned that the Europeans had found there 'reminders of St Thomas'). In 1535 Oviedo recorded it, more as a supposition than as an established fact (II, 7). Belief in its truth appears to have grown gradually, as the Spaniards discovered supposed remains, such as the crosses found in Yucatán and at La Imperial, Chile, images which were interpreted as those of the Virgin Mary, and other items. Cieza, in his *Señorío de los Incas*, gives a somewhat incredulous account of the belief in the coming of the Apostle, who in fact appears to have become confused with the figure of Viracocha, just as in Mexico his memory had become confused with that of the civilising hero Quetzalcóatl. Mendieta, in his *Historia Eclesiástica*, IV, XLI, recorded various Indian anecdotes and testimonies, and gave his own interpretation of these. Diego Durán, Ruiz de Montoya in the Jesuit province of Paraguay, Calancha, Alonso de Ovalle and others, bear witness to the continuity of the legend, and Gregorio García, in his *Predicación del Evangelio en el Nuevo Mundo, viviendo los Apóstoles* (1625), provides a compilation of all the testimonies, among which he particularly emphasises the legend of one or more men dressed in tunic and sandals who instituted auricular confession and the practice of fasting. The process of transmission of this legend was inspired, in the first place, by a desire to fill the gap of several centuries which had elapsed in the New World without its inhabitants being aware of the Redemption, and to find historical confirmation of the Biblical passages which foretold that the Gospel would be preached to all peoples before the final catastrophe (interpreted, in this context, as being the destruction of Jerusalem in A.D. 70); in addition there was the urge, strongly felt by a great number of missionaries, to pay due tribute to the religious beliefs and practices of the Indians. Gregorio García emphasised that it had been merely short-lived preaching, or the memory of it, and that therefore it had been unknown in Europe. The baroque predilection for discourse and rational argument is apparent in many of these theories.

Sigüenza y Góngora, who possessed a great knowledge of Mexican antiquities, transmitted this legend to eighteenth-century thought through his works, some of them manuscript (*Fénix del Occidente, Santo Tomás Apóstol*), and others printed (*Parayso Occidental*, 1684), and the account was thus adopted by Mier. What strikes one as curious is the discrepancy of intellectual levels in the thought processes of this arrogant 'enlightened' Mexican of the era of Independence, who, for all his 'enlightenment', continued to think in such characteristically baroque terms. His exile from Mexico was in fact provoked by a sermon which caused great commotion; in this sermon he expounded, in a modified form, the popular tradition of the Virgin of Guadalupe, and assured his listeners that the cape of the Indian Juan Diego had already borne the painted picture of the Virgin for several centuries; the picture had been painted by the missionary Apostle St

Thomas. No element in the Mexican collective religious consciousness was stronger than the cult rendered to this image by Indians and clergy: even such prominent champions of the Mexican Enlightenment as Clavígero and Bartolache wrote books to defend, according to the rules of critical historiography, this cult which had already become a national tradition. Fray Servando, who was as pro-Indian and pro-Mexican as any, nevertheless decided, perhaps under the influence of his innate combative spirit, to attempt to replace this national belief with the theory of the preaching of the Gospel by the Apostles, a thesis which gave dignity to the New World and converted the image of Guadalupe into a Mexican hieroglyph. Since the desire to save men felt by Christ and His Mother, he wrote in his *Manifiesto apologético*, extended to the men of all nations, the Redemption must of necessity have been preached by St Thomas in America 'at the same time as the other parts of the world, which were no less sinful than America'. It is impossible to find a more eloquent testimony of the incompleteness of the reception of the Enlightenment by those thinkers of the Independence period who had a pro-Indian bias, and of the way in which a religious faith emphasising the workings of Providence and the consummation of all things still prevailed over historiographical methods supposedly influenced by the Enlightenment.

The 'Translatio Imperii'

The entire historiography of the Middle Ages – and this outlook lasted until the end of the seventeenth century – developed within the context of the theory of the four world-wide empires, which originated in the Book of Daniel and was transmitted to the West during the patristic era, particularly by St Jerome. The political chronology of the world was based on the empires of the Assyrians, the Medes and Persians, the Greeks (under Alexander the Great) and of Rome (and of the States which were the successors of Rome); the final empire, in eschatological terms, would be a Messianic Fifth Monarchy. It was possible to observe, in this process, a transfer of power from the East to the West: 'every human power or knowledge began in the East and finishes in the West', wrote Otto von Freysing, who considered this process of transfer to be true not only of political but also of intellectual power – from the wise men of Babylon to the thinkers of France and Spain.

In the places where the Spaniards encountered political powers which they classified as 'imperial' (erroneously in the case of the Aztec Confederation, and correctly in that of Peru), and where the Indians had a traditional account of the development of their own history, it was possible to undertake a process of intellectual elaboration and of interpretation of Indian history, which tended to be based on the supposition of a succession of kingdoms or empires marking successive ages of history. It was not possible to reconcile this interpretation of the internal development of these empires with the succession of empires in the Old World, for there was no contact between the two processes until the moment of the Spanish Conquest. The legend of St Thomas's preaching was the only attempt, albeit a feeble one, to establish a previous connection between the two historical processes. Nevertheless, the attempt to interpret the histories of Mexico and Peru in accordance with a scheme of successive empires and ages of history did imply a desire to achieve an intellectual harmonisation of traditional materials. The other American peoples were omitted from this intellectual scheme, whether they were tribes of wild Indians or cultured peoples such as the Chibchas.

Arnoldsson (1956) has described in an excellent essay the various forms and manifestations in colonial historiography of this scheme of succession of Mexican and Peruvian imperial powers. One can observe, as a characteristic common to almost all these schemes, the account of a general upward course of civilisation, the decisive stages of this ascent being marked by heroes who were subsequently deified, or by monarchs who were wise law-givers. According to Sahagún, the first inhabitants of Mexico came from the North 'in search of the Earthly Paradise', perhaps inspired by some oracle. They founded the strongly fortified city of Tula, where Quetzalcóatl reigned, whom Sahagún compared to King Arthur of England, and who after the destruction of Tula set off for the city of the Sun, Tlapallan, from whence he would return and rebuild the destroyed city and reign again. When Cortés arrived, they thought that he was Quetzalcóatl, until they were disillusioned. He constituted, for the Mexicans, the classic model of the hero who educated his people in magical powers and moral virtues. Fernando de Alva Ixtlilxochitl, dedicating his *Historia Chichimeca* to the Viceroy in about 1616, asserted that the achievements of the New World were in no way inferior to those of the Romans, Greeks and Medes. He divided history as a whole into four Ages or 'Suns'. In the Third Age Quetzalcóatl arrived, and in the Fourth the Toltecs, Chichimecas, and so on, and finally the Aztecs. A wise king, Netzahuatlcoyotl, had laid down the design of the world, of the temples, of moral life, and had even established four Royal Councils, devoted to government, music, war and the treasury. In Peru, Ciez de León, the first historian to give a general account of the vanquished empire, in his *Señorío de los Incas*, asserted that in early times the Peruvians lived a disorderly life, being naked savages, with dwellings built on hills or rocks, living by robbing their neighbours and offering human sacrifices, until the establishment of the religion based on sun-worship by Tici Viracocha, on the shores of the great Lake Titicaca, and then eventually arose the Inca Empire and the city of Cuzco. In the writings of the Inca Garcilaso, the disparagement of the earlier communities, in order to emphasise the civilising role of the Incas, was carried to far greater lengths: all the early customs and beliefs were vile and base, and the Empire meant the abolition of rustic habits, the introduction of some notion of natural Law and the repudiation of idolatry, with the result that the natives were afterwards more disposed to receive the Catholic faith. The Indians subject to the Incas, continued Garcilaso (I, xv), had been quicker to receive the Gospel than their unsubdued neighbours: the Inca imperial power had performed in America the task of 'preparation for the Gospel', similar to that attributed by Eusebius of Caesarea to the Roman Empire. In the writings of the Inca Garcilaso and the other Peruvian chroniclers, as in Mexico, a prominent part is played by founders and law-givers, in the same way as in classical antiquity. Manco Capac, the reformer of the world, whom Garcilaso interpreted, in a very rationalistic and pragmatic manner as an intelligent man who pretended to have been sent by the Sun, was the founder of the religious ceremonies and of the entire social order, with its sacred and numerological foundations. The controversy as to whether Garcilaso was a historian or a believer in Utopias has been continued by Menéndez y Pelayo, Riva Aguero and Porras Barrenechea; Durand, a recent writer, has concluded, on the whole, that he was a believer in Utopias inspired by neo-Platonic and Stoic thought; he bases his argument on a study of what Garcilaso read, and on his famous translation of the work of León Ebreo. The Inca and his 'philosophers' ('*amautas*'), when the Empire was at its height, searched for ultimate truth and, by the light of natural reason, they caught a glimpse of Christian truths; the entire social organisation and all the conquests of the Incas were evidence of a context of peace similar to that of the Romans; Cuzco was a new Rome, for it paved the way for the dominion of the Church.

The chroniclers in the time of Viceroy Toledo, the most distinguished of whom was Pedro Sarmiento de Gamboa, considered the Empire of the Incas to have been a violent and tyrannical process of unification. Garcilaso, without directly attacking this interpretation, represented, forty years after the famous Reports of Viceroy Toledo, which aroused so much controversy, the diametrically opposite point of view.

In the work of Felipe Guzmán Poma de Ayala, one can observe, in more folkloric terms, the same scheme of the succession of empires; in general, the narrative still describes the historical ascent of a people who were at first farmers and later became warriors. This representative of the impoverished provincial nobility of Guamanga distinguished four Ages in the history of the Indians, whose ancestors had been in Noah's Ark (that is to say, from the point of view of Poma de Ayala, they descended from 'Spaniards'). Although the first generation had been deeply religious and devoted to worship, it was entirely lacking in technical ability; subsequent ages were to bring cultivation, crafts and war. In the fourth Age, the Incas made their appearance. At the same time, this *mestizo* chronicler includes, at the beginning of his work, the chronological scheme of the Roman emperors down to Charles V and the Popes, along the lines of European chronologies, albeit with picturesque variations. The illustrations and text of the last part of the work, dealing with the viceroyalty of Peru, are a curious mixture of a sarcastic attitude towards certain characteristic representatives of the régime and of admiration for others: the *encomenderos, corregidores* and *doctrineros* are placed in the former group, and hermits, friars and charitable Jesuits in the latter category.

The scheme of a succession of empires certainly imposed a measure of intellectual unification on the Indian traditions; in addition to this, it helped the Spanish monarchy to achieve a fuller understanding of itself. According to the Biblical account, not only did kingdoms succeed one another, but 'the kingdom is translated from one people to another' (Ecclesiasticus, 10: 8); this transfer of power was a punishment. Thinkers such as Mendieta and Torquemada, who justified in principle, as being the work of Divine Providence, the destruction of the old Mexican empires, insisted that the same fate threatened the Spanish Empire. Torquemada wrote that the conquistadors, because of the violent wrongs which they committed, 'have not lasted for many generations; for, although formerly they gained lands and wealth, they now have no house or estate wherein to live' (quoted in Moreno Toscano, 1963, 78). Nevertheless, baptism and liberation from idolatry were an unqualified blessing for the Franciscans, and these outweighed the condemnation of the atrocities committed by the Spaniards.

The last chapter of Acosta's *Historia Natural y Moral* (1590) solemnly proclaims the theory of 'preparation for the Gospel'. At the moment when the Spaniards appeared, the empires of Mexico and Peru were at the height of their power, and the pebble mentioned in the Book of Daniel, which was to break the feet of the statues of the empires, inaugurated the Fifth Monarchy in the New World. The Indian monarchs had introduced common languages, and this would facilitate the task of preaching. The Indians who had been imperial subjects were quickly converted, whereas the others were costing the King interminable wars and the missionaries great efforts. Even though men sought their own good rather than that of Jesus Christ, yet the Church also grows by these earthly means, asserts Acosta, quoting St Augustine; and this theory is, in essence, 'Providentialism'.

The image of the transfer of power from the East to the West was fairly common in sixteenth-century Spain. It was used by Nebrija in his *Gestas* recounting the achievements of Ferdinand and Isabella. Garibay, in his *Compendio historial* of Spain (1571), asserted that there were only two empires left, the German 'Holy Roman' one and that recently founded in the Indies by the kings of Spain (Arnoldsson, 1956, 24). Juan de Palafox, in his *Juicio interior y secreto*, written about 1640, describes Spain as one of the world monarchies, because it had extended its hegemony over several nations (Jover, 1950). It had begun under Ferdinand the Catholic, and had become perfected in 1558 at the time of the abdication of Charles V, but its decline had already begun in 1570, with the insurrection of the Low Countries, and it had continued throughout the following century, with truces that were meaningless and the loss of territories and strongholds in every continent. It could be saved, Palafox asserted, if each nation were governed in accordance with its character – governing the Castilians in the Castilian manner, the Portuguese in the Portuguese manner and so on. The same principle could have been applied, subject to certain limitations, to the inhabitants of the Americas, even though, strictly speaking, they were all legally Castilians; but Palafox only mentioned them in order to praise their habits of obedience.

The historical periodisation outlined in the Book of Daniel did not entirely lose its prophetic force even in the eighteenth century, despite the rise in popularity of the new scheme of historical periodisation – antiquity, Middle Ages, modern times. Gerbi (1960, 123/126) quotes several assertions made in the Anglo-Saxon world regarding the transfer of empire from east to west, this process being interpreted as favouring the British Empire. Berkeley, in a few lines of verse, surveyed the first four acts of the drama, and looked forward to the fifth, which would be final. The most famous saying was that of the Neapolitan Abbot Ferdinando Galiani, a talented admirer of Machiavelli and Vico, in a letter of 1776: the time had come for the fall of Europe and the total migration of religion, laws, arts and sciences to America (Gerbi, 1960, 111 ff.). Consideration of historical and political factors (sometimes, as in Adam Smith, historical and commercial factors) could still lend strong support to a secularised version of the old prophetic notion of the migration of empires from east to west. However, after the publication of Robertson's *History of America* (1777), purely pragmatic considerations, and the analysis of causes and effects, were to predominate in historiography and relegate to the background the grand, traditional, teleological theory.

The use of cultural analogies as apologias

The scheme of a succession of world-wide kingdoms, culminating in the Messianic kingdom, was the basis of a plan of political and ecclesiastical history which could not be the 'history of America', but rather that of the great empires in the Americas: the Aztec the Inca, the Spanish and even the British empires. The other peoples and cultures were left out of this scheme as lacking in universal significance. As early as the sixteenth century, the comparison of cultures opened up the possibility of considering from a historical point of view even those cultures which had not had great architectural achievements, when compared with the tradition of classical antiquity. Humanist historians such as Peter Martyr or Fernández de Oviedo used to make comparisons in the course of their narrative. The missionaries who translated the Gospels and Epistles for the liturgical year, and sermons and catechisms, into the commoner and rarer Indian languages, inevitably found themselves faced with problems of comparison, when they were selecting words which would express Christian ideas without giving rise to confusion. The danger of confusion being deliberately introduced by the Devil, which had been denounced by Sahagún, gave rise to controversies, complete with parties and factions, over the translations of Holy Scripture and sermons – the translation of the catechisms was unavoidable and involved less dangers (Ricard, 1933, 72ff.). This meant taking sides for or against the comparison of cultures, and implied a favourable or an adverse judgment with regard to the values of the indigenous cultures, especially the religious values.

The earliest systematic attempt at comparison appears to have been Las Casas's *Apologética Historia de las Indias*, written in the 1550s, after the famous controversy with Juan Ginés de Sepúlveda: although the manuscript was used as a source by some writers, such as the Augustinian Friar Jerónimo Román in his *Repúblicas del Mundo* (1575), it was not published until 1909. His defence of the rationality of the Indians is based, theoretically, on the *Politics* of Aristotle, the doctrinal principles of which were also of decisive importance to his adversary Sepúlveda. Las Casas intended to prove, using Aristotelian criteria, that the Indians were the political equals of the Greeks and Romans, and at times surpassed them. They possess, in fact, all the social strata which should be possessed by a republic that is self-sufficient and 'blessed in temporal things' – that is to say, farmers, craftsmen, warriors, nobles, priests, judges and governors. The correct ordering of society resulting from the presence of all these estates of the realm in Indian communities, to which Las Casas adds the Indians' habits of monastic prudence in the individual sphere and economic prudence in family relationships, guaranteed a viable 'public policy' and a sound social life. A detailed description of the political system of the Indians of the Caribbean, of New Spain and of Peru is furnished to justify this viewpoint. He devotes several chapters to the Incas, using Cieza de León as his principal source; he gives consideration to monarchical government (the most excellent of all, he asserts), obedience, the legislative wisdom of Pachacutec, the amazingly well-built roads and so forth. In the case of Mexico, he bestows praise on the entire legal system, on public appointments and education; he compares their perfection with Crete, Laconia and Athens, the paradigms of humanist history.

Although the absence of the true Faith – what he calls at the end of his book a kind of barbarism by default, but not because of savagery – somewhat detracts from the Indians' excellence, Las Casas nevertheless always categorically affirms the Catholic doctrine of the natural light of human reason, even though this might be contaminated to a greater or lesser degree by Satanic influences. The thesis maintained by St Paul, that the pagans could come to the knowledge of God by the light of natural reason, helps Las Casas to appreciate the wisdom and moral rectitude of Quetzalcóatl and Viracocha. The Indians 'had more inner light and natural knowledge of God than the Greeks and Romans' (ch. CXXVII). A return to the truth is always possible, he optimistically affirms, so long as the Faith is preached to them peacefully, as he proposed in his *De unico vocationis modo.* Even practices which were extremely repugnant to Catholic morality, such as human sacrifice, are excused in the *Apologética Historia* by adducing the example of so many nations of the Old World and, above all, because such sacrifices were the indication of a generous disposition, for they consisted of offering the object of one's greatest affections to a deity which one believed to be the true one. This is a curious example of a relativist outlook, similar to that of modern historiography, being adopted by a person such as Las Casas, whose conscience was so strongly moralistic and rigorist.

Thomism, as developed in the Dominican Order, had to a certain extent accepted the naturalistic notions of Aristotle and the other Greek thinkers.

This made it possible for Las Casas to base his apologia on a eulogy of the natural environment and climate of the Americas, the healthy character of which exercised a determining influence on the human senses and understanding. This theory based on climatic conditions was derived from Greek and Thomist political theory. The natives were intelligent, brave, handsome, sober, long-suffering and so on because of the favourable natural environment. It appears to be of great significance that the apologia for America, as early as the sixteenth century, should be based on the eulogy of nature, and an attitude of optimistic naturalism: this was to continue until the twentieth century.

Las Casas was not, however, a humanist. In addition to his lack of a proper critical attitude towards history (he attacked Vives because the latter had expressed his disbelief in the false accounts of early history written by Annius of Viterbo), he has recourse in his polemic to the disparagement of Greece and Rome in order to defend the New World, on the basis of arguments derived from the early chapters of the *City of God*. The value of his attempt at a comparison of cultures and at incorporation of the American Indian cultures into the framework of universal historical knowledge is diminished by his polemical disparagement of the cultures of antiquity, which reduces the humanist and theoretical quality of his defence of America.

José de Acosta was responsible for introducing into the discussion of methods to be used by the missionaries the distinction between different levels of civilisation and political organisation. He established a distinction, in the Americas, between the natives who had recognised properly established systems of overlordship and those barbarous peoples who had not previously been subject to imperial suzerainty: evangelisation had made much more rapid progress among the former than among the latter category, in which he includes the Indians of Florida and Brazil and the Araucanians of Chile. Superior to both categories were the Chinese, 'where there is such highly developed government and intellectual achievements, and also industry and riches and an innumerable population, and walled cities'. The conquest of the Chinese would be an impossible undertaking, and among them missionary efforts should take place in the peaceful manner used by the Apostles; this method, however, seems to him to be impossible in many parts of the Americas, because the Conquest has already taken place, or because the unsubdued Indians are too barbaric (see his *Reports* of 1587 on China; *De procuranda Indorum salute*, II, 8; and the *Historia Natural y Moral*, last chapter). Rather than a comparison between individual cultures, Acosta offers a model of different levels of civilisation.

The well-known theories regarding the origin of the American Indian population were largely based on comparisons between the vocabularies of Nahuatl or Quechua and those of the languages of the Old World. In 1724 Père Lafitau, a Jesuit missionary in Canada, defended the theory of the migration of the Pelasgians and other Mediterranean peoples to America by way of East Asia, as the hypothetically possible origin of the inhabitants of the New World. His real contribution, however, did not lie in his ethnographic comparisons of usages and customs such as matriarchy, religious hermaphroditism and so on but rather in the theoretical basis of the resemblances which he emphasised. He alludes, in conclusion, to the idea, occasionally expressed by the Fathers of the Church, of a previous Revelation to all mankind, before Moses and before the Flood, in which all peoples without exception shared, although this Revelation had been partially overlaid with magic and idolatry. It was not necessary, therefore, to have recourse to the theory of the early missionaries that the Devil inspired a sacrilegious miming of Christian rites, nor to the theory of certain Fathers that the Law of Moses had been known to other peoples and imitated by them. In place of such doctrines, this French Jesuit, in his *Moeurs des sauvages américains comparées aux mœurs des premiers temps*, advanced the hypothesis of a theist universalism in primitive times; this theory had been defended by such humanists as Augustinus Steuchus, in a book on the perennial philosophy, and Gerardo Vossius, in his work on Gentile theology (Valjavec, 1964). The thesis of Las Casas was based, in philosophical terms, on the Pauline and Thomist doctrine of the natural ability of human reason to attain to the knowledge of God; that of Lafitau, on the other hand, was based on the historical tradition of a primitive Revelation which was later partially diluted; they agreed, however, that the Indian religions could be turned towards the path of truth (Zavala, 1949). Lafitau totally eschewed polemics against the cultures of the Old World, and this made it possible for him to make a humanist evaluation, unmarked by prejudice, of primitive cultures.

The Spanish American Jesuits of the era of the expulsion of the Order showed themselves extremely receptive, in Italy, to the Enlightenment and to a rationalistic and pragmatic approach to historiography; this is especially evident, for example, in the general observations made by Clavígero in his *Historia Antigua de México*, such as the equality and unchanging nature of human souls, the possibility of modifying them by education and social discipline. The reception of the Enlightenment was made comparatively easy among the Jesuits, owing to the presence of certain dominant tendencies in the Company: Molinism and the exaltation of free will, habits of active intellectual endeavour, and a pragmatic attitude towards accommodation with modernising tendencies. Furthermore, the Spanish American Jesuits contributed their utmost efforts to the defence of America against the detractions of Pauw, Buffon and, to a certain extent, Robertson and Juan Bautista Muñoz (the famous controversy described in detail by Gerbi). Just as, in earlier times, Las Casas had attacked the theory of the natural servitude of the Indians, in the eighteenth century the Creole Jesuits (together with other writers) defended the natural environment of America against the attacks of the scientists of the day: the New World, they insisted, was not an unformed continent unsuited to superior forms of life, animal species did not degenerate there, nor were the Indians and the Creoles intellectually inferior – education could raise them to the same level as the Europeans. Furthermore, Clavígero used tactics of counter-attack similar to those employed in the *Apologética Historia* two centuries before: the peoples of Spain, he wrote, had been inferior as regards civilisation when the Phoenicians and Carthaginians arrived to the Mexicans of the sixteenth century. All the early inhabitants of Europe had been barbarians, wrote Iturri, a native of Santa Fé, in his *Carta crítica* (1797) attacking Muñoz. The Chilean Juan Ignacio Molina defended the climate and fauna of his country against the attacks of Pauw, and proved, contrary to Robertson's assertions, that the Indians of Chile had been farmers using the hoe, and not mere hunters. This last point was of great importance to Molina, because he classifies economic ways of life in an ascending scale which basically incorporates a value judgment: hunting – the keeping of flocks – agriculture – commerce and civilised life. This peculiar combination of an economic approach and moral and political value judgments is typical of the attitude of thinkers of the Enlightenment towards the history of civilisations, and it was incorporated bodily into the outlook of the Chilean Jesuit. More purely humanist in outlook, on the other hand, was the Mexican Pedro Márquez, the translator into Italian of the works of Antonio León y Gama on the astronomy, chronology and mythology of Mexico, and the author of original works on the architectural remains of his country, in which he compared the scientific knowledge of the Indians with that of the Babylonians and Egyptians.

The attempt of Lorenzo Boturini to apply the ideas of Vico regarding the 'vulgar wisdom' of primitive peoples to the materials on Mexican antiquities collected by Alva Ixtlilxochitl and Sigüenza, with which Boturini was familiar, turned out to be unsuccessful in practice; and his *Idea de una nueva historia general de la América Septentrional* (1746) was immediately accused in Madrid, with some justification, of having openly plagiarised Vico.

The comparison of the cultures of the Old and New Worlds, from the sixteenth to the eighteenth centuries, sheds light on certain traits that are extremely constant in the Spanish American consciousness. One of them is the habit of basing assertions of the excellence of the continent on the qualities of the climate and of the natural environment in general, to which writers attribute great influence over the typical Indian or Creole. The influence of climate is supported by quotations from Aristotle by Las Casas, and from Montesquieu by the eighteenth-century Jesuits and the Lima doctor Hipólito de Unanue. The other generalised tendency is the important emphasis given to social organisation, discipline and the educational system – all that we would describe as the social environment. All the writings defending the Indian and the Creole are based on a belief in education and social organisation as agencies capable of compensating for cultural deficiencies, which are merely accidental, and the consequent feasibility of raising the Americans to the same cultural level as the Europeans. The Jesuits, with their experience as organisers of power and of education, made an important contribution; but as early as the sixteenth century the scheme for segregating the Indians in *pueblos* contained the germ of this idea.

Comparisons between cultures led to attempts to eulogise the value of the New World and its cultures, to the detriment of European and ancient cultures; the result of this was that, instead of a humanistic outlook and an attempt to reconcile these cultures with the scheme of universal history, writers nearly always adopted a polemical and defensive attitude, which was a foreseeable consequence of the feeling of 'novelty' which America inspired.

America in the Utopias

Columbus believed that he had glimpsed beyond the mouths of the Orinoco, in his third voyage, the neighbourhood of the Early Paradise; and writers as late as Sahagún (around 1575) found it understandable that the migratory movements in Mexico should have taken place, for centuries, towards the south, because the wise men believed that Paradise lay to the south of the Equator. In 1656 León Pinelo published his work, *Paraíso en el Nuevo Mundo*. With a display of baroque erudition, he set at naught all opinions at variance with his thesis, which he claimed to be based, originally, on the Syriac Father St Ephraim, whose thought was transmitted by a certain Moses Bar Cefas, a Syriac bishop of the seventh century, whose work had been published in a Latin translation in Antwerp in 1569.

This thinker had maintained that Paradise lay on the other side of the ocean; and men had come from there to the Old World after the Flood. León Pinelo maintained that, on account of the fertility and mildness of its climate, America, and especially Peru, possessed the qualities of lands more 'sincere, pure, high and exalted', as befits Paradise; and he went on to give a detailed description of the three realms of Nature (see Porras Barrenechea, 1943). With the penchant for curious and minute detail and the erudite fantasy typical of learned men of the Baroque Age, he adduced every kind of archaeological and legendary evidence in confirmation of his thesis or capable of refuting objections to it.

The 'Golden Age' described by Hesiod and succeeding writers is another of the images customarily associated with that of Paradise during this period, together with all the abundant legendary materials concerning the Fortunate Isles, the Hesperides, the Isles of St Brendan, the *Terra Australis* and so on. The habit of nakedness, and the peaceful and docile character of the inhabitants of Hispaniola, and the sharing of wealth, were immediately communicated to readers in Europe through the writings of Columbus, Peter Martyr and Vespucio; even though these same documents, in the later reports, emphatically qualified the idyllic image, particularly as regards the peace reigning among the Indian tribes, the notion persisted, and even survived the Europeans' discovery of Aztec culture; the missionaries revived the notion. The literary reflection of this image in Europe, especially in France, has been studied by Chinard (1934), who has proved its enduring influence, from Montaigne to Rousseau. This gave rise to literature inspired by America which disparaged society and Europe, glorified the 'noble savage', and emphasised the exotic nature of the continent. Atkinson (1935, 21 ff.) and Elliott (1970, 10 ff.) have described the approximate limitations of the interest of the European reading public in the discovery of America, and have shown that, despite its novelty, this event did not arouse such great interest as might be imagined.

The theme of Atlantis is more closely connected with Utopian writings than the theory of the innocence of savages, because the Utopias were rationalistic projections of ideal social organisations, and Plato's *Critias* describes a highly civilised society. The theme of Atlantis recurred frequently in the controversy concerning the origin of the population of the Americas; it is found in the writings of Zárate, the humanists Gómara and Cervantes de Salazar, and in Sarmiento de Gamboa.

In the opinion of Ernst Bloch (1959, chs. 38–55), Columbus's enterprise was fundamentally Utopian, and gave rise to a hundred 'geographical Utopias' which implied secession, the abandonment of the old and the adoption of the new, rather than the mere expansion of the metropolis; Eden and Eldorado were confused, and combined their capacities of attraction; all the values of this present life were altered by the discovery, immediately in the case of the migrants, and then in the case of the country which sent them, provoking proposals for change. So important a scientific and technical Utopia as Bacon's *Novum Organon* bore on the title-page the columns of Hercules and the motto '*Plus ultra*',

However, the author believes that it is worth distinguishing between eschatological themes and Utopian projects: the former were motivated by a religious impulse (of the kind found in certain religions like Christianity, Judaism, Islam, Zoroastrianism and Manicheism, that is to say, the 'historical' religions); whereas the Utopias were derived from rationalistic motivations which stemmed from various sources, depending on the age. In both cases the idea of transformation is present, but the eschatologies looked forward to a supernatural consummation, whereas the Utopias embodied a rational plan or at least a constructive image.[2] This is, of course, a general typology, and individual cases are usually more complex. Thus, the Franciscan missionaries in Mexico in the sixteenth century were inspired by a definite eschatological hope, which has been described above; but at the same time they entertained an idyllic picture of the Indian world – a Utopia which missionary activity should try to preserve.

It has been definitely established that the father of modern Utopias, Thomas More, was familiar with Vespucio's *Mundus novus*, and it is possible that the latter's description influenced More's work. In any case, his book had considerable repercussions in New Spain. Bishop Zumárraga possessed a copy, and the *Oidor* Vasco de Quiroga, who was later Bishop of Michoacán, declared that the *Utopia* was the 'model' on which he based his famous legal opinion of 1535 (published in CoDoIn, X, 333–513). Quiroga also quoted, as a source of inspiration, Lucian's *Saturnalia*, translated into Latin by Erasmus and More, from which he took the description of the Golden Age; the New World was called thus, he wrote, 'not because it was newly found, but because in its people and in almost every other respect it resembles that first and golden age'. However, Quiroga, in addition to the accustomed eulogies of the simplicity of the Indians, also recognises the fact of their dispersal, which in his view led to their barbarity, in accordance with the Hispanic and Aristotelian urbanising ideal. The Spaniards could not leave them in that wild state, for that would be like a tyranny: in this respect Quiroga differed from Las Casas. He proposed instead a detailed scheme for a 'mixed polity', both spiritual and temporal, which has been analysed by Zavala (1937, 1941). The 'Utopian' nature of the proposal is evident in the precise organisation of communities of 60,000 citizens, organised in family groups, with 'juries' each responsible for thirty families, and two *alcaldes*, and a Spanish *alcalde mayor*. The two *Hospitales-pueblos* which he succeeded in establishing, and the Ordinances of which have come down to us, had communal lands for growing cereals, although there were also privately owned plots. Urban families living in the *Hospital* learning industrial crafts, and rural families engaged in growing crops took turn and turn about, the heads of families supervising the work. The harvest was distributed in accordance with the quality, condition and needs of the citizens, any surplus being for the *Hospital* and the poor. Luxury was forbidden, but public rejoicing was allowed. There were elected officials, controlled and kept in check by the heads of families; and there were *Sicofantes* responsible for controlling abuses. In contrast to More's scheme, there was no religious tolerance in the *Hospitales*, only the Catholic faith being permitted.

It would be worth embarking on a more detailed description of the role played by America in the various well-known Utopias devised between the sixteenth and eighteenth centuries, but this is not possible in the more limited context of this study. In the case of Thomas Campanella – who was certainly not by any means a mere designer of Utopias, but was also a notable chiliast – the chapters devoted to America in his *De monarchia hispanica* are deserving of a detailed analysis within the general context of his thought. In the opinion of Diez del Corral (1962), the 'City of the Sun' described by Campanella bears some resemblance to the ideal American city, as regards topography, architecture, social life and education. It would be worth making a more thorough analysis of this suggested connection, and also of the assertion, which has been repeated since it was first made by Gothein (1883), that the Paraguayan missions were inspired by the theories of Campanella.

The Jesuit reservations of the province of Paraguay were an obvious source of inspiration for the designers of Utopias. Historical research carried out in this century, from Pablo Hernández (1913) to Mörner (1953), which has concentrated its attention on the actual organisation and activities of the Jesuits, has drawn attention, from a pragmatic point of view, to connections and relations with the Utopias, and the influence of them; it has pointed out how much the Jesuits borrowed from the early missionaries of the sixteenth century and the general legislation of Spanish America, and the extent to which their activities were influenced by the geographical situation and economic possibilities of Paraguay. Mörner has observed that there is no real documentary proof that the Reservations were organised according to a single preconceived plan, since a single passage in the work of the late writer Charlevoix (1756) is not sufficient proof of this; and this means that one essential requisite of the Utopias is lacking – the fact of having been planned on a single occasion, without any internal development. However, the idea that the Jesuits constructed a Utopian State has been extremely persistent. This idea has, of course, been influenced by the generalised image of the Jesuits as a unitary, intelligent and active force, possessing all the secrets of power and education. Moreover, the disputes which the Company carried on in Paraguay with Bishop Bernardino de Cárdenas in the 1640s and 1650s, and with the *Visitador* José de Antequera in 1721 and 1735, which demonstrated the power of the Company vis-à-vis the local ecclesiastical hierarchy and the *vecinos* of Asunción, who were bitterly hostile to its Indian policy; the armed resistance offered by the Jesuit *pueblos* against the *mameluco* raiders from São Paulo; and the flourishing export trade in *yerba mate* – all these events created the intellectual context in which it was easy to imagine a vast overall design inspiring their activities. The image of a territorial power in a geographically isolated situation and under the control of the Company naturally led men to imagine that what existed there was a 'Jesuitical kingdom' inspired by Utopian projects.

In 1743 and 1749, there appeared the two parts of *Il Cristianesimo felice nelle missioni dei Padri della Compagnia di Gesu nel Paraguai*, by Lodovico Antonio Muratori, one of the principal exponents of the European 'Catholic Enlightenment'; he was a very learned man and a staunch moraliser, and knew Paraguay only through the medium of the reports, accounts of travels and letters of the Jesuits, which always reflected the same idyllic image that had been fashionable in the sixteenth century. The title itself is significant: 'felicity' was one of the key words of eighteenth-century thought; it immediately suggested lands and peoples remote from the European environment which, according to the interpretation fashionable at that time, was the chief citadel of corruption and unhappiness. The connection between Christianity and felicity, suggested in the very title of the book, implied an apologetic urge to demonstrate the possible identification of traditional and other-worldly religion with the new moral and social ideal, with this fusion taking place outside Europe. The book goes on to describe the Jesuit system as being in total contrast to the general system of Spanish government in the Americas, which it depicts in terms of the harshest possible disparagement, in the tradition of the Black Legend: devastation, lack of interest in cultivating the land and planting crops, massacres, labour in the mines, implacable racial hatred, avarice and human covetousness to a bestial degree, arrogance on the part of the *encomenderos* and junior officials, the luxurious habits and corruption of the Spaniards, and so on. The only things he finds worthy of praise are the 'beautiful rules' promulgated by the King of Spain and the existence of some pious Spaniards (see, especially, ch. VI). He contrasts all this with life in the Jesuit reservations. In this way, a writer who enjoyed prestige in Italy and Europe as a whole on account of his learning and piety distinguished, within the Spanish Empire, a historical phenomenon which differed sharply from the general picture, the Jesuit construction of 'felicitous Christianity'.

Montesquieu was one of the 'enlightened' admirers of the Company, which he certainly regarded as a world power, with a strong sense of corporate honour and power of command, which had permitted it to undertake ambitious projects and bring them to a successful conclusion. Among these were the Guaraní reservations, where the Company had succeeded in united religion and humanity – as he puts it in the *Esprit des Lois* (IV, VI) – bringing the Indians out of the jungle, clothing them, giving them guaranteed sustenance, freeing them from devastation at the hands of the Spaniards, allowing them to defend themselves by armed force, isolating them from foreigners in order to safeguard their customs, teaching them useful occupations rather than those connected with luxury and carrying on trade only in common rather than individually. Montesquieu was perhaps the first writer to point out the analogy with Plato's Republic, thus classifying the Paraguayan missions as one of the grand Utopian designs.

After the publication of these ideal descriptions by Muratori and Montesquieu, and during the difficult years immediately before the dissolution of the Company, Raynal devoted several chapters (bk. VIII, chs. XIV-XVII) of his *Histoire philosophique et politique des établissements et du commerce des européens dans les deux Indes* (1770) to this already well-known achievement of the Company, in which he had been a novice. This work, too, speaks of the Jesuits as having taken the Indians out of the forests where they had taken refuge from the devastation wreaked by the Spaniards, and shown them the attractions of 'the sweetness of human society'. 'They did not try to make them Christians before making them men', he wrote, with the superficial wit so typical of the thinkers of the Enlightenment when they engaged in polemics. The Jesuits made the Indians embrace Christianity, Raynal continued, 'when, by making them happy, they made them docile'. This writer's most interesting contribution is his comparison of the achievement of the Jesuits with that of the Incas. Two idyllic images, that of the reservations as described by the missionaries and by polemical writers of the period of the Enlightenment and that of the Empire which expanded by conquest but yet was peaceful described by the Inca Garcilaso, come together for a moment in the pages of Raynal's book. Both Utopias were theocratic, and made use of impressive religious ceremonies and music; both systems held sway over egalitarian and communistic communities; they were both severely repressive, but they were well thought out and achieved a stable equilibrium. Thus both the Inca and the Jesuit empires made 'superstition', which generally was so prejudicial to man, a beneficial agent because it partly coincided with the natural order. The last generation of Enlightened thinkers, however, being already admirers of manifestations of human passion and of emotional enthusiasm, did not fail to discern the limitations of Utopias designed according to excessively pedagogical criteria: Raynal observed that the Guaranís, whose recreation was subject to inspection and surveillance so that they should not abandon themselves to disorderly behaviour and licence, lacking any spirit of emulation and discouraged from any display of passionate feelings, must have been, at bottom, somewhat unhappy. At this point the apologia for the system yields place to an attack on it: the plea for liberty is voiced, as against mechanically perfect organisation. Even Hegel in his *Philosophy of History* repeats these same accusations against the Jesuit system.

A Catalan Jesuit who was sent out to Santa Fé in the River Plate region, José Manuel Peramás, published after the expulsion, in Italy, a thematic comparison between Plato's Republic and the Guaraní missions. This served as an introduction to a number of biographical sketches of Jesuits, published in 1791; he used as sources the writings of other members of the Order, especially Charlevoix, Cardiel, Muratori, and the 'philosophical' writers; in the case of this last group, the author accepts the favourable observations, but refutes the rationalistic interpretations. He expounded, in close juxtaposition, the sayings of Plato and the actual practice in the missions with regard to towns, houses, churches, the detection of the impious, community of goods, marriage, education, music and dancing, daily work, arts, clothing, officials and laws. This work is not very original or well written, and maintains an apologetic tone, couched in moderate terms; he attributes the Jesuits' success not to any basis in naturalism, as Raynal had done, but to their imitation of the life of the Apostles and the inspiration of Plato, which Peramás contrasted with the 'Epicurean herd of crazy philosophers' of his day.

There is, therefore, a certain characteristic peculiar to America which has made it the stimulus and pretext for ambitious eschatological and Utopian schemes, ranging from the Earthly Paradise to the projects for a more spiritual Church; it has also been the scene of the apologias for humanistic cultures comparable to those of antiquity, of retrospectively idealised Indian empires, of missionary reservations organised along Utopian lines or interpreted as Utopias in the outside world, until finally one reaches the stage, during the period of Independence, of Utopian constitutions couched in neo-classical terms. The Peruvian Juan Egaña, who was educated in the 1790s, a decade when the circle of thinkers associated with the *Mercurio Peruano* was very influential in Lima, and who later occupied university chairs and public offices of all kinds in Chile, was one of the most prominent exponents of a classical form of republicanism, which believed in the possibility of reproducing in America the ideals formulated by humanism in the Greek and Roman States. Moreover, Egaña, too, considered the Jesuit reservations to be a model of such a society. The ideal model of a republic, which had had such an important influence on the development of the French Revolution, made great headway in Spanish America in the nineteenth and twentieth centuries. Furthermore, whereas the Utopias influenced the intellectual outlook of the educated sectors, the eschatological schemes became secularised and re-emerged as the revolutionary aspirations of multiracial masses motivated by hatred: one only has to think, for an example of this, of the movements in Mexico led by Hidalgo and Morelos (Villoro, 1953). Eschatological schemes preserving a specifically Biblical and Christian framework were to be rare in the nineteenth and twentieth centuries outside Brazil. Nationalistic sentiments, which were already observable in the eighteenth century and were subsequently encouraged by the new independent States, gradually resulted in a more compact and continuous conception of history, which in general neutralised much of the force of eschatological and Utopian images, absorbing them into the new concept of a continuous historical evolution.

Both types of notion, the eschàtological and the Utopian, represented the application to America of traditional Christian hopes or of the products of an intellectualised and sentimental Western mentality. In both cases, they were ideal historical interpretations of great importance, because they incorporated the newly discovered lands into the spiritual history of Europe, even though, paradoxically, the precise manner of this incorporation resulted from the concept of them as countries which were new and different from Europe; in any case, these notions were not generated from within America, but were derived from Christian or modern European processes of thought. The designation of America as a '*Mundus novus*', which was to achieve such wide currency after the letter of Vespucio, naturally ignored, by implication, the old pre-Columbian cultures; and, despite the efforts made by the numerous chronicles of the colonial period to recapture the memory of the old empires, and sometimes to evaluate them from a humanist standpoint, the eschatological and Utopian term 'New World' proved more powerful, because it came closer to satisfying Renaissance and modern aspirations. America became a sort of compensatory design which, it was hoped, was an anticipation of the course to be followed by Europe. In British America, which lacked the counterweight of the old Indian empires, the notion of the 'New World' acquired even greater force, and it was to develop its great power of attraction after 1776.

CHAPTER 7

THE PROBLEM OF PERIODISATION OF POST-COLUMBIAN HISTORY

The periodisation of history has recently been condemned as an otiose exercise, and explained as an ideological residue of traditional historiography (Furet, 1971). It is true that this is very often the case; but it also appears to the author to be true that consciousness of history is accompanied, as an indispensable practice, by the pointing out of stages and turning-points, without which it would lose all shape and form: they are, as it were, a systematisation of historical recollection.

There is no space here for consideration of the possible systems of periodisation of pre-Columbian history, as a result of modern archaeological research.

The historians and chroniclers of the sixteenth century elaborated a certain model of periodisation. Those who evolved the concept of the 'West Indies' took as their basis the ancient geographical and technical ideas about nautical matters, and emphasised Columbus's achievement against this background. They followed the same method with subsequent discoveries and conquests, from 1500 to 1550, following a geographical order – for example, from the north to the south of the continent, like Gómara – or an approximately chronological order, which was easy enough when the theatre of activities was confined to the Caribbean, as in the case of Las Casas; however, this became more complicated after 1520, when the historical process began to develop in regions far removed from one another, which explains the disorder manifest in the work of, for example, Oviedo. Those who wrote the chronicle of one conquest or of one province were able to follow a chronological sequence more strictly, and their narrative naturally focused its attention on the dramatic events of the discovery and conquest. The historiography of the Americas began, as it did everywhere else, in the accounts of epic feats.

In addition to this, there is another element usually to be found in the chronicles, namely the description of nature, either of its marvels and prodigious and curious phenomena, or an empirical observation of the climate and natural characteristics. The description of nature was nearly always accompanied by an ethnographic account, describing native usages and customs and at times attempting to collect together information and traditional accounts regarding pre-Columbian history. Thus, besides being an epic recollection of the discovery and conquest, the more detailed chronicles were also works of natural history, ethnography and Indian history.

The two ensuing centuries saw little modification of this structure of historiography. Antonio de Herrera, at the beginning of his *Décadas* (1601), describes the geography and administrative divisions of the Indies, copying the chronicler and cosmographer Juan López de Velasco. Henceforth, almost all the chronicles included descriptions of the political and administrative geography of their respective territories, city by city – a technique of study which the eighteenth century was to call '*corografía*'. When dealing with post-Conquest historical development, which generally provided few materials for epic treatment, except in countries like Chile, the chronicles usually followed a chronological order marked by the periods of tenure of office of the viceroys and governors, without attempting to define any underlying direction or tendency or, as a result, giving any definition to the period as a whole.

Pro-Indian historiography of the eighteenth century, such as Clavígero's *Historia Antigua de México*, or the nascent science of archaeology, as represented by Antonio de León y Gama in his study of two monumental stones discovered in the Mexican capital, might have been the basis of an attempt to envisage pre-Columbian history as a development separated from subsequent events. However, the maturing of nationalistic sentiments, particularly during the years of Independence, led, both in Mexico and the other provinces, to a tendency to connect pre-Columbian history with the new notion of nationhood and its development in the course of the colonial period, and to give the entire process a teleological direction, as constituting the preparation for emancipation. Furthermore, the Indian past was also regarded at that time as embodying the original idea of nationhood, by a process of retrospective projection of contemporary notions; the political symbolism of the Independence movement was full of allusions to Indian culture.

In the mid-nineteenth century, when purely polemical literature was superseded by erudite historiography, a new system of periodisation became fashionable: discovery and conquest – colonial period – independence. Diego Barros Arana, in his *Compendio de Historia de América* (1865, II, I), emphasised, in the initial and final stages of this tripartite scheme, the dramatic character of persons and events and the combination of achievements and atrocities; whereas the two and a half centuries of the intervening period, which was now termed the 'colonial period' ('La Colonia', in the singular), was characterised by the process of commercial exploitation (which gave this period its name, taken from the term so often used in mercantilist writings, which defined the 'colonies' as centres of consumption of the industrial production of the metropolitan country), and political and administrative oppression. 'The colonists lost all sense of their individuality and were reduced to almost complete inaction'; dramatic interest, Barros Arana continued, finished with the Conquest, and subsequent history was marked by few important events. He confined himself, in writing of this period, to describing the political subdivisions of Spanish America and giving a general outline of the 'colonial system'; he supposed its characteristics to be monolithic and calculated to keep the subjects in submission indefinitely. In his *Historia General de Chile*, he takes a less apodictical approach, and makes a more successful effort to distinguish the different characteristics of each century; his overall judgment, however, is unaltered. This scheme of periodisation was connected with the affirmation of certain categories of historical thought, which were certainly of fundamental importance: individuality, and liberty or spontaneity. In the case of the Americas, this 'individuality' was that displayed by the active and enterprising men of the Conquest or the Independence movement, not the individuality of contemplatives. These values were absent in the colonial period, and this absence, from the liberal point of view, defined the era as one of despotism. This interpretation became embodied, almost with official approval, in the collective consciousness of Latin Americans through the educational system, but it has suffered some rebuttals as a result of research in the twentieth century. Spanish absolutism was less authoritarian and, above all, less efficient than historians of the nineteenth century supposed, and left more freedom of manœuvre to the American provinces; beneath the apparent immobility, there developed a social history which at times included dramatic developments. This is the angle from which the nineteenth-century history of 'the Colony' has been corrected by legal historians such as Altamira, Levene and Ots, or the historians of institutions such as Zavala.

Chaunu, in a study which has provoked much thought (1964, 49–51, 191–204), has applied to Spanish American history the sequence of Phase A and Phase B of the French school of historiography, beginning in 1500 and situating the turning-points of the centuries in 1610–20 and 1730; in this way he gives the three colonial centuries a more quantitatively measurable character, and connects them with the economic developments as displayed by the various indicators (movements of wages and prices, trade, population). The resulting long sixteenth century, which includes two decades of the seventeenth, appears as a period characterised by imbalance, with high demand and prices; it was a period of growth in population, of extrovert tendencies, of ease of behaviour; the seventeenth century, on the other hand, was a period of contraction or at least, in the sub-phase which began around 1685, of reduced growth. The sixteenth century, according to Chaunu, was the period in which the America of the high tablelands and large indigenous populations reached the maximum potential power and influence in the destinies of the world; then, in Phase B, it suffered a decline from which it has never completely recovered. In the eighteenth century, there was another Phase A, beginning in the second third of the century, but then growth took place principally on the 'frontiers' of northern Mexico, the cacao plantations of Venezuela, the great cattle-raising Marches of the River Plate region, and even the 'war frontier' of Chile, which had a small agricultural and stock-raising surplus. Chaunu's scheme of periodisation is valuable and thought-provoking. It is also worth mentioning the depiction of the seventeenth century as one of depression by Borah (1951), who based his findings principally on the demographic collapse of the Indians; this interpretation has had a decisive effect on the scheme of periodisation.

Independence (which was 'nominal', according to Chaunu) is asserted to be, for Spanish America as a whole, 'the epoch of commencements'. He not only discusses the old problems of cause and effect, but also places in time the successive swings of the pendulum in the vast structural modifications of commerce in the eighteenth century. Around 1700, the real metropolises of Spanish America were England, France and even the Netherlands, which all exported their goods to the colonial market without interference. Towards the middle of the century, Spain recovered a great deal of the lost ground and strengthened its control. However, the renewed wars with Britain in the last twenty years of the eighteenth century and the early years of the nineteenth century, and the opening of ports to commerce with neutral nations in 1797, as well as the repercussions in the New World of the constantly shifting balance of power in Europe, made it impossible for the Americas ever again to be completely Hispanic; it was an 'Empire in suspense', until 'an extraordinary combination of circumstances' precipitated, between 1808 and 1825, a series of civil wars (rather than a true 'war of independence').

Morse (1964, 164–7) suggests a scheme of periodisation according to which, after the pre-Columbian era, the sequence is: Spanish period, 1520–1760; the 'colonial' period, 1760–1920; and the national period, from

1920. The Hispanic period begins, properly speaking, with Cortés rather than Columbus, because Spanish rule in the Antilles took the form of commercial exploitation rather than effective settlement; it was after the conquest of New Spain that the continent was really incorporated into Hispanic and Christian civilisation. The period which is called, in this scheme, 'colonial', begins with the process of the opening of America to the influences and pressures of the modern Western world; at the same time, the old provinces of the Indies became real 'colonies' in the mercantilist sense, and developed a structure which was discontinuous with that of their metropolis, which was at first Bourbon Spain and later Britain and the other modern powers.

Both the scheme or Morse and that of Chaunu are striking in that they situated the real turning-point, not at the time of Independence, but in the structural changes which occurred in the eighteenth century. In the author's opinion, Chaunu unjustifiably under-estimates the historical importance of the achievement of Independence. It appears impossible, from a historical point of view, that an event should occupy so funda-mental a place in the historical consciousness of Spanish Americans if it were only a 'chronological error'. There must be some reason why that con-sciousness, often taking the form of secularised Utopian and eschatological schemes, has established that event as a fundamental turning-point. How-ever, the author agrees with the view of these writers that the beginning of the new era may be placed around 1760, as Morse suggests, even though the explosion which took place between 1808 and 1825 must still be regarded as the culmination of the process.

The author's opinion, which is not far removed from that of Morse, is that in the history of Spanish America there are two great periods which are felt in the general historical consciousness of the time, and not merely per-ceived later by the historian's intellectually refined processes of thought. These two moments in time might be designed as the 'Catholic Monarchy' or the era of the 'Indies', from 1492 until the mid-eighteenth century; and an era which might be described as more specifically 'American', from about 1760 until the present day, without taking account, at this stage, of any of its 'sub-phases'.

The era of the 'Indies' witnessed the encounter between the indigenous cultures and the conquistadors and missionaries, and the forms which that encounter took were to have exceptional importance for the future, for they resulted in the development of Creole culture, within the broader context of a multi-national monarchy. In this initial period, historical research has been able to identify distinct moments or phases, depending on the point of view of the writer. Thus, there is what is called here the 'era of foundation', from 1492 to 1570; the period of stabilisation of institutions, from 1570 to 1650; and the phases, mentioned above, of economic expansion and depression, which correspond, roughly speaking, to the sixteenth and seventeenth centuries. All these phases of development, leaving aside any possible schemes of periodisation in particular fields such as the arts, were characterised by an overall unity of style and design. The initial image of the 'Indies' was still predominant: the Spanish monarchy overseas held sway over continents, islands, seas and oceans, international trade routes which stretched from Seville to the Canaries, the Caribbean, across the Pacific to the Philippines; and trade from China and Japan reached all those places. As a monarchy, it was already 'modern', because its centre of gravity was outside the Mediterranean, which had been the principal theatre of activity of the ancient cultures; but juridically and spiritually it still belonged to medieval Christendom.

There was approximately a century's interregnum between the collapse of the 'Catholic Monarchy' and of what remained of Christendom as a guiding idea, and the establishment, as a dominant notion, of the 'concert of European nations'. This interregnum, which lasted from about 1640 to about 1740, constituted, in the Indies, a period of maturation of Creole and *mestizo* life behind the decaying façade of Hispanic administration and commerce.

About 1740 Spain began to be governed by reforming ministers, from Patiño to Godoy, and was marked by the rise of the Enlightenment, French cultural influence, Gallicanism in ecclesiastical affairs and neo-classicism. In the Americas, the structures established in the era of foundation underwent far-reaching changes as a result of the predominance of the model of the French and British colonial empires, mercantilism and the new executive bureaucracy. The Hispanic formative influences were from then onwards replaced in the Americas by other ways of thinking, new waves of sensibility, new modes of political and social organisation, the 'modern trends' and 'contemporary fashion' of Europe. The independent States which were the successors of the Spanish colonial empire became orientated towards French cultural hegemony and British trade, and this process continued throughout the nineteenth century.

The new nationalistic and modernising States increasingly realised that they were the expression of 'American' nations, firmly based in the New World, and not European or Asian ones; this led them to search for their spiritual roots in the Indian past, as they had already been doing from the mid-eighteenth century onwards. At the same time, European ideologies fashionable between 1789 and 1825 emphasised the concept of nationhood and attempted to base it on 'natural' foundations. Nationalism was then both a European ideology and a programme of action for the American States which came into being during the crisis of the Spanish *ancien régime*. Latin American nationalistic sentiments might have found expression in a confederation, and attempts at this were made in the 1820s and 1830s; but the system of the balance of power between separate national States was more realistic, and triumphed in the end.

This process, which began in the middle of the eighteenth century and is 'Americanist' and modernising, and also took place in British America, is still continuing today, and is immediately obvious to our historical consciousness. Independence was the culminating moment, but the continuous process began half a century before. The previous 'era of the Indies' can be comprehended by the more reflective historian only with the aid of research aimed at deciphering its manifestations, which were to have such a decisive influence on the subsequent course of events.

NOTES TO THE TEXT

Chapter 1, pp. 1–32

1 Ramos (1965) sees the enterprises of the Conquest exclusively as successors of the maritime incursions, the 'deeds of the sea' which bordered on piracy, and denies their relationship with the *cabalgadas* on land which were a feature of the Reconquest of Spain. While recognising, as Ramos does, the importance of the first type of enterprise, which has not yet been studied by historical researchers for the purposes of comparison, the author still believes that the resemblance of many of the American enterprises to the *cabalgadas* is undeniable.

2 The most significant documentary testimony of the distribution of booty is that of New Granada, published by C. Salazar del Camino in the *Boletín de Historia y Antiguedades* (Bogotá), 191 (1927), 662–87.

3 Alfonso García Gallo (1944, 20, note 6, disagreeing with an assertion of Angel Altolaguirre): the *capitulaciones* were not contractual in character, but were *mercedes* requested by Columbus; the confirmation of the privileges of Columbus, published in 1497, uses the term *merced*; and the *Fiscal*, in the lawsuit concerning Columbus's estate, denied that there had been any contract (CoDoIn, 2nd series, VII, 9–10). However, the evidence included in this text clearly confirms, in the author's opinion, the conviction held by the conquistadors and by Columbus before them that there was a contractual relationship, and that conviction is the basis of the present historical analysis. One of the documents relating to Columbus, the confirmation of his privileges on 28 May 1493, includes a preamble written by a jurist, Dr Rodrigo de Maldonado, extolling at great length the duty of monarchs to reward services performed (Giménez Fernández, 1944, 86).

Chapter 2, pp. 33–66

1 In contrast to this passage (1944, 123–4), Giménez Fernández states on pp. 147–8 that the Bulls, on account of the utilitarian motives which inspired them, 'solemnly announced the death of the medieval concept of the Christian *Respublica*, which was primarily governed by the spiritual power of the Supreme Pontiff'. It is, therefore, difficult to ascertain the final conclusions of this writer.

2 García Gallo (1957; 1958, 676) considers that the fifteenth-century Bulls are lacking in a clear doctrinal basis. The author considers that, in any case, the dominant doctrine in the Curia was the most emphatically

theocratic one, although the theologians usually modified this. It is highly significant that Sixtus V should have, for a time, placed the works of Vitoria and Bellarmine on the Index, a century after Alexander VI.

3 Frankl (1963) makes several most valuable observations but, in the author's view, he interpolates excessive philosophical connotations into Cortés's Fifth Letter.

4 It is somewhat surprising that a great medievalist like Menéndez Pidal, in his polemical work on Las Casas (1963), should frequently contrast the 'medieval' Las Casas with the 'modern' Vitoria (pp.132–9), using the term 'medieval' in a pejorative sense.

5 For an excellent description of political and social Thomism, see E. Troeltsch, *Die Soziallehren der christlichen Kirchen und Gruppen*, 1922.

6 For an account of the Franciscan doctrines, see Carro (1944).

7 See Law I, Section I, of Solórzano's *Libro Primero de la Recopilación de Cédulas, Provisiones y Ordenanzas Reales* (Buenos Aires, 1945), in which he expresses his teachings in legal form.

8 Jover (1950), including quotations from Palafox; Maravall (1965), 226.

Chapter 3, pp. 67–126

1 In *El Estado en el Derecho Indiano*, by the present author, there appears for the first time in Hispanic-American historical literature an analysis of the way in which Spanish laws were not carried out in the Indies by means of the judicial mechanism of supplication and the resulting suspension of the laws. This was one of the most significant elements in juridical thought and practice in the Indies.

2 See Eisenstadt (1963).

Chapter 4, pp. 127–158

1 Verlinden (1968) describes some general aspects of this process in Hispaniola, commenting on the *Repartimiento* of Albuquerque in 1514.

2 Brading (1971), 9–14, casts doubts on the theory that the mining crisis of the seventeenth century was principally due to the demographic factor; he considers other aspects, such as the poor techniques of exploitation, the high prices of mercury and the system of tribute collection. He emphasises the fact that the decrease in the volume of trans-Atlantic trade favoured local industry.

Chapter 5, pp. 159–205

1 For a description of the Creole aristocracies in the regional context, see Jorge Comadrán Ruiz (1958).

2 The author must admit to feeling little admiration for the works on the Spanish Enlightenment by Jean Sarrailh (1954) and Richard Herr (1958), which are excessively apologetic in their approach.

3 Pérez Marchand (1945) and González Casanova (1948) give accounts of many offensives by the Inquisition against 'philosophical' books in Mexico; among the targets were Voltaire, Lamettrie, Diderot, D'Alembert, Adam Smith, Volney, Raynal, Filangieri, Pope, Mirabeau, Mably, Montesquieu. For a description of colonial libraries, see Furlong (1944), Comadrán Ruiz (1961), Donoso (1963, vol. II). Perhaps the most valuable inventory is that of the library of Melchor Pérez de Soto, the chief architect of the Cathedral of Mexico City, in 1655, published in *Documentos para la Historia de la Cultura en México* (Archivo General de la Nación, 1947).

Chapter 6, pp. 206-238

1 Nothing could be further removed from the thought of Lacunza than the characteristic of 'feverishness' observed in him by Batllori (1966, 50), see Góngora, 1969.
2 Alfred Doren (1926) gives a survey of modern eschatological and Utopian literature; however, in the author's opinion, he exaggerates in identifying this polarity too closely with that existing between time and space. See also, by the same author, 'Campanella als Chiliast und Utopist' (*Festschrift W. Goetz*, 1927).

ABBREVIATIONS

ACHSC	*Anuario Colombiano de Historia Social y de Cultura*, Bogotá
AEA	*Anuario de Estudios Americanos*, Seville
AGI	Archivo General de Indias, Seville
AHDE	*Anuario de Historia del Derecho Español*, Madrid
AM	The Americas
BACH	*Boletín de la Academia Chilena de la Historia*, Santiago
BAE	Biblioteca de Autores Españoles, Madrid
BRAH	*Boletín de la Real Academia de la Historia*, Madrid
CHE	*Cuadernos de Historia de España*, Buenos Aires
CoDoIn	Colección de Documentos Inéditos de Indias, 2 series, Madrid
CSIC	Consejo Superior de Investigaciones Científicas, Spain
EA	*Estudios Americanos*, Seville
HAHR	*Hispanic American Historical Review*, United States
HI	*Historia*, Universidad Católica de Chile
HM	*Historia Mexicana*, Mexico
Jhb	*Jahrbuch für die wirtschaftliche, soziale und politische Geschichte Lateinamerikas*, Cologne
MH	Missionalia Hispanica, Madrid
RCHG	*Revista Chilena de Historia y Geografía*, Santiago
RHAm	*Revista de Historia de América*, Mexico
RI	*Revista de Indias*, Madrid
RIHD	*Revista del Instituto de Historia del Derecho Ricardo Levene*, Buenos Aires

BIBLIOGRAPHY

1. Printed Collections of Documents

It would take up too much space in a work of this nature to give the references of all the sources – literary, doctrinal, legal and so on – which have been used. They can be found in various bibliographies and in the secondary literature. Of the documentary collection published in the last century, the author has principally used, without giving here the full bibliographical apparatus, those that follow: the 'Colección de Documentos Inéditos...de Indias', Madrid, in its two series; the 'Colección de Documentos para la Historia de México', and the 'Nueva Colección' of *Joaquín García Icazbalceta*; the 'Colección de Historiadores de Chile' and the 'Colección de Documentos Inéditos para la Historia de Chile', of *José Toribio Medina*, this last in two series; the 'Colección de Obras y Documentos relativos a la Historia Antigua y Moderna de las Provincias del Rio de la Plata', of *Pedro de Angelis*. Of the collections published in this century, mention must be made of the various series of letters and papers published by *Francisco del Paso y Troncoso* in Mexico – above all, the 'Epistolario de Nueva España' (1939–42); the 'Documentos Inéditos del siglo XVI para la Historia de México' (1914), of *Mariano Cuevas, S.J.*; the various collections of *Roberto Levillier*, particularly the 'Gobernadores del Perú' (1921–26) and the 'Ordenanzas de Don Francisco de Toledo' (1929). In the same tradition are the 'Colección Somoza: Documentos para la Historia de Nicaragua', Madrid, and the 'Monumenta Centroamericae Historica' of *Federico Argüello* and *Carlos Molina*, Managua, 1965; the 'Documentos Inéditos para la Historia de Colombia', *Juan Friede* (Bogotá, 1955–, 10 vols); there are others besides. The first to select documents by theme was the 'Documentos para la Historia Argentina' of the Instituto de Investigaciones Históricas de la Universidad de Buenos Aires, from 1913. Thereafter came the work of *Silvio Zavala* and *María Castelo*, 'Fuentos para la Historia del trabajo en Nueva España' (1939–46); *Richard Konetzke*, 'Colección de documentos para la historia de la formación social de Hispanoamérica' (Madrid, Consejo Superior de Investigaciones Científicas, 1953–62); *G. Colmenares, M. de Melo and D. Fajardo*, 'Fuentes coloniales para la historia del trabajo en Columbia' (Bogotá, Universidad de los Andes, 1968). Of the highest value as the publication of a personal archive are the 'Documentos relativos a Don Pedro de la Gasca y a Gonzalo Pizarro' (Madrid, 1964), edited by *Juan Perez de Tudela*.

Bibliography

2. Select Bibliography

The following works of research have been used in writing these essays; they are those the author found of value, for their inspiration or their contents, on these themes. There is no pretence here of giving a select bibliography of all colonial history.

Acevedo, Edbert Oscar. *La Intendencia de Salta del Tucumán en el Virreinato del Río de la Plata.* Universidad Nacional de Cuyo, 1965.

Agramonte, Roberto. *José Agustín Caballero y los orígenes de la conciencia cubana.* Havana, 1952.

Aguirre Beltrán, Gonzalo. *La población negra en México.* Mexico, 1946.

Ajo y Sainz de Zuñiga, C. María. Historia de las Universidades hispánicas. Madrid, 1957 *et seq.* (Vol. 2, for documentation on universities in the New World.)

Albi Romero, Guadalupe. 'La Sociedad de Puebla de los Angeles en el siglo XVI', Jhb 7, 1970.

Aldea, Quintin, S.J. *Iglesia y Estado en la España del siglo XVII.* Universidad Pontificia de Comillas, 1960.

Alemparte, Julio. *El Cabildo de Chile Colonial.* Santiago, 1940.

Altamira, Rafael. Autonomía y descentralización legislativa en el régimen colonial español. Coimbra, 1945.

'La costumbre jurídica en la colonización española', *Revista de la Escuela Nacional de Jurisprudencia,* 1949, Mexico.

Alvarez Rubiano, Pablo. *Pedrarias Dávila.* Madrid, CSIC, 1944. (A valuable documentary study; see especially its appendixes.)

Appolis, Emile. *Les Jansénistes espagnols.* Bordeaux, Sobodi, 1966.

Arboleda Llorente, José María. *El Indio en la Colonia.* Bogotá, 1948.

Arcila Farías, Eduardo. *Economía Colonial de Venezuela.* Mexico, 1946.

Comercio entre Venezuela y México en los siglos XVII y XVIII. El Colegio de México, 1950.

El régimen de la encomienda en Venezuela. Seville, CSIC, 1957.

El Real Consulado de Caracas. Caracas, 1957.

Armas Medina, Fernando de. *Cristianización del Perú 1532–1600.* Seville, CSIC, 1953.

'*Las propiedades de las Ordenes religiosas y el problema de los diezmos en el Virreinato peruano en la primera mitad del siglo XVII*', AEA XXIII (1966).

Arnoldsson, Sverker. *Los Momentos históricos de América según la historiografía hispanoamericana del período colonial.* Madrid, Insula, 1956.

La conquista española según el juicio de la posteridad. Vestigios de la Leyenda Negra. Madrid, Insula, 1960.

La Leyenda Negra. Estudios sobre sus orígenes. Acta Universitatis Gothoburgensis, 1960.

251

Bibliography

Artola, Miguel. '*Campillo y las reformas de Carlos III*', RI 50 (1952).
'*América en el pensamiento español del siglo XVIII*', RI 115/118 (1969).
Astuto, Philip Louis. *Eugenio Espejo*. Mexico, Tierra Firme, 1969.
Atkinson, Geoffrey. *Les nouveaux horizons de la Renaissance française*. Paris, 1935.
Ayala, Francisco Javier de. *Ideas políticas de Solórzano Pereira*. Seville, CSIC, 1946.
Ideas canónicas de Juan de Solórzano. AEA IV (1947).

Bagú, Sergio. *Estructura social de la Colonia*. Buenos Aires, 1952.
Bakewell, P. J. *Silver Mining and Society in Colonial Mexico: Zacatecas*. Cambridge University Press, 1970.
Bataillon, Marcel. *Erasmo y España*. Mexico, Fondo de Cultura Económica, 1950; original French edition, 1937.
'La Vera Paz. Roman et histoire', *Bulletin Hispanique* 53 (1951).
'La découverte spirituelle du Nouveau Monde', *Annuaire du Collège de France*, 1952.
'Le "clérigo Casas", ci-devant colon, réformateur de la colonisation', *Bulletin Hispanique* 54 (1952).
'Cheminenment d'une légende: les "Caballeros pardos" de Las Casas', Syracuse, N.Y., Syracuse University, Symposium 6, 1952.
'Une Université dans le Nouveau Monde', *Annales* 3 (1952).
'Vasco de Quiroga et Bartolomé de Las Casas', RHAm 33, VI (1952).
'Zumárraga, reformador del clero seglar', HM 8 (1953).
'Les "douze questions" péruviennes résolues par Las Casas', Paris, *Hommage à Lucien Febvre*, 1954.
'Las herejías de Fray Francisco de la Cruz y la reacción antilascasiana', Miscelánea de estudios dedicada al Dr Fernando Ortiz, Havana, 1955.
Le lien religieux des Conquérants du Pérou. London, The Hispanic and Luso-Brazilian Councils, 1956.
Evangélisme et millenarisme au Nouveau Monde. Paris, Colloque de Strasbourg, 9/11-V-1957, 1959.
'Charles-Quint, Las Casas et Vitoria' in *Charles-Quint et son temps*. Paris, 1959.
Montaigne et les Conquérants de l'or. Turin, Studi Francesi, 1959.
Etudes sur Bartolomé de Las Casas. Paris, 1966.
Batllori, Miguel, S.J. *El abate Viscardo*. Caracas, Instituto Panamericano de Geografía e Historia, 1953.
La cultura hispano-italiana de los Jesuitas expulsos. Madrid, Gredos, 1966.
Bayle, Constantino, S.J. 'El Protector de indios', AEA II (1945).
'La comunión entre los indios americanos', RI 4 (1943).
El clero secular y la evangelización de América. Madrid, Biblioteca Missionalia Hispanica, 1950.
Los Cabildos seculares en la América Española. Madrid, 1952.

Bibliography

Beltrán de Heredia, Vicente, O.P. *Universidades dominicanas de la América Española. La Universidad de Santa Fe de Bogotá.* Madrid, 1923.

Un precursor del Maestro Vitoria. El Padre Matías de Paz O.P. y su tratado De dominio regum Hispaniae super Indos. Salamanca, 1929.

'Ideas del Maestro Fray Francisco de Vitoria anteriores a las Relecciones De Indis acerca de la colonización según documentos inéditos', *La Ciencia Tomista* 41 (1930).

'El Maestro Domingo de Soto en la controversia de Las Casas con Sepúlveda', *La Ciencia Tomista* 45 (1932).

Berges, Wilhelm. *Die Fürstenspiegel des Hohen und Späten Mittelalters.* Leipzig, 1938.

Bernard, Gildas. *Le Sécretariat d'Etat et le Conseil espagnol des Indes 1700–1808.* Geneva, Droz, 1972.

Berthe, Jean-Paul. 'El cultivo del pastel en Nueva España', HM 9 (1959/60).

'Xochimancas. Les travaux et les jours dans une hacienda sucrière de la Nouvelle Espagne au XVII siècle', Jhb 3 (1966).

Bishko, Charles Julian. 'The peninsular background of Latin American cattle ranching', HAHR (1952).

'The Castilian as Plainsman: the Medieval Ranching Frontier in La Mancha and Extremadura', in *The New World Looks at Its History*, ed. Lewis and McGann. University of Texas Press, 1963.

Bloch, Ernst. *Das Prinzip Hoffnung.* Suhrkamp Verlag, 1959.

Bolton, Herbert E. 'The Mission as a frontier institution in the Spanish American colonies', *American Historical Review* 23 (1917).

The Spanish Borderlands. Yale University Press, 1921.

Borah, Woodrow. 'The collection of tithes in the Bishopric of Oaxaca during the XVIth century', HAHR (1941).

Silk raising in Colonial Mexico. University of California Press, 1943.

New Spain's Century of Depression. University of California Press, 1951.

'Race and Class in Mexico', *Pacific Historical Review* XI (1954).

'Francisco de Urdiñola's Census of the Spanish settlements in Nueva Viscaya, 1604', HAHR (1955).

'América como modelo? El impacto demográfico de la expansión europea sobre el mundo no europeo', *Cuadernos Americanos* XI/XII (1962).

'Un gobierno provincial de frontera en San Luis Potosi 1612–1620', HM 52 (1964).

Social Welfare and Social Obligation in New Spain. XXXVI Congreso Internacional de Americanistas, Seville, 1966.

'Los tributos y su recaudación en la audiencia de Nueva Galicia durante el siglo XVI', *Homenaje a José Miranda.* Mexico, 1970.

Borah Woodrow, and Cook, Sherburne F. *Price trends of some basic commodities in Central Mexico 1531–1570.* University of California Press, 1958.

The Population of Central Mexico in 1548. University of California Press, 1960.

Bibliography

The aboriginal population of Central Mexico on the eve of the Spanish Conquest. University of California Press, 1963.

'Marriage and legitimacy in Mexican culture: Mexico and California', *California Law Review*, 1966.

Borges, Pedro, O.F.M. *El sentido trascendente del Descubrimiento y conversión de las Indias.* MH, 37, 1956.

Métodos misionales en la cristianización de América: siglo XVI. Madrid, 1960.

Vasco de Quiroga en el ambiente misionero de la Nueva España. MH, 1966.

Boyd-Bowman, Peter. *Indice geobiográfico de cuarenta mil pobladores españoles de América en el siglo XVI.* 2 vols. Bogotá, Instituto Caro y Cuervo, 1964.

Brading, D. A. *Miners and Merchants in Bourbon Mexico 1763–1810.* Cambridge University Press, 1971.

Brading, D. A. and Cross, Harry E. 'Colonial Silver mining: Mexico and Peru', HAHR (1972).

Brandi, Karl. *Kaiser Karl V.* Munich, 3rd ed., 1941, 2 vols.

Braudel, Fernand. 'Les Espagnols et l'Afrique du Nord de 1492 à 1577', *Revue Africaine*, 1928.

L'Espagne au temps de Philippe II. Paris, Hachette, 1965. Introd. by F.B.

Civilisation matérielle et Capitalisme (XVe–XVIIIe siècle). Paris, Colin, 1967.

Brito Figueroa, Federico. *Estructura económica de Venezuela Colonial.* Caracas, 1963.

Bronner, Fred. 'La Unión de las Armas en el Perú: aspectos político-legales', AEA XXIV (1968).

Brunner, Otto. 'Das "ganze Haus" und die alteuropäische "Ökonomik"', 1958, 1966 and 1968 and in his *Neue Wege der Verfassungs- und Sozialgeschichte.* Göttingen, 1968.

Calderón Quijano, José Antonio. 'El Banco de San Carlos y las comunidades de indios de Nueva España', AEA XIX (1962).

Carande y Thovar, Ramón. *Carlos V y sus banqueros.* Madrid, 1943, 3 vols.

'Der Wanderhirt und die überseeische Ausbreitung Spaniens', *Saeculum* 3 (1952).

Carbia, Rómulo D. *Historia de la Leyenda Negra Hispanoamericana.* Madrid, Consejo de la Hispanidad, 1944.

Carmagnani, Marcello. *El salariado minero en Chile Colonial.* Santiago, Centro de Historia Colonial de la Universidad de Chile, 1962.

Les mécanismes de la vie économique dans une sociéte coloniale: le Chili (1680–1830). Paris, Seupen, 1973.

Carrera Stampa, Manuel. 'The evolution of weights and measures in New Spain', HAHR (1949).

Los gremios mexicanos. Mexico, 1954.

'Las ferias novohispanas', HM 7 (1953).

Carro, Venancio D., O.P. *La teología y los teólogos juristas españoles en la Conquista de América.* Madrid, 1944, 1951.

Bibliography

Casado, Fernando. 'El tribunal de la Acordada de Nueva España', AEA VII (1950).

Casanovas, Ignacio. *La cultura catalana en el siglo XVIII*. Barcelona, Finestres y la Universidad de Cervera, 1953.

Castillero Calvo, Alfredo. *Estructuras sociales y económicas de Veragua desde sus orígenes históricos, siglos XVI y XVII*. Panama, 1967.

Castro, Américo. *Aspectos del vivir hispánico*. Santiago de Chile, Cruz del Sur, 1949.

Ceñal, Ramón, S.J. 'La filosofía española del siglo XVII', *Revista de la Universidad de Madrid* (1961).

Céspedes del Castillo, Guillermo. 'La Visita como institución indiana', AEA III (1946).

'Lima y Buenos Aires', AEA IV (1947).

La renta del tabaco en el Virreinato del Perú. Lima, 1955.

'Las Indias en el reinado de los Reyes Católicos. La sociedad colonial americano en los siglos XVI y XVII', in *Historia social y económica de España y América*, ed. J. Vicens Vives, vols. 2 and 3, 1957.

Chaunu, Huguette and Pierre. *Séville et l'Atlantique 1504–1650*. Paris, Seupen, Partie statistique, 8 vols., 1955–7.

Chaunu, Pierre. *Séville et l'Atlantique 1504–1650*. Paris, Seupen, 1959–60. Partie interprétative, 3 vols., 1 annexe.

Les Philippines et le Pacifique des Ibériques (XVI, XVII, XVIII siècles). Paris, Seupen, 1960.

L'Amérique et les Amériques. Paris, Colin, 1964.

Chevalier, François. 'Les municipalités indiennes en Nouvelle Espagne 1520–1620', AHDE XV (1944).

'Signification sociale de la formation de Puebla de los Angeles', RHAm 23, VI (1947).

La formation des grands domaines au Méxique. Paris, Institut d'Ethnologie, 1952.

'The North Mexican hacienda: XVIII and XIXth centuries' in *The New World looks at its history*, 1963.

Chinard, Gilbert. *L'Amérique et le rêve éxotique dans la littérature française au XVII et au XVIII siècles*. Paris, 1934.

'Exotisme et Primitivisme', IX Congrès International des Sciences Historiques, Paris, 1950.

Chinchilla Aguilar, Ernesto. *La Inquisición en Guatemala*. Guatemala, 1953.

El Ayuntamiento colonial de la ciudad de Guatemala. Guatemala, 1961.

Cline, Howard F. 'Civil Congregations of the Indians of New Spain 1598–1605', HAHR (1949).

Civil Congregation of the Western Chinantec, New Spain, 1599–1603. AM 12, 1955.

A note on Torquemada's native sources and historiographical methods. AM 25, 1969.

Bibliography

Cobb, Gwendolyne B. 'Supply and transportation for the Potosí mines 1545–1640', HAHR (1949).

Colmenares, Germán. *Encomienda y Población en la Provincia de Pamplona.* Bogotá, Universidad de Los Andes, 1969.

La hacienda de los Jesuitas en el Nuevo Reino de Granada. Universidad Nacional de Colombia, 1969.

Comadrán Ruiz, Jorge. 'La Real Ordenanza de Intendentes del Río de la Plata', AEA XI (1954).

'Las tres casas reinantes de Cuyo', RCHG 126 (1958).

Bibliotecas cuyanas del siglo XVIII. Universidad Nacional de Cuyo, 1961.

'Nacimiento y desarrollo de los núcleos urbanos y del poblamiento de la campaña del país de Cuyo durante la época hispana 1551–1810', AEA XIX (1962).

Coni, Emilio A. *Historia de las vaquerías del Río de la Plata 1555–1750.* Buenos Aires, 1956, 2nd ed.

El Gaucho. Buenos Aires, 1945.

Cook, Sherburne F., and Borah, Woodrow. *The Indian Population of Central Mexico 1531–1610.* University of California Press, 1960.

'Quelle fut la stratification sociale au Centre du Méxique durant la première moitié du XVI siècle?' *Annales* III-IV, 1963.

Essays in Population History: Mexico and the Caribbean, I. University of California Press, 1971.

Cook, Sherburne F., and Simpson, Lesley B. *The Population of Central Mexico in the XVIth century.* University of California Press, 1948.

Corbitt, Duvon. '"Mercedes" and "Realengos"', HAHR (1939).

Corominas, Pedro. *El sentimiento de la riqueza en Castilla.* Madrid, 1917.

Correa Bello, Sergio. *El 'Cautiverio Feliz' en la vida política chilena del siglo XVII.* Santiago, Editorial Andrés Bello, 1965.

Crespo Rodas, Alberto. 'La mita de Potosí', *Revista Historica,* Lima, 22, 1955–6.

Delpy, G. *L'Espagne et l'esprit européen. L'Oeuvre de Feijoo.* Paris, Hachette, 1936.

Bibliographie des sources françaises de Feijoo. Paris, Hachette, 1936.

Dempf, Aloys. *Sacrum Imperium.* Munich and Berlin, 1929.

Christliche Staatsphilosophie Spaniens. Salzburg, 1937.

Deustúa Pimentel, Carlos. 'Concepto y término de "colonia" en los testimonios documentales del siglo XVIII', *Mercurio Peruano* 330 (1954).

Las Intendencias en el Perú (1790–1796). Seville, CSIC, 1965.

Diffie, Bayley W. *Latin American Civilization: Colonial Period.* Harrisburg, Pa., 1945.

Disandro, Carlos A., and Street, Jorje L. *La Compañía de Jesús contra la Iglesia y el Estado. Documentos americanos, siglo XVII.* La Plata, Instituto Cardenal Cisneros, 1971.

Bibliography

Domínguez y Compañy, Francisco. 'Funciones económicas del Cabildo colonial hispanoamericano' in *Contribuciones a la historia municipal de América*. Mexico, 1951.

Donoso, Ricardo. *Un letrado del siglo XVIII, el doctor José Perfecto de Salas.* Universidad de Buenos Aires, 2 vols., 1963.

Doren, Alfred. *Wunschräume und Wunschzeiten.* Wartburger Vorträge, 1926.

Dupront, Alphonse. *Espace et Humanisme.* Bibliothèque d'Humanisme et Renaissance 8, 1947.

Croisade et Eschatologie. Archivio di Filosofia, Umanesimo e Esoterismo, Padua, 1960.

Europe et la chrétienté. Paris, Cahiers de Sorbonne, 1959.

Durand, José. *La transformación social del Conquistador.* Mexico, Porrúa y Obregón, 2 vols., 1953.

'Gómara: encrucijada', HM 6 (1952).

'Garcilaso entre el mundo incaico y las ideas renacentistas', *Diogenes* VII-IX (1963).

Duviols, Pierre. *La lutte contre les religions autochtones dans le Pérou colonial.* Institute Français d'Etudes Andiens, Lima, 1970.

Echánove, Alfonso, S.J. *Origen y evolución de la idea jesuítica de 'Reducción' en las misiones del Virreinato del Perú*, MH, 12, 1955.

La Residencia de Juli, patrón y esquema de reducción. MH, 13, 1956.

Egaña, Antonio de, S.J. 'El Padre Diego de Avendaño S.J. y la tesis teocrática "Papa, Dominus Orbi"', Archivum Historicum Societatis Jesu, 195, 1949.

'La teoría del Regio Vicariato Español en Indias', *Analecta Gregoriana* 95 (1958).

Eguiguren, Luis Antonio. *Diccionario Histórico-Cronológico de la Universidad Real y Pontificia de San Marcos.* Lima, 1940–9, 5 vols. (Of interest for its documentation.)

Eguiluz, Antonio, O.F.M. *Fray Gonzalo Tenorio y sus teorías escatológico-providencialistas sobre las Indias.* MH, 48, 1959.

Fray Pedro de Azuaga O.F.M., nuevo teorizante sobre Indias. MH, 62, 1964.

Eisenstadt, S. N. *The Political Systems of Empires: the rise and fall of the historical bureaucratic societies.* Free Press, 1963, 1969.

Elliott, John. 'The mental world of Hernán Cortés', Transactions of the Royal Historical Society, V, 17, 1967.

The Old World and the New 1492–1650. Cambridge University Press, 1970.

Esteve Barba, Francisco. *Cultura Virreinal.* Barcelona, Salvat, 1965.

Ewald, Ursula. 'Das Poblaner Jesuitenkollegium San Francisco Xavier und sein landwirtschaftlicher Grundbesitz', Jhb 8, 1971.

Eyzaguirre, Jaime. *Ideario y ruta de la emancipación chilena.* Santiago, 1957.

Ezquerra, Ramon. 'La crítica española de la situación de América en el siglo XVIII', RI 87/88 (1962).

Bibliography

Fals Borda, Orlando. *Indian Congregations in the New Kingdom of Granada. Land tenure aspects.* AM 13, 1957.

El hombre y la tierra en Boyacá. Bogotá, 1957.

Feijoo, Rosa. 'El tumulto de 1624', HM VII/IX (1964).

'El tumulto de 1692', HM IV/VI (1965).

Ferrari, Angel. 'La secularización del Estado en las Partidas', AHDE XI (1934).

Florescano, Enrique. 'El abasto y la legislación de granos en el siglo XVI', HM IV/VI (1965).

'Colonización, ocupación del suelo y frontera en el Norte de Nueva España 1525–1570', in *Tierras Nuevas*, Alvaro Jara, ed. El Colegio de México, 1968.

Precios del maíz y crisis agrícolas en México 1708–1810. El Colegio de México, 1969.

Foster, George M. *Culture and Conquest.* Chicago, 1960.

Francovich, Guillermo. *El pensamiento universitario de Charcas.* Sucre, Bolivia, 1948.

Frankl, Victor. 'Idea del Imperio español y el problema jurídico-lógico de los Estados misiones en el Paraguay', in *Estudios de Historia de América.* Mexico, 1948.

'Hernán Cortés y la tradición de las Siete Partidas', RHAm 53/54 (1962).

'Imperio particular e Imperio universal en las Cartas de Relación de Hernán Cortés', *Cuadernos Hispanoamericanos* 55 (1963).

El 'Antijovio' de Gonzalo Jiménez de Quesada. Madrid, Instituto de Cultura Hispánica, 1963.

Friede, Juan. *El Indio en la lucha por la tierra.* Bogotá, 1944.

'Algunas observaciones sobre la realidad de la emigración española a América en la primera mitad del siglo XVI', RI 49 (1952).

Don Juan del Valle, primer Obispo de Popayán. Segovia, CSIC, 1952.

'Fray Bartolomé de Las Casas, exponente del movimiento indigenista español del siglo XV', RHAm 34 (1952).

'Alvaro de Oyón, Capitán General de la libertad. 'Patria', RI 57/58 (1954).

Los Welser en la conquista de Venezuela. Madrid-Caracas, Edime, 1961.

Los Quimbayas bajo la dominación española. Banco de la República, Bogotá, 1963.

'Proceso de formación de la propiedad territorial en la América Intertropical', Jhb 2 (1965).

'De la encomienda indiana a la propiedad territorial y su influencia sobre el mestizaje', ACHSC 4 (1969).

Friede, Juan, and Vázquez-Machicado, Humberto. 'Beiträge zur spanischen Kolonial Ethik', *Saeculum* 4 (1957).

Furet, François. 'L'histoire quantitative et la construction du fait historique', *Annales* I/II (1971).

Bibliography

Furlong, Guillermo, S.J. *Bibliotecas argentinas durante la dominación hispánica*. Buenos Aires, 1941.
Nacimiento y desarrollo de la filosofía en el Río de la Plata. Buenos Aires, 1952.
Los jesuitas y la cultura rioplatense. Buenos Aires, Huarpes, n.d.
'Lázaro de Ribera y su Breve Cartilla Real', *Humanidades*, La Plata, XXXIV (1954).

Gallegos Rocafull, José María. *El pensamiento mexicano en los siglos XVI y XVII*. Mexico, 1951.
Gandía, Enrique de. *Historia crítica de los mitos de la Conquista de América*. Buenos Aires, 1929.
Francisco de Alfaro y la condición social de los indios. Buenos Aires, 1939.
Gaos, José. 'Los clásicos del pensamiento cubano', *Cuadernos Americanos* VII/VIII (1945).
García, Genaro. *Don Juan de Palafox y Mendoza*. Mexico, 1918.
García, Juan Agustín. *La ciudad indiana*. Buenos Aires, 1900.
García Bacca, Juan David. *Filosofía en Venezuela desde el siglo XVII al XIX*. Caracas, 1956.
García Gallo, Alfonso. 'Los orígenes de la administración territorial de las Indias', AHDE XV (1944).
'La ley como fuente del Derecho en Indias en el siglo XVI', AHDE XXI/XXII (1951).
'El servicio militar en Indias', AHDE XXVI (1956).
'Las bulas de Alejandro VI el ordenamiento jurídico de la expansión portuguesa y castellana en Africa e Indias', AHDE XXVII/XXVIII (1957–58).
García Icazbalceta, Joaquín. *Bibliografía Mexicana del siglo XVI*. Mexico, 1886, 1954.
Gerbi, Antonello. *La disputa del Nuevo Mundo*. Mexico, 1960.
Gibson, Charles. *The Inca concept of sovereignty and the administration in Peru*. University of Texas Press, 1948.
Tlaxcala in the XVIth Century. New Haven, 1952.
The transformation of the Indian Community in New Spain 1500–1810. Paris, Cahiers d'Histoire Mondiale, 1954.
The Aztecs under Spanish Rule. Stanford University Press, 1964.
Spain in America. Harper and Row, 1966.
Gil Munilla, Octavio. *El Río de la Plata en la Política Internacional*. Seville, CSIC, 1949.
'Teoría de la Emancipación', EA 7 (1950).
Giménez Fernández, Manuel. *El Concilio IV Provincial Mexicano*. Seville, 1939.
'Las Bulas alejandrinas de 1493 referentes a Indias', AEA I (1944).
'Las doctrinas populistas en la Independencia de Hispano América', AEA III (1946).

'Hernán Cortés y su revolución comunera en la Nueva España', AEA V (1948).

'Las regalías mayestáticas en el Derecho Canónico Indiano', AEA VI (1949).

Bartolomé de Las Casas, Seville, CSIC, vol. 1, 1953; vol. 2, 1960.

Gómez Canedo, Lino, O.F.M. 'Les Franciscains. Les Collèges apostoliques De Propaganda Fide', in *La découverte de l'Amérique*. Paris, Vrin, 1968.

Gómez Hoyos, Rafael. *La Iglesia en América en las Leyes de Indias*. Madrid, CSIC, 1961.

Góngora, Mario. *El Estado en el Derecho Indiano, Epoca de Fundación*. Universidad de Chile, 1951.

'Estudios sobre el Galicanismo y la "Illustración Católica" en América Española', RCHG 125 (1957).

'El Colegio Imperial de Madrid en el siglo XVII y los orígenes de la enseñanza de Historia en España', CHE (1959).

Origen de los 'inquilinos' de Chile Central. Universidad de Chile, 1960.

Los grupos de conquistadores en Tierra Firme 1509–1530. Universidad de Chile, 1962.

'El pensamiento de Juan Egaña sobre la Reforma Eclesiática', BACH 68 (1963).

'El rasgo utópico en el pensamiento de Juan Egaña', *Anales de la Universidad de Chile*, 1964.

'Pacto de los conquistadores con la Corona y la antigua Constitución indiana: dos temas ideológicos de la época de la Independencia', RIHD 16 (1965).

'Régimen señorial y rural en la Extremadura de la Orden de Santiago en el momento de la emigración a Indias', Jhb 2 (1965).

'Vagabondage et société pastorale en Amérique Latine (spécialement au Chili Central)', *Annales*, I-II, 1966; Spanish translation with modifications from the French original, 1966.

'Incumplimiento de una ley en 1639', BACH 76 (1967).

'Aspectos de la "Ilustración Católica" en el pensamiento y la vida eclesiástica chilena 1770–1814', HI 8 (1969).

Encomenderos y Estancieros. Universidad de Chile, 1970.

González, Margarita. *El Resguardo en el Nuevo Reino de Granada*. Universidad Nacional de Colombia, 1970.

González Casanova, Pablo. *El misoneísmo y la Modernidad Cristiana en el siglo XVIII*. El Colegio de México, 1948.

González Echeñique, Javier. *Los estudios jurídicos y la abogacía en el Reino de Chile*. Universidad Católica de Chile, 1954.

González y González, Luis. 'El optimismo nacionalista como factor de la Independencia de México', in *Estudios de historiografía americana*. Mexico, 1948.

Bibliography

Gredilla, Federico. *Biografía de José Celestino Mutis.* Madrid 1911.

Greenleaf, Richard E. *The Obraje in the Latin American Colony.* AM, 1967.

'Viceregal power and the Obrajes of the Cortés Estate 1595–1708', HAHR (1968).

Griffin, Charles. 'The Enlightenment and Latin American Independence', in A. P. Whitaker, ed., *Latin America and the Enlightenment,* 2nd ed., 1961.

Guarda, Gabriel, O.S.B. 'Santo Tomás de Aquino y las fuentes del urbanismo indiano', BACH 72 (1965).

La ciudad chilena en el siglo XVIII. Buenos Aires, 1968.

Gutiérrez del Arroyo, Isabel. *El Reformismo Ilustrado en Puerto Rico.* El Colegio de México, 1953.

Hamilton, Earl J. *American Treasure and the Price Revolution in Spain 1501–1650.* Cambridge, Mass., 1934.

El florecimiento del Capitalismo y otros ensayos. Madrid, 1948.

Hamnett, Brian R. *Politics and trade in Southern Mexico 1750–1821.* Cambridge University Press, 1971.

Hanisch, Walter, S.J. *Itinerario y Presencia de los Jesuitas expulsos de Chile.* Santiago, Editorial Andrés Bello, 1972.

'La Filosopia en Chile', *Historia,* Santiago, 2 (1962–3).

'El pensamiento de Juan Egaña', *Historia* 3 (1964).

Hanke, Lewis. 'The Developments of Regulations for Conquistadores', *Homenaje al Doctor Emilio Ravignani.* Buenos Aires, 1941.

Cuerpo de Documentos del siglo Xvi sobre los derechos de España en la Indias y Filipinas. Mexico, 1943.

The Spanish Struggle for Justice in the Conquest of America. Philadelphia, 1949; Spanish translation, Buenos Aires, 1949, and Madrid, 1959.

Bartolomé de Las Casas pensador, político, historiador, antropólogo. Havana, 1949.

Estudio Preliminar a la edición de la 'Historia General de las Indias' de Las Casas. Mexico, 1951.

Prólogo a la edición de la 'Relación General de la Villa Imperial de Potosí' de Luis Capoche. BAE CXXII, 1959.

Hardoy, Jorje E., and Aranovich, Carmen. 'Urban Scales and Functions in Spanish America towards the year 1600', *Latin American Research Review* (1970).

Haring, Clarence H. *The Spanish Empire in America.* New York, 1947; Spanish translation, Buenos Aires, Peuser, 1958.

Helmer, Marie. 'Un tipo social, el minero de Potosí', RI 63 (1956).

'Notas sobre la encomienda peruana en el siglo XVI', RIHD 10 (1959).

'Luchas entre Vascongados y Vicuñas', RI 81/82 (1960).

'Economie et société au XVII siècle: un "cargador de Indias"', Jhb 4 (1967).

Bibliography

Henríquez Ureña, Pedro. *Historia de la Cultura en la América Hispánica.* Mexico, 1947.
La cultura y las letras coloniales en Santo Domingo. Ciudad Trujillo, 1936.
'Hernández, Pablo, S.J. *Organización social de las doctrinas Guaraníes de la Compañía de Jesús.* Barcelona, 2 vols., 1913.
Hera, Alberto de la. 'El derecho de los Indios a la libertad y a la fe. La Bula Sublimis Deus y los problemas indianos que la motivaron', AHDE XXVI (1956).
El Regalismo borbónico en su proyección indiana. Madrid, Rialp, 1963.
Hernández de Alba, Guillermo. 'El Plan de estudios del Arzobispo Virrey', *Boletín del Instituto Caro y Cuervo* II (1946).
Hernández Luna, Juan. 'El mundo intelectual de Hidalgo', HM 10 (1953).
Hernández Rodríguez, Guillermo. *De los Chibchas a la Colonia y a la República.* Universidad Nacional de Colombia, 1949.
Hernández Sánchez-Barba, Mario. *La última expansión española en América.* Madrid, Instituto de Estudios Políticos, 1957.
Juan Bautista de Anza, un hombre de fronteras. Madrid, 1962.
Historia Universal de América. Madrid, Guadarrama, 2 vols., 1963.
Herr, Richard. *The XVIIIth Century Revolution in Spain.* Princeton University Press, 1958.
Hintze, Otto. 'Der commisarius und seine Bedeutung in der allgemeinen Verwaltungsgeschichte', 1910. (In *Staat und Verfassung*, Leipzig 1941.)
Howe, Walter. *The Mining Guild of New Spain and its 'Tribunal General' 1770–1821.* Harvard University Press, 1949.
Huddleston, Lee Eldridge. *Origins of the American Indians: European concepts 1492–1729.* University of Texas Press, 1965.
Huneeus Pérez, Andrés. *Historia de las polémicas de Indias en Chile durante el siglo XVI.* Santiago, 1956.
Hussey, Roland D. *The Caracas Company 1728–1784.* Harvard University Press, 1934.

Iglesia, Ramón. *Cronistas e historiadores de la Conquista de México.* El Colegio de México, 1942.

Jara, Alvaro. *Los asientos de trabajo y la provisión de mano de obra para los no-encomenderos en la ciudad de Santiago 1586–1600.* Santiago, Universidad de Chile, 1959.
'Importación de trabajadores indígenas en el siglo XVII', RCHG 124 (1958).
El salario de los indios y los sesmos del oro en la Tasa de Santillán. Universidad de Chile, 1961.
Guerre et Société au Chili. Université de Paris, 1961; Spanish version, Santiago, 1971.

Tres ensayos sobre economía minera hispanoamericana. Universidad de Chile, 1966.

'Dans le Pérou du XVI siècle: la curve de production des métaux monnayables', *Annales* V-VI (1967).

Tierras Nuevas (ed.) El Colegio de Mexico, 1968.

Jaramillo Uribe, Jaime. 'Esclavos y señores en la sociedad colombiana del siglo XVIII', ACHSC 1 (1963).

'La población indígena de Colombia en el momento de la Conquista y sus transformaciones posteriores', ACHSC 2 (1964).

Jiménez Rueda, Julio. *Herejías y supersticiones en la Nueva España.* Universidad Nacional Autónoma de México, 1946.

Jover, José María. 'Sobre la conciencia histórica del Barroco español', *Arbor* 39 (1949).

'Sobre los conceptos de monarquía y nación en el pensamiento político español del XVII', CHE (1950).

'Sobre la política exterior de España en tiempos de Carlos V', *Carlos V 1500–1558: Homenaje de la Universidad de Granada.*

Kahle, Gunther. 'Die Encomienda als militärische Institution in kolonialen Hispanoamerika', Jhb 2 (1965).

'Geldwirtschaft im frühen Paraguay 1537–1600', Jhb 3 (1966).

Keith, Robert G. 'Encomienda, Hacienda and Corregimiento in Spanish America; a structural analysis', HAHR (1971).

Konetzke, Richard. 'Legislación sobre inmigración de extranjeros en América durante la época colonial', *Revista Internacional de Sociología,* Madrid (1945).

'La emigración de las mujeres españolas en América durante la época colonial', *Revista Internacional de Sociología,* 1945.

El Imperio español: orígenes y fundamentos. Madrid, 1946.

'Hernán Cortés como poblador de la Nueva España', RI 31/32 (1948).

'Las ordenanzas de gremios como documentos para la historia social de Hispanoamérica durante la época colonial', *Estudios de Historia Social de España,* Madrid (1949).

'La condición legal de los criollos y las causas de la Independencia', EA 5 (1950).

'La formación de la nobleza en Indias', EA 10 (1951).

'Emigración española al Río de la Plata durante el siglo XVI', *Miscelánea Americanista* III (1952).

'Ideas políticas del Virrey Francisco Gil de Taboada', *Mar del Sur,* Lima, 20 (1952).

Los mestizos en la legislación colonial. Instituto de Estudios Políticos, 1960.

'Die Gründung des Colegio de Nobles Americanos in der Stadt Granada (1792)', *Homenaje a J. Vincke,* Madrid, 1962–3.

Bibliography

'Die Bedeutung der Sprachenfrage in der Spanischen Kolonisation Amerikas', Jhb 1 (1964).
'Forschungsprobleme zur Geschichte der wirtschaftlichen Betätigungen des Adels in Spanien', *Homenaje a Ramón Carande*, Madrid, 1963.
'Süd- und Mittelamerika I', in *Fischer Weltgeschichte*, 1965.
'Spanische Universitätsgrundungen in Amerika und ihre Motive', Jhb 5 (1968).
Kossok, Manfred. *El Virreinato del Río de la Plata. Su estructura económico-social*. Buenos Aires, 1959.
Comercio y Economía Colonial. Paris-Santiago, Nova Americana, 1965.
Krebs Wilckens, Ricardo. *El pensamiento histórico, político y económico del Conde de Campomanes*. Universidad de Chile, 1960.
Kubler, George. 'The New-Inca State 1537–1572', HAHR (1947).
Mexican Architecture of the XVIth Century. Yale University Press, 1948.

Lafaye, Jacques. *Les Conquistadores*. Paris, Editions du Seuil, 1964.
Lalinde Abadía, Jesús. 'El régimen virreino-senatorial de Indias', AHDE XXXVII (1967).
Lamadrid, Lázaro, O.F.M. *Fray José Antonio Liendo y Goicochea O.F.M. y la Philosophia Recentior del siglo XVIII*. AM 1, 1955.
Lanning, John T. *The University in the Kingdom of Guatemala*. Cornell University Press, 1955.
The XVIIIth Century Enlightenment in the University of San Carlos de Guatemala. Cornell University Press, 1956.
The Enlightenment in relation to the Church. AM, 1958.
The Church and the Enlightenment in the Universities. AM, 1959.
Leal, Ildefonso. *Historia de la Universidad de Caracas 1721–1827*. Universidad Central de Venezuela, 1963.
Leclerc, Jean. *L'idée de la Royauté du Christ au Moyen Age*. Paris, Editions du Cerf, 1959.
Leonard, Irving A. *Don Carlos de Sigüenza y Góngora*. Berkeley, Calif., 1929.
'Don Pedro de Peralta', *Philological Quarterly* XII (1933).
'On the Mexican book trade', HAHR (1947).
'On the Lima book trade 1591', HAHR (1953).
Los libros del Conquistador. Mexico, 1953.
Baroque Times in Old Mexico. Michigan University Press, 1959.
Le Riverend Brusone, Julio. 'La Historia Antigua de México del Padre F.J. Clavigero', in *Estudios de Historiografía de la Nueva España*. Mexico, 1945.
'Carácter y significación de los tres primeros historiadores de Cuba', *Revista Bimestre Cubano*, 1950.
'Problemas de historiografía', HM 9 (1953).

Bibliography

Leturia, Pedro, S.J. 'Relaciones de la Santa Sede e Hispanoamérica. I: Epoca del Real Patronato', *Analecta Gregoriana*, Rome, 101, 1959, (a collection of relevant articles from 1926).

Levene, Ricardo. *Investigaciones sobre la historia económica del Río de la Plata.* Buenos Aires, 1927, 1952.

Las Indias no eran Colonias. Buenos Aires, Espasa-Calpe, 1951.

Levillier, Roberto. *Don Francisco de Toledo, Organizador del Perú.* Madrid – Buenos Aires. 2 vols. and annex, 1935–42.

América la bien llamada. Buenos Aires, 1948.

Lewis, R., and McGann, T. F. (eds.) *The New World Looks at Its History.* Texas University Press, 1963.

Liehr, Reinhold. 'Die soziale Stellung der Indianer von Puebla während der zweiten hälfte des 18. Jahrhunderts', Jhb 8 (1971).

'Die Grundherrschaft der Herzöge von Atlizco in kolonialen Mexico', Jhb 9 (1972).

Stadtrat und städtische Oberschicht von Puebla am Ende der Kolonialzeit 1787–1810. Wiesbaden, F. Steiner, 1971.

Lockhart, James. *Spanish Peru 1532–1560.* Wisconsin University Press, 1968.

The Men of Cajamarca. University of Texas Press, 1972.

Lohmann Villena, Guillermo. *El Conde de Lemos, Virrey del Perú.* Seville, CSIC, 1946.

'Las Cortes en Indias', AHDE XVIII (1947).

Las minas de Huancavelica en los siglos XVI y XVII. Seville, CSIC, 1949.

'El Corregidor de Lima', AEA IX (1952).

El Corregidor de Indios en el Perú bajo los Austrias. Madrid, 1957.

'La restitución por conquistadores y encomenderos: un aspecto de la incidencia lascasiana en el Perú', AEA XXIII (1966).

Etude préliminaire a 'Gobierno del Perú' de Juan de Matienzo. Paris-Lima, 1967.

Les Espinosa: une famille d'hommes d'affaires en Espagne at aux Indes à l'époque de la colonisation. Paris, Seupen, 1968.

'Banca y Crédito en la América Española', HI 9 (1969).

Lopetegui, León, S.J. *El Padre José de Acosta y las Misiones.* Madrid, CSIC, 1942.

Lopetegui, León, S.J., Zubillaga, Félix, Egaña, Antonio de, S.J. *Historia de la Iglesia en la América Española.* 2 vols. Biblioteca Autores Cristianos, 1965–6.

López Martínez, Héctor. 'Un motín de mestizos en el Perú (1567)', RI 97/98 (1964).

Lynch, John. *Spanish Colonial Administration 1782–1810: the Intendant system in the Vice-Royalty of Río de la Plata.* University of London, 1958; Spanish translation, Buenos Aires, 1967.

McAlister, Lyle N. *The 'Fuero Militar' in New Spain 1764–1800*. University of Florida Press, 1957.
'Social structure and social change in New Spain', HAHR (1963).
Macera dall'Orso, Pablo. *Bibliotecas peruanas del siglo XVIII*. Universidad de San Marcos de Lima, 1962.
'Iglesia y Economía en el Perú del siglo XVIII', in *Letras*. Lima, 1963.
'El Probabilismo en el Perú durante el siglo XVIII', *Nueva Corónica* I (1963).
Lenguaje y modernismo peruano del siglo XVIII. Universidad de San Marcos de Lima, 1963.
Prólogo a las 'Instrucciones para el manejo de las haciendas jesuíticas del Perú (siglos XVII-XVIII)', *Nueva Corónica* (1966).
Prólogo a la 'Reforma del Perú' de Alonso Carrió de la Vandera. Universidad de San Marcos de Lima, 1966.
Magalhaes Godinho, Vitorino. *L'Economie de l'Empire Portugais aux XV et XVI siècles*. Paris, Seupen, 1969.
Mahn-Lot, Marianne. 'Notes sur Domingo de Santo Tomás, disciple de Las Casas', *Mélanges en l'honneur de F. Braudel*. Paris, published privately, 1973.
Malagón Barceló, Javier. *The role of the 'letrado' in the colonization of America*. AM, 1961.
Manzano, Juan Manzano. *La incorporación de las Indias a la Corona de Castilla*. Instituto de Cultura Hispánica, Madrid, 1948.
'La adquisición de las Indias por los Reyes Católicos y su incorporación a los Reinos Castellanos', AHDE XXI/XXII (1951–52).
Historia de las Recopilaciones de Leyes de Indias. Instituto de Cultura Hispánica, Madrid. 2 vols., 1950 and 1956.
Maravall, José Antonio. *Teoría Española del Estado en el siglo XVII*. Instituto de Estudios Políticos, Madrid, 1944; French translation, Paris, Vrin, 1955.
'La utopía político-religiosa de los franciscanos en Nueva España', EA 2 (1949).
El concepto de España Medieval. Instituto de Estudios Políticos, Madrid, 1954.
'La visión utópica del Imperio de Carlos V en la España de su época', in *Carlos V 1500–1558: Homenaje de la Universidad de Granada*, 1958.
'La formación de la conciencia estamental de los letrados', *Revista de Estudios Políticos* 48, 1953.
Carlos V y el pensamiento político del Renacimiento. Madrid, Instituto de Estudios Políticos, 1960.
'Del régimen feudal al régimen corporativo en el pensamiento de Alfonso X', BRAH CLVII (1958).
Marfany, Roberto H. *El indio en la colonización de Buenos Aires*. Buenos Aires, Comisión Nacional de Cultura, 1940.

Mariluz Urquijo, José María. *Ensayos sobre los juicios de Residencia indianos.* Seville, CSIC, 1952.

Martin, Norman F. *Los vagabundos en la Nueva España. Siglo XVI.* Mexico, Jus, 1957.

Martínez Cardós, José. 'Gregorio López, Consejero de Indias, glosador de las Partidas', RI 81/82 (1960).

'Las Indias y las Cortes de Castilla', RI 64 and 65 (1956).

Maticorena Estrada, Miguel. 'El contrato de Panamá, 1526, para el Descubrimiento del Perú', *Caravelle* 7, Toulouse (1966).

Mauro, Frédéric. 'Mexico y Brasil: dos economías coloniales comparadas', HM IV/VI (1961).

Maurtúa, Victor M. *Antecedentes de la Recopilación de Indias.* Madrid, 1906 (valuable for its documentation).

Medina, José Toribio. *La Instrucción Pública en Chile desde sus orígenes hasta la fundación de la Universidad de San Felipe.* Santiago, 1905.

Historia de la Real Universidad de San Felipe en Santiago de Chile. Santiago, 1928; the works on printing in America and on the Inquisition, so valuable for documentary purposes, cannot be listed here for lack of space.

Meléndez, Carlos. *La Ilustración en el Antiguo Reino de Guatemala.* San José de Costa Rica, 1970.

Melis, Federigo. 'Il commercio trasatlantico di una compagnia florentina stabilita a Siviglia a pochi anni dalle imprese di Cortés e Pizarro', V Congreso de Historia de la Corona de Aragón, 1954.

Mellafe, Rolando. *La introducción de la esclavitud negra en Chile.* Universidad de Chile, 1959.

La esclavitud en Hispanoamérica. Buenos Aires, 1964.

Menéndez Pelayo, Marcelino. *Historia de los Heterodoxos españoles.* Madrid.

Menéndez Pidal, Ramón. *La Idea imperial de Carlos V.* Madrid, 1937, 1938; Espasa-Calpe, 1948.

El Padre Las Casas. Su doble personalidad. Espasa-Calpe, 1963.

Meza Villalobos, Néstor. *Política indígena en los orígenes de la sociedad chilena.* Universidad de Chile, 1951.

La conciencia política chilena durante la Monarquía. Universidad de Chile, 1958.

Estudios sobre la conquista de América. Santiago, Editorial Universitaria, 1971 (collected studies, from 1936).

Millares Carlo, Agustín. 'Feijoo y América', *Cuadernos Americanos* 3 (1944).

Don Juan José de Eguiara y Eguren y su Biblioteca Mexicana. Mexico, 1957.

Miranda, José. 'Clavígero en la Ilustración americana', *Cuadernos Americanos*, 1946.

'Notas sobre la introducción de la Mesta en la Nueva España', RHAm 17 (1944).

La función económica del encomendero en los orígenes del régimen colonial (*Nueva España, 1525–1531*). Universidad Nacional Autónoma de México, 1947.

El tributo indígena en la Nueva España durante el siglo XVI. El Colegio de México, 1952.

Moore, Jon Preston. *The Cabildo in Peru under the Habsburgs.* Duke University Press, 1954.

The Cabildo in Peru under the Bourbons. Duke University Press, 1966.

Morales Padrón, Francisco. 'Descubrimiento y toma de posesión', AEA 12 (1955).

El Comercio Canario-Americano. Seville, CSIC, 1955.

'Historia General de América', in *Manual de Historia Universal.* Madrid, Espasa-Calpe, vols. 5 and 6 (1962).

Moreno, Rafael. 'Descartes en la Ilustración mexicana', *Filosofía y Letras* 39 (1950).

'Alzate, educador ilustrado', HM 7 (1953).

'La teología ilustrada de Hidalgo', HM 19 (1956).

Moreno Báez, Enrique. 'El providencialismo del Inca Garcilaso', EA 35/36 (1954).

Moreno Toscano, Alejandra. *Fray Juan de Torquemada y su 'Monarquía Indiana'.* Universidad Veracruzana, 1963.

'Economía Regional y Urbanización. Tres ejemplos de relación entre ciudades y regiones en Nueva España a fines del siglo XVIII', 39 Congreso Internacional de Americanistas, Lima, 1970.

Moreyra Paz Soldán, Manuel. 'La técnica de la moneda colonial. Unidades, Pesos, Medidas y Relaciones', RHAm 20 (1945).

El Tribunal del Consulado de Lima. Lima, 1950.

Mörner, Magnus. *The Political and Economic Activities of the Jesuits in the La Plata Region: the Habsburg Era.* Stockholm, 1953.

'Panorama de la sociedad del Río de la Plata durante la primera mitad del siglo XVIII', EA 92/93 (1959).

'Los motivos de la expulsión de los Jesuitas del Imperio Español', HM VII/IX (1966).

The expulsion of the Jesuits from Spain and Spanish-America in 1767 in the light of XVIIIth century Regalism. AM, 1966.

Race mixture in the history of Latin America. Boston, 1967.

La Corona Española y los foráneos en los pueblos de Indios de América. Stockholm, 1970.

El colonato en la América Meridional Andina desde el siglo XVIII. Informe preliminar. Stockholm, 1970.

'The Spanish American Hacienda: A Survey of Recent Research and Debate', HAHR (1973).

Morse, Richard M. 'Latin American cities: aspects of function and structure', *Comparative Studies in Society and History* VII (1962).

Bibliography

'The heritage of Latin America', in *The founding of new societies*, by Louis Hartz. New York, Harcourt Brace and World, 1964.

'Recent research on Latin American urbanization: a selective survey with commentary', *Latin American Research Review* (1965).

'Trends and issues in Latin American urban research', *Latin American Research Review* (1971).

Mühlmann, Wilhelm E. *Chiliasmus und Nativismus*. Berlin, Reimer, 1961.

Muñoz Pérez, José. 'La idea de América en Campomanes', AEA X (1953).

'Los proyectos sobre España e Indias en el siglo XVIII: el proyectismo como género', *Revista de Estudios Políticos* 81 (1955).

Navarro, Bernabé. *La introducción de la filosofía moderna en México*. El Colegio de México, 1948.

Navarro García, Luis. *Las Intendencias en Indias*. Seville, CSIC, 1959.

Don José de Gálvez y la Comandancia General de las Provincias Internas del Norte de Nueva España. Seville, CSIC, 1964.

Sonora y Sinaloa en el siglo XVII. Seville, CSIC, 1967.

Oberem, Udo. 'Don Sancho Hacho, ein "cacique mayor" des 16 Jahrhunderts', Jhb 4 (1967).

'Mitglieder de Familie des Inka Atahualpa unter spanischen Herrschaft', Jhb 5 (1968).

O'Gorman, Edmundo. 'La enseñanza primaria en la Nueva España', *Boletín del Archivo General de la Nación*, Mexico (1940).

'El Catolicismo Ilustrado en la Nueva España', *Boletín del Archivo General de la Nación*, Mexico (1947).

La Idea del Descubrimiento de América. Universidad Nacional Autónoma, 1951.

La Invención de América. Fondo de Cultura Económica, 1957.

'La idea antropológica del Padre Las Casas', HM I/III (1967).

Olaechea Labayen, Juan B. 'Opinión de los teólogos españoles sobre dar estudios mayores a los indios', AEA XV (1958).

'Sacerdotes indios de América del Sur en el siglo XVIII', RI 115/118 (1969).

Ots Capdequí, José María. *El régimen de la tierra en la América Española durante el período colonial*. Universidad de Santo Domingo, 1946.

Historia del Derecho Español en América y del Derecho Indiano. Madrid, Aguilar, 1968.

Otte, Enrique. 'La expedición de Gonzalo de Ocampo a Cumaná en 1521 en las cuentas de la Tesorería de Santo Domingo', RI/63 (1956).

'Aspiraciones y actividades heterogéneas de Gonzalo Fernández de Oviedo, cronista', RI 71(1958).

Introducción al 'Cedulario de la Isla de Cubagua'. Madrid, 1961.

'Die Welser in Santo Domingo', *Homenaje a J. Vincke*, 1962/63.

Bibliography

'Die genuesische Unternehmertum in Amerika unter den Katholischen Königen', Jhb 2 (1965).

'Die Negersklavenlizenz des Laurent von Gorrevod', *Gesammelte Aufsätze zur Kulturgeschichte Spaniens* 22 (1965).

'Träger und Formen der wirtschaftlichen Erschliessung Lateinamerikas im 16 Jahrhundert', Jhb 4 (1967).

'Die europäische Siedler und die Probleme der Neuen Welt', Jhb 6 (1969).

Palacio Atard, Vicente. 'Areche y Guirior', AEA III (1946).

'El equilibrio de América en la diplomacia del siglo XVIII', EA 3 (1949).

'Feijoo y los americanos', EA 69/70 (1957).

Los españoles de la Ilustración. Madrid, Guadarrama, 1964.

Palm, Erwin Walter. 'Los orígenes del urbanismo imperial en América', in *Contribuciones a la Historia Municipal de América*, Mexico, 1951.

Parra, Caracciolo. *Filosofía universitaria venezolana*. Caracas, 1934.

Parry, J. H. *The Audiencia of New Galicia in the XVIth Century*. Cambridge University Press, 1948.

The Age of Reconnaissance. London, 1963; Spanish translation, Madrid, 1964.

The Sale of Public Office in the Spanish Indies under the Habsburgs. University of California Press, 1953.

Trade and Dominion: the European Oversea Empires in the XVIIIth Century. London, 1971.

Parsons, James J. *Antioqueño Colonization in Western Colombia*. University of California Press, 1949.

Peña, Roberto. *El pensamiento político del Deán Funes*. Córdoba, 1953.

Pereira Salas, Eugenio. *Los primeros contactos entre Chile y los Estados Unidos*. Santiago, Editorial Andrés Bello, 1971.

Pérez Embid, Florentino. *Los descubrimientos en el Atlántico hasta el Tratado de Tordesillas*. Seville, CSIC, 1948.

Pérez-Jila, Francisco de Solano. 'La población indígena de Guatemala 1492–1800', AEA XXVI (1969).

Pérez Marchand, Monelisa Lina. *Dos etapas ideológicas del siglo XVIII en México a través de los papeles de la Inquisición*. Mexico, 1945.

Pérez de la Riva, Francisco. *Origen y régimen de la propiedad territorial en Cuba*. Havana, 1946.

Pérez de Tudela y Bueso, Juan. *Las Armadas de Indias y los orígenes de la política de colonización (1492–1505)*. Madrid, CSIC, 1956.

'Significado de la vida y escritos del Padre Las Casas', in BAE 95, 1957.

'La gran reforma carolina de las Indias en 1542', RI 73/74 (1958).

'Vida y escritos de Gonzalo Fernández de Oviedo' in BAE 117, 1959.

'Ideario de Don Rodrigo Fernández, párroco criollo de los Andes (1696)', AEA XVII (1960).

Bibliography

Estudio Preliminar de 'Crónicas del Perú'. BAE 164.

Documentos relativos a Don Pedro de La Gasca y a Gonzalo Pizarro. Madrid, Real Academia de la Historia, 2 vols., 1964.

Estudio Preliminar a 'Crónicas Peruanas de interés indígena'. BAE 209, 1968.

'La política indiana y el político Solórzano', RI 123/124 (1971).

Peuckert, Will Erich. *Die grosse Wende*. Hamburg, 1948.

Phelan, John L. *The Millennial Kingdom of the Franciscans in New Spain*. University of California Press, 1970.

The Hispanization of the Philippines. University of Wisconsin Press, 1959.

The Kingdom of Quito in the XVIIth Century. University of Wisconsin Press, 1967.

Picón Salas, Mariano. *De la Conquista a la Independencia*. Mexico, 1944.

Piechmann, Horst. *Die Einführung des Intendantensystems in Neu-Spanien*. Cologne-Vienna, Böhlau, 1972.

Pike, Ruth. *The Genoese in Seville and the Opening of the New World*. Cornell University Press, 1966.

Pohl, Hans. 'Zur Geschichte des adligen Unternehmers in Spanisch Amerika (XVII/XVIII Jahrhundert)', Jhb 2 (1965).

Porras Barrenechea, Raúl. *Introducción a 'El Paraiso en el Nuevo Mundo' de Antonio de León Pinelo*. Lima, 2 vols., 1943.

El Inca Garcilaso de la Vega. Lima, 1946.

El Inca Garcilaso en Montilla. Lima, Universidad Mayor de San Marcos, 1955.

Fuentes históricas peruanas. Lima, 1963.

Mito, tradición e historia del Perú. Lima, 1969.

Posada Mejía, Germán. 'El Padre Oviedo, precursor de los jesuitas "ilustrados"', HM, 25 (1957).

Powell, Philip W. *Soldiers, Indians and Silver: the Northward advance of New Spain 1550–1600*. University of California Press, 1952.

Priestley, Herbert J. *José de Gálvez, Visitor General of New Spain 1765–1771*. Berkeley, 1916.

Puente y Olea, Manuel de la. *Los trabajos geográficos de la Casa de Contratación*. Seville, 1900.

Pueyrredón, Alfredo. *Algunos aspectos de la enseñanza en la Universidad de Córdoba durante la Regencia Franciscana*. Universidad Nacional de Córdoba, 1953.

Pulido Rubio, José. *El Piloto Mayor de la Casa de Contratación de Sevilla*. Seville, CSIC, 1950.

Quelle, Otto. *Das Problem des Jesuiten-Staats Paraguay*. Ibero-Amerikanisches Archiv, X-1934.

Quirós-Martínez, Olga Victoria. *La introducción de la Filosofía Moderna en España*. El Colegio de México, 1949.

Bibliography

Radicati di Primeglio, Carlos. 'Juan Reinaldo Carli, el iniciador del estudio científico del problema de la Atlántida', *Documenta*, Lima, I, 1 (1948).

Ramírez Necochea, Hernán. *Antecedentes económicos de la Independencia de Chile*. Santiago, 2nd ed., 1967.

Ramos Pérez, Demetrio. 'La Revolución de Coro de 1533 contra los Welser y su importancia para el régimen municipal', *Boletín Americanista de la Universidad de Barcelona* (1959).

'El Padre Córdoba y Las Casas en el plan de conquista pacífica de Tierra Firme', *Boletín Americanista de la Universidad de Barcelona* (1959).

'Determinantes formativos de la "hueste" indiana y su origen modélico', *Revista Chilena de Historia del Derecho* (1965).

'Las ciudades de Indias y su asiento en Cortes de Castilla', RIHD 18 (1967).

'Trigo chileno, Navieros de Callao y hacendados limeños entre la crisis agrícola del siglo XVII y la comercial de la primera mitad del XVIII', RI (1967).

'La etapa lascasiana de la presión de conciencias', AEA XXIV (1968).

'Los proyectos de independencia para América preparados por el rey Carlos IV', RI 111/112 (1968).

'Funcionamiento de una hueste de conquista: la de Pedro de Heredia en Cartagena de Indias', RI 115/118 (1969).

Rassow, Peter. *El mundo político de Carlos V*. Madrid, Aguado, 1945.

Ravignani, Emilio. 'El Virreinato del Río de la Plata', in *Historia de la Nación Argentina* by Ricardo Levene, IV, 1.

Reeves, Marjorie E. *The Influence of Prophecy in the late Middle Ages: a study in Joachimism*. Oxford University Press, 1969.

Reibstein, Ernst. *Die Anfänge des Neueren Natur- und Völkerrechts*. Berne, 1949.

Rein, Gustav Adolf. *Der Kampf Westeuropas am Nordamerika im 15 und 16 Jahrhundert*. Stuttgart, 1925.

'Uber die Bedeutung der überseeischen Ausdehnung für die europäische Staatensystem', *Historische Zeitschrift* 137 (1927).

Ricard, Robert. *La conquête spirituelle du Méxique*. Paris, 1933; Spanish translation: Mexico, Jus, 1947.

'La Plaza Mayor en Espagne et en Amérique Espagnole', *Annales* 4 (1947).

'De Campomanes à Jovellanos', *Les lettres romanes*, XI, Louvain (1957).

'Le Règne de Charles-Quint, âge d'or de l'histoire méxicaine?' *Revue du Nord*, Lille (1960).

'L'enseignement du Castillan aux Indiens d'Amérique durant la période coloniale', *Bulletin de la Faculté des Lettres*, Strasbourg (1961).

Rico González, Victor. *Historiadoras mexicanos del siglo XVIII*. Universidad Nacional Autónoma, Mexico, 1949.

Riley, G. Michael. *Fernando Cortes and the Marquesado in Morelos*. University of New Mexico Press, 1973.

Riva Agüero, José de la. *La Historia en el Perú*. Lima, 1910, 1965.

Bibliography

Rivas Sacconi, José Manuel. *El latín en Colombia*. Bogotá, Instituto Caro y Cuervo, 1949.

Rodríguez Casado, Vicente. 'Iglesia y Estado en el reinado de Carlos III', EA 1 (1948).

'La "revolución burguesa" del XVIII español', *Arbor*, Madrid, 61 (1951).

'Notas sobre las relaciones de la Iglesia y Estado en Indias en el reinado de Carlos III', RI 43/44 (1951).

'La Orden de San Francisco y la Visita General de Reforma en 1769', AEA IX (1952).

Rodríguez Vicente, María Encarnación. *El Tribunal del Consulado en Lima en la primera mitad del siglo XVII*. Madrid, Cultura Hispánica, 1960.

Rojas Mix, Miguel A. 'La idea de Historia y la imagen de América en al abate Molina', *Revista de Filosofía de la Universidad de Chile* (1963).

Romano, Ruggiero. *Una economía colonial: Chile en el siglo XVIII*. Buenos Aires, Eudeba, 1965.

'Tra XVI e XVII secolo. Una crisi economica: 1619–1622', *Rivista Storica Italiana* (1962).

Romeo, Rosario. *La scoperta americana nella coscienza italiana del Cinquecento*. Ricciardi, 1954.

Rosenblat, Angel. *La población indígena de América y el Mestizaje*. Buenos Aires, Nova, 1954. 2 vols.

Rovira, María del Carmen. *Eclécticos portugueses del siglo XVIII y algunas de sus influencias en América*. Mexico, 1958.

Rowe, John H. 'The Incas under Spanish Colonial institutions', HAHR (1957).

Rubio Mañé, Juan Ignacio. *Introducción al estudio de los Virreyes de Nueva España*. Mexico, Universidad Nacional Autónoma, 1955 and years following, 4 vols.

Sáenz de Santa María, Carmelo, S.J. 'La fantasía lascasiana en el experimento de Verapaz', RI 72 (1958).

'El licenciado don Francisco Marroquín, primer jefe de la conquista espiritual de Guatemala', RI 91/92 (1963).

'Remesal, la Verapaz y fray Bartolomé de Las Casas', AEA XXIII (1966).

'La "Reducción a Poblados" en el siglo XVI en Guatemala', AEA XXIX (1972).

Salas, Alberto Mario. *Las Armas de la Conquista*. Buenos Aires, Emecé, 1950.

Salazar, Justo Abel, O.S.A. *Los estudios eclesiásticos superiores en el Nuevo Reino de Granada 1563–1810*. Madrid, CSIC, 1946.

Sánchez Agesta, Luis. *El pensamiento político del Despotismo Ilustrado*. Madrid, Instituto de Estudios Políticos, 1953.

El concepto de Estado en el Renacimiento español del siglo XVI. Instituto de Estudios Políticos, 1959.

Sánchez Bella, Ismael. *La organización financiera de las Indias.* Seville, CSIC, 1968.

Sancho de Sopranís, Hipólito. 'Los genoveses en la región gaditano-xerience de 1400 a 1800', *Hispania* VIII (1948).

Santos Martínez, Pedro. *Historia Económica de Mendoza durante el Virreinato 1776–1810.* Madrid, Mendoza, 1961.

Sanz, Carlos. 'Consecuencias universales del Descubrimiento de América', AEA XXIV (1968).

Sarrailh, Jean. *L'Espagne éclairée de la seconde moitié du XVIII siècle.* Paris, Klinksieck, 1954.

Saugnieux, Joël. *Un prélat éclairé: Don Antonio Tavira y Almazán.* Toulouse, 1970.

Scelle, Georges. *Histoire politique de la traite négrière aux Indes de Castille.* Paris, 1906, 2 vols.

Schäfer, Ernesto. *El Consejo Real y Supremo de las Indias.* Seville, 1935, 1947, 2 vols.

Schmitt, Carl. *Uber die drei Arten des Rechtswissenschaftdenkens.* Hamburg, 1934.

Schurz, William. *The Manila Galleon.* New York, 1939.

Sempat Assadourian, Carlos. 'Chile y Tucumán en el siglo XVI. Una correspondencia de mercaderes', HI 9 (1970).

Service, Elman. 'The Encomienda in Paraguay', HAHR (1951).

Shafer, Robert J. *The Economic Societies in the Spanish World.* Syracuse University Press, 1958.

Sierra, Vicente D. *En torno a las Bulas Alejandrinas de 1493.* MH, X, 1953.
Los jesuitas germanos en la Conquista Espiritual de Hispanoamérica. Buenos Aires, 1944.

Silva Santisteban, Fernando. *Los obrajes en el Virreinato del Perú.* Lima, 1964.

Silva Vargas, Fernando. *Tierras y Pueblos de Indios en el Reino de Chile.* Universidad Católica de Chile, 1963.
'Peru y Chile. Notas sobre sus vinculaciones administrativas y fiscales (1785–1800)', HI 7 (1968).

Simpson, Lesley B. *Studies in the Administration of the Indians in New Spain.* University of California Press, 4 vols. 1934–40.
The Encomienda in New Spain. University of California Press, 2nd ed., 1950.
Soil Exploitation of land in Central Mexico in the XVIth Century. University of California Press, 1952.

Smith, Robert S. 'The institution of the Consulado in New Spain', HAHR (1944).
'Origin of the Consulado of Guatemala', HAHR (1946).
'Sales Taxes in New Spain 1575–1770', HAHR (1948).
'Indigo production and trade in Colonial Guatemala', HAHR (1959).

Sombart, Werner. *Der Moderne Kapitalismus.* (1928).

Specker, Johann. *Die Missionsmethode in Spanische Amerika im 16 Jahrhundert mit besonderer Berücksichtigung der Konzilien und Synoden.* Schöneck-Beckenriede, 1953.

Spell, Jefferson R. *Rousseau in the Spanish World before 1833.* University of Texas Press, 1938.

Stapf, Agnes. 'La renta del tabaco en el Chile de la época virreinal. Un ejemplo de política económica mercantilista', AEA XVIII (1961).

Studer, Elena F. S. *La trata de negros en el Río de la Plata durante el siglo XVIII.* Buenos Aires, 1958.

Torre Revello, José. *El libro, la imprenta y el periodismo en América durante la dominación española.* Buenos Aires, 1940.

'Documentos relativos a Don Lorenzo Boturini Benaduci', *Boletín del Instituto de Investigaciones Históricas de la Universidad de Buenos Aires* 55/57.

'Bibliotecas en el Buenos Aires antiguo desde 1729 hasta la inauguración de la Biblioteca Pública en 1812', RHAm 59 (1965).

Torre Villar, Ernesto de la. 'Hidalgo y Fleury', HM 10 (1953).

'Algunos aspectos acerca de las Cofradías y la propiedad territorial en Michoacán', Jhb 4 (1967).

Truyol y Sierra, Antonio. 'Razón de Estado y Derecho de Gentes en tiempos de Carlos V', in *Kaiser Karl V und seine Zeit,* Cologne–Vienna, Böhlau, 1960.

Tuveson, Ernest L. *Millennium and Utopia.* University of California Press, 1949; Harper Torchbooks, 1964.

Ullmann, Walter. *Growth of Papal Government in the Middle Ages.* London, 1955.

Valcarcel, Daniel. *Reformas de San Marcos en la época de Amat.* Lima, 1955.
Reformas virreinales en San Marcos. Lima, 1960.

Valdeavellano, Luis García. *Sobre los burgos y los burgueses de la España medieval.* Madrid, Real Academia de la Historia, 1960.

'Las Partidas y los orígenes medievales del Juicio de Residencia', BRAH (1963).

Valjavec, Fritz. *Historia de la Ilustración en Occidente.* Madrid, 1964.

Vargas Ugarte, Rubén. 'El Filósofo de Los Andes', *Revista Historica,* Lima (1953).

El episcopado en los tiempos de la Emancipación Sudamericana. Buenos Aires, Huarpes, 1945.

Velázquez, María del Carmen. *El estado de guerra en Nueva España.* El Colegio de México, 1950.

Verlinden, Charles. 'Les influences médiévales dans la colonisation de l'Amérique', RHAm XII (1950).

Bibliography

'Modalités et méthodes du commerce colonial dans l'Empire espagnol au XVI siècle', RI 48 (1952).

Précedents mediévaux de la colonie en Amérique. Mexico, 1954.

L'Esclavage dans l'Europe mediévale. Bruges, vol. 1, 1955.

Esclavitud medieval en Europa y esclavitud colonial en América. Universidad Nacional de Córdoba, 1958.

'Le génois Leonardo Lomollini homme d'affaires du marquisat de Fernand Cortés au Mexique', Jhb 4 (1967).

El Repartimiento de Rodrigo de Albuquerque en Española en 1514. University of Ghent, 1968.

'El régimen de trabajo en México. Aumento y alcance de la gañanía, siglo XVII', *Homenaje a José Miranda*, Mexico, 1970.

'La population de l'Amérique Précolombine', *Mélanges en l'honneur de Fernand Braudel*, Paris, privately published, 1973. 2 vols.

Vial Correa, Gonzalo. *El africano en el Reino de Chile.* Universidad Católica de Chile, 1957.

Vicens Vives, Jaime. 'Precedentes mediterráneos del Virreinato colombino', AEA V (1948).

'Imperio y administración en tiempos de Carlos V', in *Charles V et son temps*, Paris, 1959.

Villalobos Rivera, Sergio. *Tradición y Reforma en 1810.* Universidad de Chile, 1961.

La crisis del comercio colonial. Universidad de Chile, 1968.

Villoro, Luis. *La revolución de la Independencia.* Mexico, 1953, 1967.

Los grandes movimientos del indigenismo en México. El Colegio de México, 1950.

Viñas y Mey, Carmelo. *El espíritu castellano de aventura y empresa y la España de los Reyes Católicos.* Universidad de Granada, Archivo de Derecho Público, 1952.

Vollmer, Günter. *Bevölkerungspolitik und Bevölkerungsstruktur im Vizekönigreich zu Ende der Kolonialzeit 1741–1821.* Verlag Gehlen, 1967.

Wait, Eugene M. 'Mariano Moreno: Promoter of Enlightenment', HAHR (1965).

Weber, Max. *Wirtschaft und Gesellschaft.* 4th ed., vol. 2. Tübingen, 1956.

Weckmann, Luis. *Las Bulas Alejandrinas de 1493 y la teoría política del Papado medieval.* Mexico, Jus, 1949.

West, Robert C. *Colonial Placer Mining in Colombia.* Louisiana University Press, 1942.

The Mining Community in Northern New Spain: the Parral Mining District. University of California Press, 1949.

Whitaker, Arthur P. *The Huancavelica Mercury Mine.* Harvard University Press, 1941.

Latin America and the Enlightenment. Ithaca, N.Y., 1942, 1961.

Bibliography

'The Elhuyar Mining Missions and the Enlightenment', HAHR (1951).
'The Intellectual history of XVIIth century Spanish America', in the 10th International Congress of Historical Sciences, Rome, I, 1955.
Wilks, M. J. *The problem of sovereignty in the Later Middle Ages.* Cambridge University Press, 1964.
Witte, Charles Marcel de, O.S.B. 'Les Bulles Pontificales et l'expansion Portugaise au XV siècle', *Revue d'Histoire Ecclésiastique*, Louvain, 48, 51, 53 (1955–8).
Wolf, Eric R. 'Specific aspects of plantation systems in the New World: Community sub-cultures and social classes', in *Plantation Systems of the New World*, Washington, D.C., 1959.
Wölfel, Dominik J. 'Un episodio desconocido de la conquista de la Isla de la Palma', *Investigación y Progreso*, Madrid, 1931.
'Alonso de Lugo y Compañía, sociedad comercial para la conquista de las Islas de la Palma', *Investigación y Progreso*, 1934.
Wolff, Inge. 'Negersklaverei und Negerhandel in Hochperu 1545–1640', Jhb 1 (1964).
Regierung und Verwaltung der kolonial Spanischen Städte in Hochperu 1538–1650. Cologne–Vienna, Böhlau, 1970.
Worcester, Donald E., and Schaeffer, Wendell C. *The growth and culture of Latin America.* Oxford University Press, 2nd ed.

Zavala, Silvio. *Las Instituciones Jurídicas en la Conquista de América.* Madrid, 1935.
La encomienda indiana. Madrid, 1935.
La Utopia de Tomas Moro en la Nueva España y otros ensayos. Mexico, 1937.
Ideario de Vasco de Quiroga. Mexico, 1941.
Ensayos sobre la colonización española en América. Buenos Aires, 1944.
Servidumbre natural y libertad cristiana según los tratadistas españoles de los siglos XVI y XVII. Buenos Aires, 1944.
La filosofía política en la Conquista de América. Mexico, 1947.
Estudios Indianos. El Colegio Nacional, 1948 (New edition of the following works: 'Los trabajadores antillanos en el siglo XVI', RHAm (1938); *De Encomienda y Propiedad territorial en algunas regiones de la América Española*, 1940; *Orígenes coloniales del peonaje en México*, 1944; *Las conquistas de Canarias y América*, 1936. Printed for the first time: 'La libertad de movimiento de los indios de Nueva España').
América en el espíritu francés del siglo XVIII, Mexico, 1949.
'Nuño de Guzmán y la esclavitud de los indios', HM 1 (1951/2).
Introducción a *De las Islas del Mar Océano* de Juan López de Palacios Rubio. Mexico, 1954.
El mundo americano en la época colonial. Mexico, 1967.
'La evangelización y la conquista de las Indias, según Fray Juan Silva O.F.M.', *Caravelle* 12 (1969).

Zorraquín Becú, Ricardo. *La Organización Política argentina en el período hispánico.* Buenos Aires, Emecé, 1959.

'La doctrina jurídica de la Revolución de Mayo', RIHD 11 (1960).

'Algo más sobre la doctrina jurídica de la Revolución de Mayo', RIHD 13 (1962).

'La movilidad del indígena y el mestizaje en la Argentina Colonial', Jhb 4 (1967).

Zubillaga, Felix. 'Muratori storici delle Missioni Americani della Compagnia di Gesu', *Rivista di Storia della Chiesa in Italia* 4 (1950).

Zuretti, Juan Carlos. Historia Eclesiástica Argentina. Buenos Aires, 1945.

'La orientación de los estudios de Filosofía entre los Franciscanos en el Río de la Plata', *Itinerarium* (1947).

'Algunas corrientes filosóficas en Argentina durante el período hispánico. La llamada Filosofía Moderna', I Congreso Nacional de Filosofía, Mendoza, 1949.

INDEX

Ruiz de Montoya, 219
Russians, 167, 171

Saavedra Fajardo, 177–8
Sahagún, Bernardino de, Fray, 213
Salamanca, School of, 125
Salas, Manuel de, 192
Salazar, Domingo de, Fray, 53
Salinas, 142
Salta, 174
San Alberto, José A. de, Bishop of Córdoba, 196
Sánchez de Arévalo, Rodrigo, 38, 44, 99
Sancho IV, of Castile, 68
Sandoval, Tello de, *Visitador*, 94
Santa Cruz, Alonso de, 86
Santa Cruz de la Sierra, 142, 166
Santa Hermandad, 105
Santander, Spain, 8
Santiago de Chile, 24, 105–6, 111, 113, 160
Santillán, Hernando de, 139
Santo Domingo, 6, 8, 17, 88, 89, 99, 100, 103, 129
São Paulo, 166, 234
Sardinia, 3
Sarmiento, Domingo Faustino, 186
Sarmiento de Gamboa, Pedro, 55, 222
Saturnalia, by Lucian, 232
Savonarola, 207
School of Mines, Mexico City, 193
Semanario erudito, 180
Seminary of Nobles, 181
Señorío de los Incas, by Cieza de León, 219, 221
Sepúlveda, Juan Ginés de, 49, 62, 85, 140
Seven Years' War, 171, 173
Seville, 79, 113, 155
Shipyards, 136
Sicily, 3

Siete Partidas, 3, 4, 17, 23, 33, 39, 43, 56, 68, 69, 73, 77, 124–5, 163
Sigüenza y Góngora, Carlos de, 77–8, 181, 190, 198–9, 219, 229
Silk worms, 137
Silvester of Prierias, 38
Sixtus V, Pope, 247
Slaves and slaving, 140, 142; Indian, 5, 9, 13, 15, 20, 26, 90, 110, 128–31, 136, 145; Negro, 5, 13, 103, 110, 114, 162
Smuggling, 168, 176
Sobre el verdadero método de estudiar teología eclesiástica, by Hidalgo, 182
Social Contract, 181
Social stratification, 160–7
Socorro, New Granada, 175
Solórzano Pereira, Juan de, 62–5, 77, 80, 81, 90, 97, 123, 124, 148, 151, 156, 169, 194
Soto, Domingo de, 58, 70, 85, 198
Soto, Hernando de, 11, 13, 17
Sovereignty of the State, Spanish notion of, 69–79; *see also Jus Gentium*; Conquests, crown attitude towards
Spanish Succession, War of the, 173
Spectacle de la Nature, by Pluche, 182
Spedalieri, Nicolo, 197
Spira, Jorge de, 14, 15
Steuchus, Augustinus, 228
Suárez, Francisco, 70, 78, 188, 190, 191, 196, 198
Suárez de Peralta, Juan, 218
Subdelegates, 174
Sugar-cane, 11, 21, 136, 142, 149, 162
Suma de la Política, by Sánchez de Arévalo, 99
Superintendant General of Finance, 174

Talamantes, Melchor de, Fray, 197–8